Clifford Geertz in Morocco

Between 1963 and 1986, eminent American anthropologists Clifford and Hildred Geertz, together and alone, conducted ethnographic fieldwork for varying periods in Sefrou, a town situated in north-central Morocco, south of Fez. This book considers Geertz's contributions to sociocultural theory and symbolic anthropology.

Clifford Geertz made an immense impact on the American academy: his interpretative and symbolic approaches reoriented anthropology analytically away from classic social science presuppositions, while his publications profoundly influenced both North American and Maghribi researchers alike. After his death at the age of eighty on October 30th, 2006, scholars from local, national, and international universities gathered at the University of California, Los Angeles, to analyze his contributions to sociocultural theory and symbolic anthropology in relation to Islam; ideas of the sacred; Morocco's cityscapes (notably Sefrou's bazaar or suq); colonialism and post-independence economic development; gender, and political structures at the household and village levels.

This book looks back to a specific era of American anthropology beginning in the 1960s as it unfolded in Morocco; and at the same time, the contributions examine new lines of enquiry that opened up after key texts by Geertz were translated into French and introduced to generations of francophone Maghribi researchers who sustain lively and inventive meditations on his Morocco writings.

This book was published as a special issue of the *Journal of North African Studies*.

Susan Slyomovics is Professor of Anthropology and Near Eastern Languages and Cultures at the University of California, Los Angeles, USA.

T0353062

Clifford Geertz in Morocco

Edited by Susan Slyomovics

Routledge
Taylor & Francis Group
LONDON AND NEW YORK

First published 2010 by Routledge
2 Park Square, Milton Park, Abingdon, Oxon, OX14 4RN

Simultaneously published in the USA and Canada
by Routledge
711 Third Avenue, New York, NY 10017
Routledge is an imprint of the Taylor & Francis Group, an informa business
First issued in paperback 2011

This book is a reproduction of the *Journal of North African Studies*, vol. 14, issue 3-4. The Publisher requests to those authors who may be citing this book to state, also, the bibliographical details of the special issue on which the book was based

Typeset in Times New Roman by Value Chain, India

British Library Cataloguing in Publication Data
A catalogue record for this book is available from the British Library

ISBN 13: 978-0-415-55907-2 (hbk)
ISBN 13: 978-0-415-51816-1 (pbk)

CONTENTS

List of Illustrations

Chapter 11: Perceptions, not illustrations, of Sefrou, Morocco: Paul Hyman's images and the work of ethnographic photography
Susan Slyomovics

Chapter 12: Chicken or glass: in the vicinity of Clifford Geertz and Paul Hyman
Paul Rabinow

Introduction to Clifford Geertz in Morocco: 'Why Sefrou? Why anthropology? Why me?'

Susan Slyomovics

Center for Near Eastern Studies, UCLA, Department of Anthropology, UCLA, Los Angeles, CA, USA

A very brief conclusion would be to sort of address the question that is a subject of mine: Why Sefrou? Why anthropology? Why me? I'll do this slightly autobiographical. . .. I came here in the mid-sixties after having worked in Indonesia. I wanted to get a comparison case; I wanted to see. If you work too long in one place you do begin to see everything in terms of it and that's a dangerous business, whether it's seeing all of Morocco in terms of Sefrou or whether it's seeing all of the so-called Third World in terms of Indonesia. (Clifford Geertz, closing remarks, 'Hommage à Clifford Geertz,' Sefrou, Morocco, 3–6 May 2000)[1]

The Morocco that Clifford and Hildred Geertz came to see and compare in the 1960s and 70s – the decades of America's Vietnam War – was a haven for an astonishing array of Americans abroad: beatniks and hippies, youthful draft dodgers and Peace Corps workers, hashish imbibers and drug entrepreneurs, tourists and also anthropologists (Edwards 2005).[2] Between 1963 and 1986, the Geertzes, together and alone, resided in Sefrou, Morocco, for varying periods. Sefrou is a town situated in north-central Morocco to the south of Fez, where the foothills of the Middle Atlas Mountains meet the western plain (Figure 1). The Arabic term for both the town of Sefrou and its surrounding region – *bled Sefrou* – was for Geertz and his fellow researchers more than a mere name on a map:

> Bled Sefrou is really a social space – a network of relationships mediated by markets, public insti-
> tutions, local identities, and densely interwoven bonds of kinship and alliance. No less importantly, it
> is a conceptual domain – a perceived set of populations, territories, pathways, and meeting places
> that are intimately, if not always harmoniously, linked to the nurturance and identity of those who
> live there. As an indigenous conceptual category, bled Sefrou underlines the interdependency, as
> well as the interaction, of its component parts. It stresses the conceptualisation of the region as an
> arena within which social life is played out through institutions that crosscut internal divisions of
> geography and society, even as the substance and course of social life are deeply influenced by
> the contexts in which its various manifestations are found. So conceived, bled Sefrou also presents
> itself as an appropriate unit for analysis. (Geertz, Geertz and Rosen 1979, Introduction, 8)

To study the legacy of research about bled Sefrou after Clifford Geertz's death at the age of 80 on 30 October 2006, the Gustav E. von Grunebaum Center for Near Eastern Studies organised

Figure 1. Semmarin Mosque, Sefrou (Paul Hyman 1969).

a four-day international conference titled 'Islam Re-Observed: Clifford Geertz in Morocco,' which included a photographic exhibition and a musical concert, at the University of California, Los Angeles, 6–9 December 2007.

Characterised by colleagues as 'the single most influential American anthropologist of the past four decades,'[3] Clifford Geertz made an immense impact on the American academy: his interpretative and symbolic approaches reoriented anthropology analytically away from classic social science presuppositions, while his publications profoundly influenced North American and North African researchers alike. Focusing on Geertz's scholarship about Morocco, scholars gathered at UCLA from local, national, and international universities to analyse his contributions to sociocultural theory and symbolic anthropology in relation to Islam, ideas of the sacred, Morocco's cityscapes (notably Sefrou's bazaar or *suq*), colonialism and post-independence economic development, gender and political structures at the household and village levels.

At one level, essays in this volume look back to a specific era of American anthropology beginning in the 1960s as it unfolded in Morocco.[4] Among the contributors to this volume are Lawrence Rosen and Thomas Dichter, drawn to anthropological fieldwork in Sefrou by the Geertzes, likewise Paul Rabinow in nearby Sidi Lahcen Lyusi, in addition to others who undertook fieldwork in Morocco around that same time period, including Kevin Dwyer in Taroudant, Susan Gilson Miller in Rabat and Tangier and Dale Eickelman in Boujad (along with conference presenters not included in this volume, Kenneth Brown in Salé and Robert and Elizabeth Fernea in Marrakesh). Some of these essays are by those who knew the Geertzes personally, others by scholars influenced by their writings. Many contributors describe the nature of their relationship with Clifford and Hildred Geertz, providing a rich commentary on the couple's influence on fieldwork in Morocco.

What also emerged at the UCLA conference were new lines of inquiry that opened up after key texts by Clifford Geertz were translated into French. Although research by the Geertzes in Sefrou consistently engaged with the long, multi-layered ethnographic history of North Africa, it was the case, certainly during the early years of their sojourn in Morocco, that the writings of French social scientists such as Jacques Berque and Paul Pascon were better known to Moroccan counterparts.[5] Before the Geertzes' departure from Sefrou, however, they became acquainted with Moroccan researchers, primarily the circle of geographers and historians from the Sefrou region, for example Mohamed Yakhlef and Lahsen Jennan, who continue a tradition of social science investigation, conferences convened in Sefrou and research results disseminated in a series of publications beginning in 1986 (Figure 2):[6] Mohamed Yakhlef, a former mayor of Sefrou and subsequently professor at the University of Fez, is warmly recalled in Clifford Geertz's autobiographical *After the Fact*: 'I learned a very great deal from him about how a society looks to someone for whom it is not (or not only) an object of inquiry but one of hope and uncertainty' (Geertz 1995, p. 192, note 154). In turn, Lahsen Jennan, professor of geography at the University of Fez,[7] remembers a fieldtrip with Geertz in the mid-1980s:

I accompanied Clifford Geertz in the field, and while I strove to present my hypotheses and some results in the clearest possible manner, I was hoping to learn from the anthropologist that there were some answers to my questions, since I vaguely knew that for several decades anthropology had contributed a great deal to analysing the internal logics that animate social life and elucidating the ways and whys of contemporary and past societies.

Figure 2. El Arbi El Adlouni, an informant of the Geertzes, holding his copy of *Meaning and Order*, a gift of the Geertzes (Susan Slyomovics 2007).

I made the best selection I possibly could of the moments and the sites where I would present the facts or my hypotheses. My work as a geographer consisted of describing and analysing the phenomena we observed; Sanhaja, Amekla, Almis Guigou, Boulmane, Taferdoust, Sekkoura, Tazouta and Sefrou, were the chosen sites where we stopped.

Out of respect, I avoided asking direct questions throughout the entire trip, even when the moments of silence were sometimes quite long. I was uneasy. I didn't know if what I was saying was interesting to him, but the keen attention he gave to my remarks reassured me. I was charmed. Various images of my geographer super-ego floated through my mind as we climbed higher and the air became purer. This was the most interesting journey I ever made in the Middle Atlas.

Fifteen years later, when I read Clifford Geertz's response to a question about the objectives he had in mind when he approached his various field sites, and he spoke of his will to understand why people acted as they did, and for that his approach consisted in describing 'his way of seeing their way of seeing,' or even in reading over their shoulder, I understood that on that day, the gaze of the eagle and the gaze of the horse over the prairie were not the same.[8]

In French translation, despite time lags and publications out of sequence, Geertz has been introduced to generations of francophone Maghrebi researchers who sustain lively and inventive meditations on his Morocco writings, notably his book, *Islam Observed* (Geertz 1968), translated into French as *Observer l'Islam* (1992), and his chapter, 'Suq: The Bazaar Economy in Sefrou,' from the collaborative volume by Clifford Geertz, Hildred Geertz, and Lawrence Rosen, *Meaning and Order in Moroccan Society* (1979), translated into French as *Le souk de Sefrou* (2003).[9]

Clifford Geertz's fieldwork in Sefrou came to an end by 1986. In early May 2000, to convey his gratitude to the town and its inhabitants, he returned for what would be his last visit as the honored guest of the Sefrou municipality, which hosted and co-organised the international conference (and Sefrou's 12th scholarly meeting) subtitled 'Hommage à Clifford Geertz.' In closing remarks delivered in Sefrou's magnificently restored great hall of the Palace of Pasha Omar, Geertz addressed several hundred social scientists:

Yes, I'm very pleased with this event. For an anthropologist to be honored by the people he studied is unusual and I am very pleased by the fact that after all the time I have spent here, people still feel warmly to me. I certainly feel warmly to them and am very pleased to be back here... and very pleased to have had this kind of support and this marvelous reception by the people and the leadership of Sefrou.... The municipality of Sefrou, the Transregional Institute under Abdellah [Hammoudi] of Princeton, the foundation of King Abdul Aziz al-Saud, I am grateful to all of them for this occasion which, I assure them, I do not take personally, but I am very moved by.

Anthropologists, at least of my sort, work in a place for a long time. Two places I have worked, one Indonesia and here in Sefrou, and the notion that one can be received back with warmth is perhaps the greatest reward one can have; not agreement with one's interpretations, not arguments or anything of the sort, but just the notion that they want to see you again and they are willing to stand still for that. I am most moved. When Margaret Mead died, the people of the Manus Islands planted a coconut tree, and I feel this is my coconut tree and I am very, very moved by it.[10]

In different and novel ways, the 2007 conference at UCLA extends and reinforces traditions of research derived from both American anthropologists and North African social scientists, in relation to studies on bled Sefrou, Islam, and Morocco. This volume presents some of the results of the conference, exhibition, and concert – more 'coconut trees,' metaphorically speaking.

Outline of essays

Part I, 'Islam Re-Observed,' begins with Clifford Geertz's unpublished English Introduction to the Hebrew translation of *Islam Observed* (2007). Contributors in this first section discuss

Geertz and religion, especially his anthropological and historical approaches to Islam: Lahouari Addi considers official state Islam espoused by North Africa's post-independence regimes; Hassan Rachik unpacks the complex overlaps between religion and ideology in the region; Mondher Kilani analyses contemporary perceptions of Islam in the West through examples such as the French headscarf controversy; and C. Jason Throop considers Geertz's perspective on religious belief and practice in relation to the social theories he espoused.

Part II, 'Translation, Metaphor, Humor' looks critically at Geertz's Moroccan readers through translation (Dale F. Eickelman), his rhetorical approaches and linguistic insights in the realm of humor (Kevin Dwyer), and his much quoted metaphor of 'culture as text' when applied to the gendered discourses of a Berberophone woman (Katherine E. Hoffman).

Part III, 'Photography, Paul Hyman, and Clifford Geertz,' includes images as well as essays. From 28 November through 16 December 2007, the galleria of UCLA's Fowler Museum was the venue for an exhibition titled 'Sefrou, Morocco Observed: The Photographs of Paul Hyman' (Figure 3). Forty-two images produced by the photographer during his four-month stay in Sefrou in 1969 were displayed, offering one kind of visual anthropological record, a project discussed in essays by Paul Hyman, Susan Slyomovics, and Paul Rabinow.[11]

Part IV, 'Urban Space and Sefrou,' brings together writings that reflect on Geertz's research in the town of Sefrou: Susan Gilson Miller writes about his influence on urban historians of Morocco, while Lawrence Rosen looks at his study of the suq of Sefrou as a comprehensive approach to local religious practices no less than obvious description of marketplace economic structures. Aziz Abbassi, a native son of Sefrou, contributes a short story he labels 'biofictional.' Although Abbassi writes mostly in French and Arabic, reserving Moroccan Arabic for poetry, he explains his choice of the English language for this particular genre:

> I think that, outside the fact that English is my working language of 35 years, there are several other sociolinguistic considerations: the fact that, even though my French was always strong, it was still an imposed language and I refused to use it because of all the emotions and the not-so-great memories it evokes (I talked about a certain 'bleaching of our identity,' i.e., the sudden adoption of French as a new symbol of elitism, etc.); perhaps now I feel somewhat differently as this language is no longer imposed but chosen as is the case with English; I feel that Modern Standard Arabic (MSA) could not translate faithfully all the feelings, emoting, from-the-gut expressions that I needed to relate those childhood events and images. Only *darija* [Moroccan Arabic] could do this.[12]

Figure 3. Paul Hyman at the UCLA Fowler Museum exhibition, 'Sefrou, Morocco Observed: The Photographs of Paul Hyman' (Jonathan Friedlander 2007).

Part V, 'Modernism, Meaning, and Order,' reflects on anthropology's relevance to engage Geertzian theory on topics concerned with everyday contemporary situations of Moroccans in the face of poverty (David Crawford) and transnational development schemes (Thomas Dichter). The collection concludes where the UCLA conference began, with the opening remarks of the mayor of Sefrou, Hafid Ouchchak.

Sefrou has changed since the mid-1980s when the Geertzes last resided there, and in ways that Geertz himself acknowledged in later works. The *medina* of Sefrou, as with many densely populated walled cities throughout Morocco, is draped with wires for Internet and satellite TV (Figure 4); the town faces steep population growth and overcrowded housing even as its official perimeter and boundaries keep expanding. Sefrou's female work force, although involved in the traditional production of silk caftan buttons (*'akkad*), has transformed women's handcraft cooperatives into organisations that address contemporary issues such as AIDS (Figure 5); moreover, many women now seek employment in the clothing factories located in Sefrou's peripheral industrial parks, thereby becoming members of the vast pool of labor outsourced to the Global South. In September 2007, 'bread riots' occurred in Sefrou. Initially, demonstrations were spearheaded by women's organisations from nearby Bhalil to protest the rising cost of foodstuffs; events turned violent once the forces of the provincial governor (not the municipality) entered the scene. What happened appears to have been visually documented almost as it transpired, through videos and photographs, some made with cell phones in Sefrou and posted on weblogs and YouTube. These were images that served to contest official representations even at the level of terminology: was this the chaotic urban crowd rioting over bread or a people's revolt, termed an *intifada* (uprising) in postings?[13]

Figure 4. The medina of Sefrou, draped with wires for Internet and satellite TV (Susan Slyomovics 2007).

Figure 5. Women's handicraft cooperative AIDS banner (Susan Slyomovics 2007).

In the context of many dislocating changes, Hafid Ouchchak won his first mandate as mayor in Morocco's 2003 elections. He represents local Sefrou governance that must work with a range of higher governmental appointees at the provincial level. In search of solutions to the municipal housing crunch, Ouchchak coined the term *bétonville* to describe complex new urban phenomena surrounding Sefrou's walled city (oral communication; Sefrou 2007). In contrast to the earlier and infamous Franco-Moroccan term *bidonville* (shantytown), *bétonville*, though likewise derived from a French word, *béton* ('cement'), refers to unregulated, middle-class housing constructed by developers, often financed with overseas remittance money, but characteristically without any city planning oversight, and thus without building permits, water, electricity, or sewage hook-ups. Mayor Ouchchak's urban projects are notable for articulating and often achieving specific goals: to recognise and legalise uncontrolled, anarchic, clandestine buildings and to simplify onerous and corrupt bureaucratic practices that inhibit owners and builders from speedily obtaining the various and necessary municipal permits. In addition, he completed construction of paved roads, sewage systems (separate pipes for water and waste water), and two new collection centers north and east outside the medina; and placed underground significant amounts of unsightly electricity lines. There are projects to revamp the plaza outside one of the main entrances into the walled city: soon, transforming its status as a vast parking lot, the iconic Bab Mrabaa (featured on the jacket of Geertz, Geertz, and Rosen's *Meaning and Order*) will open out to a pedestrian square adjacent to a large public garden. Thus, this particular spatial interface between the inside and the outside of Sefrou's walled city reverts to a cityscape that 'presents a historically coherent face to the world' (Geertz 1989, p. 292), or at least one that shares attributes with its former appearance in ways that might be recognisable to Clifford and Hildred Geertz when they first came upon the town in 1963:

> Sefrou in the early sixties, by then perhaps a thousand years old, still had a sharpness of definition extraordinary even for Morocco, where everything seems outlined in calcium light. When you approached the town from Fez, then thirty kilometers away, today only twenty, coming up over a small rise from the north, you found yourself confronted with the same scene that had astonished a whole series of early experience seekers. ... The town, the oasis, the mountains, each enclosed within the next, chalk white, olive green, stone brown, each marked off from the next by a line so sharp as to seem drawn with a pen, gave a sense of deliberate arrangement. Site and settlement looked equally designed.
>
> The initial effect of going on then to descend into the body of the town was, for a foreigner anyway, the total, instantaneous, and, so it seemed for an uncomfortable period, permanent dissolution of this sense of clarity, poise, and composition. (Geertz 1995, pp. 11–12)

Acknowledgments

Many institutions and individuals contributed to the success of the conference, concert and exhibition organised by the UCLA Gustav E. von Grunebaum Center for Near Eastern Studies. I thank participants in the conference whose papers are not included in this volume, Kenneth Brown, Abdellah Hammoudi, Lionel Obadia, and Stefania Pandolfo, as well as the panel chairs and discussants, Andrew Apter, Irene Bierman-McKinney, Mohktar Ghambou, Elizabeth Warnock Fernea, Robert Fernea, Douglas Hollan, Abdelhay Moudden and Susan Ossman. I thank the Fowler Museum and its director Marla Berns for co-sponsorship and the help and support of museum staff. It was my pleasure to curate the exhibition of Paul Hyman's photographs with Marla Berns, David Mayo and Janine Vigus, and to collaborate with Bonnie Poon on concurrent public programming at the museum. I thank the UCLA International Institute for co-sponsorship and include the enthusiastic participation of the staff of two centers housed at the Institute, Andrew Apter, director, Azeb Tadesse, assistant director and Sheila Breeding, administrator of the African Studies Center, and Barbara Gaerlan, assistant director of the Center for Southeast Asian Studies. Additional financial support was provided by the UCLA College of Letters and Science. The departments of Anthropology and History graciously hosted conference participants; I am very grateful for the support of the Anthropology Department and its chairs, Douglas Hollan and Alessandro Duranti.

I thank the Los Angeles-based Moroccan American Cultural Center and its director, Dr. Kamal Oudrhiri, for co-sponsorship and for organising the Saturday evening concert of 6 December 2007, an event that celebrated the American debut of Sefrou's Municipal Orchestra with singer Abderrahim Souiri and showcased a variety of Moroccan music, such as the Amazigh/Berber group, Aza, and the mellifluous Arabic and Hebrew vocals of Rafael Skoura. I thank the American Moroccan Institute and its president, Professor Mokhtar Ghambou of Yale University, for funding that helped bring North African professors to American campuses. Both the American Moroccan Institute and the Moroccan American Cultural Center contributed generously to the academic as well as the visual, musical, and gustatory pleasures that were part of these events. A grant from the Wenner-Gren Foundation for Anthropological Research (Gr.CONF-465) enabled several additional North African scholars to present their work.

Finally, I am extremely grateful to the staff of the Center for Near Eastern Studies for expert organising and publicising of the conference, exhibition, and concert events: assistant director Jonathan Friedlander, programme director Peter Szanton, financial officer Mona Ramezani, and web/graphic designer Rahul Bhushan. My profound thanks go to CNES editor Diane James, who expertly worked to translate, edit, and organise final versions of these essays.

Notes

1. I thank Abdellah Hammoudi and Princeton University's Institute for the Transregional Study of the Contemporary Middle East, North Africa and Central Asia, co-organisers of the 3–6 May 2000 Sefrou conference in honour of Clifford Geertz, for providing me with a copy of the conference videotape and for permission to quote.
2. See especially Edwards' book, *Morocco Bound*, especially his chapter, 'Hippie Orientalism: The Interpretation of Countercultures,' pp. 247–301. For my own beginnings in 1969 Morocco, see my paper in this volume, 'Perceptions, Not Illustrations,' note 11.
3. Shweder and Good 2005, Preface, p. vii. See also the academic biography and bibliography, pp. 127–139.
4. For a detailed history of American anthropology in Morocco, see Cefaï 2003.
5. Exceptions to the hold of French scholarship on the Maghreb are perhaps the work of David Hart (on Berber anthropology, and apparently the Geertzes' first guide around Morocco), and Ernest Gellner, the Anglo-Czech anthropologist of the High Atlas Berbers (see Eickelman, 'Not Lost in Translation' in this volume).
6. An exemplary Sefrou conference publication is *Ville moyenne au Maghreb: Enjeu de la décentralisation et du développement local.* Sefrou, Morocco (n.p., [1991]), fifth in the series.
7. See Jennan and Maurer 1994.
8. 'Avant-Propos,' Jennan and Zerhouni 2000, pp. 1–2.
9. Other books by Geertz translated into French are *Bali: Interprétation d'une culture* (1983), *Savoir local, savoir global: Les lieux du savoir* (1986) and *Ici et là-bas: L'anthropologue comme auteur* (1996). A full bibliography is available at *HyperGeertz*, http://hypergeertz.jku.at/geertzstart.html
10. Geertz, closing remarks, 'Hommage à Clifford Geertz' (see n. 1 supra).
11. A slideshow of Hyman's images is available at http://www.international.ucla.edu/cnes

12. Aziz Abbassi, personal email correspondence with Susan Slyomovics. See also the exchange between Abbassi and Driss Ksikes, reporter for Morocco's francophone journal, *Tel Quel*: http://www.telquel-online.com/222/arts1_222.shtml
13. See 'Les émeutes de Sefrou,' www.youtube.com/watch?v=VA3k3xoHcfs, and 'Sefrou révolte,' www.youtube.com/watch?v=pnEEpcAP2Lw

References

Abbassi, A., and Ksikes, D. *Tel Quel* [online]. Available from: http://www.telquel-online.com/222/arts1_222.shtml [Accessed xx Month 2009].

Cefaï, D., 2003. Introduction. *In*: C. Geertz, ed. *Le souk de Sefrou: sur l'économie du bazar*, trans. Daniel Cefaï. Saint-Denis: Bouchène, 1–42.

Edwards, B.T., 2005. *Morocco bound: disorienting America's Maghreb, from Casablanca to the Marrakech Express*. Durham, NC: Duke University Press.

Eickelman, D.F, 2009. Not lost in translation: the influence of Clifford Geertz's work and life on anthropology in Morocco. *Journal of North African studies*, 14 (3/4), 385–395.

Geertz, C., 1968. *Islam observed: religious development in Morocco and Indonesia*. New Haven: Yale University Press.

Geertz, C., 1983. *Bali: interprétation d'une culture*, trans. Louis Évrard and Denise Paulme. Paris: Gallimard.

Geertz, C., 1986. *Savoir local, savoir global: les lieux du savoir*, trans. Denise Paulme. Paris: Presses Universitaires de France.

Geertz, C., 1989. Toutes directions: reading the signs in an urban sprawl. *International journal of Middle East studies*, 21 (3), 291–306.

Geertz, C., 1992. *Observer l'Islam: Changement religieux au Maroc et en Indonésie*, trans. Jean-Baptiste Grasset. Paris: La Découverte.

Geertz, C., 1995. *After the fact: two countries, four decades, one anthropologist*. Cambridge, MA: Harvard University Press.

Geertz, C., 1996. *Ici et là-bas: l'anthropologue comme auteur*, trans. Daniel Lemoine. Paris: Éditions Métailié. Publisher: Location.

Geertz, C., 2003. *Le souk de Sefrou: sur l'economic du*, trans. Daniel cefaï. Saint-Denis: Bouchène, 1–42.

Geertz, C., 2007. *Islam Observed* ['Iyunim ba-Islam: hitpathut datit be-Maroko uve-Indonezyah], trans. No'am Rahmilevits. Tel Aviv: Resling.

Geertz, C., Geertz, H., and Rosen, L., 1979. *Meaning and order in Moroccan society: three essays in cultural analysis*. Cambridge, UK: Cambridge University Press.

Hyman, 2008. Images. Available from: http://www.international.ucla.edu/cnes [Accessed 30 September 2008].

HyperGeertz. 2008. Bibliography [online]. Available from: http://hypergeertz.jku.at/geertzstart.html [Accessed 30 September 2008].

Jennan, L. and Maurer, G., 1994. *Les régions de piémont au Maghreb: ressources et aménagement. Actes du colloque de Sefrou, 9–12 avril 1992*. Tours: centre interuniversitaire d'études méditerranéennes, Université de Poitiers.

Jennan, L. and Zerhouni, M., eds., 2000. *Sefrou: mémoire, territoires et terroirs des moments, des lieux et des hommes (récits et témoignages); Hommage à Clifford Geertz. XIIème Colloque de Sefrou*. [Fez]: Commission Culturelle.

Les émeutes de Sefrou, 2008. Les émeutes de Sefrou [online]. Available from: www.youtube.com/watch?v=VA3k3xoHcfs [Accessed 30 September 2008].

Sefrou révolte, 2008. Sefrou révolte [online]. Avaiable from: www.youtube.com/watch?v=pnEEpcAP2Lw [Accessed 30 September 2008].

Shweder, R.A. and Good, B., eds., 2005. *Clifford Geertz by his colleagues*. Chicago: University of Chicago Press.

Introduction to *Islam observed* (Hebrew Translation, 2007)

Clifford Geertz

A great deal has happened, both in Indonesia and Morocco particularly and in the Islamic world generally, since these lectures were first delivered in what turned out to be the *après nous le déluge* year: 1967. Indonesia has had four presidents since, two of them strong Muslims, two of them more syncretic in outlook. Morocco has had two kings, one of them emphatic and hard-handed, the other hesitant, elusive, and hard to read. The Cold War, which pumped foreign-born ideological passions into home-grown social tensions to the point where the combination threatened to disintegrate politics and dismantle the state, has ended. There are only a few Jews left of what was once a flourishing, if besieged, community in Morocco. Indonesia's rather nativistic Communist Party, once the largest outside the Sino-Soviet bloc and poised for revolution, has been completely destroyed after a failed coup and a popular massacre, its leaders killed, imprisoned, disgraced, or exiled. And, perhaps most important from the point of view of this book and its arguments, what I called in my worried closing pages 'religious mindedness,' as opposed to religiousness as such – self-conscious, doctrinarian belief as opposed to everyday, reflexive faith – and saw as just beginning to become prominent in the two countries as 'Salafism,' 'scripturalism,' 'reformism,' 'purism,' and 'double-mindedness,' has since become pervasive across the whole of the Muslim world under such generalising rubrics as 'Islamism,' 'Political Islam,' 'Neo-Fundamentalism,' and 'Jihadist Islam.' Khomeini, Le Front Islamique du Salut, the Taliban, and Osama have occurred since. So have the al-Aqsa Intifada, the attack on the World Trade Towers, the American invasions of Afghanistan and Iraq, the bombings in Bali and Casablanca, the de-Sovietisation of Central Asia, and the massive migration, increasingly permanent, increasingly contested, of Near Eastern and Asian Muslims to Western Europe and the United States.

Such, indeed, are the perils of trying to write history as it happens, as I was, in part, attempting to do. The world will not stand still till you complete your paragraph, and the most you can do with regard to the future is sense its imminence. What comes, comes: the important thing is whether, when it comes, it makes any sense as an outgrowth of the directive processes you think you have seen. History, it has been said, may not repeat itself but it does rhyme. And from that point of view, looking back from what I see now to what I saw then, though I am both worried and disheartened (I had hoped for better), I don't feel particularly embarrassed, chastened, defensive, or apologetic. I feel that I was, after all, and for all the twists, turns, and murderous surprises, rather onto something. Sensing rain, I may have gotten a flood; but it was, at least, a corroborative one. However unformed and gathering the clouds were then, they were real. So was the storm they portended.

In the last half of the 20th century, the Long Postwar, the study of religion in the social sciences was, with a few prominent exceptions – Peter Berger and Thomas Luckmann, Robert Bellah, Victor Turner, and in Israel, Shmuel Eisenstadt – still pretty much of a backwater, and the reductive version of the so-called secularisation thesis – that the rationalisation of modern life was pushing religion out of the public square, shrinking it to the dimensions of the private, the inward, the personal, and the hidden – was in full cry. Though spirits and goblins, and even high gods, still had purchase among peripheral peoples and submerged classes, and the churches remained open, the illusion had no future as a broadly consequential social force. It might, indeed, probably would, persist for a while, in this place or that, as a primitivist hangover and a drag on progress; but that it would ever again be the directive power, forcible and transformative, in social, political, and economic affairs that it once had been, in the Reformation, the Middle Ages, or the Axial Age, was scarcely conceivable. That, of course, may still turn out to be the case, and Weber's nightmare – 'specialists without spirit, sensualists without heart' – may yet come to pass. But it didn't look like that to me and my out-of-step fellow travelers in 1967. And it certainly does not look like that to anyone now. Hindutva, Neo-Evangelism, Engaged Buddhism, Eretz Israel, Liberation Theology, Universal Sufism, Charismatic Christianity, Wahhabism, Shi'ism, Qtub[1], and 'The Return of Islam': assertive religion, active expansive, and bent on dominion is not only back, the notion that it was going away, its significance shrinking, its force dissolving, seems to have been, at the least, premature.

Summing up in a handful of sentences what has happened to 'religion,' here, there, and around the world, in the closing decades of the last century and the opening one of this, as the 'with a new Introduction by the author, 2004' genre seems to demand, is, of course, quite impossible – a mug's game. But it is possible to suggest a few characteristics of the contemporary scene, within Morocco and Indonesia as well as without, within Islam as well as the other 'world religions,' that seem to be at once something rather new under the sun and logical extensions of settled trends.

Of these, I will mention here only two, though they are but part of a much larger social picture and they rather come down to two ways of saying the same thing: (1) the progressive disentanglement, for want of a better word, of the major religions (and some of the minor ones – Soka Gakkai, Mormonism, Cao Dai, Baha'i) from the places, peoples, and social formations, the sites and civilizations, within which and in terms of which they were historically formed – Hinduism and Buddhism from the deep particularities of Southern and Eastern Asia, Christianity from those of Europe and the United States, Islam from those of the Near East and North Africa; and (2) the emergence of religious persuasion, inherited or self-ascribed, thinned-out or reinforced, as a broadly negotiable, mobile and fungible, instrument of public identity – a portable persona.

The spread of the named and textualised world religions from their points of origin and most immediate relevance to foreign climes and contexts is, of course, of very long standing; that is why they are called 'world religions.' The missionary expeditions of Protestantism into Asia and Africa, the migration of Roman Catholicism along with Iberian conquest culture into Latin America, Islam's explosive thrust east and west from its backwater Arabian heartland, even the rather more elusive, harder to trace radiation of Buddhism out of India into China, Japan, and Southeast Asia, or that of Rabbinic Judaism out of the Near East into Spanish, Slavic, and Germanic Europe – all these demonstrate that beliefs, creeds, faiths, *Weltanschauungen* – 'religions' – travel, change as they travel, and work themselves, with varying degrees of success and permanence, into the finest of fine structure of the most local of local histories.

What is new in the immediate situation, or anyway different enough to represent something of a sea change, is that whereas the earlier movement of religious conceptions and their attendant commitments, practices, and self-identifications was largely a matter of centrifugal outreach in one form or another – missionisation, conquest, calico-trade proselytising, and colonial intrusion; itinerant clerics, outpost academies, *in situ* conversions – the present movement is both larger and more various, more a general dispersion than a directed flow; the migration, temporary, semi-permanent, and permanent, of everyday believers of this variety or that, this intensity or that, this sophistication or that, across the globe. There are an estimated 20 million Indians living outside of India, five million Muslims living in France. There are Buddhists (real ones – Thais, Burmese, Sri Lankans) in London and Los Angeles; Christians, Western expatriate ones, in Tokyo, Riyadh, and Bangkok, Filipino guest-worker ones in the Gulf, Australia, and Hong Kong. There are Muride street peddlers from Senegal in Turin, Turkish and Kurdish grocers in Berlin. Latin-American Indio-Catholics will soon outnumber, if they don't already, Euro-American ones in the United States. 'The world,' in a phrase I quoted years ago from Lamartine when all this was just getting started and I was just beginning to get interested in the ideologisation of religious traditions, 'has jumbled its catalogue.'

This scattering, piecemeal, headlong, fitful, and, except for a certain amount of kinship and neighborhood chaining, unorganised, of individuals (and families) born into locally rooted, culturally particularised settings alters the whole climate of public belief and spiritual self-consciousness, both for those who move and for those into whose midst they move. The formation of diaspora communities, even religiously marked diaspora communities, is also hardly a wholly new phenomenon in world history – Jews in New York, Maronites in West Africa, Hadramis in Southeast Asia, Gujaratis in the Cape. But the scale on which they now are forming (50,000 Moroccans in Amsterdam, 100,000 Malians in Paris, 150,000 Bangladeshis in London, two million Turks in Berlin – virtually all arrived there in the last two or three decades) surely is. It is not just capital that is being globalised, not just doctrine that is spreading.

The transformation of more or less routinely transmitted, compliantly received conceptions of the good, the true, and the actual into explicitly asserted, vigorously promoted, and militantly defended ideologies – the move from 'religiousness' to 'religious mindedness' of various sorts and degrees of intensity – that was 'observed' as getting underway in Moroccan and Indonesian Islam in the middle 60s as those countries began seriously to reconsider their religious history, is now a quite general phenomenon in a world where more and more people, and the selves they have inherited, are, so to speak, out of context: thrown in among others in ambiguous, irregular, poly-faith settings. It is not just Muslims, and not just North Africans and Southeast Asians, who are undergoing this sort of spiritual reorientation; nor is it only happening to migrant populations. The jumbling of the world's catalog is altering both the form and the content of religious expression, and altering them in characteristic and determinate ways, changing at once the tonalities of conviction, its reach and its public uses: that much, whatever else is or isn't happening, is quite clear.

Being a Muslim abroad (or a Hindu, a Christian, a Jew, or a Buddhist; but I must return to my sheep), outside the *Dar al-Islam*, 'The Abode of Islam,' is, as increasing numbers of Moroccans and Indonesians gone elsewhere to work, study, tour, or marry are finding out, a rather different matter than being one at home. Going among non-Muslims induces in many, probably in nearly all, a certain amount of conscious reflection, more or less anxious, on what being a Muslim in fact comes down to, on how properly to be one in a setting not historically pre-arranged to facilitate it. There can be, and are, of course a number of outcomes – an ecumenical generalising of belief to render it less offensive to a religiously pluralised or secularised setting, a 'double-minded' dividing of the self into personal and public halves, a turn toward a much more assertive and self-conscious Islamism in response to the perceived faithlessness of the new setting, and just about every possibility along the way. But a simple continuation of an established, culturally entrenched traditionalism of whatever sort and variety is impossible for all but the most sheltered and unaware.

So where does all this leave my comparative, place-focused, before-the-storm text now? An historical account of how things once were? A relic of the way we thought then? Or a usefully concrete portrayal of the social and intellectual forces now at play in the Islamic world? Of the continuing direction of things Moroccan and Indonesian now that they have outrun country borders? Detachment, perspective, and evenness of mind are hard to come by amidst the clutter and rush of the clamorous present – the enveloping jumble. Stepping back to see how it was that the jumble came to be and what has gone into the making of it may (or, at least, so I am obliged to hope) assist one in gaining them.

Note

1. Editors' note on 'Qtub,': Geertz may have intended 'Qutb' but due to re-translation, an error could have occurred.

Islam re-observed: sanctity, Salafism, and Islamism

Lahouari Addi

Institut d'Études Politiques de Lyon, University of Lyon and Triangle, UMR CNRS 5206, France

Clifford Geertz analysed religious change in Morocco by developing an approach to Islam that uses both history and anthropology. His analysis is rooted in his conception of anthropology as a discipline whose focus is culture, a system of meanings through which human beings exchange goods and symbols. In traditional societies, religion has a particular place in this system where it plays a political role of legitimation. European domination provoked change in Morocco, including the decline of sacredness and the triumph of Salafism, a doctrine more appropriate to the national feeling. A post-Geertzian perspective might consider that Salafism, which has become an official doctrine of the postcolonial state, became radicalised while it was providing mass education, giving rise to the Islamist challenge. The decline of sanctity created a void that Islamism filled.

The December 2007 conference on 'Islam Re-Observed: Clifford Geertz in Morocco' was an opportunity for many scholars from various countries to reassess Geertz's approach to the Maghreb in general and to Islam in particular. In his book *Islam Observed* (1968), Geertz laid the foundations for an anthropology of Islam radically different from the essentialist vision of Orientalism. Geertz is known as an anthropologist of Indonesia and Morocco, countries he studied through the same religion, Islam, which was the main focus of his fieldwork. His theoretical originality lies in his rejection of the analyses of macro-sociology, preferring the micro-sociological approach that deals with the empirical reality lived by individuals, as opposed to the 'total' reality. This epistemological 'bias' is justified by the fact that only the acts of individuals yield insights on meaning produced by psychological consciousness, which is not produced by collective actors (e.g. lineage, tribe, nation, state). It is from this theoretical point of view that Geertz undertakes the analysis of Morocco as a cultural system in which religion is the language and symbol of the social bond. In this paper, I will first examine Geertz's conception of religion and the features of his anthropology of Islam; then I will illustrate the approach by his analysis of the manifestation of the divine in the social world through the relationship between *baraka* (sanctity) and state power in Morocco; and finally I will propose a post-Geertzian approach to explain the evolution from Salafism to Islamism. This will justify the title of my paper, Islam Re-Observed, 40 years after it was observed in a little book that challenged academic theories of Islam as a religious phenomenon in the process of secularisation or an ideological force tamed by Westernised local nationalism.

An anthropology of Islam

A specialist in Indonesian and Moroccan 'Islams,'[1] Geertz gained renown among scholars as an original anthropologist producing an innovative analysis of the religious phenomena he perceived through cultural forms. Influenced by Talcott Parsons, whose student he was at Harvard University, Geertz distinguishes the cultural system (including religion, ideology, common sense, art, science, etc.) from the social and the psychological systems. Culture would be the symbolic outcome of intersubjectivity that constructs the social system in its morphological and objective dimensions.[2] Society would thus be a community of subjective beings organised in social groups and communicating by means of signs and symbols which make up the cultural subsystem. Geertz rejects positivism as ignoring the particularity of social life. His approach stresses cultural transformations from a phenomenological point of view that gives all-importance to world view and meanings. In spite of the importance of culture, Geertz avoids culturalism while insisting on the social bond reproduced by people in their ceaseless interaction marked by communication and the exchange of signs and symbols. If there is one assumption that Geertz refutes, it is that society resembles a machine and that anthropology is the study of its functional logic. Society is neither an engine nor a substance; it is a flux of signs, symbols, and meanings. In order to understand a society, it is necessary to start by observing public places, such as, for example, the *zawiyas* or the markets, which can provide information about social practices. In this undertaking, Geertz deploys a symbolic approach with an emphasis on meanings, practices, behaviours, and institutions. The social bond is seen in its several aspects related to economy, religion, psychology, etc.

It is within this theoretical framework that Geertz analyses Islam in Indonesia and Morocco, perceived through the cultural forms of piety. However, he has neither a general theory of society (as Parsons) nor a comprehensive approach to all religions (as Durkheim). On the assumption that science is based on local knowledge, Geertz focused on Islam, a religion that, for at least two centuries, has experienced upheavals and cultural changes that are still under way today. He pays attention to the evolution of cultural forms and hence to history. When Geertz began his research in the 1950s, Islam was not a promising academic topic. Indeed, theorists of modernisation and acculturation were then predicting, if not the marginalisation of religion, at least its secularisation in the new states of the Third World, where triumphant nationalism promised to make up for lost time with respect to the West. Against this dominant scholarly trend, Geertz's work on Indonesia showed the syncretism of the local religious phenomenon and the new imported ideology, i.e. nationalism. If he did not reject analyses of the secularisation of societies, he was wary of discourses on 'the return of religion' which revealed, according to him, a lack of perspicacity on the part of researchers who wrongly supposed that religion had faded away in the new states but was now on the rebound. For Geertz, religion was always there, but the conceptual tools of positivist analysis did not make it possible to see it (Geertz 2007). Religion is hidden in the syncretism between a faith long rooted in society and a modern ideology that believers adopt in the wake of colonial domination.

In Indonesia Geertz observed that, just as Islam had taken over Hindu civilization by preserving the local way of life, nationalism mobilised Islam by reproducing the natives' ethos. Under the nationalist varnish of the charismatic Indonesian leader Sukarno, the religious spirit persisted in a new language, revealing as much change as permanence. Geertz took an interest in Morocco after having built his reputation as an anthropologist of Indonesia, and in comparison with his writings on the latter, he produced only three works on the former which, it must be said, are of an exceptional density, pioneering a deeper understanding of the political and social significance of Islam in Moroccan society.[3] In these works, he explains why the Qur'an does not inform us about Muslim societies and why it would be superfluous to say that the attitudes of Muslims conform to the sacred text. Moroccan society, to take this example, 'absorbed' the Qur'an and gave birth to Berber Islam, an original sociological phenomenon that must be approached using history, sociology, psychology, political economy, literature, etc. Geertz endeavours to show how Moroccans legitimise their ethos by the Qur'anic text, building institutions and imagining a symbolic system that creates social reality. North African or Berber Islam is apprehended through cultural manifestations, and when there is change, it works through institutions and symbols to perpetuate a faith to which the preceding world no longer corresponds.[4] The change in question occurred once and it benefited Salafism to the detriment of maraboutism.

From the same religion in Morocco and in Indonesia, Geertz outlines a parallel between two experiences that produced different 'mystics.'

> Kalidjaga in classical Morocco would not be heroic but unmanly; Lyusi in classical Java would not be a saint but a boor. (Geertz 1968, p. 98)

This comparative remark highlights the importance of anthropological structures, including the imaginary which grants certain individuals the resources to affirm their sanctity and thus the potential to be feared. Like everywhere else, the basis of authority is belief, a subjective attitude that confers legitimacy on certain social characters who correspond to the expectations of a given public. Charisma does not depend on personal gifts alone; nevertheless, these gifts must be regarded as such by a public that validates authority on the basis of cultural criteria.

Religion is only part of the symbolic action related to the metaphysical issues and the moral paradox that interest Geertz through ethical considerations. He defines religion as a cultural system that provides believers with the cognitive framework within which the objectivity of the world and the subjectivity of the individual join and abide. Religion is a model that explains the world by giving meaning to the mystery of nature (sun, night, rain, illness, death, etc.). It also expresses of the moral sense of the person who seeks to distinguish between good and evil on an external objective basis independent of his own will. Ethos and world view are articulated to build a culture that is reproduced by the practices of individuals, to the point that culture appears to be the expression of reality, and only the mad and the feeble disbelieve the truths it contains.

Faith as a social force and in its symbolic forms is the true object of the anthropology of religion, and it is useful to study transformations of the cultural forms and semiotic expressions of faith in order to understand the social dynamics of countries rent by conflicts whose stakes go beyond religion. One should be attentive to evolutions in the social and cultural expressions of a faith that continues to refer to the same dogma. Scriptural religion does not have the autonomy that positivist Orientalism attributes to it and which would make it a determining factor in social life. Rather, one should consider the reverse: symbolic and institutional religious practices reveal the local anthropological structures. Religiousness exists only through the religious-mindedness that echoes the social imaginary as much as the material conditions of existence. Faith is displayed in rituals and expressed in symbolic forms that correspond to the ethos of a society.

The emphasis on symbolism invites us to interpret manifestations of the sacred in its changing forms, e.g. enthusiasm, mysticism, secularised piety, desire for reform, etc.

'How is it,' Geertz asks, 'that the religious man moves from a troubled perception of experienced disorder to a more or less settled conviction of fundamental order?' (Geertz 1973b, p. 109). This question is at the heart of the anthropology of religion, says Geertz, emphasising that religion comes to people not through simple observation of the tangible world but from a mental operation that implements the idea of authority dwelling in 'the persuasive power of traditional imagery' (in tribal religions), or in 'the apodictic force of the supersensible experience' (in mystical religions), or in 'the hypnotic attraction of an extraordinary personality' (in charismatic religions) (ibid., p. 110). Geertz attempts to show that faith (in authority) comes not from experience or knowledge; rather, the reverse: 'he who would know must first believe' (ibid., p. 110). The essence of religious action is 'the imbuing of a certain specific complex of symbols – of the metaphysic they formulate and the style of life they recommend – with a persuasive authority' (ibid., p. 112). Hence Geertz's definition of religion as

(1) a system of symbols which acts to (2) establish powerful, pervasive, and long-lasting moods and motivations in men by (3) formulating conceptions of a general order of existence and (4) clothing these conceptions with such an aura of factuality that (5) the moods and motivations seem uniquely realistic. (Geertz 1973b, p. 90)

If religion absolutely must be defined, Geertz would say that it is a cognitive framework that provides an explanation of the world and an ethics that echoes the moral sense. Incorporated as a cultural model, this framework finds psychological resources in the individual's subjectivity to influence his moods, stimulate feelings, and release an energy that seems to be independent of his will. Without confusing psychology with sociology, Geertz delimits the psychological sources of social action by using categories of feeling, motivation, predisposition, passion, etc. Established social values set the norm, and individuals will seek to meet the norm that determines what is true or false, good or evil. They will be motivated by their sense of truth, fairness, beauty, etc. But even if this sense is intimate, it is generated by the symbolic environment. Completion of a religious obligation, prayer in a sacred place, participation in a collective ritual, etc., give a sense of duty accomplished and thus observance of morality, order, reason, or, on the contrary, a sense of having failed, of not meeting expectations.

This analytical approach to religion involves three levels: 1) the psychological (dispositions, feelings, motivations, passions) being deeply influenced by 2) the cognitive framework (the causal explanation of surrounding reality) with the facilitation of 3) symbolic forms that make the world familiar and human. Up to the time when he was writing in the 1960s, anthropology had neglected the third level, according to Geertz, which he considers the most important for understanding religious phenomena.[5] He emphasises the interweaving between religion and what is called society to such an extent that one might wonder which of the two categories is the object of his study.[6] Through the study and analysis of religious practices, the researcher realises that society is less an organic reality than a flux of multiple interactions conveying goods and services but also words, images, and symbols expressing an ethos and a world view that make sense 'from the native's point of view.' The concepts of ethos and world view are important in Geertz's approach; he devoted an article to them in 1957 (repr. in 1973a) and would use them constantly in his later work. He acknowledges that they are not precise concepts, referring to moral and aesthetic aspects for the first and cognitive aspects for the second:

A people's ethos is the tone, character, and quality of their life, its moral and aesthetic style and mood; it is the underlying attitude toward themselves and their world that life reflects. Their world view is their picture of the way things in sheer actuality are, their concept of nature, of self, of society. It contains their most comprehensive ideas of order. (Geertz 1973a, p. 127)

Ethos and world view combine and appear in symbolic form through narration, ritual, behaviour, and other actions to form a collective style of life. It is thus, says Geertz, that 'religious symbols formulate a basic congruence between a particular style of life and a specific (if, most often, implicit) metaphysic, and in so doing sustain each with the borrowed authority of the other' (Geertz 1973b, p. 90). Although this approach is not new, he adds, it has not been sufficiently investigated to demonstrate empirically how 'this miracle' occurs. This was the task he set for himself in undertaking fieldwork in Indonesia and Morocco, on the basis of which he developed an anthropology of religion that pays more attention to culture and the problems of interpretation. He insists on the role of symbols as the positive content of any cultural activity, while trying to avoid the pitfalls of introspective psychology and speculative philosophy. He seeks to establish an empirical basis for this symbolic world which sociologists have attempted to explain by considerations of logic.[7] Nurtured by but not reduced to common sense (which was where Malinowski went wrong; Geertz 1968, pp. 92–93), religion is an intellectual construction whose field exceeds the everyday world. It mobilises superhuman characters and monsters from the social imaginary that express the sensitivity, the emotions, and the hopes of individuals in search of themselves.

What Geertz found is that ethos and world vision contain religion and emerge from the local anthropological structure. That is why Moroccan Islam is different from Indonesian Islam, just as French Catholicism is different from Mexican Catholicism. Geertz seems to be saying that scriptural religion is not as univocal as theology says it is, because lived religion is borne by a civilization or by 'the spirit of a people' which clothes it in its own ethos. 'It is really not much easier to conceive of Christianity without Gregory than without Jesus. Or if that remark seems tendentious (which it is not), then Islam without the Ulema than without Muhammed' (Geertz 1968, p. 3). For Geertz, the problem is 'not to define religion but to find it' (p. 1). Religion is not only transcendence or mystical manifestation; it is above all a cultural system enveloping a society. Culture contains social activity by giving meaning to the various acts of individuals. Geertz applied this approach to Morocco via Islam, a window that opens onto Moroccan society in all its sociological complexity and historical depth.

Sanctity, baraka and state power

Geertz left his mark on the sociology of religion with his study of Islam in Indonesia and Morocco. His seminal article, 'Religion as a Cultural System' (1966, repr. in 1973b) has often been cited by subsequent generations of scholars of religion. He put forward the idea that religion is the fusion of an ethos and a world view, and that so-called religious crises occur when these two categories no longer correspond. In addition to being a source of knowledge, religion is the source of legitimacy for political authority in non-secular societies, hence its importance for the ruling elite. It dictates what is legitimate and indicates who shall be the Prince whose mission is to ensure fairness.

Geertz asks what made a peasant from the Atlas Mountains like Sidi Lahcen Lyusi, who had neither money nor troops, defy the powerful Sultan Mulay Ismail, whose legendary cruelty has been reported by historians. What made the ruler recognise this tribal man's prerogative, strength, and grace and prevented him from arresting the man and torturing him as he did with his foes? It was sanctity, Geertz answers, the belief in sanctity as a moral force endowed with the power to bless or to curse.

Islam in Barbary was – and to a fair extent still is – basically the Islam of saint worship and moral severity, magical power and aggressive piety, and this was for all practical purposes as true in the alleys of Fez and Marrakech as in the expanses of the Atlas or the Sahara. (Geertz 1968, p. 9)

This is the first assumption – verifiable on the ground and in history – on the basis of which Geertz undertakes to understand the Moroccan socioreligious milieu, which is quite different from that in Indonesia.[8] The attribute of sanctity is *baraka*, the *mana* of the Berber people that causes life to reproduce and people to be disciplined and obey the rules, thus averting disorder (*fitna*). Baraka is 'a conception of the mode in which the divine reaches into the world. Implicit, uncriticized, and far from systematic, it too is a "*doctrine*"' (ibid. 1968, p. 44, my emphasis). It is above all a symbolic construction that orders the social hierarchy, at the top of which are those who are endowed with it and thereby designated by God to wield the authority over the people.

Baraka is a formidable resource: 'the problem is to decide who (not only, as we shall see, among the living, but also among the dead) has it, how much, and how to benefit from it' (Geertz 1968, p. 44). Geertz analyses baraka through those who are endowed with it and those who respect it. Baraka is an essential component of the political system; it creates micropowers that sometimes serve as counterweights to the central power and sometimes as intermediaries between the sultan and the believers. Baraka corresponds to Max Weber's definition of charisma, in that it makes obedience possible without the use of the physical force.[9] He who has baraka has the gift of transforming the social environment, releasing an energy that exalts the crowd. It is related to the phenomenon of the sacred as manifested in the Durkheimian *mana* that provokes social effervescence. The individual who has baraka, i.e. the saint, attracts and crystallises in his own person the religious feelings of the group for whom he is the symbol, the totem. 'Moroccan maraboutism portrays reality as a field of spiritual energies nucleating in the persons of individual men, and it projects a style of life celebrating moral passion' (1968, p. 98).

Externalised, the feelings of several thousand people are projected onto the saint who now possesses a strength that confirms his charisma. Baraka is symbolic capital whose value is measured by the numbers of the faithful and their capacity to venerate the symbol through which they exalt their membership in their respective groups. Baraka is not a psychological quality inherent in the person of the leader but the social construction of a group united around its own forms of the sacred. Saints do not impose themselves; they are produced by the social environment wherein the symbolic order that provides meanings and social hierarchies finds its justification in Islam. Sainthood is the expression of an ambient religiosity characterised by fervour and devotion; it is a cultural and psychological phenomenon that surpasses religion itself, i.e. ritual practice. The most important feature of this mechanism is the process of social validation whereby certain functions are validated and others discounted.

Sanctity in the Maghreb is as much a religious phenomenon as it is a political resource. It takes baraka, divine grace, to lead people or run a state. Baraka is decisive in the political struggle, since it legitimises authority. Baraka is necessary to the construction of hierarchy in societies where genealogical ethnocentrism – whence the generalised sense of honour – makes everyone believe he is of a higher lineage than others. While honour is relatively abundant, since practically every man is equipped with it, baraka is a scarce resource. From this point of view, baraka prevents the social system from sinking into anarchy brought on by the competition of lineages. But when baraka is abundant, it too becomes a source of anarchy. An excess of vectors of authority kills authority; relative scarcity enhances it. Historians have noticed that periods of political instability correspond to a maraboutic plethora, or what Jacques Berque calls 'the maraboutic revolution.'

Sanctity is hereditary (through genealogy), but one can also become a saint provided that evidence is shown. Geertz distinguishes two sources of baraka: on the one hand, the performance of miracles or the possession of knowledge, and on the other, assumed prophetic ascendancy. Maraboutism in Morocco, says Geertz, prevented sanctity from being the monopoly of the reigning dynasty. The king is a saint because he is *sharif*, related to the Prophet, but he is not the only one with the status of sainthood. Some of his subjects can acquire personal charisma themselves. In the competition between these two principles (the institutional and the popular) lies the secret of the tensions that mark the history of Morocco. Through this competition, popular and miraculous phenomena contest the reigning dynasty's monopoly on authority and sanctity, to some extent setting up a counterweight to the monarch. Hagiographic narrations recount how entrenched marabouts defied the monarch and accused him of failing his commitments to the believers or to God. These narrations express the dissatisfaction of people who complain of unjust rulers and find in the audacious marabout the defender of social justice (*'adl*) as set forth in the Islamic imaginary. The sociopolitical system thus has two legitimacies: one, institutional, centered around the person of the king as a descendant of the prophetic line and thus inherent in state power; the other, emanating from the popular Islam of towns and rural areas, conveyed and disseminated by those endowed with a personal charisma that makes them the agents of divine order. The history of Morocco, at least until the 19th century, was tied to the ceaseless struggle between these two legitimacies that nevertheless attract more than reject each other.

Tension between the prince and the marabout is not the rule. Geertz speaks of 'capitulation in the guise of rebellion – the sherifian principle of religious legitimacy accepted in the course of a moral collision with its quintessential representative – [as] superbly diagnostic' (Geertz 1968, p. 48). He also evokes the unification of the two principles operated by Sufism whose function is to bring 'orthodox Islam (itself no seamless unity) into effective relationship with the world, rendering it accessible to its adherents and its adherents accessible to it' (p. 48). Sufism would thus adapt the revelation contained in the Qur'an to the local ethos by producing multiple and various experiences that help to understand the stakes in North African political history. Moroccan Sufism 'meant fusing the genealogical conception of sanctity with the miraculous' (p. 48). More importantly, the entire system – in its politico-religious aspect – is structured by Sufism through three institutions whose peaceful relationships guarantee stability: the local saint incarnated in a tomb surrounded by a fervor of a cult whose intensity matches the saint's fame; the *zawiya*, the seat of a brotherhood, a religious organisation that often crosses tribal boundaries and is capable of calling up thousands ready to answer the leader's call; and finally, state power, known as *makhzen*, an institution that relies on sainthood and brotherhood to guarantee its existence. These three institutions all have baraka in common, which gives them coherence and relevance and the ability to turn religious conviction into social energy, whereby any one of the three can impose its hegemony over the others, or they may balance their relative powers with perhaps one of them scrambling for position. But Geertz tends to emphasise the unity of the system over its divisions and conflicts. 'Popular saint worship, sufist doctrine (both Spanish and Middle Eastern), and the sherifian principle all flowed together, like a swelling stream, into a single precut spiritual channel: maraboutism' (p. 54).

In the course of several pages in his essay on 'Centers, Kings, and Charisma,' Geertz outlines the rationale of Morocco's political order prior to colonisation, with movement and energy (*haraka* and *baraka*) as its two salient features (Geertz 1983, pp. 134–142). If the king, he explains, were to remain holed up in his palace, he would lose authority over the country because of his charismatic competitors and the potential spread of *siba* (lit., insolence). The makhzen must be ever on the move, demonstrating the symbolic system of state power, in order to neutralise rebellious tribes and contain them within geographical limits (mountains and deserts). The sultan moves with his court, his army, and his loyal tribes, which means that the capital, the locus of state power, is itinerant. This explains why Morocco has several royal cities: Rabat, Fez, Meknes, and Marrakesh. The sultan must move about in a country where the political units (tribes) are also constantly on the move, which implies modifications of loyalty and allegiance, since the siba will often find religious leaders whose charisma is devastating for the reigning authority.[10] The tribal phenomenon imposes mobility on state power because the stake is not land – as a source of wealth – but power and influence embodied in institutions. More than elsewhere, the instrument used to dominate people is a collective belief whose expression – baraka – is the fundamental stake in the social system. Hence the importance of religious beliefs, without which the system would collapse, because in order to sustain itself, it requires loyalty through which physical force is recruited to military ends. Supremacy comes not from economic property; rather, it is an effect of baraka. People – with their material wealth – lend allegiance to whomever possesses it. Having wealth is itself a sign of baraka in a system where strength is a source of wealth according to the logic of predation.

To protect his throne from constant military and religious defiance, the sultan must show that his baraka is stronger by demonstrating his strength and challenging potential competitors in their own locations. Moving 30,000 to 50,000 people, i.e. organising life in an itinerant city, is itself evidence of energy and power. This is the aim of the *mehalla* (way-station, camp), during which allegiances are pledged and taxes collected. The political struggle is not for control of geographical positions or economic centers; rather, it is for control of strategic axes, the subjection of space, and the acquisition of loyalties.

> If Moroccan society has any chief guiding principle, it is probably that one genuinely possesses only what one has the ability to defend, whether it be land, water, women, trade partners, or personal authority: whatever magic a king had he had strenuously to protect. (Geertz 1983, p. 136)

No matter what you have, you must defend it otherwise it will be taken from you. Having that which makes it possible to have anything else, i.e. power, the sultan is more exposed than anyone. In this context, material wealth is not the foundation of power, rather, it rewards and follows power. Strength and loyalty are the basis of power, whence the culture of *la parole donnée*, a man's word, which does not exclude personal ambitions, provided one is confident in the possession of his resources – including baraka – because nothing is worse than failing in a rebellion against the leader to whom one has pledged one's loyalty. Political relationships are shaped by the balance of power and they respond to force. Machiavelli acts and the saint justifies.

The sultan's power is a sign of grace; it means that he has baraka, the means of divine presence on earth, first of all through rituals, but also in providing assistance to orphans, the needy and the poor, etc. Power fascinates the masses; they fear and respect the sultan (*hibat ed-dawla*) who seems to be closer to the divine than to the temporal order. Others who possess baraka covet the fascination of the majority; those who think they have sufficient legitimacy to lead are tempted to venture the conquest of this mystical object. Hence the dialectic of submission and rebellion that characterises the history of North Africa. The most dangerous protagonists in this competition are the idealists who make power an instrument to realise the divine will, usually through the stricter application of religious norms which they believe the sultan has unjustly ignored. These contenders are the most tenacious, the least inclined to compromise, the least tempted by gifts. They are prepared to die for their ideal, and this gives them the strength to defy authority until they are militarily defeated or they achieve their goal. For all of these reasons – materialistic and idealistic – state power remains on the defensive, facing perpetual defiance in a social context where strength is the only reliable political resource. Hence the predatory character of state power which, in order to increase its military strength, must levy tribute from the tribes. The nature of the political struggle is such that the political interests of state power take precedence over wealth, and that the latter proceeds from the former.[11]

This model entered a crisis in the 19th century and with the advent of colonial domination it ceased to exist, out of which, indirectly, a modern form of nationalism was born. The Protectorate and the struggle for independence allowed the reigning dynasty to dominate its traditional adversaries and make them know that their loyal service was expected. The dynasty benefited from modernity in terms of administration, police, army, and radio and television, which it used to serve its own interest, that is, to endure whatever the circumstances. Formerly, saints and brotherhoods were areas of autonomy in relation to the makhzen, opposing it on occasion, integrating and reinvigorating the social system by their very opposition.[12] Basically, the Moroccan political system changed as a result of a shift in the balance of power in the religious arena.

Geertz interprets the aftermath of the North African *Nahda* (awakening, renaissance) – its emblematic figure in Morocco was 'Allal al-Fasi – as an anti-Sufi reaction that reinforced the monarchy in the face of European domination. The energy of religious fervor was rationalised, disciplined, mobilised to support the sultan in the struggle for independence. In this case, the ulema had a greater political role than in the past, campaigning against the so-called maraboutic *jahiliya* (ignorance) in order to steer religious loyalty toward the sultan, henceforward the incarnation of the nation. Now the sultan would only rarely avert to his brotherhood and maraboutic connections. Hence forward, he would refer to Salafism, the doctrine upheld by the kingdom's ulema. Thus the makhzen took advantage of modernity to marginaliwe both the saints and the brotherhoods. It was one of the most significant political changes that took place in Morocco under the colonial order.

Medieval Morocco produced saints; contemporary Morocco does not. If Islam is as present now as it was in the past, Geertz asks, what changed? His anthropology allows us to see the adaptations of the imaginary and the symbolic order as maraboutism was supplanted by the Salafi doctrine that would provide the discourse that legitimises authority. Symbolic forms of piety altered as the balance of power shifted among religious institutions.

Geertz was interested in the evolution of the imaginary and the symbolic order related to lived religion, which serves as the cognitive framework for the legitimation of authority on which the political system rests. He shed light on a process that also drew Ernest Gellner's interest (1981), which was the decline of maraboutism and the rise of Salafism, whose hegemony is related to Western domination and the formation of the nation-state. On this socio-anthropological basis, Geertz pursued the question of how to understand the dynamics of change in Moroccan society. More important than observing the effects of contact with the West, for Geertz, was his analysis of the processes by which change took place, for, as he concludes, it was no longer the same society.

> What we want to know is, again, by what mechanisms and from what causes these extraordinary transformations have taken place. And for this we need to train our primary attention neither on indices, stages, traits, nor trends, but on processes, on the way in which things stop being what they are and become instead something else. (Geertz 1968, p. 59)

Geertz suggests that religiosity significantly weakened but the religious spirit was still there. Certainly the sacred text had not changed, nor was the change a matter of faith; it was the practice of lived religion that changed, its social institutions and its rituals. Now the question was not 'What shall I believe?' but 'How shall I believe it?' (Geertz 1968, p. 61). Doubt did not undermine faith; it gripped the believers themselves; their world view no longer corresponded to reality. Had God abandoned his creatures? Would the world survive the 14th century AH? Piety remained, Geertz observes, but not confidence. 'How do men of religious sensibility react when the machinery of faith begins to wear out? What do they do when traditions falter?' (Geertz 1968, p. 3). The change offered North African societies a choice between utopia and millenarianism or disenchantment and historical consciousness. The Maghreb took the middle course, mixing millenarianism and historical consciousness, giving birth to a nationalism that was modern in form and ancient in content. Influenced by Salafism, it was the vehicle for a utopian ideal that reproduced the myth of the state overseeing fairness and happiness. In spite of its archaisms, North African society grew disenchanted with maraboutism. The surviving brotherhoods and zawiyas no longer have the influence they had in centuries past. The *bouniyya* (naïve believer) whom Bourdieu discussed in the context of Kabylia no longer exists in Algeria or Morocco.

In this context, it is not surprising that the sultan of Morocco, of maraboutic origin though he was, made common cause with the Salafi movement and entrusted the ulema with the defense the postcolonial state's interpretation of Islam. Popular religion as manifested in sainthood, *musems*, zawiyas, etc., lost its strength during the colonial period and continued to decline after independence under pressure from social, economic, and cultural changes such as rural migration, generalised monetary exchange, and the decline of traditional educational institutions. Social changes wrought by wage-earning and commercial exchange led to urban individualism and helped weaken the traditional religiosity that corresponded to the communal way of life (see Addi 1999). This sociological approach highlights the increasing lack of coherence between maraboutic culture and the social system. Cultural cohesion was disrupted by historical changes. Individuals began to doubt themselves and wonder whether they had changed the religious message, from which arose the utopian dream of going back to the source by imitating the model of the pious ancestors (*al-salaf al-salih*), and being loyal to the sacred text. Scriptural Islam, Salafi Islam, took advantage of these developments. Devoid of individual or collective ecstasy, corresponding to new social and political aspirations inspired by colonial domination, it successfully challenged the Sufi heritage.

From Salafism to Islamism

This is the historical and conceptual framework within which Geertz approaches religious change in Muslim societies. He asserts that researchers have not taken the measure of the chasm that divides a world view, with its cultural and sociological relevance, from Western domination which denies that relevance. The traditional Muslim imaginary was full of signs and meanings that confirmed the logical structure of the world. Social reality was built, or rather perceived and lived, beneath the gaze of the divine mediated by the ulema and the saints. Unfortunately, or fortunately, that world disappeared and the signs became orphans. Traditional Islam, quietist and maraboutic, saw the Ottoman Empire collapse and was itself impotent in the face of military defeat by Europeans whose new God was science and technology. The new reality shattered the psychosocial equilibrium of common sense which could neither comprehend nor admit the superiority of Europe. Why had the powerful saints failed to protect *Dar al-Islam* from European domination? Neither the saints with their omnipresent and deterrent baraka, nor the ulema with the secrets of divine power in their possession could prevent this unnatural (from the believers' point of view) supremacy. Their symbolic system could no longer influence reality. Reality was detached from the symbol that had made sense of it. It was like an earthquake, says Geertz; the psychological and sociological consequences introduced doubt into a culture that until then had been confident of its validity and its cosmological superiority. Believers wondered whether they were worthy of the faith, since they were convinced that their religion is the best and the Qur'an is the word of God. They felt guilty and questioned their traditional way of believing, and this caused profound religious changes, the most spectacular being the near disappearance of maraboutism and the brotherhoods. Scripturalism stepped forward to reconstruct the symbols and sustain the religious spirit by going back to the source, to the pious ancestors whose message had been distorted through centuries of wrong practice.

But the scriptural Islam propagated by Salafism is not secularisation. Rather, it signals the end of popular religiosity and religious bigotry and ensures the hegemony of religion over all social activities. Salafism turned Islam into an ideology in order to protect it from encroaching modernity, which is why it is not the equivalent of the Protestant reform that set in motion the dynamic of secularisation in Europe. Scripturalism or Salafism had nothing to do with the content of faith; if it had, there would have been a profound religious revolution, likely producing a schism as in Christendom. Islam experienced institutional but not dogmatic change. There was no new interpretation of the sacred text. The ideologisation of Islam tells us about the disarticulation of religious symbols from social reality. There was no Luther amongst the Muslims; there was no Weber amongst the specialists in Islam. This is where Geertz departs radically from Gellner who considered Salafism to be the source of modernity.

Salafism was certainly a nationalist reaction to European expansion, but its analysis and teachings did not break with the myth of origins. Its explanation of the Muslim predicament was, briefly, as follows: 1) Muslim society is dominated by Christendom because it has become weak; 2) it is weak because it has drifted away from original Islam; 3) it is necessary to return to the origins and root out influences posterior to the pious ancestors, including maraboutism, a pagan Berber relic; 4) maraboutism prevents the establishment of a central authority that can embody the nation and organise the struggle against colonial domination.

After prolonged resistance to colonial domination, Salafism finally had its state, but did it meet the needs of modernity? Did it create a new world view to liberate the temporal from the tyranny of the sacred imaginary? Thanks to mass education, the Salafi discourse is no longer reserved for the elite. It has been popularised and has reached the poor urban classes who now use it to denounce the government's failure to end poverty, social inequality, corruption, and so forth. By winning over the popular classes, the Salafi discourse gave rise to Islamism among the new educated generations and now they threaten the regime. And the authorities are encouraging the brotherhoods against the Islamists whose defiance of the monarchy has made them popular.

A few years after independence, Salafism became radicalised as it evolved into political Islam, sometimes using violence to protect the faith. Salafism had the political-ideological answer to the colonial situation – the creation of an independent state – but it has no answer for the post-colonial situation in terms of a modern political project (democracy, the rule of law, separation of powers, etc.). Its historical relevance stems from the fact that it corresponded to the patriotic expectations of the peoples who rejected colonial domination. Those same patriotic expectations remain, while the economic and social development gap vis-à-vis the West has widened. Social unrest is fuelled by disappointment and the feeling that the nation-state has been 'monopolised by elites who betrayed the ideal of the national struggle and became the relay for Western economic and cultural domination.' This is the creed of the Islamist movement which claims the Salafi heritage and promises 'true liberation.' Contemporary Islamism is a post-independence

Salafism or neo-Salafism that seeks to achieve liberation by entrusting direction of the state to 'true' Muslims whose faith brings them closer to the masses, now forsaken by 'a corrupt elite turned toward the West.'

In this sense, Islamism predates the independence of the Maghrebi states; its ideology was already developed by Jamal al-Din al-Afghani, Muhammad Abduh, Rashid Rida, and their disciple Hasan al-Banna. The continuity between contemporary Islamism and Salafism is obvious: education was turned over to the Salafis (it could not have been otherwise) and they formed generations who believe in the historicity and perfection of the model of the pious ancestors. For Geertz, 'rather than the first stages of Islam's reformation, scripturalism in this century has come, in both Indonesia and Morocco, to represent the last stages in its ideologization' (1968, pp. 69–70). What is called 'Muslim reformism' – the ideologisation of scriptural Islam, the rejection of post-Qur'anic commentaries, the mythologisation of the pious ancestors – did not aim to build a new sociopolitical order but rather to defend the old order by adapting the faith to the new political framework. i.e. the nation-state. This provoked significant change but not deep enough to release an internal dynamic of modernity. Scriptural Islam was not modern enough intellectually to build a symbolic system compatible with secularisation, as Protestantism did in northern European societies at the beginning of the modern era.

Salafi reformism had two aims: to liberate the country from colonial domination and to modernise society. It succeeded in the first but failed in the second because it denied the historicity of Muslim society that it confines to a mythical past. Salafism prevented common sense (in the Geertzian sense) from accepting the profane knowledge that could have neutralised the myth and the tyranny of the sacred. Of course, a century passed between Jamal al-Din al-Afghani and independence in the Maghreb, and men are marked by the historical processes that produce them as well as by the ideas they defend. 'Allal al-Fasi, who died in 1974, was a Salafi who was very open on many social issues. But then a characteristic of ideological movements is to embrace trends ranging from the most moderate to the most dogmatic.

In the end, social expectations remain the same, i.e. modernisation and social justice, and they have not been realised by the independent state. Educated in the Salafi school, the Islamists propose to meet these expectations by going back to the model of the Prophet's generation. A great deal has been written about Islamist movements, but this much is certain: they are a contradictory expression of modernity in societies under cultural and economic domination. They are mechanically modern in the sense that they make it possible for the popular classes to be heard in the political arena, but they are ideologically conservative insofar as they apply morality and psychology to political problems (see Addi 1997). The failure of the North African state is basically that of Salafism which was its ideological touchstone and whose principal weakness is that it granted too much importance to the Muslim's cultural identity, to the detriment of his universality. In its discourse and its implicit assumptions, culture is an ahistorical essence that denies the universal anthropological character of the Muslim individual. Cut off from his humanity, he is entirely absorbed by his religious identity, which speaks in his name.

As a result, Muslims are forbidden to imagine a new social and political order, which is likened to *bid'a* (innovation). Deprived of historical consciousness, they are immured in rejection and negation. This posture was effective in the national struggle but it produced illusions (stronger in Algeria than elsewhere), and has now become an obstacle to the implementation of the rule of law. Salafism did not encourage the social sciences (sociology, anthropology, history, political economy, linguistics, psychology, political science, etc.), which it suspected of being Western ideologies meant to subvert the Muslim mind. Salafism encouraged Muslims to study the natural sciences (physics, mathematics, biology, etc.) and discouraged them from studying the social sciences. The social turmoil constantly reported in the media points to the need either for the old world, or for a new world to be created by internal forces. Salafism and its by-product, Islamism, are prisoners of the medieval paradigm that subjects the temporal to the spiritual life. Both express a will to protect the faith in a world where the traditional world view is no longer corroborated by experience. The historical and theoretical weakness of Islamism lies in the desperate will to protect the faith by political means, instead of using *ijtihad* to reinterpret its dogma and adapt it to the new historical reality. This failure to articulate the signifier with the signified explains the violence and the passion of Islamism.

Neither Salafism nor Islamism has been able to invent modern forms of *religiousness* that correspond to *religious-mindedness*. As a Kantian anthropologist, Geertz distinguishes between the two concepts that relate to two different realities: social practice (religiousness) and the moral ideal (religious-mindedness). The former performs the latter through rituals. Religiousness is thus the social demonstration of religious-mindedness, giving rise to cults and institutions. The Durkheimian totem captures this social energy and crystallises it in a symbolic system which eventually becomes detached from religious-mindedness and obeys its own dynamics. Distinguishing between religiousness and religious-mindedness, Geertz is more Durkheimian than he might think, even if Durkheim was primarily concerned with religiousness as a social fact. Durkheim was less interested in religious-mindedness, which, according to him is linked to subjectivity and therefore related to psychology. He was interested in religiousness which, according to him, symbolically reinvents the idealized society as the divinised society. For Durkheim, God is society and vice versa.[13] This Kantian perspective leads to two conclusions: first, that religion is unavoidable, even if its cultural forms – collective representations – change over time; secondly, new representations for religious-mindedness must be found in modernity. Geertz's paradigm explains the crisis in Muslim societies by the break between religious-mindedness and religiousness. The saints lost their influence in the detribalised rural world, while the ulema no longer have their former prestige. A feeling of collective guilt has been aroused that will persist until religious-mindedness finds new forms of religiousness.

In conclusion, re-observing Islam forty years after it was observed by Geertz, we realise that the crisis of North African societies is profound because it is related to the underpinnings of the social bond in its ethical aspect. The ethos, in relation to the individual's moral sense, is expressed and crystallised in the cultural forms of religiousness. In Muslim societies, the moral sense is in search of a new ethnocentrism, insofar as the traditional ethnocentrism lost its substance through contact with the West. Independence promised to restore it in a kind of syncretism of Islam and modernity, but in fact the elites failed to invent a new culture. No social group can live without a proper ethnocentrism. Islamism is a defensive reaction to the failure of the postcolonial state to create a modern culture appropriate to religiousness. Geertz perceived these problems in the 1960s when he wrote *Islam Observed*. Forty years later, he would write that he sensed rain then; now we may have gotten a flood (Geertz 2005, p. 10).

Acknowledgement

This paper, was written at the Institute for Advanced Study, Princeton, in 2003. It comes from a forthcoming book on Clifford Geertz and Ernest Gellner on North Africa. I would like to thank Susan Slyomovics for asking me to organise with her the conference on 'Geertz on Morocco' held at UCLA in December 2007.

Notes

1. For Geertz, religions are different even when they refer to the same dogma. Thus there are several 'Islams,' as there are several 'Christianities,' according to time and place.

2. The concept of culture is crucial for Geertz, who divides it into subsystems: religion, art, science, common sense, ideology, etc. In secular societies, ideology becomes the basis for legitimating political power, a role formerly served by religion. Ideology acts as a state religion in countries where religious practices tend to be confined to the private sphere.

3. *Islam observed* (1968), in which his remarks on Indonesia occupy as much space as those on Morocco; 'Suq: the bazaar economy in Sefrou' (Geertz 1979); and a chapter titled 'Centers, kings, and charisma: reflections on the symbolics of power' (Geertz 1983), in which he compares the Moroccan and the English monarchies.

4. Heretofore accustomed to studying the atemporal structures of 'dead and dying societies,' anthropology now needs history, art, literature, psychology, etc., to study these transformations with the aid of documents and manuscripts that are as useful as field research. Geertz was one of the first to reconcile anthropology and history, breaking with the structuralist perspective on the identical reproduction of social systems which the ethnocentrist gaze had fixed in time.

5. Since the origin of what we call 'the science of religions' with Muller in the 19th century, it has been difficult to find a definition acceptable to all. Every definition proposed has been criticised for essentialism, sociological or psychological reductivism, or ethnocentrism. We must acknowledge that it is difficult to define a social fact as total as religion. Authors such as Durkheim and Weber gave up on providing a definition, even though their approaches contain implicit definitions of religion; likewise Geertz who presents religion as a cultural system with its own structure of meaning.

6. Society in the Durkheimian sense does not exist for Geertz who, like Bourdieu, prefers to reflect on the articulated practices that construct what ordinary language calls society. But it is important to note that for Geertz, it is the analysis of a practice – artificially isolated for methodological purposes – that provides information on the logic of the social arena. The social world is an ocean, and chemical analysis of a single drop of water reveals the molecular structure of all the water in the ocean.

7. For Geertz, religion is a dense and total phenomenon that envelops man in his social being and subjective complexity, implicating social institutions as much as consciousness. The anthropologist leaves the believer's existential anguish to the psychoanalyst or the psychologist, limiting himself to lived religion and the meaning borne by its cults. This restrictive approach draws its theoretical legitimacy from the capacity of institutions, activities, and social forces linked to faith to crystallise themselves and become autonomous from scripture or dogma.

8. The sacred takes different forms of expression in Indonesia where wet rice cultivation occupies the sedentary peasant, 'nursing his terrace, placating his neighbours, and feeding his superiors' (Geertz 1968, p. 11). Islam is manifested in a quietude that is the opposite of the maraboutic restlessness of the Maghreb. The symbolic framework and the imaginary are intimately articulated with the physical space in which a society materially reproduces itself. Hence the variation in the forms of expression of the sacred which frees the energies, called illuminism in Indonesia and maraboutism in Morocco, and which structures power relationships in the socioreligious arena that are manifested at the political level as the energy is captured by certain individuals and transformed into the legitimacy that gives authority and power.

9. Geertz claims to draw inspiration from Max Weber in addressing the problem of the meaning that individuals give to their actions, but he is closer than he admits to Durkheim, for whom society projects itself onto the terrain of religion and vice versa. For Geertz, society and religion are inseparable, one merging into the other, or rather both dissolving into culture to form a system. Sociologists of religion are wrong to cast Durkheim and Weber in opposition, since their approaches converge despite their profound differences. Geertz's reflections on baraka offer an example of this convergence (see also Segal 1988; 1999).

10. It happens that during their lifetimes such leaders founded brotherhoods in which the central power is obliged to deal with because of their ability to mobilise human and material resources into a formidable political force. When they felt sufficiently powerful, these brotherhoods would often attempt to conquer power, and when successful, they would fuse the two principles of legitimacy, making the founder's baraka a family patrimony that could be transmitted from generation to generation, at least insofar as his descendents were able to maintain its vigour and resist the competitors who would certainly arise.

11. There is a trail to follow here that could provide one explanation – among others – for the freezing of economic development in the Maghreb. The preeminence of political power over material wealth prevents competing dynamics from producing goods. Yesterday the danger arose from religious power, which it was necessary to

monopolise; today the danger arises from economic power which must not be allowed to become a strong political actor who will demand the institutionalisation of power.

12. Supposedly guaranteed by the parties and the unions, political participation is superficial because the regime desires to restrain it and distract people from the real game: the competition for power.

13. In France, these new representations are the values that form the basis for secularism, the civil religion of a disenchanted, industrialised, urbanised society. It was no fluke that Durkheim became the first theorist of secularism as civil religion in France.

References

Addi, L., 1997. Political Islam and democracy: the case of Algeria. *In*: A. Hadenius, ed. *Democracy's victory and crisis*. Cambridge, UK: Cambridge University Press, 105–120.

Addi, L., 1999. *Les mutations de la société algérienne: famille et lien social dans l'Algérie contemporaine*. Paris: La Découverte.

Geertz, C., 1968. *Islam observed: religious development in Morocco and Indonesia*. New Haven: Yale University Press.

Geertz, C., 1973a. Ethos, world view, and the analysis of sacred symbols. *In*: C. Geertz, ed. *The interpretation of cultures*. New York: Basic Books, 126–141.

Geertz, C., 1973b. Religion as a cultural system. *In*: C. Geertz, ed. *The interpretation of cultures*. New York: Basic Books, 87–125.

Geertz, C., 1979. Suq: The bazaar economy in Sefrou. *In*: C. Geertz, H. Geertz and L. Rosen, eds. *Meaning and order in Moroccan society: three essays in cultural analysis*. Cambridge, UK: Cambridge University Press, 123–313.

Geertz, C., 1983. Centers, kings, and charisma: reflections on the symbolics of power. *In*: C. Geertz, ed. *Local dnowledge: further essays in interpretive anthropology*. New York: Basic Books, 121–146.

Geertz, C., 2005. Shifting aims, moving targets: on the anthropology of religion. *Journal of the Royal Anthropological Institute*, 11 (1), 1–15.

Geertz, C., 2007. La religion, sujet d'avenir. *In*: Michel Wieviorka, ed. *Les sciences sociales en mutation*. Auxerre: Sciences Humaines, 427–434.

Gellner, E., 1981. *Muslim society*. Cambridge, UK: Cambridge University Press.

Segal, R.A., 1988. Interpreting and explaining religion: Geertz and Durkheim. *Soundings*, 71 (1), 29–52.

Segal, Robert A., 1999. Weber and Geertz on the meaning of religion. *Religion*, 29 (1), 61–71.

How religion turns into ideology

Hassan Rachik

Hassan II University, Casablanca, Morocco

When Western mass media deal with wife beatings, suicide bombings, and other forms of violence that occur in Islamic communities, liberal and progressive intellectuals react by saying that such actions do not represent mainstream Islam which is peaceful, tolerant, etc. While avoiding judgment of any particular religion as violent or peaceful, as compatible or incompatible with democracy and modernity, I propose to consider how religion turns into ideology. I will examine the political and cultural processes through which religious ideas stop being what they are and become instead an ideology.

[W]e need to train our primary attention neither on indices, stages, traits, nor trends, but on processes, on the way in which things stop being what they are and become instead something else. (Geertz 1968, p. 59)

I propose to consider how religious beliefs stop being what they are and become instead something else: an ideology. A description of the ideologisation of religion, as compared to that of the natural sciences, the social sciences, history, etc., presents particular challenges. As cultural systems, religion and ideology share many features and play similar social roles (e.g., as a guide for social action, in mobilisation, in legitimisation). Racism, for instance, might use anthropological ideas or biological findings to consolidate its ideological postulates. However, the boundaries between biology, anthropology, and racism are clearer than those that separate religious ideologies and the religion upon which they base their authority. One might not call biologists who refer to biology racists, whereas activists who refer to Islam are often called Islamists, radical Islamists, etc. My point is that just as the analysis of anthropology or biology may not help us to understand racist phenomena, consideration of Islam and its history, beliefs, rituals, etc., is likewise not very useful in understanding the political use of Islam. The subject of this study is not an abstract religion but the actual use of a religion, a set of ideas and rituals observable within actual communities (Rachik 2004).

The similarities between religion and ideology can also be confusing on the theoretical level: scholars are faced not with a one-way process, that is, one in which religions turn into ideologies, but one in which ideologies also turn into religions. Non-religious ideologies, such as Marxism, are often assimilated to religion, a pseudo-religion or a secular religion. These cultural affinities between ideology and religion make it difficult to describe the ideologisation of religion.

Geertz deserves credit for pointing out the political and cultural context of the ideologisation of Islam. The main features of this context are the fate of religious traditions, the breakdown of traditional consensus, increasing doubt, and loss of orientation resulting from the spread of modern secularism. Furthermore, the political conditions of the ideologisation of religion consist in the spread of politics, particularly the emergence of intellectuals and the public in their modern sense, and the shift of some leaders and followers from being Muslims as a matter of tradition to being oppositional Muslims. Religious ideologies tend to deal less with metaphysical and theological issues and increasingly stress social and political topics. No ideology can mobilise an entire religion, a whole system of beliefs and rituals. The notion of *bricolage* may be useful in analysing how, within this huge religious store ideologies select their tools and reject others.

The fate of tradition, increasing doubt, and loss of orientation

Many authors have held that the rise of ideologies occurs in a specific situation characterised by the fate of traditional beliefs. Karl Mannheim stresses social mobility as the main factor that leads people to doubt their own traditions. Within traditional societies, the absence or the weakness of social mobility maintains and consolidates the autonomy of communities and the isolation of their world views from those of others. The ideologisation of religion takes place within a context characterised by the rapid and profound social and intellectual disintegration of stable traditional societies (Mannheim 1985, pp. 7–8, 65, 85). Mannheim claims that theories, norms, beliefs, etc., 'degenerate' into ideologies when they 'prevent a man from adjusting himself at that historical stage.' For Mannheim, the content of ideas seems secondary, in the sense that it does not determine whether or not they are ideological. What is relevant is the adjustment of ideas to the actual and historical context. The example of the prohibition against charging interest on loans shows that this ethical attitude was not ideological when it was adjusted to a traditional society based upon intimate and face-to-face relations. Within such an economy based upon the exchange of services, gifts, and counter-gifts, it is bad to ask a relative or a neighbour for interest on a loan. According to Mannheim, the same ethical attitude is transformed into an ideology once it no longer corresponds to the new context and cannot be observed without difficulty: 'The more the real structure of society changed, the more this ethical precept took on an ideological character, and became virtually incapable of practical acceptance' (pp. 95–96). With the rise of capitalism, the ethical interdiction became maladjusted and very difficult to obey. It degenerated into an ideology when the Church tried to maintain the interdiction and use it as a weapon against its opponent, the bourgeoisie. The few examples offered by Mannheim emphasise the idea of the ideological distortion between beliefs and 'real' social relations. 'Viewed from this standpoint, knowledge is distorted and ideological when it fails to take account of the new realities applying to a situation, and when it attempts to conceal them by thinking of them in categories which are inappropriate' (p. 96). We may see instances of declining social groups who embrace antiquated ideas, but this may also concern rising social groups. Such is the case of the proprietor who becomes a capitalist but continues to treat his workers according to the ideas and terms of patriarchal society. Paraphrasing Mannheim, the ideologisation of religion is an anachronistic process consisting in the commitment to antiquated religious ideas that no longer correspond to the new realities. It should be noted, however, that, because of its exclusive stress on the past, Mannheim's explicit definition of ideology is too narrow to encompass the rising bourgeoisie and the proletariat whose ideologies he himself regards not as a mere commitment to the past but, on the contrary, as a set of new and revolutionary ideas (p. 65).

Geertz retains from Mannheim the characteristics of the changing context rather than his analysis of the ideologisation process. People who live in traditional societies 'act as … men of untaught feelings; they are guided both emotionally and intellectually in their judgments and activities by unexamined prejudices, which do not leave them "hesitating in the moment of decision, sceptical, puzzled and unresolved"' (Geertz 1973a, p. 218). In the colonial context, the traditional road maps that had oriented men in the past lost their usefulness. It is loss of orientation that gives rise to ideological activity (p. 219). Geertz describes the social process leading to the rise of religious ideologies as 'a progressive increase in doubt' (Geertz 1968, p. 61). What Muslims doubt is the depth and the strength of their belief, not its validity. Men have not come to doubt their religion, but to doubt themselves. Traditional beliefs still have spiritual power, but they no longer produce the certitude. It is this social context characterised by the disjunction between evanescent religious traditions and the will to maintain them, and the uncertainty that they can be maintained by themselves, which gives rise to religious ideologies (pp. 60–62, 77).

Following Mannheim, Geertz points out the lack of adjustment between religious traditions and the new and unfamiliar colonial context, and contends that it is the loss of power of these religious traditions that leads to the ideologisation of religion. However, Geertz avoids Mannheim's evaluative approach. He does not consider ideology as an antiquated (pathological) system of ideas. On the contrary, ideologies are 'maps of problematic social reality and matrices for the creation of collective conscience' (Geertz 1973a, p. 220). Ideologies are not old maps that people hold on to at all costs in order to interpret and act upon new realities. They are new maps that may contain both old and new ideas, depending on the context. Geertz approaches Salafism as a religious ideology and as a set of means by which intellectuals attempt to adapt Islam to the modern world. For social actors who experience the loss of the usual reference points in their traditional communities, ideology provides a guide that makes unfamiliar situations meaningful. Ideology, be it religious or not, provides 'a guide for political activity; an image by which to grasp it, a theory by which to explain it, and a standard by which to judge it' (Geertz 1973b, p. 340). It attempts 'to render otherwise incomprehensible social situations meaningful, to so construe them as to make it possible to act purposely within them …' (Geertz 1973a, p. 220). Ideologies are not antiquated maps that prevent people from taking a 'good direction,' they are systematic and sustained intellectual adaptations to new realities. Whether or not these maps are right or wrong is a secondary issue for Geertz, who tried to avoid 'Mannheim's paradox' by approaching ideologies as a system of symbols and not as a system of knowledge.

Salafi intellectuals held that Islam as traditionally understood and practised was not an appropriate guide for social action in the new context. Colonial intrusion produced a reaction not only against the Other, i.e. Christianity, but against local religious traditions. Salafism was the first ideological alternative to traditional visions of religion at the end of the 19th century. It was stimulated by the colonial encounter, yet its main target was not Western civilization but local religious traditions. Salafism or the Salafi movement, from *as-salaf as-salih* (the righteous ancestors or the virtuous forefathers, i.e. the Prophet Muhammad and his companions), is based on a literal interpretation of basic scriptures. It was known for its radical and uncompromising purism: its attempt to establish the 'plain,' 'original,' 'uncorrupted' Islam of the Days of the Prophet and the Rightly Guided Caliphs.

Geertz contends that the loss of power of traditional religion is due to the secularisation of thought, and that the major response to this secularisation is the ideologisation of religion. I find that the social processes that, according to Geertz, define the ideologisation of religion are often too general in the sense that they implicate the whole of society. I suppose that a description of the ideologisation of religion that emphasises the social groups directly involved will be more accurate. Religion is turned into ideology when an elite is in a situation that prevents it from using traditional religion which is regarded as inappropriate to the new realities. Geertz is more accurate when he writes that Salafism was the main agency of the ideologisation of religion, that Salafi intellectuals were the group who felt the tension between religion and the process of secularisation in the modern world. Salafi intellectuals were the first to be aware of changes in their society, of the maladjustment of the traditional interpretations of religion and the need for a new version of religion (Geertz 1968, pp. 69, 73, 102–105).

Following Mannheim's distinction between the unconscious acceptance and the conscious defense of tradition, Geertz contends that, in traditional societies, people take their beliefs for granted and see them as being too strong to need defending. But when traditions are threatened by alternative and secular conceptions of the world, a group of intellectuals finds it necessary to defend them. Rational and secular bourgeois ideology was a response to the weakening of religious and political traditions associated with the predominant Church and Monarchy. It should be noted that the response of the first Muslim ideologists had nothing to do with the fate of religious traditions. It was not the actual tradition which was taken for granted that became the emblem of identity, but a tradition that ideologists strove to invent, discover, create, reinterpret, and propagate to the broad public. There is a lack of evidence for the tension between the fate of tradition and the will to maintain it. What Salafism sought to propagate was not something that people knew and practised and were expected to maintain at all costs. On the contrary, what people used to practise (Sufism, veneration of saints, etc.) was largely criticised rather than defended. It is a soft ethnocentric prejudice to think that the emergence of ideologies at the expense of tradition is a universal process. Salafism was a response to the domination of Western civilization and not a reaction to the weakening of local traditions.

Furthermore, many documented studies have shown that religious traditions were not weak at the time. Religious traditions in Morocco were not based on a clear opposition between the ulema and the Sufis, between scripturalism and maraboutism. Many ulema and kings were members of Sufi orders. Some ulema and learned men, including nationalist intellectuals, even defended an orthodox Sufism (i.e. conforming to the Qur'an and the tradition of the Prophet) as opposed to 'popular' religious orders they accused of ritual excesses (see Munson 1993, 81ff, notably his discussion of the maraboutic scripturalism of a famous *'alim*, al-Kattani, pp. 87–96).

The rise of Salafi ideology was not an effect of the fate of tradition that was actually played out afterwards and to which Salafi intellectuals contributed significantly. The loss of orientation was not a consequence of the weakening of religious traditions and did not implicate the whole of traditional society but only a category of intellectuals who were in contact with Western culture and power. Furthermore, increasing doubt did not involve all learned men, many of whom stuck to their traditions, but only a few, those who aimed to raise and resolve new and modern issues. In the name of 'true Islam,' Salafi intellectuals condemned traditional views of Islam held by the established ulema, mystics, lodge leaders, etc., and dominated by the personal mediation of saints, the proliferation of concrete images of the sacred, ritual indulgences, etc. The ideologisation of religion was supposed to renew, revive, and strengthen not traditional religion (whether popular or scholarly), but an alternative view of religion.

The spread of politics

The spread of politics has a double consequence: the emergence of religious and secular leaders who want to reform Islam, and the rise of a public that is begging for reform.

Traditionally, access to the exact meaning of scriptures was restricted to a set of established interpreters. The ideologisation of religion implies the coming of new, challenging interpreters. Luther and Calvin illustrate the difference between the theologian and the ideologist:

> Luther was a theologian whose compelling concern was always with the private knowledge of God. . . . Luther never really devoted his best energies to the theoretical problems of ecclesiastical organisation. . . . . Calvin, however. . . was from the beginning of his career a man committed to systematic innovation, and his innovations were far less important in theology than in moral conduct and social organisation. (Walzer 1970, pp. 23–24)

Calvin didn't deal with ideas 'which have neither "certainty" nor "daily use".' His principle was "'to leave to God the knowledge of himself'" (p. 24).

The transition from the status of theologian to the status of intellectual is a relevant indicator of the ideologisation of a religion. Muslim ideologists, in contrast to traditional religious men (*'alim*, pl. *'ulema'*; *faqih*, pl. *fuqaha'*), are mostly not trained religious experts. Most of them are trained in the humanities or the 'hard' sciences (Schaebler and Stenberg 2004, p. 6). Mannheim held that the traditional intelligentsia were lifeless, academic, scholarly, relatively remote from the open conflicts of daily life (Mannheim 1985, pp. 10–11). Among Muslim learned men, we might find many who fit this profile, but we will also find many others involved in politics and daily life. The difference between traditional and modern ideologists is not related to the lack or the presence of activism, but to its nature. The dominant type of activism was a solitary one. Most traditional learned men formed no structured organisation. Their individual actions were sufficient to correct wrong conduct by the people and the rulers. According to the *nasiha* (advice) tradition, they should remind the ruler of his duty to implement the laws of God. The saint al-Yousi (Sidi Lahcen Lyusi, d. 1691), who, according to Geertz, represents the classical Moroccan religious style, was alone in his struggle against the king. He did not need to create any social organisation to achieve his goals. A second type of activism relied upon collective mobilisation. Many charismatic leaders carried out *jihad* against colonisation, but this type of activism was ephemeral. Sustained activism requires a new type of leaders and followers.

Geertz points out the context of the rise of oppositional Muslims, one in which the difference between the oppressor and the oppressed was seen as a difference of religious identity:

> The real line between, in the Moroccan phrasing, Nazarenes and Believers, or, in the Indonesian, Christian Men and Islamic Men, was not effaced. Indeed, it grew sharper. . . . [I]ntense involvement with the West moved religious faith closer to the center of our peoples' self-definition than it had been before. Before, men had been Muslims as a matter of circumstance; now they were, increasingly, Muslims as a matter of policy. They were *oppositional* Muslims. (Geertz 1968, pp. 64–65, emphasis in the original)

The emergence of the public is crucial to the process of the ideologisation of religion. The public emerges when the members of a traditional society, or a significant number of them, are no longer condemned to political passivity, particularly within the religious sphere. The public exists wherever there is a possibility for a person to adhere to a new system of ideas regardless of his locality, social class, nationality, religious order, etc. Thanks to modern mass media, the public of religious ideologies is growing ever larger.

Activism is usually referred to as a feature that differentiates or opposes ideology to culture and science (Bourricaud 1980, p. 30). This idea should be given more nuance with respect to religion. Islam, like many other religions, has from the beginning stimulated activism. Many political leaders in the past were religious activists. Hence it is not activism per se that puts religion and ideology in opposition, but the form of activism. In the past, religious activism was intermittent and sporadic. Now, politics tends to be a systematic and sustained activity for leaders and for the potential public of sympathisers. To paraphrase Michael Walzer, activists try to be responsible daily for their world and its reformation. Political activity is part of their religious life, not something distinct and separate. It is no longer a matter of wars, riots, revolts, periodic legitimisation of an established or a new power; on the contrary, it is a matter of systematic organisation and sustained activity. In the past, jihad, rebellion, uprisings, etc., mobilised the members of a tribe, a locality, a mystical group, etc., without separating them from their traditional attachments. Activism was a temporary or periodic act, not an organised movement. For a period of time, the potential adherent of a religious radical movement should be removed from all former boundaries, familial, tribal, local, and even national boundaries (Walzer 1970, pp. 2–12, 29). In modern urban Muslim societies, the possibility of recruiting persons detached from traditional boundaries has increased. For the potential public of religious ideologies, being a Muslim is not only a matter of faith or birth, it should above all be based on an ideological commitment. Seen at the individual level, the global process of the spread of religious ideologies can be approached as an ideological conversion. However, it should be noted that the extension of politics and its effects explains why people adopt ideologies in general, but not why they come to adhere to religious ideologies in particular.

Traditional Muslim communities strove to be grounded in a strong religious consensus. Religion was certainly used to maintain or contest an established political power or build a new one. Muslim societies knew conflict, rebellion, riots, and wars in the name of religion. But the idea of a pluralistic society where social conflicts are a normal and permanent feature of the political dynamics was impossible, even unthinkable. Where political or religious conceptions were in conflict, one of them had to win out. The ideologisation of religion requires a pluralistic society where political conflicts are the result of a more complex social structure, and where no religious ideology can exclude all the others. Following Baechler (1976), I would say that when only one 'ideology' is to be found in a given society, it should be called a tradition. To apply the term 'ideology,' there should be at least an opposing ideology within the same society.

The history of Morocco, and of other Muslim societies, shows that religion was usually at the center of political processes and institutions. Conflicting views of Islam were held by different competing dynasties, lodges, sects, saints, ulema, *mahdi*s, etc. Religious traditions were numerous, various, and often diametrically opposed. Thus the new element that makes the ideologisation of religion possible is neither the resort to religion to reform society, nor the existence of divergent and competing conceptions of religion. All of these features can be found in Muslim societies of the past. There were religious minorities, sects, 'heretical' groups, divergent schools, etc. However, religious divergences were more likely to be observed between communities than within the same community. They were limited and softened by isolation and loose communication between opposing communities. Divergence and competition within the same community in the name of the same religion were seen as abnormal, hence temporary. The ideal was either consensus or the separation of communities in conflict. In modern Muslim societies, the clash between diverse competing groups is a structural feature. Conflicting communities and groups that defend divergent conceptions should live in the same state and compete in the same public sphere. It is this modern structure of the public sphere that stimulates and maintains the ideologisation of religion – and not only of religion. The plurality of diverse views within the same polity is a necessary structural condition for the rise of ideology in general and of religious ideology in particular. Thanks to the mass media, the clash of conflicting religious ideas happens on a daily basis. This is the sociological dimension of the social situation of increasing doubt: a Muslim who used to be secure in the unity of his community's dogma now faces a plurality of views of the same religion at one and the same time.

Ideologisation as an intellectual process

The spread of modern politics and its consequence, the breakdown of traditional religious consensus, are the main political and cultural conditions for the ideologisation of religion. Let us now consider some aspects of the intellectual processes that define the ideologisation of religion.

Bricolage

According to Lévi-Strauss, a *bricoleur*, as compared to an engineer or a craftsman, is someone who uses devious means (*moyens détournés*):

> The 'bricoleur' is adept at performing a large number of diverse tasks; but, unlike the engineer, he does not subordinate each of them to the availability of raw materials and tools conceived and procured for the purpose of the project. His universe of instruments is closed and the rules of his game are always to make do with 'whatever is at hand,' that is to say with a set of tools and materials which is always finite and is also heterogeneous because what it contains bears no relation to the current project, or indeed to any particular project, but is the contingent result of all the occasions there have been to renew or enrich the stock or to maintain it with the remains of previous constructions or destructions. (Lévi-Strauss 1966, p. 17)

One needs a screwdriver but the only thing available is a knife. Bricolage is using what lies to hand instead of the appropriate tool. Lévi-Strauss's concept of bricolage is based on the distinction between the original purpose or function of a tool and its actual use. In contrast to the bricoleur's set of tools, the ideologist's tools are not collected by chance or in advance ('on the principle that "they may always come in handy"') (p. 18). The potential use of an idea is determined less by its previous uses than by the ideological project it is supposed to sustain. The notion of *jahiliya* (the state of ignorance), for instance, is a tool that is used in many ways by different and opposing religious traditions and ideologies. It can be restricted to the pre-Islamic era or it can be used in the broadest sense to include all contemporary societies, whether Muslim or not. It was his total and absolute rejection of all contemporary civilizations that oriented Sayyid Qutb to the concept of jahiliya and its extended definition. Among many available notions that define non-Muslim societies, the notion of jahiliya was selected and redefined.

The specificity of bricolage associated with the ideologisation of Islam is that the necessary tools do not depend solely on their availability. Here we are confronted with a situation midway between that of the bricoleur and that of the engineer. This intermediate situation can be explained both by the nature of the materials (rationalised religion which has a book, a history, traditions, etc.) and by the status of the one using those materials, i.e., an intellectual. When it comes to rationalised – in the Weberian sense – religion, such as Islam, tools are sought from determined stores: mainly the Qur'an and the tradition of the Prophet. Consequently, the intellectual bricoleur is someone who frequently visits these stores that are so rich that they can be used to justify any political position. However, the act of bricolage is determined less by the history of the tools available to the ideologist, than by the initial apodictic prejudices (democracy is an evil, polygamy does not conform to the modern world, capitalist banking is usury, etc.) that orient the selection of what are supposed to be the appropriate tools. An examination of the different ways of visiting the Islamic stores would shed light on how the 'original' tools are selected, transformed, and retransformed. Tapping these stores depends less and less on knowledge of their tools than on the political motivations, the diagnosis of the contemporary situation that justifies a resort to religious tools. That is why, in contrast to other cultural systems (myths, folktales, religion, etc.), ideology is made by intellectuals who stand somewhere between the bricoleur and the engineer. Like the engineer, they master techniques related to visiting the scriptural stores, and like the bricoleur their choice of tools is limited and oriented by the logic of the situation.

For instance, Salafi ideology, which advocates a return to pristine Islam, emphasises notions that have a practical impact in their struggle against their opponents. The notion of *tawhid* (belief in the oneness, the uniqueness of God) implies worship of God alone. Used as a tool, however, this notion is less theological, indeed it is mainly political in the sense that it is directed against Sufi groups and 'popular' practices. Salafis have also used the notion of *shirk* (polytheism, idolatry), which is the opposite of tawhid and refers to ascribing intermediaries in the worship of God. Contested practices such as visiting tombs and shrines, using saints as intermediaries to God, the veneration of trees, caves, and the like are targeted as shirk. The third crucial notion, *bid'a* (innovation), also shows how ideological prejudices orient the selection of religious tools. Bid'a is a central tool that is used to justify the condemnation of many innovations as heretical. In the name of the perfection of Islam, the strict interpretation of bid'a rejects all innovations, even positive ones.

Qutb gave radical political meanings to the concept of the oneness of God, to the declaration of faith (*La ilaha illa Allah* [There is no deity but God]): 'no law except from God, and no authority of one man over another, as the authority in all respects belongs to God ...' (Qutb 1980, p. 29). Declaring that sovereignty (*al-hakimiya*) belongs to God alone, he challenged all political systems based on the concept of the sovereignty of man:

> Any system in which the final decisions are referred to human beings, and in which the sources of all authority are human, deifies human beings by designating others than God as lords over men. ... In short, to proclaim the authority and sovereignty of God means to eliminate all human kingship and to announce the rule of the Sustainer of the universe over the entire earth. (Qutb 1980, pp. 66–67)

Qutb's interpretation of the sovereignty of God justifies a political position, i.e. to free man from servitude to worldly authorities who have usurped the sovereignty of God. To ascribe sovereignty solely to God means that authority must be taken from the rulers and revert to God (Qutb 1980, esp. chaps. 3 and 5; see Kepel 2005, pp. 34–70).

The first forms of ideological reformism (Salafism, Wahhabism) faced pre-ideological systems (popular religion, local traditions, scholarly interpretations, etc.). What makes the landscape more complex now is the clash between numerous ideologies, all of which claim reference to the true Islam. The notions of tawhid, shirk, bid'a, and others were ideological weapons used against Sufism, but they are inappropriate to the jihadi version of Salafism that developed in the 1980s, which mainly seeks to delegitimise political rulers and to legitimise violence against them. It rejects the dominant idea that a Muslim is obliged to obey even an unjust ruler. On the contrary, jihadi Salafism has claimed that a ruler who fails to govern according to Islamic law is a *kafir* (unbeliever, infidel), in which case jihad applies and the ruler deserves to die. *Takfir*, to declare a person kafir, and jihad are the central tools of the jihadi version of Salafism. Viewed from this perspective, the ideologisation of religion is a process of rationalisation based upon a selective set of traditional religious ideas oriented by the political attitudes of the ideologists. The process of ideologisation is somehow the reverse of the process of discovery. Ideologists know the values and the ideas they must defend. They strive to rationalise those values and ideas, to justify them, by seeking appropriate ideas and authorities. In order to understand this transformation of religion, information is required not only on the history of the religious notions used, but on the logic of the political situation and how it is represented by the actors of the transformation.

The ideologisation of religion consists in the elaboration of a 'new' religious guide. One feature of ideology is its selectiveness or over-selectiveness. In a sense, to describe the ideologisation of a religion as an intellectual process is tantamount to describing the selection process operated by its intellectuals. A historical and concrete religion is far from being a set of coherent rituals and beliefs. In fact, it is a set of various religious stores, some of which are more visited than others. Weber (1963) examined the polarity between mysticism (resignedness in a set of conditions) and asceticism (attempts to master conditions) (Parsons 1963, li). Activists may stress religious ideas and traditions that value 'asceticism' rather than 'mysticism.' Such ideas and traditions seem closer to ideological activism and more suitable for transformation into an ideology, whereas mysticism and theology would be marginalised if not rejected by religious activists. In other words, the ideologisation of religion would tend to reject 'religion out of the world' in favor of 'religion in the world.' This position should be nuanced in the sense that the bricoleur assigns no limits to his activities. He often takes advantage of theological and even mystical issues, as mentioned earlier. Bricolage is the selective creative use of materials regardless of their original use. In this respect, any religious tool is potentially transformable into an ideology. The logic of ideologisation is to beat the snake with whatever stick is handy, *faire feu de tout bois*.

One interesting illustration of ideological bricolage is the debate over the prohibition of usury (*riba*), which has been revived since the introduction of modern banking in Muslim societies (Rachik 2006). The issue is not the prohibition of usury, on which all scholars concur, but what kinds of transaction should be qualified as such. Broadly speaking, there are two leading views. The first holds that bank interest on a loan is the modern epitome of riba: any sum charged over and above the principal in a loan transaction is riba (al-Mawdudi n.d., Qutb n.d.). According to Al-Qaradawi (1960, p. 264), 'Islam permits increase in capital through trade. … At the same time, Islam blocks the way for anyone who tries to increase his capital through lending on usury or interest (*riba*), whether it is at a low or high rate. …' The second view contends that Islam prohibits 'usury' but not 'interest.' The argument is based on the distinction between usury by way of deferment (*riba al-nasi'a*) and usury by way of increase or excess (*riba al-fadl*). Salafi intellectuals such as Muhammad Abduh (d. 1905) and Rashid Rida (d. 1935) contend that the first kind is prohibited by Islam, and that the second kind (*riba al-fadl*) on a term loan is lawful. The Moroccan thinker and political leader Allal al-Fasi (1910–1974) shares this view and calls for the strict prohibition of usury by way of deferment (al-Fasi 1979, pp. 213–214, 243, Saeed 1996, pp. 35–43). The modernist view tends to emphasise the moral aspect of the prohibition of usury, arguing that the reason for the prohibition of *riba* was injustice (*zulm*) as stated in the Qur'an. What is denounced is gross and cruel exploitation; the rationale for the prohibition was to prevent the exploitation of the weak and the needy (Rahman 1982).

Religious ideologies mobilise not only religious beliefs and traditions, but they visit secular stores as well. The content of religious ideologies depends on the combination and recombination of religious and secular ideas. This is another aspect of bricolage. Ideological activity is not necessarily restricted to one domain. Any sphere of knowledge can be referred to as necessary, which makes it interesting to see how a given ideology combines religious and secular ideas and vocabularies. It is the ideologist's postulates (ultimate values) and the logic of the situation that lead him to seek his arguments in places other than the religious stores, e.g. local traditions, natural sciences, the humanities, the social sciences, human rights, etc. If Western science is valued in a religious community, if the real or imagined interlocutor is Western civilization, then the logic of compromise between Islam and modern science will prevail. Salafi intellectuals have striven to make their vision of Islam compatible with modernism. They have tried to demonstrate that democracy, scientific inventions, the declaration of the Rights of Men, etc., are all to be found in the Qur'an. To be maintained, Islam was to be founded not only on new religious ideas (and institutions) but also on ideas that are external to it (Geertz 1968, p. 105). This is the main difference between the classical Salafis (e.g. al-Afghani, Muhammad Abduh, al-Fasi) and the new Salafis. The former were only religious radicals, whereas the latter, who condemned and rejected Western civilization, are also political radicals (rejecting democracy, the Western way of life, etc.). And it is this systematic rejection of Western values that orients the new Salafi ideology. In this case, the more a religious ideology is radical, the less it relies on external secular knowledge and institutions.

Celebrating belief itself rather than what it asserts

Geertz differentiates between 'religious-mindedness' and 'religiousness,' between holding and being held by religious convictions. Religious-mindedness, celebrating belief itself rather than what belief asserts, is a response to progressively increasing doubt.

> On the spiritual level, the big change... is that the primary question has shifted from 'What shall I believe?' to 'How shall I believe it?' [....] The transformation of religious symbols from imagistic revelations of the divine, evidences of God, to ideological assertions of the divine's importance, badges of piety.... (Geertz 1968, pp. 61–62)

In dealing with the production of religious ideology, we should distinguish at least two different stages: the first stage, in which Salafi intellectuals faced traditional cultural systems, and the second in which ideologists face religious ideologies rather than less structured and less powerful traditions. At this stage, ideologists who are more interested in mobilising people than in transforming Muslim thought need few ideas, few slogans, and few emblems. There is no need to write books and edit journals, as earlier ideologists did. What is at stake, what needs to be changed first is not Muslim thought, but Muslim and non-Muslim 'corrupt powers'. Hence the style is very concise, apodictic, less argumentative, and close to common sense. Media support reflects these features: fatwas, pamphlets, declarations, tracts, etc. The more people there are, the fewer and the less complex are the ideas they can share. At this stage, what is needed is not ideas but badges that indicate one's ideological identity. The ideologisation of religion is a gradual process of the simplification and reduction of a rich and complex religious heritage down to a few badges and tokens of collective identity consciously displayed in public (a slogan, a manner of greeting, a way of dressing, praying, etc.).

Explicitness

Edward Shils wrote 'ideologies are characterised by a high degree of explicitness of formulation over a very wide range of the objects with which they deal' (Shils 1968, p. 66). Geertz contrasted traditional knowledge and ideology in similar terms: people who live in traditional societies 'act as ... men of untaught feelings; they are guided both emotionally and intellectually in their judgments and activities by unexamined prejudices, which do not leave them "hesitating in the moment of decision, sceptical, puzzled and unresolved"' (Geertz 1973a, p. 218). The notion of explicitness is more accurate when ideology is opposed to other cultural patterns such as traditions, customs, popular religion, and common sense. It is less accurate when ideology is contrasted with science and 'rationalised religion' (theology), which are also based on explicit discourse. The specificity of religious ideology does not rely on explicitness as such. The main difference consists in the extension of explicitness to secular and actual issues. New secular questions are explicitly addressed: 'Who are we?' 'Why has the Western world progressed and the Muslim world regressed?' The explicit content of religious ideology is a response to contemporary experience. Are democracy, the banking system, and so forth compatible with Islam? Reforming society is the primary goal of religious ideologies. Their central themes are what to reform (religious traditions, the political system, etc.) and how to effect the change (peacefully or not).

Religion is turned into ideology when an elite is in a situation of defending its religion against a political power, a political situation that would weaken and transgress the elite. A religious ideology can be defined as a set of ideas that refer to religious and secular tools and accompany political actions and processes in a sustained and systematic way. Islam has not been completely separated from politics. It has been used, as mentioned earlier, to legitimise established political powers, rebellions, etc. However, in the past, religious beliefs were embedded in an amorphous traditional political culture (or proto-ideology), i.e. a set of shared meanings related to political processes. By contrast, religious ideologies are the systematic, focused, and sustained expression of shared religious and non-religious meanings as they are related to actual political processes and issues. The social function of religious ideologies is to develop a new guide (often presented as the old guide), provide a new vocabulary (often mixed with the traditional vocabulary), and address new questions and solve new problems (by invoking old problems). But the present is what is at stake; the past serves as a store to be visited according to the needs of the present.

References

al-Fasi, 'A., 1979 [1952]. *Al-Naqd al-dati* (Self-criticism). Rabat: n.p.

al-Mawdudi, A.A., n.d. *Al-Riba*. Beirut: Dar al-'Arabiyya.

Al-Qaradawi, Y., 1960. *The lawful and the prohibited in Islam=al-Halal wa al-haram fi al-Islam*. Indianapolis, IN: American Trust Publications.

Baechler, J., 1976. *Qu'est-ce que l'idéologie?* Paris: Gallimard.

Bourricaud, F., 1980. *Le bricolage idéologique: essai sur les intellectuels et les passions démocratiques*. Paris: Presses Universitaires de France.

Geertz, C., 1968. *Islam observed: religious development in Morocco and Indonesia*. New Haven, CT: Yale University Press.

Geertz, C., 1973a [1964]. Ideology as a cultural system. *In*: C. Geertz, *The interpretation of cultures*. New York: Basic Books, 193–233.

Geertz, C., 1973b [1967]. Politics past, politics present: some notes on the uses of anthropology in understanding the new states. *In*: C. Geertz, *The interpretation of cultures*. New York: Basic Books, 327–341.

Kepel, G., 2005. *The roots of radical Islam*. London: Saqi Books.

Lévi-Strauss, C., 1966 [1962]. *The savage mind*. Chicago: University of Chicago Press.

Mannheim, K., 1985 [1936]. *Ideology and utopia: an introduction to the sociology of knowledge*. New York: Harcourt, Brace & World.

Munson, H. Jr., 1993. *Religion and power in Morocco*. New Haven, CT: Yale University Press.

Parsons, T, 1963. Introduction. *In*: M. Weber, ed. *The sociology of religion*. Boston: Beacon Press, xix–lxvii.

Qutb, S., 1980. *Ma'alim fi al-tariq*. Cairo: Dar al-Shoruq. [*Milestones*]. Available online at: http://www.youngmuslims. ca/online_library/books/milestones/hold/index_2.asp [Accessed 31 July 2008].

Qutb, S., n.d. *Tafsir ayat al-riba*. n.p.

Rachik, H., 2004. Observer autrement le monde musulman. *Revue française de sciences politiques*, 54 (June), 469–472.

Rachik, H., 2006. Money, charity and purity in Morocco. Ohio: Intel Corporation, photocopy.

Rahman, F., 1982. *Islam and modernity: transformation of an intellectual tradition*. Chicago: University of Chicago Press.

Saeed, A., 1996. *Islamic banking and interest: a study of the prohibition of riba and its contemporary interpretation*. Leiden, The Netherlands: E. J. Brill.

Schaebler, B. and Stenberg, L., eds., 2004. *Globalization and the Muslim world: culture, religion, and modernity*. Syracuse, NY: Syracuse University Press.

Shils, E., 1968. Ideology: the concept and function of ideology. *In*: D.L. Sills, ed. *International encyclopedia of the social sciences*. New York: Macmillan and the Free Press, vol. 7, 66–76.

Walzer, M., 1970 [1965]. *The revolution of the saints: a study in the origins of radical politics*. New York: Atheneum.

Weber, M., 1963 [1922]. *The sociology of religion*. Boston: Beacon Press.

Religious act, public space: reflections on some Geertzian concepts

Mondher Kilani

Institut d'Anthropologie et de Sociologie, Bâtiment Anthropole, Université de Lausanne, Switzerland

This paper examines theoretical and methodological implications of Clifford Geertz's approach to religion as he formulated it in 'Religion as a cultural system' (Geertz 1966), where religion and culture seem to be defined as functional equivalents. The paper considers religious symbols in the public space, using two examples from contemporary reality – one being a certain expression spoken by the copilot of Egypt Air Flight 990, the other being the headscarf controversy in France – in order to explore how the anthropologist relates the microsituations he observes to an all-embracing context.

In this paper I will consider religious symbols in the public space, understood essentially in its conflicted and controversial aspect. In doing so, I take inspiration from several notions developed by the anthropologist Clifford Geertz. My purpose is to answer the question of how we account for human action, how we fathom the meanings behind it. In short, how does the anthropologist produce his interpretation? These notions in turn will be subjected to a critical reading. I will illustrate my points using two examples from contemporary reality, one being a particular expression used by Muslims in various situations in daily life, and the other being the French controversy over wearing hijab in the public space.

In 'Thick description' (Geertz 1973), Geertz espouses the idea of culture as public, writing that 'culture is public because meaning is,' it being understood that meaning is incorporated into action and can be deciphered from it. If we can read human actions, it is because they have 'texture,' they present themselves as 'discourse.' To put it another way, ethnography begins with the actors' discourses and is carried out as the anthropologist contextualises them. Given these preliminaries, and following André Mary (1998), we ask, what is the connection between what a social actor 'says' through words, gestures, and behaviour, and the 'cultural forms,' 'symbolic systems,' or 'structures of meaning' that inform the 'said' of the social actor?

In point of fact, the notion of 'social discourse' is not very explicit in Geertz. What do we make of multiple contradictory interpretations, particularly concerning social actors, and how do we decide between them? Paul Ricoeur (1984) emphasised the multivocality of actions as of texts and the polemical nature of interpretation. So what do we make of social discourse? Is it the social actor's discourse, or is it already the 'context' created by the anthropologist in order to read a person's action? This raises the question of how the anthropologist relates the micro situations he observes, describes, and contextualises, to an all-embracing context – e.g. religion or culture – and what he does to avoid taking this referential context as an invariable background and thereby ossifying it.

In this connection, I will look at Geertz's approach to religion as he formulated it in 'Religion as a cultural system,' his contribution to the collective work, *Anthropological approaches to the study of religion* (Geertz 1966), in order to underline the obvious tension in Geertz between a conception somewhat influenced by an intellectualist bias and a conception oriented more toward the logic of action, which latter I shall draw on to support the development of my argument. In his essay, Geertz offers a first definition of religion as a system of representations:

> (1) a system of symbols which acts to (2) establish powerful, pervasive, and long-lasting moods and motivations in men by (3) formulating conceptions of a general order of existence and (4) clothing these conceptions with such an aura of factuality that (5) the moods and motivations seem uniquely realistic. (Geertz 1966, p. 4)

This amounts to making religion and culture equivalent, at least in the sense that Geertz defines culture in the same essay, where he writes that it

> denotes an historically transmitted pattern of meanings embodied in symbols, a system of inherited conceptions expressed in symbolic forms by means of which men communicate, perpetuate, and develop their knowledge about and attitudes toward life. (1966, p. 3)

The definition of both religion and culture as 'world view' places them in the position of equally satisfying the same functional requirements. Yet such a definition of religion (or culture) would only be relevant were it not only the dominant but the only world view within a society. In that case, and only in that case, the definition of religion as 'that which explains the world and orients the action of men' would relate to a character specific to it. But such is not the case, since societies are for the most part pluralist, in one way or another, when it comes to 'world views.'

This is a shortcoming that has characterised traditional approaches to religion, and Geertz appears to have been caught in the same trap, at least in certain formulations in his famous paper. In confounding religion and culture, the traditional approach to religion essentialises the collective identity as a form established once and for all and often conceived independently of any historicity. The Muslim culture (or religion) is thus considered to be a substance that inscribes individual behaviour in a quasi-integral social habitus. We seem to be dealing with a separate world inhabited by beings whose mentality is totally different from ours, one where the specialists apparently do not know how to 'put religion in its place,' for example, considering it merely a 'belief in superhuman beings,' in the manner of Edward Tylor (1871). On the contrary, they allow it to float here, there, and everywhere. Such an overly inclusive definition of religion forecloses the possibility of exiting the separate world created by Orientalists. Such a definition cannot conceive that religious behaviours are perfectly distinguishable from other social behaviours even when the latter are religious in form.

On the level of this new formulation of religion we meet Geertz again, now with consider-ations that contradict his first approach. In the same essay, he shows how the impact of religious ritual has its greatest effect outside of religion per se:

> The dispositions which religious rituals induce thus have their most important impact – from a human point of view – outside the boundaries of the ritual itself as they reflect back to color the individual's conception of the established world of bare fact. (Geertz 1966, p. 35)

In other words, the particular atmosphere that characterises certain religious practices permeates many spheres of people's lives, far beyond what is strictly religious, endowing those spheres with a particular style, a predominant tone. Thus we can say, for example, that if a Muslim recog-nises certain practices in the formal code of Islam, he lives them essentially as an aesthetic form of action (Ferrié 1991, p. 232); hence his preference for using the right hand rather than the left, the fact that he avoids a puddle of blood, does not eat rare meat, kisses people on the cheeks twice rather than thrice, is buried and not cremated, recites the *bismillah* (in the name of God) before taking an action, etc. All of these apparently religious behaviours are simply instances of civil conduct. This is congruent with Geertz's analysis of Balinese rituals in which he sees first of all an expression of ordinary life (Geertz 1966).

Looking through this new prism, we see that religion, which in the traditional approach and in the first Geertzian version is supposed to engulf 'the total person, transporting him, so far as he is concerned, into another mode of existence' (and which, as such, truly occurs only in strictly religious practice), has nothing to do with 'the pale, remembered reflection of that experience in the midst of everyday life' (Geertz 1966, p. 36). Such a change in perspective allows us to move from a conception in which the symbolism would be 'in the mind' (borrowing Ricoeur's term), to one in which the meaning is 'incorporated into action and decipherable from it by other actors in the social interplay' (again using Ricoeur's terminology 1984, p. 57). It follows that religion as a social phenomenon must be seen as thought in action, rather than as a system of thought that imposes itself upon the actor's consciousness.

Such a readjustment assumes the adoption of the social actor's point of view, or the 'native's point of view,' as Geertz suggested again in one of his last essays (2007, p. 432). In this oper-ation, it is a matter, on the one hand, of 'putting ourselves in contact with the human subjectivi-ties in play, with what the believers really think and feel' (this is the phenomenological analysis), and on the other hand, of 'exposing and describing the interpretive frames through which they understand and judge acts and events' (the hermeneutic analysis) (p. 432). This means that we must examine the actors' mental states, intentions, and perceptions of the environ-ment, and refrain from any kind of global reasoning as to what might be the general way of think-ing of any particular group. This implies bringing together the explanation of the structuring anteriority – appropriate to the approach of sociological holism – and the logical structure of the situation, as it impresses itself upon the perception of the actor in a given context – an approach appropriate to methodological individualism.

In order to illustrate these various considerations, let us now focus on some ordinary forms of 'religious' expression taken from Islam. As we consider certain phrases that people utter daily in countless situations, such as *bismillah* (in the name of God) or *tawakkaltu 'al allah* (I rely on God), we will attempt to grasp their meaning in the various contexts in which they occur and highlight their divergent interpretations in cultural spaces where they take on unexpected mean-ings, such as in Europe or the United States. The crash of Egypt Air Flight 990, a Boeing 707 en route from New York to Cairo that went down in the Atlantic Ocean on 31 October 1999, gave rise to a controversy between Americans and Westerners on one side and Egyptians, Arabs, and

Muslims on the other, which even now has not subsided, some eight years after the incident. In the following analysis, I focus on words spoken in the public arena by various actors, essentially media professionals, cultural experts, and civil society representatives.[1] My analysis neither comments on the official investigation reports nor assesses the relevance of their conclusions. At the very most, I will cite the reports where they enter into the polemic. It is the public controversy provoked by the event that is the primary object of my analysis, even though it clearly reinforces the discrepancies between the conclusions of the US and the Egyptian reports on their respective investigations, the former concluding that the copilot was responsible for the crash, and the latter exculpating him from any malicious act.[2]

Attention quickly focused on a brief utterance attributed to the copilot. The phrase '*tawakkaltu 'al allah*' (I rely on God; I trust in God; I put myself in God's hands), decoded from the recording of the final words exchanged between the two pilots, came to symbolise the 'cultural gap' that supposedly divides America from the Arab world. Because God was invoked, the American investigators hastily characterised the phrase as a 'prayer.' Some in the American media translated '*tawakkaltu 'al allah*' as 'I have made my decision, I place my faith in the hands of God,'[3] and described it as a formula that a Muslim would pronounce when preparing to commit the irreparable, in this case, an act of suicide.[4] Confusion was sown between the words 'faith' and 'fate,' producing the phrase, 'I place my fate in the hands of God.' Indeed, this was how the American investigators first translated the transcription of the copilot's utterance, before they revised it as 'I rely on God,' apparently under the influence of information provided by the official Egyptian investigators.[5] One can imagine that if the expression inspired a certain interpretation on the American side, it was because it referred to God and was spoken by a Muslim, and whenever a Muslim is involved, suspicion turns toward extremism.[6]

By contrast, the Egyptians were immediately skeptical of the American investigators' impartiality. They disputed the suicide theory that was based on this Arabic phrase being repeated eleven times. According to the Egyptians, the suicide theory could even be a cover-up for something the manufacturer, Boeing, might be responsible for, or some other cause of the disaster that could be laid at the feet of the United States. Under questioning, the Arab experts insisted that the phrase in question is not a prayer but a formula that can be used in numerous ways in very different contexts.[7] Depending on the context, it could even mean that the copilot was trying to save the airliner. In everyday life, the expression '*tawakkaltu 'al allah*' is a way of entrusting one's soul to God before a journey, an exam, or an ordeal, but it can also be used before an ordinary action with no particular risk. In the context of the airline disaster, it would seem perfectly normal for the copilot to use the expression in response to the situation of extreme danger and attendant stress, although the report on the American investigation repeatedly indicates that no evidence of this type of response was recorded,[8] just as it notes that the copilot's reactions to the first sign of a problem (before the pilot returned to the cockpit) did not indicate that he was surprised or upset by what was happening.

As in English or in French, likewise in Arabic, many religious expressions have been secularised and are commonly used without the least religious import, even though religious hardliners may assert the contrary, that every such utterance necessarily expresses an absolute state of belief and should be taken literally. But here as elsewhere, the social actor who uses such expressions does so within the logic of the situation. The Arabic language is rife with the name of God, whether in the ubiquitous *insha'allah* (God willing), or *al-hamdu li'llah* (praise God, thank God), *astaghfiru'llah* (I ask God's forgiveness), or *a'udu bi'llah* (God forbid, God help me). Other common expressions include 'God keep you,' 'God protect you,' 'God save you,' 'God spare you,' 'God help you,' 'God be with you,' etc. In short, *tawakkaltu* '*al allah* seems to be the type of religious expression spoken in practically any situation in Arab and Muslim countries, somewhat as people in the Christian West might use the expression 'My God,' or 'Jesus,' or 'Holy Mother.'

In her novel, *Lettre posthume*, Dominique Eddé very judiciously brings out the point that there is enough 'God in God to suffice for all the world.' God is 'a rallying point, a password, an indestructible absence. ...' God is 'an absolute word that answers for nothing and no one,' because '"Allah" is not only the Arabic name of God, it is what we call the ineffable, everything within a hair's breadth of existence or non-existence.' Allah is 'the flight of thought in the midst of speech,' 'the god of words,' 'religion in language' (Eddé 1989, pp. 65–68):

> 'Allah' when the light is beautiful, 'Allah' when the light fails, 'Allah' to question catastrophe, 'Allah' to run for your life, 'Allah' to applaud the artist, 'Allah' to conjure the future, 'Allah...' when you remember something, 'Allah, Allah' when nothing happens, 'Allah' if you trip, 'Allah' if you fall, 'Allah' if you don't fall, 'Allah' whatever happens, 'Allah' when a beautiful girl walks by, 'Allah' to break the silence, 'Allah' at the end of a sigh, 'Allah' when you learn the truth and 'Allah' when you discover a lie.... (Eddé 1989, pp. 66–67)[9]

In summary, we can say that the phrase spoken by the copilot neither proves that he had suicidal intentions, nor that he was a Muslim extremist, any more than it proves the reverse. The issue is whether he uttered the phrase after having determined that the end was inevitable because of some kind of technical malfunction, or if the phrase was an invocation preceding an act of suicide, as the American theory would have it, even though that theory was categorically ruled out by the Arab and Muslim side. The Egyptian investigators argued that it would be impossible for a Muslim to associate the recitation of this phrase with the intention to commit suicide,[10] and certain Muslim commentators went so far as to assert that Muslims never commit suicide because their faith forbids, assuming that what is forbidden never happens. Nevertheless, there is a phrase that would have been conclusive concerning the copilot's suicidal intention if he had in fact uttered it, and that is, 'I have made my decision.' Indeed, at the beginning of the affair, certain American media outlets quite wrongly attributed this phrase to the copilot.[11] Without such 'conclusive' evidence, however, all the anthropologist has to work with is the social discourse and the contradictory interpretations that such an incident occasions on the part of the various actors. The anthropologist's task is to contextualise the various meanings while trying to find a middle way between the raw experience of the actor – to which, in any case, he has no access – and the experience he reconstructs.

At this point, it is useful to recall what Geertz thought of the ethnographic account. According to him, its value

> does not rest on its author's ability to capture primitive facts in faraway places and carry them home like a mask or a carving, but on the degree to which he is able to clarify what goes on in such places, to reduce the puzzlement – what manner of men are these? – to which unfamiliar acts emerging out of unknown backgrounds naturally give rise. (Geertz 1973, p. 16)

For our purposes, this suggests that we adopt a semiotic concept of culture understood, again as Geertz specified, as 'interworked systems of construable signs.' Culture as such 'is not a power, something to which social events, behaviours, institutions, or processes can be causally attributed; it is a context, something within which they can be intelligibly – that is, thickly – described' (Geertz 1973, p. 14). Consequently, cultural analysis would consist in formulating conjectures and evaluating them in relation to the context.

Obviously this raises the question of verification, or, to retain the interpretive perspective, the question of the plausibility of the proposed explanation. Following Arnold Davidson (2005), who himself built upon ideas developed by the historian Carlo Ginzburg, I do not believe that the researcher can discover clear proof that allows direct access to the reality. He can only approach the reality through the mediation of contradictory voices clashing in a given situation. If there is a 'common ethic,' it is accessible only through the social actors who construct and reconstruct the reality through the intermediary of their mutual relationships. These are 'thick' relationships: they are made of relations of strength and negotiation, expectation and frustration, understanding and incomprehension. Each actor projects his own conceptual categories on the others, and through a game of reflecting back and forth the actors together reconfigure the reality. Like a detective, the anthropologist must be alert to the discrepancy between the various voices expressing themselves in a given context. It is this discrepancy that allows him to read beneath the smooth surface of image and discourse the subtle interaction between threats and fears, attacks and projections, scorn and admiration, certainties and misunderstandings. It is this same discrepancy that will help the anthropologist give meaning to phenomena that would otherwise remain obscure or whose meaning would be subject to endless controversy; balancing between a naturalistic representation according to which only rational observation is capable of deriving the organising principles of the domain under study and deducing the native interpretation (Guille-Escuret 2000, p. 199), and a relativistic representation that disbelieves in the possibility of attaining the reality and thus confines itself purely to reconstructing the social actors' subjectivities which it juxtaposes one beside another, regardless of any 'common ethic.'

Having considered these methodological issues, let us move on to the second example, which concerns the wearing of the 'veil' by young women of Muslim origin in France. Here I will focus on the contradictory 'social discourses' produced by various actors around this 'object,' and attempt to relate them to the contentious sphere of contemporary culture. To this end, I will examine conflicts arising from the question of the visibility or the invisibility of a 'religious' expression – the analysis of which must determine its true meaning – and how these conflicts concern French society as a whole. The lines of reflection concern the boundary between public and private space, between global and communal cultural norms, between socially dominant and socially dominated groups.

Can we assign a single function to the 'veil'? In the course of the debate over the ban on the Islamic headscarf in France, some analysts claim to have pinpointed the 'true' and 'ultimate' meaning of the veil, that is, 'a sign of woman's subjection, of the archaism if not the radical Islamism that would manipulate young women for political ends' (Khosrokhavar 2004, p. 90). This desire to fix the ultimate meaning of wearing hijab is problematic on two counts. On the one hand, it results in the 'refusal to hear what the women who wear it have to say' – women who say they do so voluntarily and on their own initiative, whatever the reasons they cite – and, on the other hand, it constitutes 'a denial of the diversity of situations in which the headscarf is worn,' including those situations in which the motivation is primarily religious (Nordmann 2004, p. 165). The result is that neither the social logics that lead girls and young women to wear a headscarf nor the conditions of their existence are taken into account; indeed, these are of no interest; they are relegated to the background of stereotypes linked a priori to this wardrobe accessory.

Emerging from behind this lack of interest in context is the central interest in this conflict which is, at least on the majority side, 'to tone down the Islamic appearance of certain distinguishing practices in order to make them socially tolerable' (Tersigni 2003, p. 116), and confine them to the private space. That is the intent of the law against wearing hijab in the public space (schools, government offices, hospitals, etc.) in the French Republic.

The republican doctrine of assimilation effectively privileges the relationship of the individual citizen and the state, hoping to ban any overt demonstration of communal membership from the public space, while passing over the fact that the society has never stopped classifying individuals according to ethnic, religious, or cultural group. In practice, the republican principle of equality can tilt toward the suspicion that some people, even though legally French, tend in their 'cultural' behaviours to alter the republican order and the universally secular character of the public space. In the headscarf debate, the majority national cultural norm discounts the strategy of young women who wear hijab in response to specific social situations and who seek to challenge certain forms of discrimination. Taking full political stock of the veil is difficult because it shakes the foundations of secularism, in particular its neutrality with respect to personal associations. Paradoxically, this failure to consider hijab in the political context, thus confining it to the religious context, is in alignment with the position of Muslim fundamentalists, notably the Wahhabis of Saudi Arabia, who consider it to be no more than the observation of a religious requirement and the sign of woman's submission to man – whereas in Turkey or Tunisia, the very rationale for banning the headscarf in universities and government offices is political. One more example, if one were needed, to illustrate the pertinence of the logic of the situation to understanding why women wear the headscarf and why the headscarf is banned.

To return to the French context, wearing a headscarf must in many cases be seen as a political statement grappling with two 'normative powers': the French model of integration which organises and defines the public space by excluding certain groups, and the Muslim parental figure who has heretofore put forward a somewhat private Muslim identity. Wearing hijab in public – reinventing a tradition in the context of contemporary France – is not necessarily a challenge to the separation of public and private. It is an attempt to make visible a minority, a 'culture,' a 'religion' that until now have been condemned to invisibility and secretiveness, and to connect them to modernity, notably through the civic engagement of young women who wear hijab. This spectacular 'showing' of the veiled body of women in the public space might seem paradoxical in light of the unilateral reading of the veil as signifying the seclusion of women in the domestic space. In any case, we can say that this intrusion of the 'private' into the 'public' (Babès 2004, p. 94) represents a real change in the status of women within both spaces, a change toward liberation rather than confinement, with the headscarf suggesting emancipation rather than seclusion.

In keeping with the suggestion that cultural analysis gains insight into meaning by examining discrepancy, let us extend the reading of the veil in the public space by placing it in perspective with another feminine sign that involves the female body, i.e. the 'thong,' a bottomless panty that allows skin-tight pants to be worn without showing any lines; this too is part of the private/ public, emancipation/domination debate. The veil and the thong are generally read as mutually exclusive vestimentary features because of what they supposedly represent: on the one hand, submissive religious conduct; on the other, liberated behaviour. Behind these representations we find the 'great divide' between Muslim 'sexism' in the *banlieues* and 'equality of the sexes' in the secular space.

And while feminist criticism of the 1970s pointed out the hypersexualisation of women in the public sphere of consumer society, few now theorise that those who wear hijab 'could be proceeding from the same critique,' since everyone knows 'their motivations have nothing to do with ours,' as Christine Delphy asserts (2006, p. 63). Hijab is reduced to an unequivocal sign of masculine sexual domination and attributed to an Other culture, reputedly a harshly sexist culture, whereas the thong, despite its sexy reputation, is not considered sexist apparel because it is a matter of secular vestimentary conduct. Yet wearing a thong isn't always innocuous; it can be part of a system of corporeal techniques and modifications to which a woman's body

48   *M. Kilani*

and sexuality must be subjected, which in this context at least would make it the same sign of woman's domination as wearing a veil.

At this point we might well ask whether identifying markers that are culturally familiar more easily pass unnoticed than those that are culturally unfamiliar. The answer is probably yes, yet it is not quite so simple with regard to the thong, which is still considered 'indecent' in the public space, something that women need to be protected from. Even when emancipated, women are not seen as full subjects, but rather as minors, victims whose innocence must be protected if they dare to wear an outfit that is too 'provocative,' whereas boys' clothing, even when considered indecent, is not as readily associated with 'sexual provocation.' When we compare these different perspectives and open up the aperture, it appears that the question of hijab raises the question of the difference between the sexes in secular, hedonist, postmodern society, a society in which, despite everything, woman's body remains subject to man's omniscient gaze and constitutes a measure of power and domination.

An anecdote I heard from several sources in different contexts will serve to illustrate the simultaneously protective and concupiscent attitude with which a man may speak of the subjugation of a woman's body. It takes place in the souk of an Arab city – Cairo, Damascus, Algiers, or other – where a bearded salesman is trying to overcome the last reservations of a young woman in hijab who is contemplating the purchase of a thong. He touts the effect it will have on her husband: 'You'll drive him crazy with this tonight.'[12] Cover the body in public space, the better to reveal it in private!

Veil or thong, thong or veil, both wardrobe items inevitably raise the question of woman's status. Can she reclaim herself as a woman and not be prevented from being a man like any other? Can she be recognised both as particular (woman) and universal (*homo*), a condition apparently taken for granted with respect to a man (*vir*)?

Clearly Geertz's influence throughout this paper has been essentially heuristic, allowing us to clarify the type of question to put to the real – not why the actor acts, but what is the situational logic according to which he acts – and to define the (interpretive) position from which to answer the question. This in turn raises the question of the value of the ethnographic account, particularly with regard to its plausibility. From this point of view, the notion of discrepancy also seems to offer a certain heuristic value. One characteristic of discrepancy is its dynamism. Making discrepancy work (*faire travailler l'écart*), to borrow a phrase from François Jullien (2007), consists in comparing two positions, not in order to reify or essentialise their difference, but the better to show the persistence of the discrepancy between them, which allows us to better understand the discrepancy, not from a perspective of growing distance, but of thicker description.

Acknowledgements

I thank the participants in the two recent conferences on Clifford Geertz, the first at the University of California, Los Angeles 'Islam re-observed: Clifford Geertz in Morocco' in December 2007, and the second at the University of Lyon 'Autour de Clifford Geertz' in January 2008. Their suggestions and critiques allowed me to refine the arguments I develop in this paper, for which I of course am solely responsible. My thanks also go to Marianne Kilani-Schoch for her critical reading of this paper.

Notes

1. See, e.g., Wren 1999, Piotrowski 2000, and Mari 1999. See also 'L'énigme des derniers mots du copilote d'EgyptAir oppose Égyptiens et Américains,' *Le Monde*, 19 November 1999, and 'L'Égypte s'interroge sur de mystérieuses images radars "classifiées" de l'US Air Force,' *Le Temps*, 15 August 2000.

2. The report on the US investigation (NTSB 2002) concludes that the crash of Egypt Air Flight 990 was not the result of any mechanical cause, but of the manipulation of the airplane controls by the copilot (first relief officer). The reasons for his action were not determined. The report on the Egyptian investigation (ECAA 2001) holds, on the contrary, that no evidence indicates the copilot could have plunged the airpliner into the ocean, and emphasises instead the accumulation of technical failures as the probable cause of the accident.

3. This translation was offered by the American daily *USA Today* and by several television networks including ABC.

4. According to the *Los Angeles Times*, in the midst of the crisis the copilot even recited the *shahada*, the Muslim statement of faith ('I bear witness that there is no God but God and that Muhammad is the Prophet of God'), which reinforced suspicions of suicide or sabotage. According to the experts, however, when a Muslim recites the shahada, it does not generally precede any kind of action. Moreover, the National Transportation Safety Board (NTSB) intervened several times to quash this story, which was based on 'unidentified sources.'

5. See NTSB 2002, 4 n 11: 'This phrase (recorded on the CVR [cockpit voice recorder] in Arabic as "Tawakkalt Ala Allah") was originally interpreted to mean "I place my fate in the hands of God." The interpretation of this Arabic statement was later amended to "I rely on God." According to an EgyptAir and ECAA presentation to Safety Board staff on April 28, 2000, this phrase "is very often used by the Egyptian layman in day to day activities to ask God's assistance for the task at hand".'

6. Ibrahim Hooper, National Communications Director of the Council on American-Islamic Relations, pointed to 'an information gap when it comes to Islam and Muslims, and this gap is easily filled with ignorance.' He added, 'If the inference was by a Christian pilot who said, "God help me," we wouldn't even have this conversation.' Quoted by Wren 1999.

7. The report on the Egyptian investigation puts great emphasis on the very common use of this expression in Egypt, and underlines the fact that it is only used in the context of a 'good action,' e.g., when preventing someone from falling, or in a more routine manner, when embarking on a journey by bus or by train (see ECAA 2001, p. 83).

8. Based on the rate of the copilot's speech and the frequency of his repetitions of the phrase, the report on the American investigation concludes that there was no significant increase in his level of psychological stress.

9. I would like to thank Kenneth Brown who alerted me to this passage during the UCLA conference on Clifford Geertz. Tunisians, in their everyday lives, use the word *wallah* (or *wallahi*) as an opening to lend more weight to their words, make themselves more interesting, swear their loyalty, affirm their reliability, threaten someone, impress the public, express admiration, show astonishment, declare love, hail a person, warn them, convince a partner, attract their attention, etc.

10. The Egyptian report emphasises the fact that the phrase is only used in the context of a good action and never in that of a bad action, and provides examples of situations in which it could never be used, such as killing someone or planning a robbery, etc. (see ECAA 2001, p. 83).

11. According to Jean-Paul Mari (1999), the *Wall Street Journal* and *USA Today* reported this story based on a leak from the American investigation, but then 'a new "leak" explained that the terrible phrase, "I have made my decision," never even existed on the tape! It wasn't just a mistranslation but a big lie. NTSB president Jim Hall expressed outrage' over these media reports.

12. Here I would like to thank my colleague, the linguist Khaoula Taleb-Ibrahimi, who, during the January 2008 Lyon conference on Clifford Geertz, reminded me of this incident, a scene she had witnessed and one that others had also described to me.

References

Babès, L., 2004. *Le voile démystifié*. Paris: Bayard.

Davidson, A.I., 2005. *L'émergence de la sexualité. Épistémologie historique et formation des concepts*. Paris: Albin Michel.

Delphy, C., 2006. Antisexisme ou antiracisme? Un faux dilemme. *Nouvelles questions féministes*, 25 (1), 59–83.

Eddé, D., 1989. *Lettre posthume*. Paris: Gallimard.

Egyptian Civil Aviation Authority (ECAA), 2001. *Report of investigation of accident*, Available from: http://www.ntsb. gov/events/ea990/docket/ecaa_report.pdf [Accessed 18 July 2008].

Ferrié, J.-N., 1991. Vers une anthropologie déconstructionniste des sociétés musulmanes du Maghreb. *Peuples méditerranéens*, 54/55, 229–46.

Geertz, C., 1966. Religion as a cultural system. *In*: M. Banton, ed. *Anthropological approaches to the study of religion*. New York: Frederick A. Praeger, 1–46.

Geertz, C., 1973. Thick description: toward an interpretive theory of culture. *In*: C. Geertz, ed. *The interpretation of cultures*. New York: Basic Books, 3–30.

Geertz, C., 2007. La religion, sujet d'avenir. *In*: Michel Wieviorka, ed. *Les sciences sociales en mutation*. Auxerre: Sciences Humaines, 427–434.

Guille-Escuret, G., 2000. Épistémologie du témoignage. Le cannibalisme ni vu ni connu. *L'Homme*, 153, 183–206.

Jullien, F., 2007. *Chemin faisant, connaître la Chine, relancer la philosophie*. Paris: Seuil.

Khosrokhavar, F., 2004. L'islam des jeunes filles en France. *In*: Charlotte Nordmann, ed. *Le foulard islamique en questions*. Paris: Amsterdam, 89–94.

Le Monde, 1999. L'énigme des derniers mots du copilote d'EgyptAir oppose Égyptiens et Américains. *Le Monde*, 19 November.

Le Temps, 2000. L'Égypte s'interroge sur de mystérieuses images radars 'classifiées' de l'US Air Force. *Le Temps*, 15 August.

Mari, J.-P., 1999. Contre-enquête sur une catastrophe aérienne; EgyptAir: le suicide était presque parfait. *Grands reporters.com*, 9 December. Available from: http://www.grands-reporters.com/EgyptAir-le-suicide-etait-presque.html [Accessed 19 September 2008].

Mary, A., 1998. De l'épaisseur de la description à la profondeur de l'interprétation. À propos de la description dense de C. Geertz. *Enquête*, 6, 57–72.

National Transportation Safety Board (NTSB), 2002. *Aircraft accident brief*, 13 March. Available from: http://www.ntsb.gov/publictn/2002/AAB0201.htm [Accessed 19 September 2008].

Nordmann, C., 2004. Le foulard islamique en questions. *In*: Charlotte Nordmann, ed. *Le foulard islamique en questions*. Paris: Amsterdam, 160–177.

Piotrowski, W.K., 2000. What's in a name?: The Crash of EgyptAir 990. *Religion in the news*, 3 (1). Available from: http://www.trincoll.edu/depts/csrpl/RINVol3No1/egyptair.htm [Accessed 19 September 2008].

Ricoeur, P., 1984. *Time and narrative*. vol. 1. Chicago: Chicago University Press.

Tersigni, S., 2003. Prendre le foulard: Les logiques antagoniques de la revendication. *Mouvements*, 30, 116–122.

Tylor, E., 1871. *Primitive culture,* part 2. *Religion in primitive culture*. New York: Harper Torchbooks.

Wren, C.S., 1999. The crash of EgyptAir: the statement; Arabic speakers dispute inquiry's interpretation of pilot's words. *New York Times*, 19 November. Available from: http://query.nytimes.com/gst/fullpage.html?res=9C05E1DC1F3DF93BA25752C1A96F958260 [Accessed 19 September 2008].

Interpretation and the limits of interpretability: on rethinking Clifford Geertz's semiotics of religious experience

C. Jason Throop

Department of Anthropology, University of California, Los Angeles, CA, USA

This paper critically interrogates Clifford Geertz's analysis of religious belief as it relates to both his broader semiotics of culture and his views on how such beliefs are implicated in the formation of particular dispositions, propensities, and habits informing social action. It is argued that Geertz's account of religion can be held to reveal some of the most central assumptions of his social theory, his hermeneutics of culture, and his philosophy of action.

Introduction

In this paper I critically interrogate Clifford Geertz's analysis of religious belief as it relates to both his broader semiotics of culture and his views on how such beliefs are implicated in the formation of particular dispositions, propensities, and habits informing social action. To do so, the paper is organised in two parts. In the first part I discuss the extent to which Geertz's perspective on religious belief and practice as outlined in the context of *The interpretation of cultures* (1973) is deeply revealing of some of the most central assumptions of his social theory, his hermeneutics of culture, and his philosophy of action. Most importantly, I will point to how these same writings evidence what I believe are two neglected aspects of Geertz's culture theory, namely his interest in subjectivity and practice.

In the second half of the paper I will turn specifically to his more recent critique of William James' 'subjectivist' account of religion in *The varieties of religious experience* (1987[1902]). Geertz's critique of James will help to clarify how the Geertzian project seeks to contribute to understandings of the cultural constitution of particular subjectivities in contemporary culture theory. In the conclusion of the paper I attempt to make a case for the significance of extending Geertz's perspective on two fronts: on the one hand, as Geertz himself called for, toward a more nuanced understanding of subjective experience as evidenced in James' original writings on the philosophical psychology of religious experience, and on the other hand, toward a micro-analytic understanding of subject formation, power, and truth as suggested in Michel Foucault's last and most mature writings on *The hermeneutics of the subject* (2005).

Geertz's semiotics of culture: the familiar story

Geertz is, of course, renowned for his semiotic approach to culture and social action. What he is perhaps not as well known for, however, is his view that such a semiotics must be grounded in the formation and interplay of various dispositions, propensities, habits, and skills. This perspective brings Geertz's thinking in line with some rather unlikely consociates, namely, practice theorists such as Pierre Bourdieu (1977, 1990) and Anthony Giddens (1984). The reasons behind the lack of attention to this side of Geertz's culture theory in anthropology is not exactly clear to me. However, it may have something to do with the fact that many of Geertz's most powerful and explicit articulations of his position are embedded in his discussions of religion. In particular, they are found in the context of his examination of the relationship between religious symbolism and practice in his book, *The interpretation of cultures* (1973). Before turning to explore this neglected side of Geertz's culture theory, however, I would like to review what might be considered some of the most general aspects of his interpretivist perspective.

Generally speaking, following Max Weber, Geertz asserts that his vision of an interpretive science whose purpose is to explore the 'webs of significance' that constitute culture is founded on the idea that culture is a public, ideational, and yet non-mentalistic system of construable signs. Paraphrasing the philosopher Gilbert Ryle, Geertz holds that it is precisely the inherently public nature of culture that challenges the notion that somehow cultural symbols exist 'in someone's head.' It is in this context that we get an entrée into what is one of the central concerns in Geertz's writings on religion: the effort to examine the interrelationship between cultural symbols and the moods, propensities, dispositions, and habits of social actors.

Geertz believes with Ryle that 'mind' is a term that most accurately denotes not some privately accessible 'ghost in the machine,' but a publicly accessible 'class of skills, propensities, capacities, tendencies and habits. . . [in short] an organized system of dispositions which finds its manifestation in some actions and some things' (1973, p. 58). He argues that it is these 'external' (i.e. public) symbolic manifestations of complexes of skills and habits that ultimately underlie all reflective thought. What many scholars assume to be 'mental' processes are, according to Geertz, more accurately a dynamic matching of 'states and processes of [public] symbolic models against [equally public] states and processes of the wider world' (Geertz 1973, p. 78).

Geertz argues that it is only this public view of symbols as 'material vehicles of thought' that can ensure the possibility for uncovering properties of cultural and personal systems through systematic empirical analysis (1973, p. 362). In Geertz's view then, his perspective provides anthropology with a way in which to uncover 'what *is* given, what the conceptual structure embodied in the symbolic forms through which persons are perceived actually is' (p. 364, emphasis in the original). It is his view that this potential 'method of describing and analyzing the meaningful structure of experience' can provide anthropology with the basis for establishing what he referred to at the time as a valid 'scientific phenomenology of culture' (p. 364). This early reference to phenomenology is quite interesting given Geertz's critiques of the broader phenomenological movement in philosophy, and as we will see, with regard to his critical reading of William James' subjectivist take on religious experience. That said, it is also interesting that Geertz's writings on religion seek to advance a particular view of experience that may yet still be reconcilable with the very subjectivist and phenomenological approaches he is so critical of.

Attempting to move beyond what he labels the 'cognitivist/subjectivist' fallacy, Geertz argues that anthropologists must recognise that culture, mind, and experience are, in the end, symbolically mediated public interpretations and actions through and through. For these reasons Geertz makes a point of distinguishing his position clearly from that of phenomenologists such as Edmund Husserl (1962), who tend to advocate 'strong subjectivist tendencies' that 'place stress upon a supposed inner state of an actor rather than on a certain sort of relation – a symbolically mediated one – between actor and situation' (Geertz 1973, p. 110 n 35). Building instead on Gilbert Ryle and George Herbert Mead, Geertz argues that the assumption that culture is both public and social leads inevitably to the insight that cultural processes do not 'happen in the head' but consist, in contrast, in a traffic of significant symbols that serve to 'impose meaning upon experience' (1973, p. 45). Geertz argues in fact that 'undirected by culture patterns – organized systems of significant symbols – man's behaviour would be virtually ungovernable, a mere chaos of pointless acts and exploding emotions, his experience virtually shapeless' (p. 46). It is this externalised, socially infused understanding of culture as a coherent system of significant symbols informing conscious experience that allows Geertz to later establish his memorable metaphor of 'culture as text' (pp. 448–449).

Symbols, moods, and motives in Geertz's semiotics of religion

I have already alluded to Geertz's emphasis upon dispositions, tendencies, and habits in the context of his hermeneutic theory of culture and social action. It is in turning specifically to his writings on religion, however, that we find a more clearly articulated attempt to integrate his thinking on the relationship between culture, symbolic systems, and what we might call in contemporary terms, subjectivity and practice. Perhaps the best place to start in this regard is with Geertz's now famous definition of religion in his article, 'Religion as a cultural system.' According to Geertz,

> a religion is: (1) a system of symbols which acts to (2) establish powerful, pervasive, and long-lasting moods and motivations in men by (3) formulating conceptions of a general order of existence and (4) clothing these conceptions with such an aura of factuality that (5) the moods and motivations seem uniquely realistic. (Geertz 1973, p. 90)

Most striking here is Geertz's reliance upon moods and motivations, especially given the antipsychologistic stance that he has long been noted for. Key for understanding the relationship between systems of symbols and the moods and motivations that are instilled in individuals who partake in such systems is the recognition that all cultural patterns have, as Geertz terms it, 'an intrinsic double aspect.' That is, cultural patterns are simultaneously both *models of* and *models for* reality. Cultural patterns both conform to social and psychological realities and alter those self-same realities to their own dictates.

A central way that religious systems do this is, in Geertz's words, 'by inducing in the worshiper a certain distinctive set of dispositions (tendencies, capacities, propensities, skills, habits, liabilities, pronenesses) which lend a chronic character to the flow of his activities and the quality of his experience' (1973, p. 95). Again, Geertz holds that the way that religious systems 'lend a chronic character to the flow of activities' and to the 'quality of experience' is significantly rooted in the way that such systems impact an individual's motivations and moods.

Motivations are understood by Geertz to be 'persisting tendencies' or 'chronic inclinations' 'to perform certain sorts of acts and experience certain sorts of feeling in certain sorts of situations' (1973, p. 96). Motives are, in his estimation, not reducible to acts or feelings, however. They are instead 'liabilities to perform particular classes of act or have particular classes of feeling' (p. 97). Motives are the generative source of acts and feelings. They are not the acts and feelings themselves. They are then, in a word, dispositions. Motives are dispositions to feel and act in particular ways, according to specific goals or ends, in particular sets of circumstances.

Where motives are specifically oriented to particular ends, to particular goals that feelings and actions are directed toward achieving, moods are characterised by Geertz to be diffuse and objectless. It is well worth quoting at length Geertz's eloquent distinction between these two sorts of subjective experience.

> The major difference between moods and motivations is that where the latter are, so to speak, vectorial qualities, the former are merely scalar. Motives have a directional cast, they describe a certain overall course, gravitate toward certain, usually temporary, consummations. But moods vary only as to intensity: they go nowhere. They spring from certain circumstances but they are responsive to no ends. Like fogs, they just settle and lift; like scents, suffuse and evaporate. When present they are totalistic: if one is sad everything and everybody seems dreary; if one is gay, everything and everybody seems splendid.... But perhaps the most important difference, so far as we are concerned, between moods and motivations is that motivations are 'made meaningful' with reference to the ends toward which they are conceived to conduce, whereas moods are 'made meaningful' with reference to the conditions from which they are conceived to spring. *We interpret motives in terms of their consummations, but we interpret moods in terms of their sources.* (Geertz 1973, p. 97, my emphasis)

Whether understood in terms of the diffuse, context-oriented, and totalistic encompassment of moods or the focused, goal-oriented, and discrete enactment of motivations, such varieties of subjective life are, for Geertz, significantly patterned by religious symbols and the broader cultural patterns within which they are embedded. That Geertz is so keen to impress upon us the 'depth' to which religious ideas and symbols penetrate social actors' lived experience is certainly striking to those of us who are much more familiar with the text-centered symbolic side of Geertz's thinking. It is also interesting, I think, given the scant attention that even more psychologically oriented anthropologists like myself have paid to the place and significance of 'moods' in patterning subjective life and social action (see Groark and Throop n.d.). Indeed, of interest to those of us who are engaged in a dialogue with Geertz's culture theory is the extent to which his take on religion reveals what might be termed the sentimental side to his semiotics.

It is important to emphasise, however, that Geertz's interest in moods and motivations is not a theme that is carried forward and substantially elaborated upon elsewhere in his work. It is also important to recall Geertz's questionable attempt to define motivation in dispositional, and not experiential or emotional, terms; a stance that highlights a more practice theoretical and less experiential take on social action. And yet, even given Geertz's well known anti-mentalistic stance, and what we will soon see to be his anti-Jamesian view that religion is not reducible to 'religious feeling,' the extent to which he turns to such generally 'non-cognitive' experiences as motivations, moods, and dispositions in his discussion of the significance of religious ways of being is nonetheless quite noteworthy. At the very least, I contend that this points to Geertz's willingness to develop an incipient, if ambivalent, interest in subjective experience, one that we will see him take up yet again in his later critique of William James' philosophical psychology of religion.

The problem of suffering and the surfeit of meaning

The significance of motives and moods takes on further import in Geertz's discussion of the 'problem of meaning' in religious practice. He notes that numerous thinkers have suggested that religious systems often arise to address both extraordinary events and humankind's recurrent confrontations with the limits of interpretability. Without the coherence provided by culturally elaborated systems of significant symbols, humans find themselves, Geertz asserts, on the brink of chaotic dissolution. Such a lack of 'interpretability' leads to forms of moodedness that are permeated by anxiety, angst, and disquiet (Geertz 1973, p. 100). The quest for meaning, in particular the quest for religious meaning, is understood in this light as a response to the forms of moodedness that arise in the face of the 'opacity' of certain events, such as 'the dumb senselessness of intense or inexorable pain' (p. 108).

The existential problems humans face when confronting 'a chaos of thingless names and nameless things' is at the heart of problems of interpretability and meaning, says Geertz (1973, p. 103). There are, he suggests, three specific points where the limits of interpretability threaten to bring forth just such a chaos. These include: 1) the limits of our analytic capacities that arise as 'bafflement in the face of the intransigently opaque;' 2) the limits of our powers of endurance and the 'problem of suffering;' and 3) the limits of our moral insight when confronted with 'intractable ethical paradoxes' (p. 100). Whereas the limits of our analytic capacities lead to the cultivation of 'more intellective aspects' of meaning, the experience of suffering is founded in the attempt to give definition and precision to our life of 'moods, sentiments, passions, affections, [and] feelings' (p. 104). The limits of moral insight are, in contrast, tied to the refining of evaluative capacities as we seek to construct systems of value that aid in the making of 'sound moral judgments' (p. 106).

Again the place of moods and motives in this discussion is striking. Moreover, the significance of Geertz's working through these three aspects of the problem of meaning with such an explicit interest in moods, affects, values, and forms of intellection lies, I believe, in foregrounding this often neglected side to Geertz's semiotics of culture, namely his interest in subjectivity, or what we might also term 'experience.'

***

So far I have argued that Geertz's writings on religion in the context of *The interpretation of cultures* advances both practical and experiential dimensions to what has most often been viewed as a strictly symbolic or interpretivist approach to culture and social action. What is perhaps even more interesting is that it is in the context of these same writings that Geertz works to integrate the practical, experiential, and interpretive aspects of his semiotics of culture. This he accomplishes in discussing the concept of perspectives, attitudes, or modes of seeing and in analyzing the role that ritual plays in the synthesis of mood, motivation, and symbol. It is with regard to the former that Geertz seeks to clarify how his take on subjectivity or experience differs from putatively more subjectivist accounts in phenomenology. It is in the context of the later that he highlights the key role that practice plays in instilling dispositions, propensities, and habits embedded in particular systems of cultural meaning, religious or otherwise.

On the religious perspective

Geertz takes on the problem of experience by means of a discussion of 'perspective.' Perspective, Geertz explains, refers to a specific 'mode of seeing' in which individuals are inclined to perceive, comprehend, discern, and grasp the world in a particular way. For instance, the religious perspective can be compared to other perspectives, such as aesthetic, common-sense, historical, and scientific perspectives. It is possible for individuals to shift between such perspectives and as such shift between distinctive modes of being-in-the-world. In this discussion of perspective we find Geertz owning up to the clear inspiration he has taken from the phenomenological writings of Edmund Husserl and Alfred Schutz who wrote much about the phenomenological modifications underpinning a social actor's ability to shift between various 'attitudes,' from the natural attitude to the scientific attitude for instance. That said, Geertz is clear to distinguish his views from what he takes to be the overly 'subjectivist' underpinnings of phenomenological approaches to experience. So even despite his interest in the moods and motivations that are necessarily implicated in these various perspectives or attitudes, he does not want to be mistaken for emphasising 'a supposed inner state of an actor rather than... a certain sort of relation – a symbolically mediated one – between an actor and a situation' (Geertz 1973, p. 110, n 35).

Geertz's own somewhat ambivalent stance toward phenomenology, in particular Schutzian social phenomenology, is evident throughout this discussion of perspective, however. Despite his criticisms he maintains that he does not wish to suggest that a phenomenological account of religious experience is not essential to a complete understanding of religion and religious belief. Citing the Peircian-inspired writings of Walker Percy, he cautions that such a phenomenological analysis must be one that is intersubjective and nontranscendental. It is, in his words, a phenomenology that must be undertaken in 'genuinely scientific terms.'

Following Schutz's lead, Geertz sets out to define the contours of the religious perspective by means of comparison to other such modes of seeing. He begins with the common-sense perspective, what Husserl and Schutz would have termed the 'natural attitude.' The common-sense perspective is one wherein a social actor takes for granted what is given to him in his experience of the world. It is the unquestioned immersion in the givenness of a reality that is significantly culturally defined and yet naturalised to appear to the social actor as that which is 'just there.' Associated with this mode of seeing is a particular motivation – the pragmatic motive to engage with the reality of the 'just there' for purposes of attending to everyday concerns, needs, desires, and wants.

The scientific perspective, in contrast, is a mode of seeing that challenges the givenness of the common-sensical through 'deliberate doubt and systematic inquiry.' In shifting from the common-sensical to the scientific perspective, disinterested observation replaces pragmatic motivations and abstract models displace everyday assumptions. Much of the scientific perspective is grounded in discovering what lies behind the given, what hidden processes give rise to the perceptible.

The 'suspension of naïve realism and practical interest' inherent in the common-sense perspective is accomplished in yet another distinctive way through the aesthetic perspective, Geertz argues. If the scientific attitude is one of revealing what is behind the perceptible, the aesthetic perspective is one that revels in the surfaces of it. Where the scientific attitude is oriented to a disinterested doubting of what is given in everyday forms of perception and appreciation, the aesthetic attitude holds the everyday in abeyance 'in favour of an eager dwelling upon appearances, an engrossment in surfaces, an absorption in things, as we say, "in themselves"' (Geertz 1973, p. 111).

Religious perspectives differ from common-sensical perspectives in that they are oriented beyond everyday realities to realities that 'correct and complete them.' And it is not action but faith and acceptance that are seen as the mode of engagement with such realities.

Whereas scientific perspectives question everyday realities through 'institutionalised skepticism' and probabilistic hypotheses, religious perspectives question the everyday in terms of non-hypothetical truths. It is not detached scientific analysis that drives religious perspectives but committed encounters with such truths. And finally, the religious perspective differs from the aesthetic perspective in that it does not work to question factuality but instead to deliberately 'create an aura of utter actuality.'

As will be evident in Geertz's later critique of William James' account of religious experience, Geertz's take on experience is one that some of us more phenomenologically oriented anthropologists might deem to be rather 'thin.' His emphasis upon the ways in which cultural realities pattern particular perspectives that include distinctive moods, motivations, and corresponding modes of appreciating, judging, and acting, however, evidences an orientation to subjectivity that seems rather more pronounced than some of Geertz's most ardent critics may have traditionally given him credit for. And yet, it may still be fair for us to wonder whether or not Geertz's anti-subjectivist version of hermeneutic anthropology grants him the necessary tools to adequately disentangle the complex subjective textures and temporalities embedded in such moods, motivations, and modes of perceiving.

Ritual and the synthesis of symbol, mood, motivation, and reality

As mentioned above, the primary means by which Geertz sees such a religious perspective being concretely instilled in particular practitioners is through what can be understood to be a decidedly practice-based interest in ritual activities. It is not purely cognitive or symbolically mediated reflection upon a set of religious principles that propels the perspectives entailed in religious belief. It is rather ritual practices that do so. According to Geertz, ritual practices are held to generate the context within which the appropriate set of moods and motives (an ethos) are able to articulate with an acknowledged 'image of cosmic order' (a world view). It is through ritual performance then that what may have previously been merely beliefs can be transformed into experiential and existential actualities.

Geertz holds that a social actor's participation in ritual performance is the very vehicle through which a given symbolic system is verified and vivified for him. The practices entailed in such performances are not only imaginative but also bodily enactments that are reflected in and are generative of the very moods, motivations, ideals, and values encompassed in any given community's religious attitudes. It is through ritual practice then that the symbolic and the experiential are brought into a mutually informing dialogue. And it is through such practice that social actors are instilled with the attitudes, perspectives, habits, and dispositions that more or less align with religious and cultural belief systems.

Geertz's interest in more formally articulated ritual performances, such as Javanese shadow puppet plays and Balinese theatrical performances, is also extended, however, to more mundane everyday actions that social actors consistently engage in while interacting with their consociates. As he states in his discussion of the various types of practices that are implicated in the phenomenologically rich concept of *rasa* in Java,

> On the world-view side, there are yoga-like mystical techniques (meditation, staring at candles, repeating set words or phrases) and highly involved speculative theories of the emotions and their relations to sickness, natural objects, social institutions, and so on. On the ethos side, there is a moral stress on subdued dress, speech, and gesture, on refined sensitivity to small changes in the emotional state both of oneself and of others, and on a stable, highly regularised predictability of behaviour. (Geertz 1973, p. 136)

I should be clear here in noting that some of Geertz's critics have charged him with overly emphasising, in even what are arguably his most practice-based reflections on everyday and ritualised forms of social action, the functionally homogenising and static effect of such practices. It is important to recall, however, that Geertz does in fact show an interest in such engines of change driving transformation in any given religious or cultural system. He does so most directly in *The interpretation of cultures*, perhaps, in the context of his thick description of the social tensions and disruptions occurring during the ritualised interactions at a Javanese funeral or *slamatan*. It is also worth noting that despite this interest in social transformation, particularly as generated through socio-political and economic alterations to Java's social terrain, he still does not often give much of an account of individual agency (*à la* practice theory) or of the necessary diversity of experience that is arrayed within any given community of practice (*à la* cultural phenomenology or person-centered ethnography). He does, however, interestingly trace how the emerging social and political complexity in Java at the time of his fieldwork was concretely reflected in the attitudes, moods, and emotions of those specific individuals involved in Paidjan's funeral. As he explains,

> The disorganization of the ritual resulted from a basic ambiguity in the meaning of the rite for those who participated in it. Most simply stated, this ambiguity lay in the fact that the symbols which compose the slametan had both religious and political significance, were charged with both sacred and profane import. The people who came into Karman's yard, including Karman himself, were not sure whether they were engaged in a sacralized consideration of first and last things or in a secular struggle for power. (Geertz 1973, p. 165)

It is perhaps in evoking the place of ambiguity, situationally-dependent forms of meaning, and shifting fields of power arising in the dynamics of ongoing social interaction that Geertz comes closest to advancing a perspective that aligns with many contemporary agency theorists who often draw from some combination of micro-interactional, phenomenological, or practice-based approaches. Still, such potentiality for proximity between these perspectives is more an *approchement* than a realisation, for Geertz does not ever seek to closely examine what may have been the highly personalised forms of ambiguity and conflict underlying Karman's particular engagement with the ritual, nor does he focus on detailing the real-time embodied sequences of concrete practices and forms of talk and interaction that constitute the underlying dynamics of the social scene.

Now, while I believe that Geertz's writings on religion do point to a productive place to begin reconciling his hermeneutic or meaning-based approach to cultural analysis with contemporary practice and phenomenologically based theoretical concerns in anthropology and the social sciences more broadly defined, I do also acknowledge that it is perhaps too much of a stretch to see his perspective in any straightforward or unproblematic way as strictly aligned with them. In my attempt to work to productively extend Geertz's approach in ways that may allow us to engage in just such a dialogue, I believe that it is helpful to turn to one of his last published pieces on religion, his critique of William James' philosophical psychology of religious experience.

The varieties of religious subjectivity: Geertz contra James?

Geertz (2000) begins his essay-length meditation on James by noting the individualism and sentimentalism inherent in James' definition of religion as rooted in an individual's feeling of a 'pinch of destiny.' Religion, says James, is necessarily located *not* primarily in institutions or great works but in an individual's 'recesses of feeling, the darker, blinder strata of character.' To be sure, James' experiential pragmatism, his radical empiricism as he called it, is ardently subjective and pluralistic to its core. It is, for James, truly *varieties of experience*, religious or otherwise, that best represent the state of our being as meaning-seeking and meaning-making human agents. James' take on meaning is thoroughly embodied, lived, and, he would say, 'experiential.' Meaning is not reducible to thought, or the ossifying abstractions embedded in cognitive schemas, images, and ideas. Meaning is experienced in the richest and most dynamic sense of the term. Anything we call meaningful in our lives, James held, is as much defined by moments of focused clarity as it is by ever fluctuating undercurrents of vagueness and ambiguity. It was James (1890), we should recall, who wished to reinstate 'the vague and inarticulate to its proper place in our mental life.'

James' (1987[1902]) book-length and very much person-centered description of the richly textured experiences of individuals' religious lives, rests on what Geertz takes to be a far too radically personal, private, subjective, and experiential understanding of religion. As Geertz states, 'cordoning off a space for "religion" in a realm called "experience" – "the darker, blinder strata of character" – seems, somehow, no longer so reasonable and natural a thing to try to do' (Geertz 2000, p. 169). Embedding his critique in what is putatively the current contours of 'our' taken-for-granted assumptions about contemporary religious life, Geertz, ever a master of rhetorical prose, suggests that when we think of 'religious struggle' in contemporary terms, it is not 'private wrestlings with inner demons' nor ongoing 'battlements of the soul' that are most likely to come to our collective imaginations. It is instead the struggle that arises in the context of protest, collective violence, terrorism, revolt, genocide, torture, and warfare that does. Religious struggle, in Geertz's words, 'mostly refers to quite outdoor occurrences, *plein air* proceedings in the public square – alleyway encounters, high court holdings' (p. 169).

Geertz's much earlier calls for turning from phenomenological subjectivism to the development of what he called, with a textual wink, an 'outdoor psychology,' is certainly on one level well in line with these critiques. In other ways, however, there is something new going on here for Geertz. First off, such a perspective certainly constitutes a movement away from his earlier ambivalently phenomenologically inspired writings on the religious attitude discussed above. Second, this is not primarily an argument from philosophy, whether Wittgensteinian, Rylean, Schutzian, or otherwise, that seeks to question the merits of pursuing subjectivist accounts of social life. It is more significantly a call to recognise the place of cultural meaning, power dynamics, and social identity in anything that we might choose to label as religion. In his words,

> 'Experience,' however ineradicable it may be from any discourse on faith that is responsive to its regenerative claims. . . no longer seems adequate to frame by itself our understanding of the passions and actions we want, under some description or other, to call religious. Firmer, more determinate, more transpersonal, extravert terms – 'Meaning,' say, or 'Identity,' or 'Power' – must be deployed to catch the tonalities of devotion in our time. (Geertz 2000, p. 170)

While attempting to draw our attention to the collective processes underpinning the formation and negotiation of meaning, self-representation (identity), and power, Geertz is not, however, quite ready to throw out the Jamesian baby with the bathwater. It is very interesting that he argues in the second half of this same article that an understanding of religion that is thoroughly divested of interiority, of the life of sentiment, faith, and belief, 'is hardly worth the name' (p. 178). Geertz wishes to argue here that while there are some serious shortcomings to myopically focusing on an individual's experience of religion, it is still not possible to understand the convictions, the motivations, and the moods that are instilled in social actors who have taken up a stance on the world through the lens of a religious perspective, without turning to examine closely such personal forms of meaning. In contemporary social theory, Geertz laments,

> [t]he whole vast variety of personal experience, or, more carefully, representations of personal experience, that James, on the one hand, so exquisitely explored, and, on the other, so resolutely walled off from those 'dictators of what we may believe,' the public, the social, and the everyday, is not only isolated once more from the convolutions of history – it goes unremarked altogether. (Geertz 2000, p. 179)

To understand religious meaning, religious identity, and the power struggles associated with contemporary religions, social institutions, and the state, it is impossible, Geertz asserts, to ignore the experience of individual practitioners. To understand what Geertz takes to be a fundamental shift in religious sensibility underlying the 'conflicts and dilemmas of our age,' it is necessary to follow not James' 'radically individualistic, subjectivistic, 'brute perception' concept of religion and religiousness,' but instead his 'intense, marvelously observant, almost pathologically sensitive attention to the shades and subtleties of thought and emotion' that inform individuals' always culturally inflected choices, decisions, reveries, and acts (p. 185), that is, their experience.

***

Now it is perhaps time to show my hand here. As a psychological and medical anthropologist with a longstanding interest in contributing to and developing a phenomenological approach to cultural meaning and social action, I have always had a rather complicated appreciation of Geertz's culture theory. On the one hand, I have thoroughly respected his attempts to advance a philosophically mature anthropology that can share the floor with philosophy in its attempts to understand those forms of being-in-the-world that most fundamentally characterise us as humans. On the other hand, I have found, like many of my peers in psychological anthropology, that his largely anti-subjectivist and anti-experiential take on meaning is somewhat lacking. Being deeply inspired by the work of James, Husserl, and Schutz, I have also found myself critical of Geertz's critiques of phenomenology. And along with those in my field who have devoted their careers to examining social suffering, collective violence, genocide, and myriad other forms of human cruelty, suffering, and pain, I have at times been sympathetic to critiques that charge Geertz with failing to pay adequate attention to questions concerning the dynamics of power, agency, and vulnerability.

What I would like to do in the concluding sections of this paper is to suggest a few possible paths for generatively extending Geertz's semiotic theory of culture and social action along lines that would help to correct for some of these shortcomings. The seeds for such an enterprise, as I have implied throughout this paper, are already importantly suggested in Geertz's account of how religious experience is understood in relation to the problems of interpretation and the limits of interpretability and how religion can be viewed as a mode of practice and a form of subjectivity based upon culturally instilled tendencies, habits, dispositions, feelings, moods, and motivations. Moreover, they are evident in his later calls for recognising the place of identity, power, and meaning in understanding religious experience, while still acknowledging the importance of examining the 'subtleties of thought and emotion' underlying such putatively rarified forms of existence.

There are indeed many lines we could take to forward such a project. Here I would like to suggest just a few. First, on the subjective side of the equation, the richness, complexity, and diversity of experience foregrounded in James' philosophical psychology of religion has been pursued in recent years by psychological and medical anthropologists subscribing to cultural phenomenological, embodiment, and person-centered approaches. Turning to how it is that social and cultural life is constituted both subjectively and intersubjectively, such approaches have called for the recognition that, as Thomas Csordas (1990) following Merleau-Ponty (1962) puts it, our subjective life does not begin with but rather ends in objects. That is, forms of cultural understanding and practice, established canons of norms, values, and morality, our taken-for-granted assumptions about what is true, good, and beautiful, are not simply objectively given to social actors. They are instead active achievements that are mediated through our always embodied modes of subjective life. When we turn our analytic lens away from pre-given objects of experience toward those processes of subjective and intersubjective constitution underlying them, we are better placed, cultural phenomenologists argue, to examine the diverse ways that social actors can come to inhabit what is taken to be a shared reality, religious or otherwise.

Interestingly, in his discussion of the different subjective orientations that are distilled in differing 'perspectives,' whether religious, scientific, common-sensical, etc., Geertz points to how it is that one and the same object can become constituted in distinctive ways by means of the particular perspective that a given social actor takes in orienting to it. The resonance between Geertz's discussion of perspective and recent work in phenomenological anthropology highlighting the constitutive side of both subject and object formation is not at all surprising when we again recall that Geertz is drawing here from phenomenology and the work of Husserl (1962) and Schutz (1967) who would call such differing perspectives 'attitudes.'

The very dynamism and complexity of subjective orientations to objects of experience is evident in Husserl's (1962) insight that shifts in such attitudes, what he calls phenomenological modifications, operate continuously for experiencing subjects who may take more or less reflective stances or more or less engaged stances when relating to objects of experience, be those objects of the 'mind' or of the 'world.' Indeed, from a phenomenological perspective distinctions between subjective and objective aspects of reality, between what is of the 'mind' and of the 'world,' are themselves in part determined by the attitude that a social actor takes up. There is, from the phenomenological perspective, no strict line demarcating the subjective and the objective, for both are significantly constituted by attitudes toward experience that render certain aspects of it thoughts, images, feelings, sentiments, moods, sensations, perceptions, judgments, forms of appreciation, etc., on the one hand, or properties of physical objects, bodies, persons, animals, celestial phenomena, spirits, natural occurrences, etc., on the other.

Cultural phenomenologists are certainly appreciative of Geertz's own phenomenologically inspired call to recognise that concretely enacted participation in religious life works precisely to shift participants' perspectives from a common-sensical to a religious one. As Geertz attests, 'religious belief in the midst of ritual, where it engulfs the total person, transporting him, so far as he is concerned, into another mode of existence, and religious belief as the pale, remembered reflection of that experience in the midst of everyday life are not precisely the same thing' (Geertz 1973, pp. 119–120). That said, cultural phenomenologists would still ask Geertz, however, to provide a more rigorous phenomenological account of the concrete embodiment of such practices and the experiential particularities tied to 'transporting' or shifting a given actor's perspective from the common-sensical to the religious.

For instance, in the context of his description of the Rangda-Barong performances in Bali, Geertz alludes to the ways that the encounter between performers and audience in the enactment of the relation between these two mythical beings necessarily engages not only an imaginative but a bodily appropriation of the drama. In particular he describes an 'extraordinarily developed capacity for psychological dissociation,' possession, and 'trance' as a means for the Balinese 'to cross a threshold into another order of existence' (p. 116). Aside from describing the scene as one of 'frenzied activities' and mass 'violent trances,' he does not, however, go into any specificity with regard to what it is like for the particular actors to concretely experience such a transformation. What exactly is entailed in an individual's experience of embodying a demon, a 'minor' witch, or 'various sorts of legendary and mythical figures' in trance? To use Csordas' (1993) felicitous phrase, what specific *somatic modes of attention* are implicated in the process of recognising that an individual is about to, or has already, become possessed? Are there particular embodied sensations of tingling, numbness, or pain, or are there particular smells, visions, or sounds that serve as indications of the presence or impending arrival of a particular possessing demon or spirit? Are there differing experiences of self-efficacy and will at play when individuals begin to feel their bodies operating in ways that they do not intentionally command? To what extent do individuals recall the process of possession and the aftermath of its enactment? How do subsequent narrative recountings of the experience by those who were possessed and those who were not serve to shape both personal and collective attitudes toward such practices? These are all questions that would be taken up in detail in the context of a more explicitly cultural phenomenological approach to ethnographic description and analysis.

On the person-centered side of things, psychological and medical anthropologists have sought to examine the compelling cares and concerns – in Geertz's language, the moods and motivations – that shape an individual's lived experience of her social and physical worlds (see Wikan 1990, Hollan 2001). Indeed, as Geertz suggested, most certainly tied up with particular phenomenological modifications and modes of constitution are particular feelings, emotions, and sentiments. And it is often the very complex ambivalences, ambiguities, and diversities inherent in any given actor's life of sentiment and feeling that make overly reductive and predictive models of human behavior suspect from a person-centered perspective. To understand human meaning and action, person-centered ethnographers remind us, it is necessary to delve deep into not only what Malinowski (1935) would have termed the *context of the situation* and the *context of culture*, but also to what Douglas Hollan (personal communication) has termed the *person-as-context* – that is, the often unique ways that the particularities of an individual's life trajectory and upbringing have led her to feel, think, appreciate, imagine, fantasize, and anticipate in distinctive ways. In social interaction, what is taken up by any given interlocutor as meaningful, significant, of concern, is based not only upon the context of the other's contribution to the interaction, but also necessarily on an individual's own tendencies to interpret, feel, and emote in particular ways. How such personally inflected cultural forms of being and experiencing are instilled in, recognised or contested by particular actors is, I believe, at the very heart of the anthropological enterprise.

In the case of Paidjan's funeral, a person-centered ethnographer would, with Geertz, most certainly be interested in undertaking a thick description of the various actions, conflicts, and problems leading up to the politically fraught attempts to appropriately bury the boy. That said, there would additionally be efforts on the part of a person-centered ethnographer to explore the always highly personalised ways that the various actors engaged in the social scene are motivated to give meaning to their experiences. It would not be assumed, for instance, that all of the mourners attending the event would be able to cultivate feelings of *iklas* – 'a kind of willed affectlessness, a detached and static state of "not caring",' as Geertz describes it (1973, p. 153). There would be instead an active attempt, in talking to, interviewing, and observing the various participants over an extended period of time, to discover how the event in question was anticipated, registered, and recalled in terms of particular experiences of mourning, longing, and grief, of frustration, anger, and regret, or of fear, anxiety, and shame. It would be assumed that individuals participating in the event would have highly complex, shifting, and ambivalent attitudes that are rooted in longstanding imaginal, emotional, and motivational patterns tied to their personal histories of attachment and loss. An attempt would thus be made to situate Geertz's description of Karman's frustration and anger in the wake of the Modin's refusal to officiate the boy's funeral on the ground of Karman's anti-Muslim political affiliations, within the context of Karman's personal history of dealing with authority, with perceived slights from others, and overt refusals to requests in times of vulnerability and need.

Yet another point whereby we might think to begin profitably extending Geertz's hermeneutics of culture is through some of Michel Foucault's later writings on the hermeneutics of the self and subject formation. While I certainly do not consider myself an expert on Foucauldian thought, over the past few years I have been actively thinking through the relevance of some of the ideas articulated in these later works for my own ethnographic investigations into the role that pain and suffering play in the formation of particular ethical subjectivities on the island of Yap in the Western Pacific (Throop forthcoming). For those who may be unfamiliar with Foucault's later lectures and writings, it may indeed come as a surprise that a psychologically oriented anthropologist such as myself would choose to rely upon a Foucauldian framework for extending what I take to be an incipient interest in practice and subjectivity in Geertz's writings on religion. It is true that the works that Foucault is most recognised for in contemporary anthropological theorizing are often those that systematically work to dispense with all references to 'experience' and 'subjectivity' in favour of a reliance upon the constructs of 'discourse' and 'power.' Indeed, Foucault's clearly anti-subjectivist stance arose in part from his well known public dispute with Sartre over the existentialist idea that all knowledge is necessarily mediated through actively constitutive processes of conscious subjects (see Paras 2006, p. 38). In addition, it is significantly tied to Foucault's attempts to examine the history of systems of knowledge and power that provide the very conditions for the possibility of certain ideas to arise and gain legitimacy in given sociohistorical periods.

That said, there is an increasingly recognised shift in Foucault's appreciation of subjectivity and experience in the context of his later writings and lectures (see Foucault 1978, 1985, 1986, 1997, 2005; cf. Dreyfus and Rabinow 1983, Paras 2006).[1] In these works – works that are rooted in studies of ancient philosophy, aesthetics, morality, and yes, religion – Foucault explicitly uses the 'language of experience' as a means to look 'at the subject from *within*, as an actor' (Paras 2006, p. 144). Much like Geertz, however, I believe that Foucault still presents us with a view of subjectivity that is far too 'thin.' And his perspective could similarly be augmented through an approach that focuses explicit attention to the necessarily dynamic, ambiguous, always complexly textured, and uniquely conflictual nature of the *particular* subjectivities that are engaged in such forms of moral self-fashioning (see Throop 2003, forthcoming). For my purposes in this paper, however, what is very helpful and productive about Foucault's later writings is their ability to provide a basis from which to extend Geertz's thinking on the place of practice in relation to processes of self-formation in a given community.

Foucault's understanding of the formation of subjectivities is embedded in his view of the basic building blocks of moral systems more generally (Foucault 1985; cf. Robbins 2004). For Foucault, all moral systems can be understood to have two basic elements: (1) *Codes of behaviour* that consist of explicitly recognised, prescribed, and prohibited forms of conduct; and (2) *Forms of subjectivation* that are tied to 'setting up and developing relationships with the self, for self-reflection, self-knowledge, self-examination, for the decipherment of the self by oneself, [and] for the transformations that one seeks to accomplish with oneself as an object' (Foucault 1985, p. 29).

As Joel Robbins points out, while codes of behaviour are deemed to be fairly straightforward by Foucault, forms of subjectivation are viewed to be much more complex and include a number of possible components (Robbins 2004).[2] Of these, the most pertinent for my purposes here are his notions of *technologies* and corresponding *hermeneutics of self*. According to Foucault, technologies of self are understood to refer to those particular activities, ideas, and practices implicated in the fashioning of moral subjects. They consist, in his words, of the ethical work 'that one performs on oneself, not only in order to bring one's conduct into compliance with a given rule, but to attempt to transform oneself into the ethical subject of one's behaviour' (Foucault 1985, p. 27). Different technologies of self, Foucault argues, are implicated in differing hermeneutics of self – that is, different ways of interpreting the self in moral terms. What the self is understood to be, its relationship to others, the broader community, ongoing, past, or anticipated activity, as well as its ability to reveal itself to others, to speak to the truth of its own self-experience (both to itself and to others), are all implicated in such differing hermeneutic strategies or disciplines of interpretation.

With his focus upon early Greek, Roman, and Christian periods, key examples of technologies and hermeneutics of self proffered by Foucault include such practices as the renunciation of personal desires, sexual abstinence, the examination of conscience, acts of confession, and enduring pain and suffering. Similar such practices, we should recall, were highlighted by Geertz in his discussion of Javanese understandings and orientations to the notion of *rasa*. A key insight of Foucault's that certainly resonates with Geertz's reflections on religious life is the idea that the practices implicated in the formation of ethical subjectivities are seldom solely relegated to the realm of explicitly morally defined behaviours. Instead, they may actively recruit aesthetic forms of appreciation and practice.[3]

Of direct pertinence in this regard is the fact that Foucault's examination of antiquity led him to focus upon morality as an 'art of existence.' Such a view of morality is less concerned with providing instruction on what individuals should or should not *do*, than on how they should *be* (Paras 2006, p. 128). An art of existence is thus held to 'enable men to turn their life into a work: an object that might be judged according to aesthetic and stylistic categories' (p. 126). As Paras explains,

> Such arts ideally allowed one to acquire a set of qualities. These qualities were neither aptitudes, nor precisely 'virtues,' but rather attributes of being. Foucault called the aggregate of acquired qualities, 'modalities of experience.' (Paras 2006, p. 127)

It is precisely here in Foucault's discussion of differing 'modalities of experience' that we might be afforded a significant point of articulation with cultural phenomenological, embodiment, and person-centered approaches that seek to also detail those modalities of experience implicated in generating differing modes of social action. It is also here that we find a possible space to begin thinking through how it is that power is implicated in the 'subtleties of thought and feeling' that Geertz found to be such a productive place to turn in furthering our understanding of the dynamics and complexities of meaning and practice in contemporary religious life. To come to cultivate a 'this-worldly, even practical mysticism' in the form of 'detached tranquility which is proof against disturbance from either within or without' for Javanese persons, evokes not only a particular phenomenological outlook but also certain relations of power that are reflected in the vicissitudes of individuals' struggles to align their own self-experience with the moral expectations of their community of practice. And it is just toward such a point of articulation between the particularities of subjective experience, the dynamics of social life, and differing regimes of interpretation, that such a newly founded Geertzian semiotics of culture may be profitably extended.

Conclusion

Admittedly what I have provided here is only a sketch of a few of the ways that it might be possible to turn toward developing a neo-Geertzian theory of culture that takes into account both the rich diversity and complexity of subjective life and the dynamics of power implicated in the practices underlying modes of subject formation. By drawing so heavily from other thinkers in pursing such a development, some readers may wonder why we should bother calling such an approach 'neo-Geertzian' and not 'neo-phenomenological' or 'neo-Foucauldian.' Given that my primary motivation for writing this essay was to engage in what has hopefully been an active and productive dialogue with one of our discipline's most thoughtful, insightful, and influential culture theorists, I frankly do not much care as to what, if anything, we might term the fruits of such an endeavour. That the seeds for seeing points of articulation between what might otherwise be viewed as quite historically and substantively distinctive approaches in philosophy and social theory lie in Geertz's writings may be, however, one very compelling reason to continue thinking with him as we work collectively to advance and transform what it is, and how it is, that we go about understanding what we and what our informants 'are up to, or think we are up to.'

Acknowledgements

I would like to thank Susan Slyomovics for graciously inviting me to participate in the conference that led to the development of this collection of essays and for reading and commenting on earlier drafts of this essay. The paper also greatly benefited from the insightful comments made by my fellow panelists, Lahouari Addi, Abdellah Hammoudi, and Paul Rabinow. Finally, I would like to thank Douglas Hollan for providing me with critical and constructive comments that helped to substantially improve the paper.

Notes

1. As Eric Paras observes, 'The definition of the subject that Foucault offered at the beginning of 1980s, if it is to be judged coherent, necessarily carried within it the ideas of autonomy, reflexivity, and lived experience... the Foucauldian subject of 1980 was a free individual. It had the ability to pursue (or not pursue) techniques that would transform its subjectival modality – but which would not, one way or the other, disrupt its status as an independent locus of experience' (Paras 2006, p. 123).
2. According to Foucault, forms of subjectivation include at least four different aspects: 1) determination of the ethical substance; 2) reliance upon particular modes of subjection; 3) specified technologies of self; and 4) orientation toward a predetermined telos. In his words, the formation of ethical subjectivity is 'a process in which the individual delimits that part of himself that will form the object of his moral practice [i.e., ethical substance], defines his position relative to the precept he will follow [i.e., mode of subjection], and decides on a certain mode of being that will serve as his moral goal [i.e., telos]. And this requires him to act upon himself, to monitor, test, improve, and transform himself [i.e., technologies of self]' (Foucault 1985, p. 28).
3. While it has often been the case that Western philosophers since the 1800s have sought to make a rather strict distinction between aesthetic and moral forms of judgment, it is interesting that when we turn back to early Greek philosophy there is much overlap between notions of the beautiful and notions of the good. For instance, the Greek term *to kalon*, which is often translated as 'beauty,' did not, however, 'refer to a thing's autonomous aesthetic value, but rather to its 'excellence, which is connected with its moral worth and/or usefulness' (Feagin 1995). Moreover, for Aristotle, virtues (*aretai*) were themselves conceived as traits, capacities, and dispositions (e.g., justice, courage, temperance, generosity, intelligence, wisdom, etc.) that bring about happiness or 'flourishing' (*eudaemon*) on account of their relative 'refinement, beauty, or excellence' (*kalos*) (see Aristotle 1985).

References

Aristotle, 1985. *Nicomachean ethics*. T. Irwin, trans. Indianapolis, IN: Hackett Publishing Company.

Bourdieu, P., 1977. *Outline of a theory of practice*. Cambridge, UK: Cambridge University Press.

Bourdieu, P., 1990. *The logic of practice*. Stanford, CA: Stanford University Press.

Csordas, T., 1990. Embodiment as a paradigm for anthropology. *Ethos*, 18 (1), 5–47.

Csordas, T., 1993. Somatic modes of attention. *Cultural Anthropology*, 8 (2), 135–156.

Dreyfus, H.L. and Rabinow, P., eds., 1983. *Michel Foucault: beyond structuralism and hermeneutics*. Chicago: University of Chicago Press.

Feagin, S.L., 1995. Beauty. *In*: Robert Audi, ed. *The Cambridge dictionary of philosophy*. Cambridge, UK: Cambridge University Press, 66.

Foucault, M., 1978. *The history of sexuality: an introduction*. New York: Random House.

Foucault, M., 1985. *The use of pleasure*. R. Hurley, trans. New York: Pantheon Books.

Foucault, M., 1986. *The care of the self*. R. Hurley, trans. New York: Vintage Books.

Foucault, M., 1997. *Ethics: subjectivity and truth*. R. Hurley et al., trans. New York: New Press.

Foucault, M., 2005. *The hermeneutics of the subject: lectures at the Collège de France 1981–1982*. New York: Palgrave.

Geertz, C., 1973. *The interpretation of cultures*. New York: Basic Books.

Geertz, C., 2000. The pinch of destiny: religion as experience, meaning, identity, power. *In*: C. Geertz, ed. *Available light*. Princeton: Princeton University Press, 167–186.

Giddens, A., 1984. *The constitution of society*. Berkeley: University of California Press.

Groark, K., and Throop, C.J., n.d. Mood, memory, and meaning in everyday life. Unpublished manuscript.

Hollan, D., 2001. Developments in person-centered ethnography. *In*: C.C. Moore and H.F. Mathews, eds. *The psychology of cultural experience*. Cambridge, UK: Cambridge University Press, 48–67.

Husserl, E., 1962. *Ideas: general introduction to pure phenomenology*. New York: Macmillan.

James, W., 1890. *The principles of psychology*. New York: Holt and Co.

James, W., 1987 [1902]. *The varieties of religious experience*. New York: Penguin Books.

Malinowski, B., 1935. *The Coral Gardens and their magic*. New York: American Book Company.

Merleau-Ponty, M., 1962. *The phenomenology of perception*. C. Smith, trans. New York: Routledge.

Paras, E., 2006. *Foucault 2.0: beyond power and knowledge*. New York: Other Press.

Robbins, J., 2004. *Becoming sinners: Christianity and moral torment in a Papua New Guinea society*. Berkeley: University of California Press.

Schutz, A., 1967. *The phenomenology of the social world*. Evanston, IL: Northwestern University Press.

Throop, C.J., 2003. On crafting a cultural mind: a comparative assessment of some recent theories of 'internalization' in psychological anthropology. *Transcultural psychiatry*, 40 (1), 109–139.

Throop, C.J., forthcoming. *Suffering and sentiment: exploring the vicissitudes of experience and pain in Yap*. Berkeley: University of California Press.

Wikan, U., 1990. *Managing turbulent hearts: a Balinese formula for living*. Chicago: University of Chicago Press.

Not lost in translation: the influence of Clifford Geertz's work and life on anthropology in Morocco

Dale F. Eickelman

Dartmouth College, Hanover, NH, USA

A May 2000 conference in Sefrou publicly recognised the impact of Clifford Geertz's work and professional life on doing sociology and anthropology in Morocco. Yet recognition of his work in how sociology and anthropology were taught in Morocco grew only incrementally from the late 1960s to the present. One obstacle was language. Geertz's *Islam Observed* (1968a) was translated into French only in 1992; a translation into Arabic is virtually unobtainable in Morocco; and his book-length essay, 'Suq' (Geertz 1979), appeared in French only in 2003. In the late 1960s, Morocco's educational system was also in the midst of Arabisation. Part of this essay seeks to capture the audience for anthropology in the late 1960s and early 1970s, describing the context in which the writings of Geertz and Gellner were initially received in Morocco. Then, drawing on my experience in leading a faculty seminar in Arabic for faculty in history and sociology and especially a parallel one for graduate students in sociology in 1992, I indicate how Geertz's ideas and others began to enter the Arabic-language curriculum. Finally, relying on a recent book by sociologist Abdelrhani Moundib (2006), a student in the 1992 student seminar who currently teaches at Rabat's Université Mohammed V–Agdal, I analyse how Geertz's ideas are transmitted in a primarily Arabic university curriculum.

This essay traces how Clifford Geertz's work was taught and understood in Morocco from the 1960s to the present, with an emphasis on the period through the 1990s. The May 2000 conference honouring Geertz in Sefrou was a public event that celebrated his influence in Morocco, but concrete understanding of his life and work had already incrementally spread in the pre-Internet era. Especially with the 1992 French translation of *Islam observed* (*Observer l'Islam*), reviewed soon after in *Prologues*, the influential Casablanca review of books and ideas, at least parts of Geertz's work became accessible to a wider audience in Morocco. Already in 1992, the graduate students at Mohammed V University in Rabat participating in the informal off-campus seminar that I led that year, showed me thick binders of photocopied extracts of books and articles, including *Islam observed* (Geertz 1968a) and my own *Moroccan Islam* (Eickelman 1976), heavily annotated with notations of Arabic equivalent terms. Today, as Susan Slyomovics affirms from recent visits to Sefrou (see her Introduction to the present collection), affordable CDs have replaced the ubiquitous photocopy machine in making Geertz's words, like those of the rest of us, available to anyone with the appropriate languages – and the knowledge of where to shop.

My intent is to recreate the past in the present, emphasising mostly the late 1960s to the late 1990s, just before computers and the Internet became common. The significance of Geertz's work on Morocco outside of Morocco has been dealt with elsewhere, including in this volume, and I have written an earlier account of his approach to Islam (Eickelman 2005). My focus here is to portray how his ideas and approach were communicated and received in Morocco itself. From the perspective of the 21st century this boundary is artificial, for several key Moroccan anthropologists and sociologists work and live outside of Morocco, including Abdellah Hammoudi and Mouna Bennani-Chraïbi. Others, most notably the sociologist Mohamed Cherkaoui, who for years deliberately avoided writing on Morocco in order to avoid being type-cast as 'Moroccan' and to be taken seriously in his chosen field of European sociology (Cherkaoui, personal communication, 2 June 2008), now contribute to studies of Morocco (Cherkaoui 2007a, 2007b).

Parts of this essay are necessarily autobiographical. Clifford and Hildred Geertz arrived in Morocco a few years earlier than I did, but my experience of the time and intensive contacts with Moroccan university colleagues and students beginning in the 1970s offer a perspective on how anthropology in general, and Geertz's work in particular, were received and changed over time.

Beginnings

Telegrams allowed no room for emoticons, but the one that Cliff sent to Cairo in November 1968 confirming his presence in Sefrou added one technically unneeded word: 'Welcome' (see Figure 1). That single word sufficed. Christine, my wife, and I had intended to remain in Iraq for two years studying the pilgrimage center of Karbala, but permission from the government of 'Abd al-Rahman 'Arif (1966–68) meant little after the coup d'état that returned the Ba'thist party to power on 17 July 1968.

Through the advice of an Iraqi friend, who would later become rector of the University of Tikrit, we delayed reaching Iraq until October, arriving in Baghdad after a two-day trip from Tehran with a busload of friendly Shi'i pilgrims. But we barely lasted three weeks in Iraq and never made it to Karbala. A short stay in Cairo after leaving Iraq uncovered only one project in which an American graduate student could participate – a study of how to get Egyptians to smoke more Egyptian than foreign cigarettes. Morocco looked more promising. In Baghdad, a worn copy of a British Naval Intelligence Handbook for North Africa that briefly mentioned Boujad, a regional pilgrimage center, was enough for me. The Foreign Area Fellowship Programme, the joint Social Science Research Council and American Council of Learned Societies programme that funded my field research, agreed that the unexpected shift from Iraq to Morocco was consistent with my initial fellowship goals.

In 1968, there were not yet any direct flights from Cairo to Morocco. An unexpectedly sympathetic Algerian consul, who first told us that it would take a week to process our visas, issued them within a few hours when we explained the state of our finances. After the flight to Algiers and a night in a run-down hotel, we traveled on two Algerian trains – the last of which had sturdy wooden carriages from the 1930s decorated in the interior with scenes of Algeria. After a border crossing that rivaled those between Eastern and Western Europe

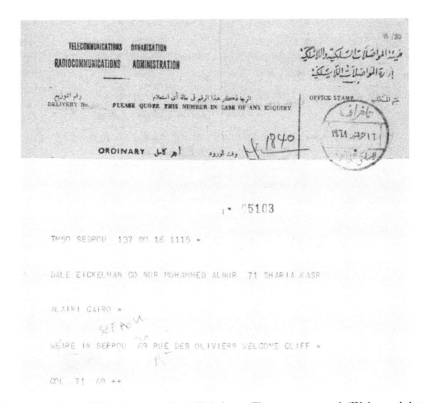

Figure 1. Telegram from Clifford Geertz to Dale Eickelman: The one extra word, 'Welcome,' that Clifford Geertz sent from Sefrou to Cairo, 16 November 1968, lifted our spirits after our stay in Iraq.

before the collapse of Communist rule, a Moroccan train, also with wooden coaches decorated with colonial-era photos, delivered us to Fez in the middle of the night. We arrived in Sefrou three days after our departure from Cairo.

Anthropological Morocco was already familiar to us, at least in outline. I took Marvin Mikesell's excellent course on the geography of North Africa in 1967, and regularly attended the off-the-books seminar on Morocco and related subjects that Clifford and Hildred offered monthly in their Chicago home for most of 1966–68.

Christine and I stayed in a small hotel in Sefrou for several days, and saw Cliff and Hildred almost daily. Once we got our bearings, we left on a bus trip through Morocco's south, returning via Marrakesh, Rabat and, inevitably, Boujad. In December we began securing permissions to conduct research in Morocco. Part of this task included the formal procedures then in place. The US cultural attaché, musicologist, and cellist E. Lee Fairley sent a letter on 19 December 1968 to the Moroccan Ministry of Foreign Affairs, which responded in mid-February 1969 that it had no objection to my conducting a study of Boujad and its region. By that time my work in Boujad was well underway.

It was a call to the Ministry of the Interior that sped up the permissions process. At Cliff's suggestion, as I recall, we paid a call on Patrice Blacque-Belair, the son of an Affaires Indigènes officer in the Middle Atlas during the French Protectorate, who had been working in various advisory capacities in urban planning with the Moroccan government since 1956 (and who in 1970 left for New York, where he continued his career with the United Nations Development

Programme). When I met him in December 1968 he was working for Maati Jorio, the distinguished Moroccan civil servant who was then secretary general of Direction de l'Urbanisme et de l'Habitat. Jorio's boss was Minister of the Interior Muhammad Oufkir (1918–72), whose sinister reputation became fully evident only later. When I saw Jorio in 1984, soon after he became his country's ambassador to Washington (1984–86), he assured me that there was a 'firewall' (*cloison pare-feu*) between the ministry's Urban Affairs division and the internal security apparatus.

In 1968, one could still walk into the main building of the Ministry of the Interior, which was until 1956 the Résidence-Général of the French Protectorate. There was a doorman of sorts but no directory or names on doors. We encountered a frail-looking French woman – not more than four feet tall in my memory – who appeared to be distributing the mail. Why a French woman should still distribute the mail in the most powerful ministry in independent Morocco struck me as odd. She kindly interrupted her rounds to lead us to Blaque-Belair's office. He told me that Jorio, in the office next door, could give us permission to conduct field research in Morocco, but not to mention that we had seen him first. 'He's angry with me today and is likely to hold an introduction from me against you.'

We knocked on Jorio's door. After a short wait with a secretary, we were ushered into his presence. In my best approximate French I explained what I wanted. Jorio, who was courteous but formal, unsmilingly replied,

'You've done everything wrong. You must go back to Washington and wait for our embassy to transmit your request to the Ministry of Foreign Affairs.'

'Monsieur Jorio, we came here by way of Baghdad, and. ...'

'Ah, Monsieur Eickelman,' he replied, still without a smile, 'we have no protocols for American students who come to Morocco by way of Baghdad. Therefore I will give you the letters that you need today.'

Finally he smiled ever so slightly and said that he didn't know where Boujad was administratively. The ministry had just created new provinces and changed the boundaries of others. He wasn't certain whether it was in Beni Mellal or Khouribga province. He solved the problem by giving me two handwritten four-by-six-inch notecards that would serve as letters of introduction to hand-deliver to the governors at my own pace. He followed these up with a more formal letter dated 13 January 1969, expanding my study to include Beni Mellal – a solution that obviated the need to locate Boujad more precisely.

At no point in our first months in Morocco did anyone suggest that we contact university colleagues, although by mid-1969 I introduced myself to Abdelkebir Khatibi, director of the short-lived Institut de Sociologie in Rabat (1966–70). André Masson, the urban planner who was head of the technical division of the Urbanism and Habitat section of the ministry, arranged for me to speak to his staff in February 1970. Beginning in 1972, I returned frequently to Morocco, where I met and kept in sustained contact with a senior generation of scholars including Germain Ayache (d. 1990), who supervised in Arabic the dissertations of the next generation of Moroccan historians, including Mohamed Kenbib and Ahmad Toufiq. At the Institut National Agronomique et Vétérinaire Hassan II (INAV), I met anthropologist Abdellah Hammoudi and sociologist Paul Pascon (d. 1985). After Morocco's independence, when French citizens were offered an opportunity to choose French or Moroccan nationality, Pascon had chosen to become Moroccan and trained a generation of young Moroccans in the craft of sociology.

Rewriting the past in the present is always a dangerous task, but there is no record or memory of Cliff having spoken in a formal academic setting in Morocco prior to his departure from Casablanca in February 1969 (Hildred Geertz, personal communication, 3 August 2008,

Karen Blu, personal communication, 9 August 2008). This is through no reticence on his part but the lack of opportunity. Oufkir viewed anthropology and sociology with suspicion and the Institut de Sociologie, then directed by Abdelkebir Khatibi, shut down after three years of operations. INAV, where Paul Pascon and Abdellah Hammoudi were located, was relatively free from political pressure. As with anthropology under military rule in Turkey, where anthropologist Bozkurt Güvenç (personal communication, 1988), son of a trusted senior military officer, kept the discipline alive by locating it in the Faculty of Medicine at the University of Ankara, it was shielded from political vicissitudes at INAV. Princeton-trained sociologist Mohammed Guessous was popular as a lecturer at the Université Mohammed V, but his intense political activities precluded his writing much sociology or inviting visiting American scholars to make presentations – although he shared his vast knowledge of Moroccan society with anyone who sought him out. To be fair, academics at the Université Mohammed V were busy complying with a government-ordered Arabisation. Its historians, sociologists, and geographers, trained largely in French (with the exception of Guessous), were fully preoccupied with adapting their courses to an Arabic-speaking student body that was growing exponentially and straining the meager resources allocated to higher education.

On a personal level, Cliff developed strong ties with Moroccan scholars, especially geographer Mohamed Naciri and also Guessous. But in a general sense, social sciences that incorporated field research existed only in the Department of Geography at Mohammed V University, still the only university in Morocco, and at INAV. French and Moroccan geographers produced distinguished studies on Morocco's regions and towns, but in other fields, notably sociology, the focus was more on economic 'development,' which of course included Naciri's work. The vogue among Moroccan graduate students at the time veered more to global studies of economic and political development, in which Morocco figured principally as a 'case.' Several students from the Khouribga and Beni Mellal region who knew of my work chastised me in 1969 for being a 'folklorist' at worst or, alternatively an 'Orientalist,' because I was interested in religion as practiced in a 'dead and dying' regional center rather than a place more representative of the 'new' Morocco. The proliferation of local and regional studies, and a profound explicit public respect for the 'pious ones' (*al-salihun*) – often an integral part of understanding the meaning of 'home' in Morocco – only returned in the last decade of Hassan II's reign (r. 1961–99).

On reading Geertz in Morocco

Geertz's first book-length essay on Morocco (and Indonesia), *Islam observed* (Geertz 1968a), was promptly reviewed in the *Annales marocaines de sociologie* (Coatalen 1969a). It was the only review in the issue to lack all bibliographic information, but it was an adequate account of Geertz's scope and approach. Paul Coatalen, who also offered brief reflections on Berber society in the Tafraout region (Coatalen 1969b) in the same issue, later worked and taught in Malaysia. The same issue of *Annales* also contained an article by Ernest Gellner (1969b), 'The tribal system and social change in North Africa,' translated into French by the indefatigable Coatalen, that essentially summarised *Saints of the atlas* (Gellner 1969a).

In general, the specifics of Gellner's work appear to have become more quickly known in Morocco than Geertz's. 'Qu'est-ce que le tribalisme nord-african?' – the first major subtitle of Gellner's 1969 *Annales* article – directly resonates with a seminal 1953 essay by Jacques Berque, which in turn evoked Ernest Renan's famous 'Qu'est-ce qu'une nation?' (see Eickelman 1985). Moreover, Hammoudi (1974), basing himself on a close reading of *Saints*, produced an influential critique that became a staple component of the photocopy collations that circulated among Moroccan graduate students in the early 1990s and presumably in earlier years.

Studying social anthropology in Morocco: the changing view from below

In Morocco from March through June 1992, I led a weekly faculty seminar in Arabic at Mohammed V University on 'History and anthropology in Morocco.' My own contribution to the seminar (Eickelman 1993) offered an overview of key works in Moroccan social history and social anthropology, and how significantly the two disciplines complemented one another. Conceptually this notion of complementarity was hardly an innovation, but articulating it in the context of Moroccan universities was a major challenge. I drew heavily on the work of the seminar participants themselves. Most were historians, although a few sociologists and political scientists also participated. I repeated my own contribution later at a conference at the Sidi Mohammed ben Abdallah University in Fez, an invitation facilitated by an historian who regularly travelled from Fez to Rabat to participate in our seminar. Geertz's name was often invoked and I was occasionally referred to as part of the Geertzian 'school.' Yet the references to Geertz tended to be iconic and not related to specific themes. Admittedly, it was hard to invoke Geertz in the context of an otherwise fascinating presentation on how Europeans and Moroccans manipulated Moroccan coinage in the 19th century. In commentary, however, it was easier to invoke aspects of Geertz's work to pose questions about how Moroccan and Ottoman rivalries played out in 16th- and 17th-century displays of authority. Such conjoining of approaches takes time. One of the seminar's regular participants was historian Mohamed el-Mansour. His 2004 article, 'Moroccan Islam observed,' which uses Geertz (and Gellner) as points of departure to discuss the development of specifically Moroccan practices of Islam, including what he calls the 'glorification of genealogy' and a specifically Moroccan Sufism, incorporates at least in part some of the discussions of 1992 and evinces a close reading of Geertz's *Islam observed*. Perhaps because of cost and inaccessibility, most of the seminar participants knew about Geertz's book-length essay on the *Suq* (Geertz 1979), but were not familiar with it.

During the midway break in the second seminar meeting, a group of students waited for me outside the conference room. They wanted to know if they could meet with me. I asked whether they would like to join us for the seminar, as there was space in the conference room. With embarrassment, they said that would not be possible. Moments later, I saw why. Two faculty members called me aside. 'It would not be possible for the students to join our seminar,' they said. Nor would it be possible for me to meet with them separately on campus. As a guest of the university, I was reluctant to challenge them or ask for an explanation of the invisible line that prohibited graduate students from commingling with faculty.[1] Instead, I asked whether I could meet them in my apartment. In the back of my mind, my model was the Geertz-like informal seminars in Chicago's Hyde Park. 'You don't want to do this,' one of my colleagues replied. 'Some of them might be police spies.' 'In that case,' I said, 'I'll get some sense of what interests the police and the quality of their training.'

A few days later, I met with the students in my apartment. Six showed up, and five participated in all of the sessions. The first session, as we all agreed later, was awkward. The students, all men, had prepared a list of 42 questions with little evidence of sequence or order. At the outset, I indicated that just as they had their questions, I had some for them. We got through perhaps a dozen questions in the first hour. Then, after soft drinks, I asked my own. Clearly the days in the 1970s of Germain Ayache meeting his advanced students at home for tutorials were far behind. The students said that they lacked the opportunity for seminars and met with their instructors only infrequently outside of class. After the first two meetings, we established a pattern. The students selected a reading or theme that we would pursue for most of the session. Then we would turn to my questions intended to invoke what it was like to be a graduate student in Morocco in the 1990s.[2] Even if they pursued their studies, they wondered, would their degrees have value? The best that I could do was to repeat what several faculty members said to me during the parallel official seminar: 'The university as an institution has major weaknesses, but as individuals we remain committed to academic life.'[3] They were, I reassured them, getting a good education.

It was during this seminar that I learned that the most committed students in Rabat were meeting regularly in self-directed peer study groups, just as students at Yusufiyya Mosque-University had done in Marrakesh in the 1920s (Eickelman 1985, pp. 98–104). They gathered books and articles and discussed them together. I saw very few books in their original format. Most were photocopies, even the Arabic translation of my *Moroccan Islam* (Eickelman 1989). Photocopies cost less than the original (MAD 84, or approximately $18 at the exchange rate of the time) – and the Arabic version of my book was published in Morocco.

Geertz's *Islam observed* figured prominently in the student canon and was one of the most dog-eared and annotated of the readings. His essay on the Suq did not make the canon, not out of lack of interest but because copies, even for photocopying, were unavailable.[4] 'Religion as a cultural system' (Geertz 1966) was part of the canon, as was his 'Religion: anthropological study' (Geertz 1968b) and 'In search of North Africa' (Geertz 1971). My 'New directions' chapter (Eickelman 1984) made it into the canon, used, I was told, as a sort of Cliff's Notes[5] (ironically) to make sense of how to talk about conflicting approaches to understanding Moroccan society. Various articles in French by Gellner also made it into the student collections.

Of the five students in our informal seminar, I learned several years later that only one of them remained in graduate studies. One passed an examination to join the Ministry of the Interior and became a *qa'id* (*chef d'arrondissement*) in Casablanca, and another emigrated to Europe.

Geertz as currently taught: Abdelrhani Moundib

In Morocco, as in the US, the path to a doctorate is slow. Abdelrhani Moundib[6] was the participant who finished his doctorate in 1994, subsequently published in Arabic as *Religion and society: a sociological study of religiosity in Morocco* (Mundib 2006). Like many of his American counterparts, Moundib taught for many years prior to receiving his doctorate, and this teaching experience shapes his book. It also indicates how Geertz is presented in Arabic to an audience unlikely to have access to the French and English originals. The 'field' component of his study concerns shrines and religiosity in Dukkala and al-Jadida, Moundib's region of origin, but it is the framing of the argument in terms of the work of predecessors and contemporaries that is significant.

As a Moroccan colleague once said to me, readers of scholarly books in the US and Europe can assume the availability of the books they cite, so it is bad form to explain them at length – even if this remains the convention for doctoral dissertations. Books are hard to find in Morocco and quickly go out of print, so a good part of Moundib's book, used currently also as a text, explains at length earlier approaches to the study of religion in Morocco. Edward Westermarck and Alfred Bel figure prominently in the first 52 pages, including Hammoudi and Hassan Rachik's commentaries on these predecessors. The section dealing with Geertz, Gellner, and myself is primarily from pages 52 to 68, 'Anglo-Saxon anthropology and the development of academic points of reference.' Here, Moundib does more than set out the ideas of others. Of

Gellner's segmentary approach, he invokes Geertz (1971, p. 21) to the effect that Gellner offered a ready-made theory for which he tried to make Morocco an example. In the body of his study on Dukkala (Mundib 2006, pp. 71–194), he repeatedly returns to specific points made by Gellner that relate to his own work, just as he invokes the work of Geertz, Hammoudi, and others.

According to Moundib, Clifford Geertz, Hildred Geertz, Lawrence Rosen, Paul Rabinow, and Dale Eickelman all represent an 'interpretive' approach, 'which tried to understand the nature of the Moroccan social system and to pinpoint the mechanisms of change starting from the concepts of individuals and the cultural representations of their world view and social relationships' (Moundib 2006, p. 53). Of Geertz in particular, he writes that there are three main levels to his work as it applies to Morocco (p. 54). First is the theoretical level (*al-mustawa al-minhajiyya*) of religion as a cultural, social, and psychological phenomenon. Second is a religious history of Moroccan society, and third is his field research in the 1960s. Since Geertz, Geertz, and Rosen (1979) is not invoked, it is reasonable to assume that it is the understanding that Geertz derived from conducting extensive field research and that this served as an example for others.

Moundib argues that from the end of the Second World War to the mid-1960s, prior to the appearance of Geertz's essay on 'Religion as a cultural system' in 1966, there was little development in the study of the history of religions. Most scholars were content to rely on the insights of Durkheim, Weber, and Malinowski. Geertz, writes Moundib (2006, p. 54), enlarged and developed the work of his predecessors, so that his theoretical ideas are now part of our shared 'intellectual storehouse' (*khazzan ma'rifi*), a deliberate play on the familiar Moroccan term that carries the meaning of both government and storehouse (*makhzan*). Geertz's idea of religion as a cultural system is then described in detail.

Unlike some American commentators, Moundib (2006, p. 57) gets Geertz right: religion cannot be studied as an ahistorical semiotic subject. It must be understood within the context of continuing historical and social change. Where others see ambiguity in Geertz's approach, Moundib sees a valiant effort to understand Moroccan history from the time of the arrival of Islam in Morocco to the present. Geertz's historical account is similar in scope to that of his colonial predecessor, Alfred Bel (1938), but it is radically different in approach and interpretation. Geertz's interpretation of religion, Moundib writes (2006, pp. 58–59), starts from the assumption that religion is a social institution and its practice is necessarily a social activity. Hence religious belief must be seen in the context of social practice, which for Geertz meant a combination of fieldwork and the reading of history.

Key to understanding the nature of religion in Morocco is the paradoxical link between *baraka*, a sense of God's grace or spirituality, and a strong secular pragmatism. The history of religions should not be the collection of piecemeal fragments but a history of the social imagination. The idea of possessing *baraka* based on divine grace or through a genealogical link with the Prophet, reflects a dynamic tension at the heart of Moroccan religious history, and Geertz's invocation of the struggle between Sidi Lahcen Lyusi and Sultan Mulay Ismail exemplifies this tension.

Shaping Geertz's approach to religion to an Arabic-speaking Moroccan audience, Moundib (2006, p. 60) writes that religion comes not only from God, but from ideas about God. As a result, the profound changes in understanding Islam that have been underway since the end of the colonial era should come as no surprise. Moundib cites several critics who argue that Geertz is inherently ambiguous. Moundib replies that this very ambiguity is at the heart of understanding religion in social history. Geertz, he acknowledges, writes in a complex literary style that, while loaded with metaphors, makes reading him a pleasure. He possesses a beauty of expression even if he opens many brackets and brackets within brackets. Geertz's style, Moundib concludes (2006, p. 63), breaks with common academic writing conventions but can be explained by the inherent improvisational nature of comparative religious studies.

Moundib's discussion of my writings (pp. 63–67) affords him an opportunity to continue his discussion of Geertz. Whether I like it or not, Moundib argues that I am part of the interpretive 'school,' although my writing is characterised by simplicity (*al-basata*) and clarity (*al-wuduh*). In approach, Geertz and I share a number of methods and analyses. For example, we agree that though field research is always limited to specific places, the key issue is how, not whether, one describes and interprets – a salient Geertzian point.

Here it is useful to point out that Moundib, whether he has a student audience in mind or a more general Moroccan one, faces the same challenge that many academics do in reaching a wider public more familiar with quantitative approaches to social analysis, such as opinion polls and other surveys. Yet in understanding religiosity in Morocco, Moundib argues, Geertz helps us to see that whether it is Salafi Islam, the Tablighi movement, or others, they are understood and interpreted first by shared Moroccan practices of 'common sense' and the strong, deeply rooted religious beliefs that form part of them.

Conclusion

Of the anthropological monographs written initially in Arabic primarily for a Moroccan audience, Moundib's *Religion and society* is more relentlessly conceptual than most of its predecessors in its elaborate discussion of theoretical concepts and the sustained effort to link them to the ethnographic specifics of his study of religiosity in Dukkala. Geertz's study of the 'Suq' is only beginning to percolate into the vulgate of Moroccan university pedagogy. Perhaps only a few copies of the translated version (Geertz 2003) will make it directly into the hands of students, but CD copies are probably not far behind. When that occurs, there will be a pragmatic exemplar linking economic with religious practice at a highly persuasive micro-level. 'Suq' does not make for a quick read in any language, as I am reminded by introducing it to a small undergraduate seminar of non-Moroccan students in Fez in Spring 2008, but it is likely to have the same profound effect as *Islam Observed*. Max Weber's ideas acquired new currency after their translation into English in the 1930s, just as the work of Jürgen Habermas, once available in English, gained a new life.

Geertz's *Islam observed* was slow to be translated and his 'Suq' essay had to wait 24 years for translation into French. The nature of Arabic book distribution and censorship is such that I have yet to see, or meet any Moroccan who has seen, the Beirut translation into Arabic of *Islam observed* (Geertz 1993). But the rapid expansion of mass higher education in the Arab world affords a large and significant audience eager to read what others say about them – and to learn how to say more in public about themselves. The slow journey of Geertz's work into French and Arabic, accelerated over the last decade by the formal recognition of his work in Morocco, commentary on it, and incorporation into a new generation of ethnographic research and writing as represented by Moundib, suggests that Geertz's work is taking root with a new and expanding audience.

Acknowledgement

The author wishes to thank Laurel Stavis for reading an earlier draft of this essay.

Notes

1. In 1997, I participated in a colloquium in Germany where we discovered that graduate students were herded into a cellar, out of sight, to listen to the proceedings. Only after some of the participants discovered their presence were they allowed to join us at least during the breaks. The organisers explained that space limitations prevented them from being in the same room as us. The explanation was plausible, but our first supposition was a particularly harsh academic hierarchy.
2. Toward the end of the seminar I met Michael Fahy, then a graduate student beginning his work on an ethnography of undergraduate education in Morocco. At a point when his work appeared to be seriously blocked, I managed to facilitate his getting space in a university dormitory to continue his work (see Fahy 1998).
3. By 2006, Mohammed V University became the first Moroccan institution to complete an extensive self-study, followed by an invited external review (see Université Mohammed V 2006, 2008).
4. Soon after the appearance of my *Moroccan Islam* (Eickelman 1976), I learned from the librarian at Mohammed V University that they ordered six copies for faculty use. By 1982 they had all disappeared from the shelves in spite of the fact that the library did not lend books.
5. 'Cliff's notes' is a series of annotated summaries of various literary classics that has been popular among students since its first appearance in the 1970s, and is now available online at http://www.cliffsnotes.com/WileyCDA.
6. 'Abdelrhani Moundib' is the spelling in Roman letters. I use standard transliteration in citing his written work in Arabic.

References

Bel, A., 1938. *La religion musulmane en Berbérie*. Paris: Paul Geuthner.
Cherkaoui, M., 2007a. *Good Intentions: Max Weber and the paradox of unintended consequences*. Peter Hamilton, trans. Oxford: Bardwell.
Cherkaoui, M., 2007b. *Morocco and the Sahara: social bonds and geopolitical issues*. 2nd ed. Oxford, UK: Bardwell.
Coatalen, P., 1969a. Clifford Geertz: Islam observed. *Annales marocaines de sociologie*. (no vol. indicated). 91–96.
Coatalen, P., 1969b. Réflexions sur la Société Chleuh (Région de Tafraoute). *Annales marocaines de sociologie*, (no vol. indicated). 27–31.
Eickelman, D.F., 1976. *Moroccan Islam: tradition and society in a pilgrimage center*. Austin: University of Texas Press.
Eickelman, D.F., 1984. New directions in interpreting North African society. *In*: J.-C. Vatin, ed. *Connaissances du Maghreb: sciences sociales et colonisation*. Paris: CNRS, 278–89.
Eickelman, D.F., 1985. *Knowledge and power in Morocco: the education of a Twentieth-Century notable*. Princeton, NJ: Princeton University Press.
Eickelman, D.F., 1989. *Al-Islam fi al-maghrib*. (Moroccan Islam), Mohammed Aafif, trans. Casablanca: Dar Toubkal. 2 vols.
Eickelman, D., 1993. *Al-Anthrubulujiya wa al-ta'rikh wa wad'uhuma fi al-majall al-akadimi* [Anthropology and history in their academic contexts]. *Majalla kulliya al-adab al-'ulum al-insaniya, Jami'a Muhammad al-Khamis* [Journal of the Faculty of Arts and Sciences, Mohammed V University] (Rabat), 18, 117–23
Eickelman, D.F., 2005. Clifford Geertz and Islam. *In*: Richard A. Shweder and Byron Good, eds. *Clifford Geertz by his colleagues*. Chicago: University of Chicago Press, 63–75.
Fahy, M.A., 1998. Marginalized modernity: an ethnographic approach to higher education and social identity at a Moroccan university. Thesis (PhD). University of Michigan.
Geertz, C., 1966. Religion as a cultural system. *In*: Michael Banton, ed. *Anthropological approaches to the study of religion*. London: Tavistock, 1–46.
Geertz, C., 1968a. *Islam observed*. New Haven, CT: Yale University Press.
Geertz, C., 1968b. Religion: anthropological study. *In*: David L. Sills, ed. *International encyclopedia of the social sciences*. New York: Macmillan and the Free Press, 13, 398–406.
Geertz, C., 1971. In search of North Africa. *New York review of books*, 16 (7), 22–24.
Geertz, C., 1971. Suq: the *bazaar* economy in Sefrou. *In*: Clifford Geertz, Hildred Geertz and Lawrence Rosen, *Meaning and order in Moroccan society*. New York: Cambridge University Press, 123–313.
Geertz, C., 1993. *Al-Islam min wajha nazar al-inasa*, Abu Bakr Ahmad Ba Qadir, trans. Beirut: Dar al-Muntakhab al-'Arabi. Cited as 93Tara1. Available from: http://hypergeertz.jku.at [Accessed 5 September 2008].
Geertz, C., 2003. *Le souk de Sefrou. Sur l'économie de bazaar*. Daniel Cefaï, trans. Saint-Denis: Bouchène.
Geertz, C., Geertz, H., and Rosen, L., 1979. *Meaning and order in Moroccan society*. New York: Cambridge University Press.

無

Gellner, E., 1969a. *Saints of the Atlas*. Chicago: University of Chicago Press.

Gellner, E., 1969b. Système tribal et changement social en Afrique du Nord. *Annales marocaines de sociologie* (no vol. indicated). 3–19.

Hammoudi, A., 1974. Segmentarité, stratification sociale, pouvoir politique et sainteté: réflexions sur les thèses de Gellner. *Hespéris-Tamuda*, 15, 147–180.

El-Mansour, M., 2004. Moroccan Islam observed. *Maghreb review*, 29, 208–18.

Moundib, 'A.al-G., 2006. *Al-Din wa al-mujtama'a: dirasa susiyulujiyya li al-tadiyyun bi al-Maghrib* [Religion and society: a sociological study of religiosity in Morocco]. Casablanca: Afrique-Orient.

Université Mohammed V, 2006. Évaluation institutionnelle interne de l'Université Mohammed V–Agdal. Rabat: Université Mohammed V–Agdal (June).

Université Mohammed V., 2008. Évaluation institutionnelle externe de l'Université Mohammed V–Agdal. Rabat: Université Mohammed V–Agdal (February).

Geertz, humour and Morocco

Kevin Dwyer

The American University in Cairo, Cairo, Egypt

This paper explores the role of humour in Clifford Geertz's work on Morocco and seeks to understand why, although Geertz was very witty in person and in writing, and although humour provides the kind of material Geertz would have been able to put to excellent use had he chosen to study it, he never directly addressed questions related to humour in society and only glancingly referred to humour in Morocco. The paper examines the humorous techniques Geertz employs and the kinds of humour he attends to in his writings on Morocco, the characteristics of humour and the 'comic attitude' and their relationship to Geertz's views of Moroccan culture and society, how Geertz's rhetorical dispositions and 'serious' anthropological stance are rooted, historically, in the late colonial and immediate postcolonial periods, and concludes that Geertz's relative neglect of humour provides interesting insights into both the strengths and weaknesses of his approach to culture, to anthropology, and to Morocco.

Of the many aspects of Clifford Geertz's work that have intrigued me over the years one, at this time, stands out: as far as I can tell, he never directly addressed questions related to humour in society and only glancingly referred to humour in Moroccan society. I am intrigued by this for several reasons. Not only was Geertz himself very funny in person, but his writing often moves us to smile, if not actually laugh. Also, I believe that humour provides the kind of material that Geertz would have been able to put to excellent use had he chosen to study it, and he himself makes some suggestive remarks in this direction. Finally, humour often occurs in ways that would satisfy his frequent calls for anthropologists to pay attention to what he termed 'small facts' and to not divorce analysis from the particular, the everyday. I would like to explore here what this relative neglect of humour might suggest about his interpretations of Morocco, his notion(s) of culture and anthropology, and our own.[1]

Geertz's humour

Many of the other contributors to this volume are in a better position than I to testify to Geertz's sense of humour in person. But I remember his spirited story-telling and his sharp sense of humour from our occasional contacts over the years and I recall with real pleasure his presentation at Yale in the late 1960s of a pre-publication version of 'Deep play,' one of the fun-niest papers I ever heard, rivalled only by some of Bob Murphy's performances. So I will take his in-the-flesh sense of humour as a given and support it only with Quentin Skinner's statement, since it reflects my own impression, that 'Cliff had an unfailing and infectious sense of humour, and loved hearing as well as telling funny stories. ...'[2]

In Geertz's writing there are numerous examples of humorous turns. His techniques include:

a) Interjecting apposite witty quotes, such as the two he provides from a Sefrou informant who said, referring to the exodus of the French and the Jews after Morocco regained independence in 1956, 'We have lost both our brains [the French] and our pockets [the Jews],' and who then com-mented on Berber immigration into the city, 'The city used to eat the countryside, now the coun-tryside eats the city.' (Geertz 1989, p. 294).

b) Rapid shifts between and intermingling of high and low cultural referents: Geertz moves from an assessment of John Dewey to a Peanuts cartoon (Geertz 2000, p. 24); invokes, in an other-wise elevated discussion, the eccentric figure of Yogi Berra ('you can say a lot just by writing'), only to return in the next paragraph to Isaiah Berlin (whose voice Geertz characterises, inciden-tally, as 'relentlessly comic') (Geertz 2005, p. 110); sums up what he sees as the current confusion in anthropology by recounting in detail a scene from a Red Skelton movie (Geertz 1995, p. 120).

c) Rhythmic phrasing that often creates a joke-like tension, then releasing it in surprising punch line-like endings, often of a deflating, anticlimactic nature. The opening paragraph of *After the fact* provides an excellent example of this (and apologies for the ellipses, which weaken the rhythm and overall effect):

> Suppose, having entangled yourself every now and again over four decades or so in the goings-on in two provincial towns. . . you wished to say something about how those goings-on had changed. You could contrast then and now. . . .. You could write a narrative. . . .. You could invent indexes and describe trends. . . .. You could produce a memoir. . . .. You could outline stages. . . .. You could describe the transformation of institutions, structures in motion. . . .. You could even build a model, conceive a process, propose a theory. You could draw graphs. (Geertz 1995, p. 1)[3]

d) Clever puns and double entendres: the title, *After the fact*, is a good example – in fact, it is a triple entendre, as Geertz explains in the book's final pages.

e) Quick transitions between the particular and the general, frequently in the form of synecdoche, where a part stands for the whole.

As an example of some of these rhetorical turns – the juxtaposition of high and low vocabu-lary, the wordplay, the rapid transition between the particular and the general – here is one of his early descriptions of Morocco:

> Morocco, Middle Eastern and dry rather than East Asian and wet, extrovert, fluid, activist, mascu-line, informal to a fault, a Wild West sort of place without the barrooms and the cattle drives, is another kettle of selves altogether. (Geertz 1983b, p. 64)[4]

Geertz, had he so wished, would no doubt have probed a society's use of humour to great effect. On occasion he hints at the important role humour plays – the final sentence of 'From the native's point of view' reads,

> Understanding the form and pressure of, to use the dangerous word one more time, natives' inner lives is more like grasping a proverb, catching an allusion, seeing a joke – or, as I have suggested, reading a poem – than it is like achieving communion. (Geertz 1983b, p. 70)[5]

However, as far as I am aware, he never explicitly developed an argument for using humour as a way to gain access to 'natives' inner lives,' nor did he employ humorous material in other than a tangential manner.

Finally, his notion of culture and, in particular, his emphasis on everyday lived experience opens the door to an exploration of humour. In 'Thick description' he remarks,

> If anthropological interpretation is constructing a reading of what happens, then to divorce it from what happens – from what, in this time or that place, specific people say, what they do, what is done to them, from the whole vast business of the world – is to divorce it from its applications and render it vacant. (Geertz 1973b, p. 18)

This close attention to what he calls elsewhere in this essay 'small facts,' and his effort to marry these to 'large issues' (p. 23), might have led him to focus on those humorous moments and episodes that occupy so much of daily life.

Humour in Geertz's writings on Morocco

How, where, and to what extent does Geertz deal with humour in Moroccan society and culture? Let me now quickly review from this perspective, in chronological order, Geertz's major writings on Morocco before turning, in subsequent sections, to explore what his approach to humour and his use of it may tell us about his view of Morocco and his vision of culture and of anthropological activity.[6]

In 'Thinking as a moral act,' Morocco figures explicitly only in a discussion of how 'recalcitrant' agrarian reform is and Geertz argues, in essence, that technological progress and increasing social welfare appear to be incompatible goals, at least in the short run (Geertz 2000, p. 25).[7] This discussion is set within the context of a broad consideration of the ethical implications of anthropological fieldwork, an activity Geertz sees as pervaded by 'anthropological irony,' exemplified in a 'comical misunderstanding' with a Javanese informant that leads to rupturing their relationship (pp. 34–36).[8]

This leads Geertz to an extended argument promoting an anthropological ethic of 'scientific detachment' or 'disinterestedness,' with the anthropologist compared to a 'laboratory technician' or a 'eunuch in a harem' (p. 38) or 'a cancer surgeon' (p. 29), with anthropologists 'rather more effective in exposing the problems than... in uncovering solutions for them' (p. 24). This is all summed up, and we smile again, as he returns to the Peanuts cartoon and Lucy's punch line: 'I don't give advice, I just point out the roots of the problem' (p. 39).

In his effort in *Islam observed* to see the contribution that 'parochial understandings can make to comprehensive ones' (Geertz 1968, p. vii) (a phrasing that prefigures 'small facts' speaking to 'large issues' in 'Thick description'), Geertz attempts to understand what he sees as the 'crisis' in Islam in both Morocco and Indonesia – a 'crisis' coming from a loss of faith and an increase in doubt, signaled by a shift toward 'religious-mindedness' – and the strategies being developed in each society when what he calls the 'machinery of faith' (p. 3) begins to wear out.[9]

In questioning the place of religion in the life of society, Geertz constructs some characteristically rapid generalisations: the 'basic style' of Moroccan life 'was about everywhere the same... above all, self-assertive' (p. 8); Moroccan classical religious style was 'activist, rigorist, dogmatic' (p. 20). He even manages, in one sentence, to do this for both countries, in a parallel construction where Indonesia undergoes 'the radical dissolution of individuality,' and Morocco 'the radical intensification of individuality' (p. 54).

Moroccans respond to this crisis, 'the struggle for the real,' by viewing science as dealing only with the natural world, as strictly segregated from religious concerns, with Indonesians viewing science as emanating from religion (p. 105). Morocco is viewed as suffering almost from 'spiritual schizophrenia,' Indonesia as engaging in 'vacuous abstractions' (p. 116). Among

Moroccans there is also, as Geertz sees it, some skepticism regarding at least the maraboutic strain within the dominant religious system, and as evidence for this he cites a humorous 'maxim': 'Beware a woman from the front, a mule from behind, and a marabout from all directions' (p. 102).

In 'Thick description,' Geertz presents in some detail (in a page and a half of closely packed small font) an event recounted by one of his informants in 1968 but having happened more than 50 years earlier, involving a diverse population of Jews, Berbers, and French. The event itself, full of conflict, murder, imprisonment, crossed purposes and the like, serves as an example of the challenges anthropologists face in constructing understandings of other people's behaviour and even in constructing an understanding of what understanding means and how one would move toward it. Geertz uses this incident as an object lesson in how anthropologists should proceed and toward what ends. While the incident itself is not a humorous one, in probing it Geertz employs a vocabulary that, tongue-twisting at times, is itself quite humorous:

> [T]he object of ethnography [lies in] a stratified hierarchy of meaningful structures in terms of which twitches, winks, fake-winks, parodies, rehearsals of parodies are produced, perceived, and inter-preted, and without which they would not (not even the zero-form twitches, which, *as a cultural cat-egory*, are as much nonwinks as winks are nontwitches) in fact exist, no matter what anyone did or didn't do with his eyelids. (Geertz 1973b, p. 7, emphasis in the original)[10]

In 'From the native's point of view,' Geertz focuses on the importance in Morocco of relational terms, *nisba*s (nouns transformed into relative adjectives) which 'attribute relational properties to persons' (such as occupation, religious sect, geographical origin, or prophetic descent) and which then 'tend to be incorporated into personal names' (Geertz 1983b, p. 66), claiming that they should be seen as 'part of a total pattern of social life' (p. 67).

Geertz does not employ humour in this essay, although there is a somewhat characteristic move – inference by paradox – that leads the reader to smile, as when he suggests that 'nisba-type categorisation leads, paradoxically, to a hyperindividualism in public relationships' (p. 68). And then, in the suggestive final sentence I have already referred to, which points to poetry (and humour) as possible ways to pursue 'the native's point of view,'[11] he cues up his exploration of Moroccan poetry, to which I now turn.

Understanding Moroccan poetry requires, Geertz argues in 'Art as a cultural system,' a 'semiotic science of art' (Geertz 1983a, p. 102), and he proposes to examine the poetry in light of three essential, interrelated aspects: the status of the Qur'an, the performance context of poetry, and its agonistic nature. Taken together, 'they make poetry a kind of paradigmatic speech act, an archetype of talk, which it would take, were such a thing conceivable, a full analysis of Muslim culture to unpack' (p. 110).

Leaving aside the merits of positing an epistemology that may not even be conceivable, and leaving aside too whether the term 'Muslim culture,' in its singularity and breadth, is being con-strued here in so decontextualised a manner as to become hollow, we might question Geertz's awarding Moroccan poetry the ambitious role of epitomizing all Moroccan speech and the even more ambitious one of standing for Moroccan interpersonal relations, where rhetorical fluency is said to lead to coercive force, summed up in the expression *'andu klam* (p. 114).[12] Here too we find the rapid generalisations and simplifications, and the use of synecdoche, that are so characteristic of Geertz's interpretations and writing style. And although he shows Moroccan oral poetry voicing some humorous tropes, such as irony, understatement, and exag-geration, as the poets seek to 'satirise' (p. 116), mock, or ridicule opponents and gain the upper hand, he does not consider these tropes in any detail.

Shortly after 'Art as a cultural system,' Geertz published two articles on Moroccan markets: the first, 'The bazaar economy' (Geertz 1978), in an economics journal, and the second, 'Suq: the bazaar economy in Sefrou' (Geertz 1979), an almost book-length study published in *Meaning and order in Moroccan society*. In both he highlights the agonistic aspects of market behaviour. In the first article, which summarises some of the basic ideas contained in the second, Geertz tries to show behaviour in the Sefrou market as rational, and focuses on the 'search' as a necessary strategy for gaining advantage in a situation of inefficient communication of information; in the second, he concentrates on exploring Moroccan vocabulary and cultural categories.

In the diagram-, table-, figure-, and endnote-studded 'Suq,' which covers nearly 200 pages, Geertz makes the far-reaching claim, similar to ones he already made for *nisba* and '*andu klam*, that 'if one is going to indulge in [the dubious procedure]' of '[c]haracterising whole civilizations in terms of one or another of their leading institutions,' then, 'for the Middle East and North Africa, the bazaar is surely a prime candidate,' just as is 'the caste system for classical India' (Geertz 1979, p. 123). Geertz's basic approach in 'Suq' is to delineate the vocabulary and categories used by Moroccans to navigate the complexities of the *suq*, both as an economic and as a cultural system. He argues this explicitly, saying that to 'convey the exact shape of the conceptual world of the suq... [a]ll that can be done is to work through a small catalogue of words...' (p. 199).

Although Geertz notes that humour, along with flexibility and patience (p. 228), is one of the valued qualities in 'the conventions of bargaining' (p. 227), consonant with his relative neglect of concrete instances of actual behaviour he offers humorous elements at only a few points in his presentation and then only distantly: when treating lying (pp. 211–212), he places in an endnote some half-dozen proverbs and sayings taken from Westermarck (p. 259 n 146); and again in the end matter, in Annex D, he places 'The song of the baker,' in which a customer uses exaggeration, humorous metaphor, slapstick, and other rhetorical devices to criticise an incompetent baker (pp. 308–310).

In many ways, 'Suq' is an atypical work in Geertz's corpus: in its encyclopedic tone (the 113 pages of text contain 13 tables and seven figures, buttressed by 28 pages comprising 185 endnotes filled with a library of bibliographic references [pp. 236–264], to which are added 45 pages of annexes); in its almost ethnoscientific, cognitive anthropological approach; in its suggestion of a world systems theory vocabulary – the suq is 'peripherally integrated into the modern capitalist system' (p. 234); and in its ending with a policy recommendation that the suq needs to change in the direction of becoming a better 'communications system' (p. 234).[13]

In 'Toutes directions,' using Sefrou as 'a case in point' (Geertz 1989, p. 293),[14] Geertz examines the city's changing character and how, in incorporating its outlying areas and populations, the city changes both morphologically and in the way its population imagines it. The only humorous moments are those I referred to earlier – the remarks an informant offers concerning the emigration of the French and Jewish communities and the immigration of Berbers.[15] Geertz's concluding sentence, making small facts speak to large issues in yet another statement of characteristic sweep, may make us smile, wryly, at its combination of crystalline economy and prescient elegance, as well perhaps at its contrast with the view he presented in *Islam observed*: 'What is happening to the "Islamic City" [...] is what is happening to "Islam." It is losing definition and gaining energy' (Geertz 1989, p. 302).

About five years later, Geertz published *After the fact* (1995), in which, in his own words, he was 'trying to describe the work I've been doing with myself in the picture' (Olson 1991, p. 204). He describes that picture's changing composition:

The two towns of course have altered. . . . But so. . . has the anthropologist. So has the discipline. . ., the intellectual setting within which that discipline exists, and the moral basis on which it rests. So have the countries. . . and the international world in which the two countries are enclosed. . . . It is Heraclitus cubed and worse. (Geertz 1995, pp. 1–2).

As he tries to put himself in the picture – 'to convey . . . what it is to be an anthropologist not off somewhere beyond the reach of headlines but on some sort of fault line between the large and the little' – he proposes that 'what is needed, or anyway must serve, is tableaus, anecdotes, parables, tales: mini-narratives with the narrator in them' (p. 65). Pursuing this aim in his own fashion, he presents two anecdotes meant to be amusing. There is a mildly humorous incident of a disastrous mixed marriage between a Moroccan man and a U.S. woman (pp. 67–70), and then another, again mildly humorous, about the complications of gaining an audience with King Hassan II (pp. 75–79). In both anecdotes Geertz is laughing more at Morocco, Moroccan practices and Moroccan institutions, than showing humour in them; nor is he laughing at himself or the society from which he comes. Instead, this is humour mainly at Morocco's expense.

As he reconstructs his anthropological career in *After the fact*, we encounter some replays of humorous moments we saw in earlier writings, but we also come across some new ones. He reports, for example, that Egyptians are said to be in a can't-win struggle with Israel because 'if they lose to the Jews everyone will say they were defeated by women, if they defeat them everyone will say "all they did was beat a bunch of women"' (p. 48). And, very close to the end of *After the fact*, relegated to an endnote, we find a true joke, labeled as such: 'The popular joke in Sefrou about [Hassan II's newly built mosque in Casablanca] was of two worshipers who go to it but can't get in for the crowd. One says they should complain; the other says, "Don't do that! He will only build another one!"' (p. 194).

In drawing out the meaning of these anecdotes and humorous asides, Geertz passes over humour's significance but restates a point many of us were making well before this (although no doubt not as elegantly): that the anthropologist is wedded to the world-historical context that enables fieldwork to take place. In Geertz's words,

It is a matter of living out your existence in two stories at once. One of these stories is the familiar one of the anthropologist projecting him- or herself onto the local scene as a minor actor, odd but harmless, and a solemn observer, searching out assorted facts. The other is the less familiar one, rarely recounted, of his or her attempt to maintain such a reduced and specialised persona amid the currents and cross-currents of world-scale politics – the struggle for hegemonies, broad or narrow, persistent or fleeting. (Geerz 1995, p. 94)

In the final sentence of *After the fact*, Geertz tallies the benefits he has gained from an anthropological career spanning four decades:

There is not much assurance or sense of closure, not even much of a sense of knowing what it is one precisely *is* after, in so indefinite a quest, amid such various people, over such a diversity of times. But it is an excellent way, interesting, dismaying, useful, and **amusing**, to expend a life. (Geertz 1995, p. 168, Geertz's italics, my boldface)

The 'comic attitude' and Geertz's 'take' on Morocco

Let me tell you a joke. . ..

There is no denying that Geertz, having himself been amused, has also amused many of us, and immensely. With this in mind, we would do well to ask what kind of amusement this has been and, in Geertz's case, what are some of the characteristics and implications of his 'amusement.'

In particular, how may we interpret his use of humour and what may this tell us about his vision(s) of Morocco?

Conventionally distilled, there are three main theories of humour: incongruity, superiority, release. In the incongruity-based view (associated with Kant, Schopenhauer, and Bergson, among others), emphasis is on the unexpected juxtaposition of unlikely neighbours, of things that ordinarily don't go together; with regard to superiority (and here we think of Hobbes and Bergson too), we laugh when we are made to feel superior to someone else, when we find ourselves protected from the harm that befalls another; and we gain release in humour (Freud and other psychologically-based views) when we experience a psychological tension that, when suddenly relieved, leads to laughter as a sign of that release.[16]

All these approaches highlight the existence of a tension that arises when anomalies, contradictions, inconsistencies, contrasts, incompatibilities, are brought into proximity with one another, and then some form of relatively economical and/or elegant resolution of this tension ensues that triggers the laughing or smiling response. It is this juxtaposition of anomalous or contradictory visions, expressions, perspectives, that has led some – among them Peter Berger (1997, pp. 7–13) – to think of humour as providing a challenge to our everyday attitudes, to the taken-for-granted nature of our everyday reality.

Upon seeing these words, many readers will recall Alfred Schutz's work and Geertz's frequent references to Schutz in many of his earlier writings. Schutz's argument, greatly simplified, is that we have many different ways of relating to the world around us, paramount among them being our 'natural attitude,' our 'everyday, common-sense attitude' that accepts the world as given, that takes it for granted.[17] However, this is not our only 'attitude.' There is also the 'scientific' attitude, where we investigate causes and effects, assess the reliability of theory through certain procedures, and remain 'detached' from our conclusions. The 'ideological,' 'religious,' and 'aesthetic' are other attitudes that Geertz discussed in a detailed manner.[18]

We may think of the 'comic attitude' as another 'finite attitude,' an important one, for think how often we are moved in our human interactions to smile or laugh. For many of us, melancholic or not, I suspect these moments occupy a good part of our day.

Now, what happens in these situations? To take a simple example, let me tell you a joke, for convenience a short one. The context is Egypt during Gamal Abdel Nasser's rule, at a time when basic goods were in short supply.

> A fisherman caught a fish and brought it to his wife to cook. But she had no oil to cook it in and her husband, in a fit of frustration, threw the fish back into the sea. Whereupon the fish surfaced and shouted, 'Three cheers for Gamal Abdel Nasser!'

What has occurred here? Instantly, as we enter the joke 'frame,' we detach ourselves from our immediate reality; we expect to hear a story, a story not necessarily 'real' or 'true,' that will move us toward laughter. For a moment or longer we are taken out of our 'natural attitude,' put in another frame of mind, called to attention, and we suspend the category of true/false. The psychological tension that ensues – in part a product of our uncertainty over getting the joke – primes us for some sort of release, hopefully in laughter or something similar.

Furthermore the joke itself, in putting forward conflicting statements, or in juxtaposing two or more conflicting visions, or in displaying incongruities, may call into question our everyday attitude, challenge it, ridicule it, relativise it. In this joke, this happens in several ways: the unexpected shift of perspective from fisherman to fish – and a talking fish at that – might be taken as questioning human wisdom and challenging species-centric views; the irony of the fish's praise entailing its opposite (criticism) raises our awareness of language's complexity and ambiguity; the critique of leadership attacks the dominant political order, etc. In this way, the comic attitude may be creating new points of view or subverting accepted ones. But it also may, to the contrary, play a conservative role and reinforce the everyday if, after the punch line, we return to the everyday with a renewed consciousness of it, reaffirming its primacy.[19]

Of course, when we say creative, subversive, or conservative, this is with regard to an everyday that is constituted by specific values, beliefs, context, that is, by culture. In fact, in his discussion in *Islam observed* of the religious attitude, Geertz makes this argument explicitly:

> There is a dialectic between religion and common sense – as there is between art, science, and so on and common sense – which necessitates their being seen in terms of one another. Religion must be viewed against the background of the insufficiency, or anyway the felt insufficiency, of common sense as a total orientation toward life.. ... (Geertz 1968, p. 95)

Geertz's 'take' on Morocco

Now, how does Geertz's particular 'comic attitude' articulate with his views on culture and anthropology and inform his interpretations of Morocco?

It is hazardous to single out, from among Geertz's many statements on culture and the nature of anthropology, a few that epitomise his views, but let me try nonetheless. In *Islam observed* he provides a clear ontological statement and offers an epistemology: culture consists of 'public, historically created vehicles of reasoning, perception, feeling, and understanding – symbols, in the broadest sense,' and the effort to understand requires a 'semantic' approach, 'concerned with the collectively created patterns of meaning the individual uses to give form to experience and point to action' (Geertz 1968, 95).

This vision – that the aim of anthropology is to uncover (or construct) public vehicles and their meanings – is certainly a defensible one, but it is not the only one.[20] One might also seek to portray what might be called 'Moroccan ways of thinking, feeling, and doing,' an aim that life histories, for example, attempt to fulfill; or to convey the encounter between people of different communities and how such an encounter proceeds; or to 'establish communication between worlds, making lived experience as it appears in one site accessible to people living in another.'[21]

Geertz's own vision, as I have just summarised it, fits easily with his views on culture as text which he has expressed in statements that many of us are almost able to recite by heart once the first few words are pronounced, as, for example:

> The culture of a people is an ensemble of texts, themselves ensembles, which the anthropologist strains to read over the shoulders of those to whom they properly belong. (Geertz 1973a, p. 452).

And where

> Doing ethnography is like trying to read (in the sense of 'construct a reading of') a manuscript... written not in conventionalised graphs of sound but in transient examples of shaped behaviour. (Geertz 1973b, p. 10)[22]

However, despite invoking 'transient examples of shaped behaviour' or what he elsewhere calls 'small facts,' and despite referring to anthropologists as the 'miniaturists of the social sciences' (Geertz 1968, p. 4), Geertz clearly de-emphasises these aspects in favour of broader 'collectively created patterns of meaning' and in favour of the large issues to which these small facts may be made to speak. In addition, the actual miniatures Geertz constructs and the few instances of 'transient behaviour' he presents are, on the whole, rather decontextualised, often of a historical nature, and usually 'divorce[d] from what happens – from what, in this time or that place, specific people say, what they do, what is done to them, from the whole vast business of the world,' despite his warning that to do so is to 'render [them] vacant' (Geertz 1973b, p. 18).

In favouring the 'large issues' and the 'collectively created patterns of meanings,' Geertz tends to construct visions where culture is relatively coherent, with an emphasis on 'dominant' culture at the expense of what may be called 'subcultures' and/or 'counter-culture' (admittedly simplifying terms, but they suit the purpose here). This entails a turning away from culture as a contest over meanings and actions, where different groups, social forces, and institutions struggle and negotiate with one another as part of an effort to promote their own meanings and assert their power and influence. On the whole the vision that dominates his essays on Morocco is one of a cultural system marked by a broad, pervasive, and largely coherent set of public meanings, and this is reinforced by his penchant for making certain notions, concepts, and/or terms (such as *'andu klam, sdeq, nisba*) serve not merely as central cultural notions but as stand-ins for broad societal patterns, carrying the weight of a 'total pattern of social life' (Geertz 1983b, p. 67).[23]

Both of these aspects of Geertz's interpretations – the focus on large issues and the facility with synecdoche – might have been undermined by a detailed examination of humour, built as the latter is on juxtapositions of contradictory or anomalous items. In a similar vein it is interesting to observe that, in putting forward his own particular view of anthropological interpretation over, say, that of exploring 'Moroccan ways of thinking, feeling, and doing,' he has turned away from another domain that also might have challenged his interpretations – the domain of life histories, often filled with inconsistencies, contradictions, and humorous episodes and insights.[24]

Related to this, we also see in his work on Morocco a recurring pattern of summarising complex cultural situations in a relatively short list of characteristics. While simplification, categorisation, and stereotyping are often necessary steps in attempting to understand and act in our complex world, and often, when used with Geertz's characteristic elegance, have the benefit of amusing us (although on occasion we may grimace rather than smile), these steps need to be assessed for their implications, and Geertz's quick summaries often seem as revealing for what they omit as for what they include.

For example, in the final sentence of 'Suq,' he says, 'in the details of bazaar life something of the spirit that animates that society – an odd mixture of restlessness, practicality, contentiousness, eloquence, inclemency, and moralism – can be seen with a particular and revelatory vividness' (Geertz 1979, p. 235).[25] In this catalogue of characteristics, together with the implication that they capture in part the 'spirit' of Moroccan society, many qualities that should no doubt be included are absent – sociability, caring, fraternity, among others. Also absent, not incidentally, are the qualities of fun, amusement, and humour, even though he has referred earlier to humour as important in the 'conventions of bargaining.'

Geertz's somewhat provocative lists are buttressed by a number of asides that convey implicit and sometimes rather explicit negative value judgments. As I have already mentioned, in his earliest work on Morocco he describes it as suffering from a kind of 'spiritual *schizophrenia*' (Geertz 1968, p. 116); later it is seen as 'informal to a *fault*' (Geertz 1983b 1974, p. 64); and even later, the use of *nisba* terms is seen as a 'collective habit, not to say *obsession*' (Geertz 1979, p. 142, my emphasis). Admittedly, when these judgments occur they are often in such a concise, even snappy form that they may register only subliminally, if at all. But, subliminal or not, these value judgments are there.[26]

Geertz's 'being-in-the-world, anthropologically': history, rhetoric, psychology

With all this in mind, how might we explain or understand Geertz's relative lack of attention to humour in Morocco and his reluctance to apply to humour the same kind of interpretive approach he adopted for so many of our other ways of being-in-the-world, particularly when he himself was so attuned to humour, such a skilful wielder of it, and when he sensed that humour was, as art, religion, common sense, etc., just the kind of 'cultural system' or 'finite attitude' that could be plumbed to provide cultural meaning? What does this say about Geertz's view of anthropology as a way of 'being-in-the-world,' that is, about anthropology as a human activity? And what might all this say about our own?

My answers to these questions are offered here in a tentative rather than conclusive spirit. Perhaps some of Geertz's writings on Morocco have escaped me; also, I am leaving aside almost all he has written on Indonesia, Java, and Bali. Consequently, what I will be suggesting may need revision if we find Geertz writing more directly on humour in Morocco or in his earlier fieldwork locations, or in any way addressing humour in a systematic manner.

Despite his later reservations about medical metaphors, Geertz often employs such metaphors in describing anthropological activity.[27] I have already cited several of these,[28] but for me, one among them stands out from the rest. In 'Thinking as a moral act,' one of his first essays to deal with Morocco, he argues that,

> One of the more disquieting conclusions to which thinking about the new states and their *problems* has led me is that such [anthropological] thinking is rather more effective in exposing the problems than it is in uncovering solutions for them. There is a *diagnostic* and a remedial side to our scientific concern with these societies, and the diagnostic seems... to proceed infinitely faster than the remedial. (Geertz 2000, p. 24, my emphases)

This is also the essay in which the anthropologist's situation is compared to that of a laboratory technician and is seen as 'not entirely incomparable to that of the cancer surgeon who spends most of his effort delicately exposing severe pathologies he is not equipped to do anything about' (p. 29).

Geertz has put forward this view on many occasions, that the anthropologist is in a position to 'diagnose' problems, to perceive how recalcitrant they are. But what are the assumptions that underlie this view that the anthropologist, having such difficulty understanding a society, can nonetheless define it by its 'problems'? This stance of 'problem-recognition, problem-diagnosis' is a questionable one, particularly when it is not accompanied by any serious move in the direction of reflecting on one's own society. It resembles, to continue the medical metaphor, that of a doctor diagnosing a malady, where the society undergoing 'examination' is presumed to be, in some sense, pathological, sick. In adopting this stance Geertz places himself, consistently, in a 'one-up' position, a position that predisposes him to Hobbesian forms of humour – laughing at rather than with – and that, unwittingly and somewhat ironically, gives a new twist to the 1960s political maxim, 'If you're not part of the solution, you're part of the problem.'

This view returns us, conveniently, to the 1960s and even to the 1950s, for this aspect of Geertz's approach needs to be situated historically and related to his attaining professional maturity during a period marked by the end of colonialism in its orthodox form and the emergence of the 'new states' theme, which he addressed at length. Geertz, aware of this as he looks back in the 1990s over his anthropological career and situates his work within the development paradigm, says that,

> It is in the shadow of this task ['that something serious had to be done, and quickly, to remodel their character' (139)] that countries like Indonesia and Morocco, and people from outside, like me, who

found themselves absorbed with their fate, and in an odd and derivative way caught up in it, lived during the fifties, sixties, seventies, and eighties, and continue to live today. . . .. (Geertz 1995, p. 139)

George Marcus addresses this aspect of Geertz's work, noting that,

> The anthropology of the 1950s and 1960s was part of the great mission of development in the new states – in the midst of which Geertz was a very American as well as an anthropological writer, accepting this mission with a certain resignation that did not particularly define a politics of field-work. That politics instead emerged in terms of the always slightly absurd but very human predica-ments of a well-meaning outsider thrust among people with very different life chances. According to the presumptions of the development mission, themselves based on Western notions of liberal decency, the outsider was in some sense the model of a desired future. (Marcus 1999, p. 91)

Marcus is referring here to Geertz's remark, in 'Thinking as a moral act,' that, 'moreover, one [the anthropologist] is a type of benefactor of just the sort of improvements they [the informants] are looking for,' and Marcus comments: 'Here again, as in the cockfight anecdote, the broader context of implication – that of colonialism and neocolonialism – that has so exercised the subsequent critics of ethnography is submerged in Geertz's account, implied but not explicitly noted' (Marcus 1999, pp. 90–91).

For Geertz, then, fieldwork and anthropological research, fitting as they did into the develop-ment paradigm and committed as their practitioners were to diagnosing problems if not to solving them, were very serious enterprises. There is no better sign of his recognition of this seriousness than in the astonishingly apposite Diderot epigraph he placed at the beginning of *Local knowledge*, which I cannot resist presenting in its entirety:

> 'Je me demande dans quel genre est cette pièce? Dans le genre comique? Il n'y a pas le mot pour rire. Dans le genre tragique? la terreur, la commisération et les autres grandes passions n'y sont point excitées. Cependant il y a de l'intérêt; et il y en aura, sans ridicule [qui] fasse rire, sans danger [qui] fasse frémir, dans toute composition dramatique où le sujet sera important, où le poète prendra le ton que nous avons dans les affaires sérieuses, et où l'action s'avancera par la perplexité et par les embarras. Or, il me semble que ces actions étant les plus communes de la vie, le genre [qui] les aura pour objet doît être le plus utile et le plus étendu. J'appellerai ce genre *le genre sérieux*.'
> Diderot, *Théâtre* (Geertz 1983c, p. vii)

Yet, I think there was something of a shift in Geertz's orientation away from the 'one-up' stance that pervaded his work for three decades, a shift perhaps occurring during the writing of *Works and lives* (Geertz 1988), although one might argue that the germ of this was already present in 'Thinking as a moral act' and perhaps also in *Islam observed*.[29] On the one hand, as we have already seen, Geertz begins to place the anthropologist in the text. He admits that, with a few exceptions, he had avoided doing this.

> [M]ost of that kind of problem has centered on the question we usually refer to as 'reflexivity.' In *Works and lives* I have some sardonic things to say about some attempts in that direction, though I think it's the direction to move. . . .. [W]e are part of what we study, in a way; we're there. . . . Now, I've never done it. Well. . . once in a while I've done it. But I've never really thoroughly done it, and I've written a lot of books which are written from the moon – the view from nowhere. I am persuaded that at least for some works, for a lot of works, we've really got to get our-selves back into the text, to have ourselves truly represented in the text. . . . In the book I'm writing now, *After the fact, that's* what I'm trying to do. It's not confessional anthropology, and it's not about what I was feeling or something of that sort; it's trying to describe the work I've been doing with myself in the picture. (Olson 1991, pp. 203–204)[30]

Secondly, I believe it is arguable that, in his late writings, Geertz edges away from the 'diagnostic' stance toward one resembling perpetual puzzlement, perplexity. Whereas in earlier writings he tended to offer, however tentatively, avenues that would lead to improved understanding (for example, in *Islam observed*, after cataloguing a series of 'unpromising' approaches, among them indexical measures, typologies, modernisation/acculturation theory, and evolutionary approaches, he finishes by proposing to concentrate on 'process' [Geertz 1968, pp. 57–59]), in his later writings we more often find statements that emphasise bewilderment. For example, take the opening of *After the fact*, which I cited earlier (and which I abbreviate even more radically here):

> Suppose, having entangled yourself... over four decades or so in the goings-on in two provincial towns... you wished to say something about how those goings-on had changed. You could contrast then and now.... [there follows a series of techniques, ending with:] You could even build a model, conceive a process, propose a theory. You could draw graphs. (Geertz 1995, p. 1)

With these techniques, even taken together, unable to convey the complexity of change – remember, 'the two towns of course have altered... [b]ut so... ha[ve] the anthropologist... the discipline... the intellectual setting... the moral basis... the countries... the international world' (Geertz 1995, pp. 1–2) – Geertz concludes: 'It is necessary, then, to be satisfied with swirls, confluxions, and inconstant connections; clouds collecting, clouds dispersing. There is no general story to be told, no synoptic picture to be had' (p. 2). Or, later in *After the fact*:

> If the relation of what we write to what we write about... can no longer be credibly compared with that of a map to a distant territory hitherto uncharted or to that of a sketch to an exotic animal recently come upon, what can it be compared with? Telling a believable story? Building a workable model? Translating an alien language? Construing an enigmatical text? Conducting an intelligible dialogue? Excavating a buried site? Advancing a moral cause? Restructuring a political debate? Staging an instructive illusion?' (Geertz 1995, p. 130)

Among this series of deficient options (to which I would like him to have added, 'constructing synecdochic cultural categories like *nisba*, *sdeq*, or '*andu klam*'), again no clear choice emerges and Geertz's rather 'shaggy dog' answer is,

> All these possibilities and more have been suggested and countersuggested; but the only thing that seems certain is that the game has changed. (Geertz 1995, p. 130).

In this later effort to situate himself in his text Geertz, looking back over his work, says, 'I've always argued that in part I'm represented in my texts by my style, that at least people won't think my books were written by anybody else...' (Olson 1991, p. 204). Here Geertz directly draws our attention to his role as a rhetorician and we may well argue that a sensitivity to rhetoric was always central to his conception of anthropological activity. This is not only my assessment, but something close to his own. He may have only realised this rather late in his career – in an interview published in 1991 he says, 'I'm probably a closet rhetorician, although I'm coming out of the closet a bit' (Olson 1991, p. 202). It is this sensitivity to rhetoric (not to say his 'obsession' with it) that allows him to sound the characteristically wry, humorous, and ironic notes in his writing.

Given the importance Geertz awards to writing style and the seriousness he attaches to the 'problem-filled' field, I think it is worth looking more closely at the contrast in his work between these two key moments of anthropological activity – fieldwork and writing – a contrast that might even be termed a radical disjunction. Geertz says, for example,

> I can't write in the field. I write a lot of field notes, but I can't compose anything. [...] I think there's a much greater separation in anthropology, especially among field anthropologists, than in a lot of social sciences, between the research and the writing – at least as I do it. [...] So, for me at least,

it's a fairly divided life. I don't write in the field; I write after I return. Mostly, *here* I write and *there* I research. (Olson 1991, p. 190, emphases in the original)

Add to this his serious approach to the field's 'problems' and we see someone for whom the element 'work' in fieldwork carries the main charge, and whose sharp sense of humour finds expression in the playfulness of his writings. We might say, then, that for Geertz the field, where the real 'problems' are, is his *workstation*; his study at home, where he writes, is his *playstation*. He has described his sessions at the *playstation*, his manner of writing, in the following way:

> I don't write drafts. I write from the beginning to the end, and when it's finished it's done. [...] I never leave a sentence or a paragraph until I'm satisfied with it.... The process is very slow.... I wish I could ['write a first draft and not care whether it's idiotic' (190)], but for reasons that are probably deeply psychological, it's impossible. I usually write about a paragraph a day, but at least it's essentially finished when it's done. (Olson 1991, p. 190)

Since Geertz has opened the way here for a psychological probe, let me engage in this for a moment, even though this is something that I am not inclined to. Geertz may be displaying a particular character disposition in this radical disjunction between the 'serious' enterprise of fieldwork and his playfulness in his study. I took the liberty of quoting Quentin Skinner slightly out of context earlier; the full quote reads,

> Although Cliff had an unfailing and infectious sense of humour, and loved hearing as well as telling funny stories, he never struck me as the kind of person around whom funny stories accumulate... because [I think] of the intensity of his intellectual commitments, which left him preoccupied and a little withdrawn. Like many basically melancholy people, he saw the world as filled with absurdities, but he nevertheless felt that they needed to be seriously addressed.[31]

Simon Critchley, commenting on Freud's view of melancholia, remarks that perhaps the melancholic is wiser than the rest of us, closer to the truth. He points to philosophers who appear to have been melancholics – Pascal, Montaigne – and literary figures such as Hamlet and Dostoyevsky's *Underground man* (Critchley 2002, p. 98).[32] Furthermore, in Freud's view, the escape from melancholia is often into mania – joy, exaltation – a liberation from the super-ego's control (p. 100), evidence of which we might see in the buoyancy of Geertz's writing.

Ending

I have tried here not to see Clifford Geertz as a coherent vehicle of meaning(!), nor to emphasise the large issues – anthropology, colonialism, and the relationship between the two, for example – at the expense of the relatively 'small fact' of one individual's work. I have tried to see something of that one individual's complexity, something of the contradictory and conflicting gifts, attitudes, and dispositions that have gone into creating an exceedingly rich (and witty) body of writings. I have tried, in doing this, to treat him much as I would any of my favorite informants – paying attention both to what they say and what they don't, to what I ask and what I don't – trying to understand, from my own perspective, something of what it was like to stand in Clifford Geertz's shoes, to reflect both his serious and humorous leanings and the unsteady balance between them – all this to satisfy my aim, as I suggested earlier, of 'making lived experience as it appears in one site accessible to people living in another.'

As I do this I imagine Cliff in his study, going through his texts sentence by sentence, paragraph by paragraph, frequently chuckling to himself as he constructs a clever turn of phrase. For example, I imagine him responding in this way when he came up with, 'To anyone who has been in Bali any length of time, the deep psychological identification of Balinese men with their cocks is unmistakable....' Wordplays such as this had us laughing in the aisles at Yale, hopefully not too sophomorically, when he presented them there in the late 1960s.

Having looked at Geertz's writings from this perspective, I feel a chance was missed that he didn't pay more attention to humour, that he didn't write something along the lines of 'Humour as a cultural system,' or explore the 'comic attitude' and its relationship to 'the insufficiency, or anyway the felt insufficiency, of common sense as a total orientation toward life.' I have suggested some reasons why he never did write such articles nor, as far as I can tell, anything else that explored humour in a sustained way. But perhaps his relative silence here has nothing at all to do with what I've suggested. Maybe the subject struck him as too oxymoronic; or maybe he came to the view that 'I don't do systems.'[33] On the other hand – to give this story a 'shaggy dog' ending suited to Geertz's own rhetorical (and perhaps even tonsorial) tastes – it may be simply, and rather ironically, that, sadly, he just never got around to it.[34]

Notes

1. A related reason I find his neglect of humour surprising has to do with his heightened attention to games, which have a family resemblance to humour in that both have an important agonistic component. Geertz treats the agonistic side of human behaviour in many of his essays: Moroccan poetry is seen as agonistic; so is Moroccan market behaviour (where the horse racing metaphor comes in); anthropology is likened to a game of chess; and of course there is his 'Deep play' essay. Given the significant similarities between humour and games/ contests, although there are some suggestive differences as well, it is interesting and perhaps revealing that he pays so much more attention to games than to humour. Why he does this would have to be a subject for another paper. To these considerations one might add, somewhat tongue-in-cheek, that Geertz himself has been one of the rare anthropologists of sufficient renown to become a target of humour. I will return to this in a later note (see n. 10 infra).

2. Skinner, *The Institute Newsletter*, winter 2007.
   I first met Clifford Geertz in the mid-1960s as I was finishing my Masters in Romance Languages at the University of Chicago. I was encouraged by the chair to go on for the Ph.D.; however, when I mentioned my desire to study the francophone literature of the Maghreb (I had spent a few months in the winter of 1963– 64 hitchhiking from Ceuta across the Maghreb to Tunis, I knew literature in French was being written there, and I thought this would be a very interesting topic), the chair's response was discouragingly direct: 'Mais, ce n'est pas du français!'
   I had a friend who was in Chicago's doctoral anthropology programme at the time – Steve Barnett – and he suggested that I explore anthropology. I went to the department, mentioned my area of interest, and was immediately directed to Geertz's office. My knowledge of anthropology was so thin that I had no idea how important a figure he was – lucky ignorance because, had I known, my first encounter with him might have dissuaded me from entering anthropology at all. Geertz's welcome was, to put it gently, reserved, and he sent me, rather summarily, to Paul Friedrich, who was much warmer, more receptive, and even encouraging. Following the meeting with Friedrich I applied for and was accepted into the graduate programme.
   I gained some acquaintance with Geertz over the following year when, in addition to being in the class he taught for a month or so as part of the Systems prerequisite (or was it Careers?), he also welcomed me into his home for a weekly gathering (or was it biweekly or monthly?) of people interested in Morocco. There I certainly met Tom Dichter and Larry Rosen and perhaps Paul Rabinow as well. I transferred to Yale the following year and continued to learn, directly and indirectly, about Geertz's importance in anthropology. While at Yale I attended his Terry Lectures (which later became *Islam observed*) and, perhaps during the same visit, an early version of what was to become 'Deep play.'
   Over the next few decades I saw him occasionally and somewhere along the way we shifted to first names. I never saw Cliff in Morocco but attended a small conference on Morocco that he and his then wife Hilly hosted at Princeton sometime in the mid-1970s, had lunch with him a couple of times in the late 1970s (when he was in the UK and I was working in London – this was when he was generous enough to read and comment on some chapters of my *Moroccan dialogues* manuscript), and had a dinner or two at Princeton during the late 1980s with him and his wife Karen, whom I had gotten to know independently when she and I were teaching in New York during

the 1970s. These were, as far as I can remember, the only times we met after our initial brief encounter in the mid-1960s, until some 30 years later, in 1995–96, when I saw Cliff quite often while my wife was a member of the IAS. These were, unfortunately, our last occasions for personal contact.

3. These anticlimactic endings are a characteristic of what is often termed the 'shaggy dog story,' defined as 'a whimsically extravagant story humorous from its length and the inconsequence of its ending' (*Chambers 20th Century Dictionary* 1972, 1242–1243). The just-quoted opening paragraph of *After the fact*, with its extended series of possible techniques terminating in a sharp descent from high 'theory' to the lowly 'graph,' is a fine example of this. The form is a staple of Geertz's rhetorical style and there are several other instances of shaggy dog structure given or suggested later in this paper; see below, for example, in the section on 'Geertz's "being-in-the-world, anthropologically",' the extended quote from *After the fact*: 'If the relation of what we write to what we write about. . .' (Geertz 1995, p. 130).

4. Jim Boon (2000, 2005) provides many insightful comments on Geertz's style, but focuses more on its entertaining effects than its humorous qualities.

5. He hints at this again in 'Art as a cultural system,' where he places humour and art on a similar footing, describing a dictionary definition of art as 'a way of putting the matter which seems to suggest that men are born with the power to appreciate, as they are born with the power to see jokes, and have only to be provided with the occasions to exercise it.' He continues immediately, 'As what I have said here ought to indicate, I do not think that this is true (I do not think that it is true for humour either); but, rather, that "the sense of beauty," or whatever the ability to respond intelligently to face scars, painted ovals, domed pavilions, or rhymed insults should be called, is no less a cultural artifact than the objects and devices concocted to "affect" it' (Geertz 1983a, p. 118).

6. Geertz's major writings on Morocco treated here are 'Thinking as a moral act' (2000 1968), *Islam observed* (1968), 'Thick description' (1973b), 'From the native's point of wiew' (1983b 1974), 'Art as a cultural cystem' (1983a 1976), 'The bazaar economy' (1978), 'Suq: the bazaar economy in Sefrou' (1979), 'Toutes directions' (1989), and *After the fact* (1995).

7. His normative view of the Moroccan situation – that having large-scale and technologically advanced farming would be the most advantageous agricultural form – underplays both the high productivity of many family farms (in part because of their heightened level of 'self-exploitation') and the benefits for a country of producing its own food. Geertz seems here to be promoting rather uncritically an export-led economic development model.

8. For Geertz this irony is characterised by the anthropologist being 'used as an object' and treated 'as a fool' by the informant, leading to one of the 'fringe benefits of anthropological research,' i.e. learning how to behave in such situations (Geertz 2000, p. 30); by the anthropologist being seen by the informant as someone who possesses the life chances the informant desires but will probably never get, with the anthropologist thus becoming like 'the bourgeois informing the poor to be patient' (p. 31); and by the anthropologist having to ask the Other for charity and only being able to offer him- or herself in return, consequently forming the illusion of being the informant's 'friend' (p. 33).

9. As he says, the religious history of both countries over the past 150 years is characterised by 'a progressive increase in doubt' (Geertz 1968, p. 61), a symptom of this being 'the transformation of religious symbols from imagistic revelations. . . to ideological assertions' (p. 62).

10. This seminal essay is the target of Lee Drummond's humour in *Anthropology News*, May 2002, p. 60, in the form of a covering letter sent to Geertz by an apocryphal editor of the just as apocryphal journal *Anemic Anthropology*, parodying journal reviewers' comments on whether the essay was suitable for publication. The incident Geertz explores is described, not incorrectly, as 'not a record of events you observed but instead notes on your conversation with an 80-year-old man about an incident he was involved in 56 years ago.' The editor goes on to suggest that 'much of your anecdotal eye-winking and its "interpretation" adds nothing to an established and ongoing research programme on cognition and learning within evolutionary psychology,' and recommends that Geertz either rework the article substantially or submit it 'as it stands to *Occasional Papers of Central Kansas State Teachers' College*.'

11. 'Understanding the form and pressure of, to use the dangerous word one more time, natives' inner lives is more like grasping a proverb, catching an allusion, seeing a joke – or, as I have suggested, reading a poem – than it is like achieving communion' (Geertz 1983b, p. 70).

12. '[I]t is not possible to describe here the general tone of interpersonal relations in Morocco with any concreteness; one can only claim, and hope to be believed, that it is before anything else combative, a constant testing of wills as individuals struggle to seize what they covet, defend what they have, and recover what they have lost. So far as speech is concerned, this gives to all but the most idle conversation the quality of a catch-as-catch-can in words, a head-on collision of curses, promises, lies, excuses, pleading, commands, proverbs, arguments,

analogies, quotations, threats, evasion, flatteries, which not only puts an enormous premium on verbal fluency but gives to rhetoric a directly coercive force; '*andu klam*, 'he has words, speech, maxims, eloquence,' means also, and not just metaphorically, 'he has power, influence, weight, authority'' (Geertz 1983a, p. 114).

13. Geertz may still have thought of this study as an essay, despite its length and variety of materials, for he had been saying just a few years earlier and perhaps even as he was formulating 'Suq,' that 'the essay, whether of 30 pages or 300, has seemed the natural genre in which to present cultural interpretations and the theories sustaining them...' (Geertz 1973b, p. 25).

It should perhaps also be noted that in 'Thick description,' Geertz goes to some pains in an effort to distinguish his approach from ethnoscience and cognitive anthropology (Geertz 1973b, pp. 11–12). In essence, he sees a main difference in his own focus on public meanings versus the ethnoscience/cognitive anthropological focus on psychological representations. Nonetheless, in 'Suq' the differences between his approach and the others are not easy to discern.

14. '[A] case in point.... [A]fter [looking at it] one may see in other instances matters otherwise occluded. Examples instruct, they do not prove' (Geertz 1989, p. 293).

15. 'We have lost both our brains and our pockets,' and 'The city used to eat the countryside, now the countryside eats the city' (Geertz 1989, p. 294).

16. There are also a number of linguistically oriented approaches, and those that focus on the themes embodied in humour (ethnic humour, gender humour), as well as sociological approaches that focus on humour as facilitating the construction of group boundaries, identity, etc.

17. See Geertz's 'Common sense as a cultural system' (1975) for one instance of his use of these concepts.

18. See Geertz, 'Ideology as a cultural system' (1964), 'Religion as a cultural system' (1966), and 'Art as a cultural system' (1983a).

19. I have already referred to Berger 1997 as focusing on humour's challenge to everyday attitudes, as providing a possibility for transcending the everyday; Critchley 2002, on the other hand, emphasises humour's conservative role, that the comic inevitably returns us to the mundane. Here are three longer jokes that provide further examples of how humour works. They are all set in Egypt (and I would like to take this occasion to thank three of my students at the American University in Cairo – Ali Atef, Fouad Halbouni, and Hala Osman – for helping me explore various aspects of Egyptian humour).

1) Mubarak, Atef Ebeid (then prime minister), and Fathy Sorour (leader of parliament) were cruising above Egypt in a helicopter and looking down at the people.

Mubarak said, 'Oh, the people look miserable, let's throw them 10 pounds to make at least one of them happy.'

Atef Ebeid responded, 'Mr. President, if I may speak freely, may I suggest something? If we change the 10-pound note into two fivers, we can make two people happy.'

Sorour interjected, 'If I may express myself freely, I suggest we change the 10-pound note into one-pound notes and make 10 people happy.'

The pilot then asked the president if he might be allowed to speak. Granted leave to speak he said, 'Then I suggest if all three of you throw yourselves out of the helicopter you'll make 70 million people happy.'

2) Mubarak has died and gone to hell. The devil looks him up and down and says,

'I really don't know what to do with you. You are after all a head of state!'

'Yes... I am,' Mubarak replies in a pompous tone.

'OK... so would you like to be boiled, fried, or what?'

'What...? Of course not.... Can't I get a softer punishment? What about the two idiots before me [Nasser and Sadat]? What ever happened to them?'

'OK, OK.... Follow me.'

Mubarak accompanies the devil down a long corridor lined with many rooms. The devil tells him these are all 'torture suites' for former presidents and famous personalities. Mubarak opens the first door and finds Mohammed Naguib [Egypt's first president] being dipped in a barrel of hot lava by four devils. Mubarak frowns, saying, 'No, that's too gruesome – can you show me Nasser's suite?'

Mubarak is taken to Nasser's suite where he sees the former president being whipped by seven devils and bleeding profusely. Mubarak frowns again. Then he asks if he can be taken to see Sadat. The devil leads him to a door at the very end of the corridor. Looking in, Mubarak finds a beautiful perfumed suite with lovely furniture. In the center of the room is a big jacuzzi where Sadat is writhing in a bubble bath with Marilyn Monroe.

'Son of a devil... even in hell. God.... Why does Sadat always get all the attention? What kind of punishment is this anyway?'

'Who said we were punishing him? We're punishing her.'

3) Presidents Bush, Jr., Jacques Chirac, and Hosni Mubarak have all died and gone to heaven. After God has judged them they are each expected to ask Him one question before being transferred to their heavenly suites. Bush asks Him, 'When will my country become fully prosperous?' God sighs and takes Bush to his private office where there are infinite stacks of books and files. After checking a few files God responds, 'Well, by my calculations, after about five years of honest labour.' Bush rejoices and leaves.

Chirac then asks God the same question. God takes Chirac to his private office and looks in his files. 'Well. . . I think if your country can practice some chastity and honest labour you'll get there in about 15 years.' Chirac rejoices too and leaves.

Lastly, Mubarak asks God the same question. God scratches his head and takes Mubarak to the same office. This time God looks through several stacks of files but finds no answer. He asks the Archangel Gabriel for more files but still He finds no answer. God continues to search and many weeks pass. Finally, He summons Mubarak, meets him with heavy eyes and much yawning, and says, 'I couldn't find what you were looking for. . .. Egypt may well become prosperous, but not in my reign.'

20. A nod to Larry Rosen is called for here – his very funny appropriation of the expression 'vehicle of meaning' in referring to an automobile he inherited from Geertz when he began his fieldwork in Morocco, now unfailingly appears whenever I think of Geertz's use of the term (see Rosen 2005).

21. The quote comes from Dwyer (2004, p. 309), a book in which I tried to strike a balance between individual experience and wider contexts in a way rather distinct from Geertz's focus on public meanings and their systematic nature. The second aim – conveying an encounter between people from different communities – was one I tried to fulfill in an earlier book (Dwyer 1982). To these anthropological aims one should certainly add those of advocacy and preservation, among others.

22. The full quote is: 'Doing ethnography is like trying to read (in the sense of "construct a reading of") a manuscript – foreign, faded, full of ellipses, incoherencies, suspicious emendations, and tendentious commentaries, but written not in conventionalised graphs of sound but in transient examples of shaped behaviour' (Geertz 1973b, p. 10). Geertz's views on culture as text are heavily indebted to Paul Ricoeur's *The model of the text*, as he indicates (1973, p. 19).

23. This emphasis on meaning as systematic and coherent does not do justice to the importance of 'contest' and conflict in the construction of culture – contests between groups and various social forces over objects and meanings. This is somewhat ironic, for Geertz often writes about the agonistic aspects of Moroccan culture (for example, with regard to poetry) and is in general extremely sensitive to the agonistic element in life. In *Islam observed* (1968), 'Toutes directions' (1989), and *After the fact* (1995), he makes overtures in this direction. For example, in the latter he talks about contesting visions of modernity: 'What was surprising, and disorganizing as well, was that modernity turned out to be less a fixed destination than a vast and inconstant field of warring possibilities, possibilities neither simultaneously reachable nor systematically connected. . .' (Geertz 1995, p. 138).

It may be useful here to contrast Geertz's overall approach with Bourdieu's. Despite the superficial similarity of the obeisance both pay to 'science' (superficial in that their visions of science are very different and the kind of obeisance they pay very different too; in Geertz's case it focuses on the stance of 'detachment' but otherwise seems largely rhetorical, in Bourdieu's case an empiricist methodology dominates), the most important difference seems to me to lie in the fact that Bourdieu's theoretical constructions rest on a view of culture as a struggle between contending visions and forces, with concepts such as *habitus* providing for a fertile relationship between agency and cultural imperatives (this argument is similar to the one made by Ortner 1984), whereas Geertz, in his emphasis on concepts and meanings, is less able to encompass both individual action and cultural imperatives. At the same time, let it be said that, unlike in Geertz's work, it is very difficult, perhaps impossible, to find in Bourdieu's work much reference to humour, and certainly his writing betrays not a hint of it. I did not know him well enough to say whether he had anything like the personal gift for humour that Geertz had.

24. The closest Geertz comes to a 'life history' approach is found in *Islam observed*, in his discussions of Sunan Kalidjaga and Sukarno in Indonesia and Sidi Lahcen Lyusi and Muhammad V in Morocco as exemplary figures for their countries and for their times. But these are not really life histories in the usual sense of the term.

25. Taken from: 'But the great social formations of the Maghreb do bear a family resemblance to one another that the suq, as one of the most formidable and most distinctive of them, can, when properly understood, throw into more exact relief. This is not to suggest that Maghrebian society is a big bazaar, any more than it is a big tribe. Nevertheless, in the details of bazaar life something of the spirit that animates that society – an odd mixture of restlessness, practicality, contentiousness, eloquence, inclemency, and moralism – can be seen with a particular and revelatory vividness' (Geertz 1979, p. 235).

26. Here is a somewhat longer, better disguised, but nonetheless negative judgment, from the closing paragraph of *Islam observed*. He poses the following question based on his view that faith is decreasing in both countries: '[W]hat will happen to men like these students when this fact becomes clear [that their strategies in "the struggle for the real" are "but desperate holding actions" or "disguised retreats" (p. 117)]?' And he goes on, 'Frank O'Connor once remarked that no Irishman is really interesting until he has begun to lose his faith. The revelatory shocks that awaited Lyusi and Kalidjaga and rendered them interesting await our anxious traveler and muddled physicist, too, and with them the unquiet societies whose embodiments they are' (1968, p. 117).

27. Geertz argues against medical metaphors in the course of explaining why he was dissatisfied with Richard Rorty's use of the terms *normal discourse* and *abnormal discourse* and proposed instead the terms *standard* and *nonstandard discourse*: 'The main reason I didn't like the normal/abnormal business is that both in my field and in general it has all the overtones of abnormal as *sick*. I don't like the medical model applied in general, so I wanted to get away from that' (Olson 1991, p. 196).

28. To which I might add the 'clinical inference' metaphor he employs as a synonym for the anthropological aim of 'generalizing within cases' (Geertz 1973b, p. 26).

29. *Islam observed* also strikes what is for Geertz a rare societally self-reflexive note, with his suggestion that the 'predicaments' of Morocco and Indonesia are also 'our own' (1968, p. 22), by which he means that the U.S. too is characterised by this progressive loss of faith (p. 102). He does not explore this phenomenon in the U.S. at any length – he may in fact be wrong about it as he may also be wrong in his general assessment of the trends in Indonesia and Morocco. Perhaps it is relevant here to recall his own view of one of the limits of 'cultural theory' (and another use of a medical metaphor), that 'it is not, at least in the strict meaning of the term, predictive. The diagnostician doesn't predict measles; he decides that someone has them, or at the very most *anticipates* that someone is rather likely shortly to get them' (1973b, p. 26, emphasis in the original).

30. Although indeed sardonic at times about attempts to place the anthropologist in the text, Geertz could also be very generous toward efforts in this direction, even when strongly disagreeing with them. In a letter he wrote responding to a publisher's query about producing a paperback edition of my *Moroccan dialogues*, he provides an excellent example of giving value to work very different from his, while not compromising his own position and, as always – even here in a genre that doesn't rank very highly in the anthropological repertoire – introducing some surprising constructions and characteristic rhetorical flourishes that move us to smile. He writes, '[*Moroccan dialogues*] is an extremely original, extremely forceful work, a book of genuine importance which adds a new voice to the anthropological "multilog." If I myself dissent from some of the positions... that's what makes not only horse races, but anthropology.... [W]ere I to be teaching... I would certainly assign it even if after having assigned it I might spend a good deal of time saying why I dissented from some of the things said in it.... *Moroccan dialogues* is one of the more interesting, controversial (this, in the good sense), incisive, and provoking (in *both* the good and bad senses) books to appear in anthropology in some time....'

31. Skinner, *The Institute Newsletter*, winter 2007.

32. As Critchley notes, Freud wrote on the last two. I might add that this list includes some of my own favourites and I have written on the first and the last.

33. I would like to thank Lahouari Addi for bringing to my attention the interview Geertz gave under the title, 'I don't do systems' (see Micheelsen 2002).

34. Geertz explained that he did not continue the 'X as a cultural system' series of articles 'partly because I tired of the conceit... and partly because I realised that I didn't really believe in the "unity of the sciences"' (Geertz 2005, pp. 114–115).

References

Berger, P., 1997. *Redeeming laughter: the comic dimension of human experience*. New York: De Gruyter.

Boon, J.A., 2000. Showbiz as a cross-cultural system: circus and song, Garland and Geertz, Rushdie, Mordden,... and more. *Cultural anthropology*, 15 (3), 424–456.

Boon, J.A., 2005. Geertz's style: a moral matter. *In*: R.A. Shweder and B. Good B., eds. *Clifford Geertz by his colleagues*. Chicago: University of Chicago Press, 28–37.

Chambers 20th Century Dictionary, 1972. Edinburgh W&R Chamber Ltd.

Critchley, S., 2002. *On humour*. London: Routledge.

Drummond, L., 2002. To wit: revise and resubmit II. *Anthropology news*, 43 (5). Arlington, VA: The American Anthropological Association, 60.

Dwyer, K., 1982. *Moroccan dialogues: anthropology in question*. Baltimore, MD: Johns Hopkins University Press.

Dwyer, K., 2004. *Beyond Casablanca: M. A. Tazi and the adventure of Moroccan cinema*. Bloomington: Indiana University Press.

Geertz, C., 1964. Ideology as a cultural system. *In*: David Apter, ed. *Ideology and discontent*. New York: Free Press, 47–76.

Geertz, C., 1966. Religion as a cultural system. *In*: Michael Banton, ed. *Anthropological approaches to the study of religion*. New York: Frederick A. Praeger, 1–46.

Geertz, C., 1968. *Islam observed: religious development in Morocco and Indonesia*. New Haven, CT: Yale University Press.

Geertz, C., 1973a [1972]. Deep play: notes on the Balinese cockfight. *In*: C. Geertz, ed. *The interpretation of cultures*. New York: Basic Books, 412–453.

Geertz, C., 1973b. Thick description: toward an interpretive theory of culture. *In: The interpretation of cultures*. New York: Basic Books, 3–30.

Geertz, C., 1975. Common sense as a cultural system. *Antioch review*, 33, 47–53.

Geertz, C., 1978. The bazaar economy: information and search in peasant marketing. *American economic review*, 68 (2), 28–32.

Geertz, C., 1979. Suq: the bazaar economy in Sefrou. *In*: Clifford Geertz, Hildred Geertz and Lawrence Rosen, eds. *Meaning and order in Moroccan society: three essays in cultural analysis*. Cambridge, UK: Cambridge University Press, 123–313.

Geertz, C., 1983a [1976]. Art as a cultural system. *In*: C. Geertz, ed. *Local knowledge: further essays in interpretive anthropology*. New York: Basic Books, 94–120.

Geertz, C., 1983b [1974]. 'From the native's point of wiew': on the nature of anthropological understanding. *In*: C. Geertz, *Local knowledge: further essays in interpretive anthropology*. New York: Basic Books, 55–70.

Geertz, C., 1983c. *Local knowledge: further essays in interpretive anthropology*. New York: Basic Books.

Geertz, C., 1988. *Works and lives*. Stanford, CA: Stanford University Press.

Geertz, C., 1989. Toutes directions: reading the signs in an urban sprawl. *International journal of Middle East studies*, 21 (3), 291–306.

Geertz, C., 1995. *After the fact: two countries, four decades, one anthropologist*. Cambridge, MA: Harvard University Press.

Geertz, C., 2000 [1968]. Thinking as a moral act: ethical dimensions of anthropological fieldwork in the new states. *In*: C. Geertz, ed. *Available light: anthropological reflections on philosophical topics*. Princeton, NJ: Princeton University Press, 21–41.

Geertz, C., 2005. Commentary. *In*: R.A. Shweder and B. Good B., eds. *Clifford Geertz by his colleagues*. Chicago: University of Chicago Press, 108–124.

Marcus, G., 1999. The uses of complicity in the changing mise-en-scène of anthropological fieldwork. *In*: S. Ortner, ed. *The fate of 'culture': Geertz and beyond*. Berkeley: University of California Press, 87–109.

Micheelsen, A., 2002. 'I don't do systems': an interview with Clifford Geertz. *Method and theory in the study of religion*, 14 (1), 2–20.

Olson, G.A., 1991. The social scientist as author: Clifford Geertz on ethnography and social construction. *In*: Gary A. Olson and Irene Gale, eds. *(Inter)views: cross-disciplinary perspectives on rhetoric and literacy*. Carbondale: Southern Illinois University Press, 187–210.

Ortner, S., 1984. Theory in anthropology since the sixties. *Comparative studies in society and history*, 26 (1), 126–166.

Rosen, L., 2005. Passing judgment: interpretation, morality, and cultural assessment in the work of Clifford Geertz. *In*: R.A. Shweder, and B. Good B., eds. *Clifford Geertz by his colleagues*. Chicago: University of Chicago Press, 10–19.

Skinner, Q., 2007. Remembering Clifford Geertz. *The institute letter* (winter 2007). Princeton, NJ: Institute for Advanced Study, 6.

Culture as text: hazards and possibilities of Geertz's literary/literacy metaphor

Katherine E. Hoffman

Department of Anthropology, Northwestern University, Evanston, IL, USA

This paper considers the conceptual, ethnographic, ethical, and methodological implications of Geertz's influential metaphors of culture as 'text' and of fieldwork as 'reading.' In Morocco, one of Geertz's two long-term field sites, large segments of the rural population, Berber-speaking even more than Arabic-speaking, are unschooled and nonliterate. Women's rich expressive culture, including religious culture, is oral. Drawing on long-term fieldwork among Tashelhit-speaking Berber women in southwestern Morocco, I consider the language ideologies that shape women's attitudes toward the production and dissemination of religious oral texts. These ideologies complicate the supposed transparency of Geertz's literary/literacy metaphor. The paper reconsiders the possibilities of this metaphor for the anthropology of language, and locates Geertz's contribution and critical responses to it within the history of ideas and ethics shaping ethnographic research.

At the heart of the interpretive anthropology Clifford Geertz pioneered, or at least popularised, is the metaphor of culture as text. He wrote in 'Deep play,' his description of the Balinese cockfight, that,

> The culture of a people is an ensemble of texts, themselves ensembles, which the anthropologist strains to read over the shoulders of those to whom they properly belong. (Geertz 1973a, p. 452)

Moreover, in his article, 'Thick description,' he commented on these 'texts':

> [W]hat we call our data are really our own constructions of other people's constructions of what they and their compatriots are up to . . . . (Geertz 1973b, p. 9)

This metaphor has typically been considered a literary one, particularly in light of other parts of Geertz's oeuvre where he emphasises the layers of interpretation or translation inherent to the practice of ethnography (Keesing 1987, p. 166), always intended to tack back and forth between emic (insider) and etic (outsider) perspectives. The use of metaphor and imagery was central to Geertz's vision of a revamped social science, and especially anthropology, that would take its cues as much from the humanities as the hard sciences. It is fair to say this was part of the literary move, but also methodologically it drew attention to the anthropologist's task of writing or encoding. As Mitchell has noted,

> [C]riticisms of Geertz's work fault it for failing adequately to distinguish the natives' cultural text from the interpretive text of the anthropologist (a difficulty Geertz admitted himself from the beginning). They do not tend to question what is meant by a text. (Mitchell 1990, p. 576 n 5)

This is deeply problematic when one considers the work of anthropologists to be the rendering and sense-making of cultural texts.

Here and elsewhere, the culture-as-text metaphor has been roundly embraced and critiqued. It is not my intention to evaluate these assessments except insofar as they pertain to the argument I will elaborate regarding ideologies of text from the perspective of the Tashelhit Berber–speaking women with whom I work in southwestern Morocco, many of them nonliterate. For those praising and critiquing Geertz's insights, the humanistic component of his work becomes the focal point, particularly his emphasis on multiple layers of interpretation involved in fieldwork and the production of ethnographic 'truth' more broadly speaking, truth that by necessity can only be partial, synchronic, and piecemeal.

Geertz's attendant claim was that culture is public and evident in human behaviour (influenced by Wittgenstein's belief of language as public): 'Culture is public because meaning is' (Geertz 1973b, p. 12). Even belief, then, should be understood through the practices that it shapes and thus there is no need to get inside the head of the Other (as if that were possible). This focus on culture as comprised of public systems of meaning was an important intervention at the time, when structuralists and ethnoscientists were insisting on the interiority of culture and its grounding in the mind. Moreover, the notion of belief as manifest through behaviour is one I often heard while conducting long-term fieldwork in southwestern Morocco in the late 1990s. My own field notes are full of instances in which people explained others' actions as revealing their desires, so that what mattered was not what one wanted, but what one did (Hoffman 2002, 2008).

As I want to argue here, however, the metaphor of culture as text is not only a literary metaphor, but also a literacy metaphor. It seems to presume that we, whoever we are, share an orientation toward the practice of writing and the nature of texts. What is curious about Geertz's notion of 'reading' another people and culture is its supposedly universal and accessible means of explaining interpretation; presumably, we all read, and we know what reading involves. The levels of interpretation involved appear to be self-evident or at least familiar to the anthropologist. When seen in this light, and considering the places and times in which Geertz conducted his research, these presumptions constitute more of a starting point for interrogation than a fait accompli. It seems to me that scholars of the Maghreb must take into account the orientations toward text held by the nonliterate people with whom many of us work, and with them, to consider their understandings of the political economy of texts, meaning their production, dissemination, and circulation, as well as the ways people interpret, authenticate, and grant texts authority.

When these 'texts' are written artifacts, the question of access is acute, as questions of power immediately arise, particularly because individuals' access to literary practices is conditioned by wealth or poverty, geographical location (often a related concern), but also intrafamily relations – as when parents and especially fathers choose which daughters to send to school, and for how long. Keesing's critique of Geertz's notion of culture as shared as well as public is particularly acute:

> I suggest that views of culture as collective phenomena need to be qualified by a view of knowledge as distributed and controlled – that we need to ask who creates and defines cultural meanings, and to what ends. (Keesing 1987, p. 161)

Keesing contends here that symbolic anthropology, in order to make a lasting contribution, must be situated in a wider theory of society; cultural meanings need to be more clearly connected to the humans whose lives they inform. Moreover, he convincingly contends, views of cultures as collective symbols and meanings must be qualified with a sense of knowledge as distributed and controlled: 'Even in classless societies, *who knows what* becomes a serious issue' (Keesing 1987, p. 161).

Written text artifacts, especially religious texts, can take on a fetish quality for those without the means to decipher them, but such mystification is not limited to written texts. Literacy is a set of practices, as Street (1984) argues in his approach to cross-cultural studies of literacy; literacy is not simply the possession of the skills of reading and writing, nor a transformed state of individuals and societies. By considering literacy as a set of practices, we can ask what constitutes these practices, who engages in them and how, and who determines which practices are worthwhile and which texts authoritative.[1] When approached from this perspective, the operative concept of text is any kind of written artifact: a book, but also the numbers and street names on a bus, a receipt, a prescription insert (Wagner 1993). Looking at written text is one plausible, and highly fruitful, line of inquiry into the meanings of text, reading, and writing in Morocco, where there is a marked distribution of literacy resources and differential access to any of these texts and literacy practices.

Another way to consider the issue of the authority of texts, however, is to abandon the presumption that a text need be written. Instead we can broaden the notion of 'text' to one used by folklorists and linguistic anthropologists, and that includes the spoken word. Urban (2001) has argued that all 'culture' is really metaculture in that it consists of instantiations of renditions of convictions of what culture involves – that is, recognising the reproduction of culture across time and space and constantly shifting with each iteration. Such understandings presumably move us away from the idea of text as static, with boundaries, and fixed, to be consulted in its entirety and considered as a whole, much as Ricoeur suggested and on which Geertz built. Ricoeur's claim was that in writing we fix 'not the event of speaking, but the "said" of speaking. ... It is the meaning of the speech event, not the event as event' (quoted in Geertz 1973b, p. 19; see also Silverstein and Urban 1996, p. 1). But, we might ask, where do our Moroccan informants stand on this matter of what constitutes text and its authority?

In this paper, after preliminary comments on the culture-as-text metaphor, I will turn to a few observations from my ethnographic fieldwork among Tashelhit Berber–speakers in Taroudant Province to consider oral religious texts and the writing of culture. Rather than culture as text, these are texts as culture. Geertz's metaphor suggests turning our anthropological subjects into texts to then read, but this dismisses the uniqueness of anthropological fieldwork, as Handelman cogently argues:

> [F]ieldwork anthropology is unlike any of the humanities and other social sciences in that it is not a text-mediated discipline in the first place. Consequently, it is the sole discipline that struggles with the turning of subjects into objects rather than the turning of objects into subjects. (Handelman 1994, p. 341)

By 'text-mediated,' Handelman is referring to 'work whose material and products are both literally textual.'

The metaphor and its critics

Before developing this line of inquiry with ethnographic observations, a brief discussion of the metaphor and its critiques is in order. Keesing calls the metaphor 'dangerous reification'

(Keesing 1987, p. 165). Handelman characterises it as 'the single worst move of [Geertz's] distinctive, highly creative, often brilliant scholarship' drawn in the interest of blurring genres and extolling cultural relativism (Handelman 1994, p. 246). Roseberry's Marxian critique is perhaps the most widely recognised; he argues that Geertz took too much of an idealist position, rather than a materialist one, considering culture as product rather than process. He argues instead that we should 'ask of any cultural text, be it a cockfight or a folktale, who is talking, what is being talked about, and what form of action is being called for' (Roseberry 1989, p. 28). That is, Roseberry contends, the kind of interpretive anthropology Geertz espoused ignores historical production and the relations of power that produce 'culture' and in which 'culture' is bound. His is essentially a political-economic critique that chastises Geertz for being so focused on symbols that he fails to link them to the broader forces that have shaped them – in Geertz's metaphor, the webs we humans have spun and in which we are suspended. That is, as Shankman et al. (1984) claim in their evaluation of Geertz, the 'text' (or culture) seems separated from its social context. And as Keesing argues, cultures do not just constitute webs of significance, but ideologies, 'disguising human political and economic realities as cosmically ordained.' These ideologies empower some, disenfranchise others, and extract the labour of some for the benefit of others. He implores, 'We need to ask who *creates* and *defines* cultural meanings, and to what ends' (Keesing 1987, pp. 161–162). For in the end, few people do the spinning of webs of significance; most people are just caught in them (p. 162, quoting Scholte).

The second approach to text that I take here is from folklore and linguistic anthropology, where a 'text' may be either oral or written. Bauman and Briggs (1990, 1992) have elaborated the concept of entextualisation, which involves extracting a piece of discourse from one context and embedding it in another. The oral text then has the quality of being bounded and moveable between contexts, as does a written text. These texts may be quotations, jokes, or stories; they shift with each entextualisation. Moreover, the text's meaning – which is ultimately what we are after, if we follow Geertz's lead – depends on this intertextuality. Taken further, these iterations result in the phenomenon Urban calls metaculture: each instantiation or reproduction of a bit of culture is 'meta' in that it constantly comments on itself by containing a notion of an ideal or norm which it strives to attain – or intentionally flout. Each time an *aḥwaš* collective dance is performed in the Atlas Mountains, for instance, there are certain consistencies and other differences from previous performances. Both performers and audiences have clear ideas about the evaluation criteria for any given entextualisation, and can assess its success or shortcomings. This approach acknowledges that cultural products are integral to cultural processes. Perhaps here we are reconciled with Geertz, but maybe not.

Geertz drew attention to the practice of ethnography as both fieldwork and textual artifact, and attended most importantly to the relation between them. He wrote,

> The ethnographer 'inscribes' social discourse; *he writes it down*. In so doing, he turns it from a passing event, which exists only in its own moment of occurrence, into an account, which exists in its inscriptions and can be reconsulted. (Geertz 1973b, p. 19)

However, Geertz's position becomes problematic when we recall that the 'it' recorded by the fieldworker already consists of entextualisations performed by the people being studied. The fieldworker writes things down – things that were already his or her translations of the informants' interpretations of what people were doing, saying, and meaning – and then the fieldworker returns repeatedly to these field notes consisting of experiences and conversations rendered into text, and tries to make sense of things. By that point, however, the complexity of experience and the barrage of semiotic information has been selected and distilled into smaller and more simplified portions that then become the definitive representation of the experience or conversation. (Even the making of audio and video recordings, on which Geertz did not comment, requires selection and reification, and forces the researcher to consider how much of an event to record, what and whom to exclude, and how to deal fairly with a wide range of audibility in the data collected.) Fieldworkers do their best, at least when they work with *niya* or good intentions, but such are the conditions of the trade. Geertz was right to lay at least some of these conditions bare, and most importantly as he saw it to consider their effect on the analysis and description through which anthropological text artifacts, ethnographies, are produced.

There is another, arguably more sinister or at least Euro- and literacy-centric bias to Geertz's culture-as-text metaphor that renders it problematic and begs the question of insiders' understandings of text and power. Conquergood, for one, sees the emphasis on text as potentially silencing the subaltern and removing the performance of culture from considerations of its construction and reproduction (Conquergood 1998; also Palmer and Jankowiak 1996). This is particularly true in places like rural Morocco where access to texts is highly limited, relegated to specialists, and subject to criteria such as linguistic code to be decoded (classical or colloquial Arabic, French, Tamazight, etc.). As Ortner (1997, p. 4) correctly observes, Geertz largely stayed away from the trend starting in the 1970s toward examining questions of power. Even the ethnographic material he presented, some argue, cries out for an analysis of power differentials that Geertz instead described as 'clash of cultures' or 'confusion' of tongues, as Ortner argues in the episode over a French colonial officer taking a Jewish shepherd's sheep and unjustly sending its owner to jail (p. 4). Yet, does *not* engaging directly with political issues render an anthropologist dispassionate or, worse, unaware? Renato Rosaldo (1997), for one, argues that in Geertz's case it does not, for Geertz's plan was deeply moral and ethical, about humanity and interconnectedness. That may be, but I still want to suggest that Geertz's work displayed a marked insouciance toward the cultural meanings of text. This is despite, as Ortner argues, Geertz's placement of agency as central to questions of power, and his emphasis on accessing the actor's point of view. As Mitchell argues, for instance, 'the conception of a people's culture or political consciousness as a text employs a problematic and distinctively modern notion.' Moreover, meaning is never abstract but rather emerges from situated performances (Mitchell 1990, p. 561).

I am intentionally leaving aside the question of culture itself – or rather, presuming it exists (whatever 'it' is), that it matters, and that it is built of symbols that people endow with meaning. Instead I take the premise Ortner advances: that even if cultures were never and are never whole, complete, boundable, and distinguishable from each other, we can still accept 'the fundamental assumption that people are always trying to make sense of their lives, always weaving fabrics of meaning, however fragile and fragmentary' (Ortner 1997, p. 9).

When 'text' is religious, there is an undeniable power attached to it. Among the Tashelhit-speaking Berbers with whom I work in the Sous Valley and Anti-Atlas Mountains, this is certainly true of anything related to Qur'anic or other religious Arabic. Arabic text may be considered powerful not only in the sacred book, but in ritual contexts as well, as when a *fqih* writes a verse on paper that he dips in water to unleash the ink that the infirmed then drinks; or, in more mundane circumstances, as when an ill person feels intimidated by a prescription insert, or fears inscription for census, tax, or fieldworker data-collection purposes (Wagner 1993, pp. 29–30). Spoken 'text' may be powerful as well. Berber-speakers may evaluate fellow Berber-speakers as *šiki* or snobbish for speaking in Arabic; Qur'anic recitation and prayer are considered calming by many (Haeri 2003); reciting or listening to Tashelhit-language '*hadith*' (chanted religious parables and sometimes song) can be seen as a pious act. In each of these intertextual encounters, there is a stress on the oral text's integrity or physicality. From an emic perspective, the mere inscription or recitation is the act or the product; its importance is self-evident and does not require interpretation. Meaning, in this view, comes from the engagement with the written or oral text itself.

Rural Berber women themselves – not just the anthropologist – insist on the transportability and entextualisation of cultural texts. Scholars may see these performances as fragmentary, but the Berber women I worked with did not, instead comparing each instance against an ideal, an originary moment – a perfect model. How such entextualisations measure up is not a matter of anthropological concern, but it does matter to our informants. A key criterion for them is textual integrity: the oral text must be complete to be good. By way of illustration, I take the example of Tashelhit women's oral religious poetry and story-telling.[2] I focus here on a *hadith* or parable specialist, the elderly Lalla Kiltum who lived her late adulthood and died in an Ida ou Zeddout village during my fieldwork. Her roots were in the Tata region, and she had a reputation as something of a local religious authority, albeit differently skilled than the male *ṭalîb*, with whom women had contact only insofar as they were required to rotate serving meals to him and consulted him in times of illness. In examining Lalla Kiltum's orientation to religious text, and text as culture, I want to suggest that more is at stake than the largely professional question of appropriate practice in anthropology or area studies. Missing from Geertz's approach is a consideration of how nonliterate people themselves select, extract, render, embed, and otherwise turn fragments of 'culture' and 'text' into meaningful practice.

I turn now to a few ethnographic considerations of the entextualisation of sacred texts as cultural process and product. In selecting these examples, I necessarily recall the fieldwork process about which Geertz wrote:

> Doing ethnography is like trying to read (in the sense of 'construct a reading of') a manuscript – foreign, faded, full of ellipses, incoherencies, suspicious emendations, and tendentious commentaries, but written not in conventionalised graphs of sound but in transient examples of shaped behaviour. (Geertz 1973b, p. 10)

This was what Geertz called 'nook-and-cranny' anthropology, intended to build knowledge in spurts rather than cumulatively. Many fieldworkers recognise how partial their perspectives are when in the field, and yet, in leaving the field and rendering experience into scholarly text, there is a tendency to strive for what is ultimately an unattainable coherence.

Ethnographic considerations

Literary representations of sacred entextualisations

Geertz's insistence that fieldworkers 'write things down' is deceptively simple, and those of us working with transcription often work with assistants. Native transcribers can operate according to different language ideologies than those of the fieldworker. There may be disagreement over what to write down from a recording, how to write it down, and how to interpret it. As fieldworkers, we are concerned,

> not with how anthropologists write down what they hear, or not only with that problem, but also with how natives, trained in the practice of writing or ... reproducing and then translating, render spoken discourse that has been lifted from one co(n)text via the then extrinsic technology of tape-recording. (Silverstein and Urban 1996, p. 3)

I experienced these challenges with my university-educated and highly attentive transcription assistant, Latifa, while in the field. When we first set to work together on my Tashelhit-language cassette recordings in 1996, there was no standardised transcription convention for Berber, and many thinkers were preoccupied with the question of script choice, a question on which many experts and intellectuals, as well as Amazigh activists, weighed in. Should printed Berber be written in Arabic, Latin, or Tifinagh script? I had my own opinion on this matter, but more immediately, there was the question of how to transcribe by hand fluently and efficiently from my audio recordings with Latifa. We chose Arabic script, since she said she was most comfortable in it and could work quickly in it, and because it was well suited for the sounds found in Tashelhit (and could be easily adapted to represent Berber-specific sounds). There were no standard conventions at that point, nor word segmentation principles, and we had to develop our own. Issues arose immediately: do we transcribe exactly what was said, and if so, how do we graphically represent individual performances of speech to capture such characteristics as prosody? If someone makes an error in grammar, pronunciation, or lexicon, should it be corrected in the written record? I said no, and Latifa sometimes said yes, especially since we were using these transcripts as scripts for my own language learning: they were prescriptive as well as descriptive and thus served two purposes.

We also had to resolve a question that is most relevant to the topic of the present article: what should we do when a piece of 'text' such as a Qur'anic verse or Arabic proverb is embedded in the person's Tashelhit? What are the transcription rules? Initially, I wanted to apply the same orthographic conventions and principles we used for Tashelhit in transcribing classical Arabic, specifically, that we would write utterances as they were pronounced and performed in the specific interaction being transcribed. Yet, I immediately sensed tension with my assistant over this issue, for writing religious language incorrectly seemed like blasphemy to her. After discussing the issue a few times, it was clear that the tension was not productive, and we revised our conventions for the religious text. Typically when we worked, we listened together to the slowed audio recordings, and I held the pencil and wrote out the words with her repeating sections I found difficult. During our first year working together, this mostly meant that she dictated and I wrote. Working this way allowed me to use writing as an aid to understanding and memory, and it ensured that I remained mentally alert during the long and sometimes tedious hours of transcription. Gradually, however, there was less dictation and more writing, or simultaneous dictation and writing. We developed colour codes for aspects of the verbal interaction we wanted to capture, underlining Arabic borrowings and assimilated terms in green pencil, and underlining words and phrases in red that we intended to recopy and elaborate on separate sheets of paper to use for our language lessons.

When we came to religious phrases in Arabic, in the end, I simply passed the paper and pencil to Latifa and she wrote them down in *fuṣha*, classical Arabic. I considered putting a more accurate graphic representation of pronunciation in parentheses. But who, here, was marking the text? To my assistant, there was something profoundly unsettling about seeing the sacred word rendered profane through a non-standard orthography that privileged voiced entextualisation over standard and idealised written form. We had to find a compromise, or rather, decide who would retreat. I did. Even spoken Qur'anic verses needed to be identical to the written, definitive text of reference: 'the book' (*al kitab*). The transcription rules we had developed together simply did not apply to some intertextual instances. Qur'anic quotation was common in my field recordings in all kinds of everyday encounters as well as in more stylised speech such as marketplace oratory, as Kapchan (1996) reports from her Beni Mellal market material. Much as Haviland (1996, pp. 64–65) found in his work with Mexican transcriber-informants, recorders of discourse like Latifa often reject what they consider 'errors' in the texts they co-create.

Sacred verbal texts: Lalla Kiltum's house of hadith

In this second consideration from fieldwork, I want to consider what happens when the text that is entextualised is oral and a perceived rendition of a written sacred text. What kind of text is it, then, and what is the anthropologist 'reading' and 'writing' during fieldwork: the text itself, or the social process of intertextual embedding? To examine these questions, I present another fieldwork interaction from a recording of the recitation of parables and religious lessons (as per Schieffelin 2008) in Tashelhit, called *hadith* by its Anti-Atlas practitioners. I want to consider the understandings of text that emerge from these recitation and listening practices, and how they may contribute to what a Moroccan metaphor of culture as text might look like.

For my analysis of Lalla Kiltum's *dar lhadit*, as villagers called this recitation in Ida ou Zeddout, I am heeding Eickelman's call to focus on contexts in which knowledge is learned, elaborated, and reproduced, and on the value this knowledge has to the communities involved (Eickelman 1985, p. 18). In a traditional style of transmission for religious knowledge, the *shāykh* instructs the *ṭalîb* (e.g. Eickelman 1985). In the oral transmission of texts, there is a tendency to use exact quotation, framed in Arabic by *qāl lū* (Eickelman 1985, pp. 41–42; Kapchan 1996, pp. 142–145) and in Tashelhit Berber by *ina yas*, 'he said' (see the use of *niġ am* in Hoffman 2006, p. 156). There is an interesting authority in oral texts in Morocco where, unlike in Greece according to Ong, they are not considered suspect relative to written texts (in Eickelman 1985, p. 95). As Keesing reminds us, the distribution of cultural knowledge is complex, and there are multiple levels of expertise beyond religion (e.g. genealogies, rituals, magic). Given the diversity of explanations that informants give for culture, it is problematic to consider culture as shared (Keesing 1987). To Geertz's credit, he did advocate looking for the ways meaning is created in daily life. This is one of many directions in which his followers, including Michelle Rosaldo (1980), followed his lead with even more systematic and analysed ethnographic data that, she contended, is rarely transparent and needs decoding.

I met the lively Lalla Kiltum in 1996 in an Ida ou Zeddout village in the eastern Anti-Atlas Mountains where she entertained villagers with her stories over lunch. She was probably in her early sixties, although she claimed not to know her age, and suffered from excess weight and a dermatological condition that appeared to be vitiligo, both of which made her self-conscious with outsiders. (She had never allowed anyone to photograph her, and I was no exception.) The young boy in my host family had mentioned on one of our long walks that there was a *tafqirt* (old woman, Ar. *fqira*) who gave hadith lessons (the term used for parables or religious moralizing tales) during Ramadan. I told him I'd like to meet her; he brought me to her room, and I was pleased to learn that this was the same Lalla Kiltum. She greeted me warmly, saying that one hadith states that if you do not know something, you should ask someone who is learned (*iqra*), and clearly this was what I was doing in seeking her out. I asked her how she learned the hadith, and she emphasised repeatedly that she never studied and was not educated; she just memorised. I told her I would like to tape her recitation, and she agreed. Her father had been a *ṭalîb*, she said, and he called to prayer five times daily. Lalla Kiltum said she learned hadith verses from another woman who had also memorised them. She used to recite on Fridays for the village women, but interest had waned, she said: 'They're busy with housework, or they'd rather just sit now, not like it used to be.'

Lalla Kiltum lived alone; her second husband lived in another house in the village. The villagers considered them both eccentric; a few suggested they might both be possessed by spirits. Her home was a room above a stone compound whose courtyard housed a few cows, chickens, and a donkey. Once inside, only the open door provided light. The room was full of pots and black plastic bags hanging from beams and from nails on the walls. When I arrived with my young host brother around 11 a.m., Lalla Kiltum was just rousing from sleep; she dusted off a teapot and glasses and put a kettle of water on her butane-gas burner. It was clear she did not receive visitors often. She had slept poorly because a draft wafted in under the door all night. She started to warm some *azzkif* (barley porridge) for her breakfast, presuming correctly that we had already eaten. A neighbour girl peeked in to see if she needed anything, and Lalla Kiltum asked her to bring a radio; when the girl returned with it, Lalla Kiltum found the Friday morning religious programming in Tashelhit. Hadith readings and listener question-and-answer sessions were underway. We listened attentively, Lalla Kiltum's ear near the speaker, the children silent. When the programme finished and she emptied her porridge bowl, I asked her to explain the radio hadith. At first she didn't answer, and I faulted my Tashelhit phrasing. I turned to the boy and asked him to ask her so she would understand; he looked uncomfortable and averted his gaze. When I tried asking her again, she responded, 'Look, you should tape the radio, don't ask me. I can't tell you because I don't know those hadith. You have to listen for yourself.' She looked down at my tape recorder and asked why I had brought it. I said I wanted to record her recitation to replay it and better understand. I had understood little from the radio the first time through, I told her: that they were discussing the morning prayer and women in marriage, but not much more. She asked, 'Do you want me to tell you hadith?' I nodded yes, and she put her hand slightly over her mouth and leaned forward, rocking back and forth. She then recited for about 15 minutes.

When Lalla Kiltum finished, she asked whether her recitation was good. I said that it was, and asked her to rephrase in everyday language what she had just recited. She knew that I was learning Tashelhit and had only partial familiarity with it, but again she said that everything one could know about the verses was 'in there,' meaning on the cassette. She asked to listen to the cassette recording, so I rewound it halfway and we listened. When the recording ended, she complained that I had not taped everything; I explained that since the recording was long, I had not rewound it in its entirety. She insisted that I do so, and we listened to it all again. She verified the integrity of the hadith she had recited, repeating that 'everything you need to know is in there.' She declined to rephrase the hadith in everyday Tashelhit, and told me I just needed to listen to the tape closely and repeatedly in order to learn the hadith. Her body and speech relaxed somewhat when I put the tape recorder away. She asked me to drop a piece of dried ginger root in the teapot and serve us. I asked if there were other religious teachings she knew, and she said that she knew some words from the Qur'an 'that they say in mosque' (*timzgida*). As though proving her point, she said *bismillah* and began more recitation off-tape.

A few days later, Lalla Kiltum's husband told me that Lalla Kiltum wanted me to return for tea and recitation. When I saw her next on the village's main path, she greeted me warmly. We walked back to her room, folding back the plastic and burlap sacks that demarcated a chicken coop from the terrace by her door. She pulled her padlock key from a cloth belt around her waist and unlocked the loosely attached door. I teasingly asked her whether she feared intruders and she told me that of course she did.

We ducked at the threshold to enter and she took sheepskins and laid them out side by side in the dark room. She pulled the gas burner nearer to the skins as well as a small aluminum platter holding three dusty tea glasses and a small metallic red kettle. The decorated candy box I had brought her back from Venice stored a small gray box of green tea and a few chunks of sugar. She located half of a sugar cone in her stash of foodstuffs and handed it to me, asking me to break off more chunks using the tea glass. I told her I feared breaking the glass, so she instead chipped away the sugar pieces. Meanwhile I set the kettle to boil on the burner, rinsed the dusty glasses with water from a two-litre jug, and then rinsed the tea tray, pouring the dusty water into a shallow plastic basin on the floor within reach. I asked Lalla Kiltum whether she still had any ginger root left; she dug into several of the black plastic sacks hanging from wooden poles studding the wall, and found two small pieces. She put them into the spare tea glass and told me to rinse them. While I rinsed, she fetched some shelled raw almonds from another plastic bag. I took the teapot off the burner and put in only a small piece of sugar, as she refused a second. She put a small black skillet on the burner, then quickly browned the almonds before transferring them to a small plastic saucer on which she had poured roughly ground salt from a white plastic jar that formerly held a yoghurt drink. She pushed the saucer in my direction and urged me to eat. We ate the sweet and salty almonds, bursting with the oils brought out by the roasting, and sipped ginger and green tea in silence for a moment.

I asked her whether she would recite another hadith, and she silently nodded her head up and down to indicate that she would. I reminded her of the two we had already recorded; both were about conversion to Islam. The first was a parable of a student who had reached the gates of heaven only to find that his parents had been sent to hell because, unlike their son, they had not converted to Islam. The second told a tale of a girl in the time of the *rumiyyin* (lit. Romans, but also pre-Islamic people and Westerners) who, unlike her parents, publicly recited the shahada despite threats of tarring and burning from the *qadi* and *amġar*; when the girl protested that hell awaited the unconverted, eventually they all saw her wisdom, converted, and were assured a place in heaven.

After my summary of these parables, Lalla Kiltum started reciting from the middle of the second one. My paraphrasings, not surprisingly, did not seem to satisfy her; she recited the parable in full, word for word, without summarising. Fortunately I remembered parts of verses so I could recite a few lines with her. She understood at first that what I wanted was to revisit the second hadith, and so I reiterated that I hoped she would recite for me a new one. Did she know a hadith about the creation of the world, or the creation of people? I asked her. She thought for a minute, and said, 'They know that, those who have studied' (*ġaran*, lit. gone up). I quickly urged her, 'Please recite whichever hadith you want, any one.' She asked, 'Do you want to study?' I said yes, and turned on the tape recorder. Lalla Kiltum got pensive and I stopped rattling the tea glasses and almond dish so as to concentrate fully on her words. She recited a rhythmic chant on *tawḥid* (oneness or unity, one of the names of God) (see Appendix: Qualities of God).

When Lalla Kiltum finished, I turned off the tape recorder and she asked to hear it, as she had each of the times we had taped. She nodded her head up and down in satisfaction as she listened to the entirety of the recording, then I turned off the tape. She sat quietly and so I prompted a discussion about the hadith's meaning. 'It talks about people, about εql (reason) and ššk (doubt),' I remarked. 'What did it say?' I still hoped that she would paraphrase the themes of the verses into simpler Tashelhit, but Lalla Kiltum again refused and I relented. Instead, she repeated a few lines and said, pointing toward the tape recorder, 'It's all there. Study it.'

Conclusions: language ideologies and transmission of religious knowledge

In retrospect, I wonder whether my fieldwork and Tashelhit language learning would have bene-fited from memorising Lalla Kiltum's verses, as she admonished. Yet I was blocked by the fear of appearing open to religious conversion. This was a delicate matter given that many people among whom I worked believed that learning Tashelhit and Arabic suggested a latent desire to convert from Christianity, as did the young woman in Lalla Kiltum's parable. While I surely disappointed Lalla Kiltum in this respect, I did learn a few things about language ideologies and knowledge. The themes Lalla Kiltum's hadith raises about culture, oral religious poetry, and recitation bring us back to Geertz's literary/literacy metaphor of culture as an ensemble of texts.

In our interactions, it was clear that Lalla Kiltum treated the 'hadith' parables as texts whose integrity and completeness were essential to their authority. Moreover, 'learning' them involved memorisation rather than content analysis. This orientation explains Lalla Kiltum's desire to verify each oral text's integrity. She was disappointed and disapproving when she suspected that my recording was incomplete. She refused to interpret or paraphrase, which accounts for the young boy's discomfort at my insistence that she explain the verses' meanings. A text, in this view, has an integrity even when oral; wholeness is a precursor to accuracy.

In the case of oral religious texts like the chanted 'hadith,' the transmitter's authority is crucial. Here, the reliable narrator was a non-literate, impoverished, elderly woman whose life had been full of difficulty; she had in turn learned the parables from another non-literate woman. Yet when Lalla Kiltum insisted that the religious authorities broadcast on the radio were more knowledgeable because they had 'studied' religion, she reinforced a conventional hierarchy of authority in which those who 'read' written texts placed higher than those with knowledge of exclusively oral texts.

With the textual turn in humanistic social sciences stimulated by Geertz, one crucial remark that is often overlooked is that access to texts is not equally shared. Oral religious culture is to some extent shared, but it is also in the domain of specialisation, at least insofar as some individuals are considered more authoritative purveyors than others. Cultural capital is inherent in this knowledge, even if the demand for it – in this case, by other women villagers – has decreased and may now have disappeared. More people use 'texts' than the literate, whether these texts are written (Wagner 1993, p. 15) or instead oral, as I have discussed here. These forms of expressive culture necessarily challenge Geertz's proposition that culture be rendered into text, for they ask us to inquire into the multiple meanings and associations people have for texts, and how they may differ from those embraced by textual wordsmiths and anthropologists.

Notes

1. This position contrasts with that of Ong (1982) and Goody (1977) who posit literacy as more of an all-or-nothing proposition.
2. In this article, I will not discuss the *waḍifa*, a month-long corpus of religious songs, chants, and prayers recited collectively by both Berber and Arab women during Ramadan in a saint's tomb in Taroudant.

References

Bauman, R. and Briggs, C., 1990. Poetics and performance as critical perspectives on language and social life. *Annual review of anthropology*, 19, 59–88.

Bauman, R. and Briggs, C., 1992. Genre, intertextuality, and social power. *Journal of linguistic anthropology*, 2 (2), 131–72.

Conquergood, D., 1998. Beyond the text: toward a performative cultural politics. *In*: S.J. Dailey, ed. *The future of performance studies: visions and revisions*. Annandale, VA: National Communications Association, 25–36.

Eickelman, D., 1985. *Knowledge and power in Morocco: the education of a twentieth-century notable*. Princeton, NJ: Princeton University Press.

Geertz, C., 1973a. Deep play: notes on the Balinese cockfight. *In*: C. Geertz. *The interpretation of cultures*. New York: Basic Books, 412–453.

Geertz, C., 1973b. Thick description: toward an interpretive theory of culture. *In*: C. Geertz. *The interpretation of cultures*. New York: Basic Books, 3–30.

Goody, J., 1977. *The domestication of the savage mind*. New York: Cambridge University Press.

Haeri, N., 2003. *Sacred language, ordinary people: dilemmas of culture and politics in Egypt*. New York: Palgrave Macmillan.

Handelman, D., 1994. Critiques of anthropology: literary turns, slippery bends. *Poetics today*, 15 (3), 351–381.

Haviland, J., 1996. Text from talk in Tzotzil. *In*: Michael Silverstein and Greg Urban, eds. *Natural histories of discourse*. Chicago: University of Chicago Press, 45–78.

Hoffman, K.E., 2002. Moving and dwelling: building the Moroccan Ashelhi homeland. *American ethnologist*, 294, 928–962.

Hoffman, K.E., 2006. Berber language ideologies, maintenance, and contraction: gendered variation in the indigenous margins of Morocco. *Language & communication*, 26 (2), 144–167.

Hoffman, K.E., 2008. *We share walls: language, land and gender in Berber Morocco*. Malden, MA: Blackwell.

Kapchan, D.A., 1996. *Gender on the market: Moroccan women and the revoicing of tradition*. Philadelphia: University of Pennsylvania Press.

Keesing, R.M., 1987. Anthropology as interpretive quest. *Current anthropology*, 28 (2), 161–176.

Mitchell, T., 1990. Everyday metaphors of power. *Theory and society*, 19 (5), 545–577.

Ong, W.J., 1982. *Orality and literacy: the technologizing of the word*. New York: Methuen.

Ortner, S., 1997. Introduction. special issue: the fate of 'culture': Geertz and beyond. *Representations*, 59, 1–13.

Palmer, G.B. and Jankowiak, W.R., 1996. Performance and imagination: toward an anthropology of the spectacular and the mundane. *Cultural anthropology*, 11 (2), 225–58.

Rosaldo, M.Z., 1980. *Knowledge and passion: ilongot notions of self and social life. cambridge studies in cultural systems*, Clifford Geertz. Series Editor. New York: Cambridge University Press.

Rosaldo, R.I., 1997. A note on Geertz as a cultural essayist. *Representations*, 59, 30–34.

Roseberry, W., 1989. Balinese cockfights and the seduction of anthropology. *In*: W. Roseberry. *Anthropologies and histories: essays in culture, history, and political economy*. New Brunswick, NJ: Rutgers University Press, 17–29.

Schieffelin, B.B., 2008. Tok Bokis, Tok Piksa: Translating parables in Papua New Guinea. *In*: Miriam Meyerhoff and Naomi Nagy, eds. *Social lives in languages: sociolinguistics and multilingual speech communities*. Amsterdam: John Benjamins, 111–134.

Shankman, P., *et al.*, 1984. The thick and the thin: on the interpretive theoretical program of Clifford Geertz. *Current anthropology*, 25 (3), 261–280.

Silverstein, M and Urban, G., 1996. The natural history of discourse. *In*: Michael Silverstein and Greg Urban, eds. *Natural histories of discourse*. Chicago: University of Chicago Press, 1–17.

Street, B.V., 1984. *Literacy in theory and practice*. New York: Cambridge University Press.

Urban, G., 2001. *Metaculture: how culture moves through the world*. Minneapolis: University of Minnesota Press.

Wagner, D., 1993. *Literacy, culture and development: becoming literate in Morocco*. New York: Cambridge University Press.

Appendix: Qualities of God

Note: Orthographic conventions for Tashelhit used here follow the principle of one grapheme per letter. Where ṣ and ḥ occur together in a word, as in *ṣhin*, they are pronounced distinct from each other (not as in the English word 'shoe'): ḍ= ض: ṣ= ص: ḥ=ح : x = خ: š = ش: ġ = غ : ε = ع

The door to oneness I am opening to you	*Lbab n tawḥid aġ bdiġ a ti nawi*
Help me, my Master	*awsi gis a bab inu*
I depend on you, my Lord	*a bari kiyyi aftklaġ a ilahi*

Oneness is the key to heaven's door	tawhid ntat a igan tasarut n imi n ljnt
It's the best of sciences it can turn a person	laxiyar n lɛlm a tga tnra kra s
around [save him]	injm yan
It came first before humans,	ntat as izkur bnadm
he questions it and gets caught on it	is gis itawsqsa itġwid gis
Justice is limited to three parts	lḥukm krad laqsam aġ itgli
Reason, justice, it's limited to three parts	lɛql, lḥukm, kra laqsam aġ itgli
It's ( ) heaven and one whose reason is true	a igan ljay jnt d kra ṣhan ġ lɛql
Truth is forever, it won't pass anyone by	lṣha gis tin abadan ur sar gis izri yat
It's the impossible,	a igan lmustaḥil
something that one never dreamed of	ur ilin ġ lɛql
The one that is not eternal it never lasts	ur gis ṣhin tin abadan ur sar gis izri yat
The qualities of God are all indisputable	lwajib aġ kulu natn ṣifat n lbari
The opposite of them are impossible for God	lmustaḥil n nsnt ig ḍd nsnt ġ rbbi
He obliges all people to [follow] the shari'a	wajib šrɛ f lmkkalf
whomever it is	wana ira igit
for men and for women, all are one	ġ irgazn ula timġarin kulu yan ad gan
Free people and slaves	lḥrarat ula ismgan
They must know	iqn tnd ad isan
20 qualities of God, proof and more proof	ɛšrin ṣifat n rbbi dlil d lburhan
20 descriptors and others for good measure	ɛšrin laṣda ula kra s izrin
The prophets knew the wonders of God	isan lmustaḥil ġ lmur salin n rbbi
and that which has passed	ula ma das izrin
The one following the righteous One	yan dar iṣh tawḥid
won't fear Satan	ur iksud iblis
One who memorises them without proof	yan tnt iḥsan bla dlil
he is the learned one	nta a iġli
One who doesn't memorise them	yan tnt ur iḥsin
without proof he is of the animals	bla dlil nta a igan ġ lbhaym
he thinks he is of the people	iḥal is nit iga ġ ladmin
The one who memorises them without proof	yan nit iḥsan bla dlil
he is the one *lmuqalid*	nta a igan lmuqalid
how many groups there are	mnaw laqwam lan gis
Believer turn your back on	a mumn iɛṣan ini idrk
those who memorised they won't learn;	a tnt ḥsun ur a ieṣan
Say God don't take care of me	ini ur idrk ur a inklf rbbi f nfs
the one who is able	ila d mami tzdar
in the holy Quran there's enough to grab you	ġ lquran lɛḍim aġ nit ila d ġwi yan
Sidi Sherif it says in some books	sidi šrif a tinan ġ lbɛḍ n lktb
We took it and we followed it	nasit imtbɛat gis
20 qualities of God we want to present	ɛšrin ṣifat n rbbi as riġ a tnd nawi
We'll follow each one,	ku d yan nstbɛais
the opposite of each is apparent to us.	ḍid ns iḍhr nit
Ancient is God,	lqdim a iga rbbi
older than even the skies	lqdim ila urta ka lin ignwan
and there is not one creature except you	ula ila gis yan umxalq a ilahi bla kiyyi
Ancient is God, we have nothing	lqadim a igan rbbi tinġ ur a skrt yan
except what he leaves us	tins a infldn ġ lemur
Food for example,	lmtl n ṭɛm
if one eats he creates from it	iġd iša yan ixlq gis
God not food creates	rbbi urd ṭɛm ar tḥlqt
His will is his he does as he wishes	larada tins ur a iskr s ma ira
All that he doesn't want	kulu ma ur iri
won't be impossible for us	ur ikun f lmuḥlt aġ

One won't be ignorant of it	*ur as gis ijhl yan*
Now ( ) or doubt or ( )	*ġikn d ḍn ula ššk ula lmahuras*
He knows all under the earth	*iɛlm f kulshi ilit ġ du sa ikaln*
or in the sky	*nġ ila ġ waḍan sa ignwan*
One, belief, oneness is God	*lwaḥid a niyya lwaḥid a iga rbbi*
The Ancient is God	*lqadim a iga rbbi*
An example is food	*lmtl n ṭɛm*
if one eats he creates from it	*iġt iša yan ixlq gis*
God not food creates us	*rbbi tawant urd ṭɛm aġ txlqt*
His will he doesn't do what he doesn't will	*liradat ns ura iskr s ma ur irin*
He isn't in the realm of the impossible	*ur ikun f luḥlt*
There's nothing he doesn't know	*aġ ig ur as gis ijhl yat*
A place ( ) or doubt or ( )	*makan ḍ dn ula ššk ula lmahuras*
He speaks without a mouth,	*ar isawal bla imi*
he sees without eyes	*ar itanay bla ṭit*
he hears without ears	*ar isflid bla imzgan*
Even an ant if it runs along	*mqar t ṭuft iġ tzri*
the bottom of a stone press he hears it	*ġ isli isfld as*
Be it in one's heart or above the skies	*ilit d kra ġ lqlb nġd ila ġ waf ignwan*
or under the earth God knows about	*niġd ila ġ dusa italn kwashi*
everything he saw everything	*iɛlm flas rbbi kulshi izrat*
He has seen everything	*kulshi iqrb isi*
20 qualities of God we are offering them	*ɛshrin d ṣifat n rbbi azriġ a tnd nawi*
To the one who doubts,	*yan gisnt iškan*
the one who understand tells.	*ɛud nasnt wali ifhmnin*

A (fashion) photographer's reflections on fieldwork

Paul Hyman

Paul Hyman recalls his sojourn in Sefrou, Morocco in 1969, his encounters with anthropologists conducting fieldwork in the region, and his experience re-viewing his own photographs of Sefrou reframed in the context of the 2007 exhibition at UCLA's Fowler Museum, 'Sefrou, Morocco Observed: The Photographs of Paul Hyman.'

Paul Hyman, a professional photographer, took these pictures over a period of four months in 1969 at our invitation, mainly as a kind of *experiment* to *see* what someone innocent of academic social science who approaches the world through a lens rather than a typewriter would *see*. (Geertz, Geertz, and Rosen 1979)[1]

The one-page Introduction to my photo essay in *Meaning and order in Moroccan society* is unsigned. It was only last year that I found out from Hildred Geertz that it was Cliff himself who wrote it. When I meet someone from the field of anthropology, I playfully introduce myself by saying, 'You're looking at "someone innocent of academic social science",' in the hope that this might provoke some interest, since, in their academic circles, they probably don't know many people with that distinction. At least two people at the Geertz conference, including Susan Slyomovics, referenced this Introduction.

I now wonder if this one page, seemingly simple yet provocative and enigmatic, might offer some additional insight for those with a deeper knowledge of Geertz's work, his innovative thinking, his whimsy and his humour.

When I arrived in Sefrou in February 1969 wearing fringe leather pants, ready to 'drop acid' and search for Allah, little did I realise that I was in the presence of three anthropologists who were slated to become superstars: Clifford and Hildred Geertz and Paul Rabinow. What brought about this unexpected convergence of personalities in this unlikely setting? During the two previous years, I had been working as studio manager for a top New York fashion photographer. The purpose of my visit was twofold: to do something 'meaningful' with my photography before entering the commercial world of NY fashion photography, and to visit my childhood friend, Paul Rabinow. I wanted to offer my support for his major endeavour to date, two years of fieldwork in Morocco, a large part of which was spent in Sidi Lahcen Lyusi, a *duar* near Sefrou. I spent roughly a total of three weeks with Rabinow in this primitive village, without running water and electricity. This was quite a shock, especially after witnessing the botched slaughtering of a cow. Although the cow was held down by several men, it managed, after having its throat cut, to scramble to its feet and run off into the fields, blood spurting from its neck. This was a far cry from shooting a gorgeous model walking down the steps at Bethesda Fountain in Central Park, she getting paid $250 an hour, me shooting at a ratio of 100 to 1 with a Nikon Motor Drive, an assistant by my side holding a gold reflector, a hair and makeup person at the ready in case the hair wasn't blowing right. However, I did not get a single shot of the blood-spurting cow. The entire event was so completely unexpected and I purposely didn't bring my Nikon Motor Drive to Morocco. It sounded like a cannon, and since my main interest was portraiture, I felt the motor drive would only be an added distraction and somewhat intimidating. Gaining the confidence and trust of the people I was photographing would be difficult enough to overcome with the ever present black Nikon F around my neck. I was not only a *n'zrani* (the Moroccan word for 'Christian,' i.e. a person from Nazareth) but a Jewish *n'zrani* at that. The Moroccans didn't know I was Jewish, but I did. At times, this hidden identity made me even more self-conscious. Goes with the territory.

Two Peace Corps guys who had been in Sefrou for two years had very specific advice on how to photograph the Moroccans. They insisted that the only way possible was to photograph them surreptitiously from a balcony or similar hiding place using a powerful telephoto lens. The presumed rationale for this was their belief that, because of calls to modesty in the Koran, the Moroccans would not take favourably to being photographed. It was, they thought, 'against their religion.' Based on my personality, my photographic abilities, and my ethics, I chose a completely opposite approach. I was very public. Hopefully my work stands as a productive and valuable refutation of their advice.

Cliff and Hilly were finishing a five-year stint in Sefrou. Clearly we were from opposite ends of the spectrum in terms of background and sensibilities, so I give them credit for indulging me, their optimism about my would-be talent, and setting the 'experiment' in motion.

> We anthropologists who were in the field at that time – Clifford and Hildred Geertz and Paul Rabinow – discussed our work and that of the study as a whole with him, but offered him no thesis to document nor findings to illustrate. We just introduced him to our acquaintants. Hyman learned enough conversational Arabic to become welcome in their homes on his own. (Geertz, Geertz, and Rosen 1979, Photographic Essay, p. 1)

At our first meeting, I told Cliff that I was interested in learning Arabic. He was initially quite discouraging. 'Don't bother,' he said, 'after six months you won't be able to put together a sentence.' Rabinow to the rescue!!! On the spot, we evolved what I call 'the custom conversation' (*la conversation personalisée*.) With the help of the Geertzes, Rabinow, and the Pasha, along with the miracle of a Polaroid camera, I was able to give instant samples of what I was doing to the first people I photographed. Digital photography did not exist in 1969, and so the Polaroid proved invaluable. It provided a bridge on which to build trust. It also produced some funny problems. If there were two men in a given Polaroid, they began to argue as to who would keep the photo, so I often wound up tearing it in half so that each man could have his own image. So much for the advice of the Peace Corps.

To me, a portrait is a form of communication. It's a one-on-one conversation, a joint venture based on trust. Let me stress that this is *my* view. If you can make your subject feel good, then he will be confident that he will also look good, and that it's safe to be natural, to be himself.

I recently saw an exhibit of the work of Irving Penn, the world-renowned fashion and portrait photographer for *Vogue* magazine. Penn's work, in my opinion, is most notable and recognisable for his incredibly rich lighting, his stylised composition, and his incomparable printing. Style is the most enviable and the most elusive goal for any photographer, and Penn's style is unmistakable, in fact it dominates the photo, even overpowering the person being photographed. The exhibit featured portraits of prize subjects like Jasper Johns, Truman Capote, Salvador Dali, Arthur Miller, Ingmar Bergman, Simone de Beauvoir. To the viewer, these celebrity portraits have immediate and innate interest. I saw visitors peer at the small print to see exactly which celebrity was photographed. But Penn, a formidable still-life photographer, treats these subjects almost as if they were still lives. And their lives are *still*. We see little of what is inside them, what they feel, or their souls. I contrast my work to Penn's because he was in my milieu and I was unfamiliar with the work of Margaret Mead or Malinowski, et al.

When I first started photographing on my own, before apprenticing to my mentor, James Moore, my initial goal was to go beneath the surface, penetrate people's façades, in order to reveal how unhappy they really were. After two years in the fashion world, a new priority evolved: making my subjects 'look good,' and that was predicated on making them 'feel good.' During my stay in Sefrou, I met several Frenchmen who had been in Morocco, working with Moroccans every day for over 20 years, yet couldn't speak two words of Arabic, and didn't care to! As you may well imagine, this French attitude did not make the Moroccans 'feel good.' Adding salt to the wound, the Moroccans *looked up* to the French. Since the French expressed no interest in learning Arabic, it felt to me as if they were *looking down* on the Moroccans. To the contrary, my fledgling efforts to learn their language made them 'feel good.' This attitude helped form the basis of the trust I was able to establish. It was a clear way to demonstrate my respect for their language, and indirectly for their culture.

'*K'atz arf l'arabia?*' (Do you speak Arabic?)

'*Rir shi shwiya. Mashi bzef.*' (Only a little bit.)

Invariably, these simple phrases elicited a huge smile and a resounding, proud, and encouraging, '*Iyeh, B'zeeeeef!!!*' (No, not a little. Really a lot!!!)

Clearly, there was no evidence of any proficiency on my part, yet they were delighted that I was trying. Arabic is a language where intonation can add meaning, so *b'zef* means 'a lot' while *b'zeeeeef!!!* means 'really a lot!!!' This aspect of the language offered me an opportunity to colour my simple phrases without extensive knowledge of grammar or vocabulary. As my custom conversation slowly evolved, it helped me develop my identity for the people of Sefrou. Since I was out in the public eye everyday, my Nikon F very conspicuously hanging around my neck, people would naturally ask,

'*W'alash tsuerni?*' (Why are you taking my picture?)

'*N'ta mezzyen*' (Because you're nice), was my reassuring response. Had I studied Arabic for five years at Harvard, I doubt I would have learned these colloquial phrases, yet they were essential to my work. This very basic conversation, repeated again and again, encapsulated our identities as photographer and model[2] and formed the basis of my relationship with the Moroccans I photographed. Happily, given my time frame, a deep knowledge of the Koran was not necessary for the rapport that I was able to establish.

At this point, the discerning anthropologist might wonder (or more likely, not care at all) whether I would still be deemed 'innocent of academic social science.' After all, I had spent one month with Clifford and Hildred Geertz and four months with Paul Rabinow during their fieldwork in the Middle Atlas. Well, in fact, I still remain innocent of academic social science, but perhaps not quite so innocent of what I like to think of as non-academic social science, by which I mean: my intuition. I am not extolling innocence *per se*, but in my case, the innocence informed my work. Certainly, my photographic contribution as well as my written contribution to the present collection would be very different had I been schooled either in 'academic social science' or in ethnographic photography.

Rabinow's acknowledgment to me in his *Reflections on fieldwork in Morocco* was overly generous when he wrote, 'Most of all I wish to thank Paul Hyman, for his *stunning* and *perceptive* pictures, his *acute* and *unique* insights, and his friendship' (Rabinow 1977, p. vii; my emphases). The photos and friendship are well documented, but *acute and unique insights* fall outside of my professional domain, so what is the point here? Surely those versed in academic social science are quite capable of their own 'acute and unique insights.' To my mind, it brings up the value of turning to *outsiders*, in any field, for the purpose of thinking outside the box, of offering a different perspective, unhindered by the danger of becoming, for the academic, at times, a self-righteous dynamic confined by its own structure and tradition.

The following anecdote illustrates my point. The 'acute and unique insights' that Rabinow references were observations I made about his informant, Ali. These were not photographic observations, but rather behavioural observations. I noticed Ali's preference for dark colours when he chose from the selection of gifts that Rabinow brought back for him from a sojourn in Tangier. For me, it was a simple observation, yet Rabinow could relate it to his fieldwork. It was a pleasant surprise that someone *innocent of academic social science* could offer meaningful *insight* to someone who clearly wasn't.

Arabic vs. 'anthropologic'

Although Cliff discouraged me from learning Arabic, he was nonetheless impressed enough with my intelligence, for some strange reason, to suggest anthropology as a career. At 23 years of age, and still struggling with my identity, I nonetheless sensed that this would not be the most productive use of my talents and I dare say that anthropology is none the worse for this decision.

'But Cliff, that wouldn't work because I have trouble remembering names.'

'That's not a problem,' he assured me. 'Your informant can remember the names of the additional participants in your fieldwork.'

'Those aren't the names that would give me difficulty. It's the names of the other anthropologists and their works.'

'Oh,' he acknowledged, 'that could be a problem.'

Of course, I was flattered by his suggestion, especially since it came from someone of his stature. But the *Arabic* I needed for *my* identity and fulfilling *my* challenge in Morocco took only a few weeks to activate. How long would it have taken me to learn *Anthropologic*? A lifetime? Perhaps longer in my case since I'm a slow reader. Fieldwork for the anthropologist is infinitely more complex than my *photofieldwork* since it involves so many levels: the society, its religion, culture, and history all intermingled and informed by the work of other anthropologists, not only concerned with that particular culture, but with the phenomenon of culture in general. Someone said at the conference that Cliff never 'wrote' in the field. Fieldwork, for him, meant collecting data. The writing was done back in his office, post-fieldwork.

Conversely, my work with my subjects and the ensuing results were in real time: sharing and capturing a moment. Of course, there was the editing process back in the states, but it involved only the selection of which 'moments in the field' to use. This was pre-Photoshop so there was no doctoring or enhancement of the images. Layout, however, is a powerful art form in itself. How photographs are presented in a book or a magazine or an exhibition can enhance the visual experience for the viewer. A successful layout adds meaning to the photographs and their ability to communicate. For the layout of the photographs in *Meaning and order*, I was very privileged to have the talent and encouragement of Bea Feitler. Bea was one of the outstanding graphic designers of the late 20th century, having been an art director at *Harper's Bazaar* and *Rolling Stone* magazines. She also designed impressive monographs like *Cole* (Kimball 1971) and Helmut Newton's *White Women* (1976). Bea was a significant influence in the career of Annie Leibovitz, who, I believe, doesn't need a footnote. The fact that someone of Bea's stature would volunteer to design my photo essay meant a great deal to me and gave me added confidence that these photos were, in and of themselves, quite special. Unfortunately, Bea died prematurely in 1982 at the age of 44, and so we are denied any further contributions she would have made to the world of graphic design. The contribution that Bea's layout brought to *Meaning and order* would not have been possible without the insistence of Cliff and Hilly that my photo essay be self-standing, self-contained, and self-structured. The resulting layout is classic *Harper's Bazaar* of that period: one inset photo surrounded by white facing a full page, while the entire section is interspersed with several double-page spreads. Here, visual rhythm adds to the beauty of the photo essay, just as textual rhythm does in the written essay. The independence of my photo essay was a concept that Walter Lippincott, then editor-in-chief at Cambridge University Press, strongly opposed. Happily, the Geertzes' view prevailed. The concept and the result seem unprecedented: encouraging and facilitating a fashion photographer to have free reign in an academic work, even honoured with a credit on the cover. *Meaning and order* has sold for over $600 on eBay, recognition, in this case monetary, for its unique and rare quality.

The exhibition at the Fowler Museum is another excellent example of the power that a successful presentation can bring to someone's work. Having reviewed, edited, and printed these photographs over so many years, I never imagined that I could see them in a new light. I was astounded, at my first viewing of the exhibit, to see Sefrou and these people of the Middle Atlas as I had never seen them before. The size of the photographs, the magnificent prints, their placement (layout), their framing, and the tasteful use of colour brought a sense of majesty to the work. And so, even this 'mindful eye,' the photographer himself, was changed by the experience of viewing his own one-man show at the Fowler. So very deserving credit must also go to Jonathan Friedlander, Rahul Bhushan, and Susan Slyomovics for their exceptional contributions. Clearly, this event was not a 'one-man show.'

Beauty or lucidity? Or both?

This topic came up while strolling the UCLA campus with Rabinow during a break at the conference. 'These are beautiful' is the comment I hear most often when people see the work I did in Morocco. So I asked Professor Rabinow, my childhood friend, what might be the equivalent praise for an academic paper or a book he had written. '*Très lucide*,' he said with a wry smile. So what fascinates me is the question: What is the relationship between 'These are beautiful' and '*Très lucide*'? I offer no answers but hope the question may prove provocative. Stated in very rough and overly simplistic terms: if the anthropologist is a scientist, or a social scientist, seeking *lucidity*, then how can my role as an artist seeking *beauty* make a contribution to that science? In what innovative ways can *lucidity* and *beauty* co-exist, enhance each other? Can science and art each add to the other's understanding, especially when art can often defy lucidity?

Perceptions vs. illustrations

The word 'see' is used twice in Geertz's Introduction to the photo essay in *Meaning and order*: 'a kind of experiment to *see* what someone innocent of academic social science ... would *see*' (my emphases). Aha, 'they' wanted to *see* what I *saw*. As I said at the conference, 'I don't know what I *saw*. What I *saw* is represented in my photographs. More pertinently, what I *saw* is what I *felt*.'

Portrait photography is a form of communication, but it's essentially a non-verbal form of communication. 'If you trust me and feel good, then you will look good' is unstated yet must be 'felt' by both parties. I will leave it to the anthropologists to find 'meaning and order' in these images, if in fact they exist. Neither the Geertzes nor Rabinow attempted any rationalisation or analysis of the images themselves, yet each used them in a unique way. If Rabinow's *Reflections* can be considered a type of 'screenplay,' then my images are characters in his play. Good casting, don't you think? Geertz took an even more unconventional approach, making no attempt to integrate them into his own writing, or Hildred's or Larry Rosen's.

What did I *see*? What did Clifford Geertz *see*? What did Hildred Geertz *see*? What did Larry Rosen *see*? What did Paul Rabinow *see*?

Now, to playfully complicate things, Geertz uses the words *say something*, *view*, *comment*, *visual notations*, and *looks like*:

> Most photographs in anthropological works are intended to illustrate something, to prove something, or to beautify something. These are not. They are intended to *say something*. They are a *view* and a *comment*, *visual notations* of Sefroui life.... This is what, to a mindful eye [whose mindful eye? Geertz's? mine? the viewer's?], Sefrou *looks like*. (Geertz, Geertz, and Rosen 1979, my emphases)

If we add Rabinow's *stunning* and *perceptive* pictures, we now have two *sees*, one *say something*, one *view*, one *comment*, one *visual notations*, one *looks like*, one *stunning*, one *perceptive*, and one *perceptions, not illustrations*.[3] These are verbal descriptions of my work. Wow, did I do all that just by clicking the shutter?

I just want to comment here that most if not all of the credit for Rabinow's flattering description of 'stunning' pictures should go to the Moroccans themselves, for they are truly a stunning and proud people. My mentor, James Moore, a nationally recognised fashion photographer, often noted, with humble wisdom, that 'the model is more important than the photographer.' This is not a typical comment you would hear from photographers of Moore's renown, whose egos are often boundless. A simple illustration of this is the fact that I could not have photographed the Moroccans if I were in Algeria, or China. Sounds silly, I know, but think about it.

Conclusion

I am referred to as a professional photographer in the various comments made about my work in Morocco. To fine-tune my identity: my training to that point was in fashion photography. I was neither an ethnographic photographer, nor even a reportage photographer. I did apply my aesthetics, seeking beauty, to the assignment, which *was* reportage. Had I been trained in anthropology, or ethnographic photography, these photos would undoubtedly have been much different.

The work I did in Morocco has been widely circulated in the academic world, but until this conference the audience was unseen and unknown to me. This work was first published in 1975 in Rabinow's *Symbolic domination*, next in 1977 in his *Reflections on fieldwork*, and most comprehensively in 1979 in *Meaning and order*. Most of my work in Morocco was in black and white. Since I was predominately interested in portraiture, and I felt that black and white, being more abstract than colour, was somehow more intimate, I felt it would bring me closer to the essence I was seeking, without the distraction of colour. Also, at that time, black and white photography was considered more artistic, while colour was still considered to be more commercial.

It is now 40 years since my 'photofieldwork' experience in Sefrou and Sidi Lahcen Lyusi, and six months since my one-man show at the Fowler Museum as part of the Geertz conference. Although I consider the Fowler exhibit to be the crowning achievement for my output to date, I am still trying to decide which was the more shocking cultural experience. At this juncture, I tend to think that the conference was more shocking for several reasons. I could not anticipate the culture of an academic conference as I could a visit to Morocco. I felt more of an outsider, less integrated than I had in Morocco where the key to activate my ability to work was so much simpler. The reading of 18 academic papers in three days, the jargon, the various analyses, comments, complex ideas, and cross references, etc., was baffling. There was nothing visual (excepting my photographs and Susan's paper), simply no way for me to relate to what was being said.

In presenting the history and dissemination of these photographs and exhibiting them, the Fowler provided me with the opportunity to finally meet the audience in the flesh. It was gratifying to be able to get their direct feedback. When I was in Morocco, I often felt that I was intruding in some way, that these people, and their culture, should remain private, be left untouched. What a pleasant surprise to hear from none other than the Mayor of Sefrou himself, Hafid Ouchchak, that the anthropologists and myself as photographer were 'revered' in Sefrou, and that our presence had given them global recognition. To learn of and feel their pride was a joy and a relief.

A final personal note on the conference

I can only say how honoured and grateful I am for the opportunities and recognition that these outstanding and innovative anthropologists have accorded me, most notably, Susan Slyomovics.

If 'the aim of anthropology is the comprehension of others in order to return, changed, to ourselves' (Rabinow 1975, p. 100), then for me, it was worth the trip, especially after 'Islam Re-Observed: Clifford Geertz in Morocco,' which changed me even more than my four months in Morocco. Participating in the conference was a renaissance for me. The Moroccan experience had come full circle. Now, 'Hyman re-observed' provides a whole new world on which I can reflect.

Acknowledgements

'A (fashion) photographer's reflections on fieldwork' is my first published essay. I was very fortunate to have the help of two professionals, each making a very welcome contribution. A great debt is owed to Bambi Schieffelin, Professor of Anthropology at New York University. A truly caring educator, her intellect, tempered with patience and generosity, helped clarify my thoughts and give them coherence. Bridget Potter is an Instructor of Academic Writing at Columbia College. If this essay bears any resemblance to the English language, it is due to her arduous, but not thankless, efforts on my behalf. Ms. Potter is also an MFA Candidate in Non-fiction Writing at Columbia University's School of the Arts. *Il va sans dire*, that without Clifford Geertz and Paul Rabinow, my project would never have come into existence, and without the visionary and monumental efforts of Susan Slyomovics, would not have reached its fruition. If anyone is interested in further information about my photographic essay, please visit http://www.paulhymanphotography.com or contact me at paul@paulhymanphotography.com.

Notes

1. Page 1 of the photographic essay, 'People of Sefrou and the Middle Atlas' (my emphases).
2. I use the word 'model' generically; 'subject' or 'the person being photographed' would serve equally well and are, at times, employed.
3. See Susan Slyomovics, 'Perceptions, not illustrations, of Sefrou, Morocco: Paul Hyman's images and the work of ethnographic photography,' in this collection.

References

Geertz, C., Geertz, H., and Rosen, L., 1979. *Meaning and order in Moroccan society: three essays in cultural analysis. With a photographic essay by Paul Hyman.* New York: Cambridge University Press.
Kimball, R., ed., 1971. *Cole*, Biographical essay by Brendan Gill. Designed by Bea Feitler. New York: Holt, Rinehart & Winston.
Newton, H., 1976. *White women*, Designed by Bea Feitler. New York: Stonehill.
Rabinow, P., 1975. *Symbolic domination: cultural form and historical change in Morocco.* Chicago: University of Chicago Press.
Rabinow, P., 1977. *Reflections on fieldwork in Morocco.* Berkeley: University of California Press.

Appendix 1. Reflections on some of the photos that were most special to me

These illustrations are referenced by number as they appear in the photographic essay, 'People of Sefrou and the Middle Atlas,' in *Meaning and order in Moroccan society.* The descriptive titles are by Hildred Geertz.

Figure 1. A town-dwelling Berber woman of village origin (no. 4)

This woman was unknown to me. I just happened upon her in the souk one Thursday. There was an immediate magnetism. When I look at this photo I see so much warmth, confidence, pride, and love, not an ounce of shame or regret for her tattered wardrobe. The gaze is direct and seemingly all-knowing. We did not speak.

Figure 1. A town-dwelling Berber woman of village origin (in Geertz, Geertz, and Rosen 1979, no. 4).

Figure 2. Covered vegetable market in Sefrou medina (no. 6)
This guy looks like he's right out of central casting, and he knows it. Clearly into his own distinctive style, he's ready for anything. I photographed him on several occasions so we knew each other in that sense. I'm sure there were simple greetings like '*La bes, 'lhamdulillah.*'

Figure 2. Covered vegetable market in Sefrou medina (no. 6).

Figure 3. Berber countryman in Ville Nouvelle cafe (no. 8)
This was the typical 'How are you? Can I take your picture?' When he nodded yes, I sat down at his table and took this shot. Does his expression of pride have an element of playful flirtation?

Figure 3. Berber countryman in Ville Nouvelle cafe (no. 8).

Figure 4. Berber shepherd (no. 11)
This photo was taken in Sidi Lahcen Lyusi with the help of Rabinow's informant, Ali, who knew the man and asked his permission. The photo is unintentionally majestic on the shepherd's part. As a took several shots, I repeated, '*Shoof, shoof*' (Look at me, please look at the camera). He kept his head steadfastly bowed so I gave up trying, thinking that perhaps he didn't understand my Arabic. When I asked Ali why he refused to acknowledge the camera, Rabinow translated the explanation: the shepherd had brought his flock to 'camp' on Sidi Lahcen's land, because his homeland was further up in the mountains and since the ground was frozen for the winter, his sheep were unable to graze. As a grateful guest, he was expressing his humility, *kay hashem*. This photo elicits some of the strongest reactions to my work, even though the viewer is unaware of the social ramifications of the moment. It remains one of the most popular and powerful images in the series.

Figure 4. Berber shepherd (no. 11).

Figure 5. The Pasha of Sefrou (no. 12)
The Pasha and I became 'buddies' of sorts. From the outset, he was invaluable in legitimising my presence to the Sefrouis that he introduced me to, or to those who saw us together in the medina. His demeanour and expression are classic: complete and total satisfaction, with himself.

Figure 5. The Pasha of Sefrou (no. 12).

Figure 6. The day of Sacrifice ('Id l-kebir) in urban household, Sefrou medina (no. 32)
This was the closest I came to 'photographing Allah.' The pattern of the blood suggests his name in Arabic script from the sheep's perspective and to us, if we view it upside down.

Figure 6. The day of Sacrifice ('Id l-kebir) in urban household, Sefrou medina (no. 32).

Figure 7. Berber woman in medina house (no. 42)
Although she was uncomfortable looking at the camera, her pride and strength are evident, happily set in this lovely array of Moroccan textures.

Figure 7. Berber woman in a medina house (no. 42).

122   *P. Hyman*

Figure 8. Thursday market; this rural visitor enjoys visiting Sefrou (no. 48)
Known to all, affectionately, as the *majdoub* (crazy person), he was certainly one of the most recognisable figures in Sefrou. I photographed him many times. The expression on his face was always the same, as was his babbling and dribbling. I don't think anyone understood him but he was loved and considered to have special powers, *baraka*. Both the majdoub and any bystanders took special delight when I allowed him to hug me. Apparently he spent nearly all of his time walking back and forth between Sefrou and Sidi Lahcen.

Figure 8. Thursday market; this rural visitor enjoys visiting Sefrou (no. 48).

Figure 9. Singer (sheikh) (no. 52)
The power of the sheikh was undeniable. Whether you wanted to bless someone or curse them, the sheikh 'got it done.'

Figure 9. Singer (sheikh) (no. 52).

Figure 10. Herdsman in olive grove, village of Sidi Lahcen Lyusi (no. 64)
Of all the photographs I took in Morocco, this is my favourite and to me one of the most beautiful and expressive. Even with the man's back to the camera, this image reveals so much of the Moroccan persona. The shepherd is barefoot on a wintry day, his clothes in tatters and his animal scrawny and underfed. Everything about the photo suggests poverty and the struggle of life. Yet the shepherd has a spring in his step, suggesting an optimism. He is certainly not feeling sorry for himself, although the circumstances might result, for other cultures, in anger, disappointment, and self pity.

Figure 10. Herdsman in olive grove, village of Sidi Lahcen Lyusi (no. 64).

Perceptions, not illustrations, of Sefrou, Morocco: Paul Hyman's images and the work of ethnographic photography

Susan Slyomovics

Department of Anthropology, University of California, Los Angeles, CA, USA

In 1969, photographer Paul Hyman spent over four months in the Sefrou region of Morocco at the invitation of anthropologist Paul Rabinow. Sixty-four of his black-and-white photos were selected for the insert in the 1979 publication on Sefrou authored by Clifford Geertz, Hildred Geertz, and Lawrence Rosen, *Meaning and order in Moroccan society*. Geertz described Hyman's work as 'visual notations,' and Hyman as 'a professional photographer rather than an anthropologist' who catches 'the look of the place, its people, and its life,' yet the possessor of 'a mindful eye.' This essay explores Geertzian approaches to Hyman's images in particular and to visual anthropology in general.

[I]f what we see is to a considerable degree a reflex of the devices we use to render it visible, how do we choose among devices? Thirteen ways of looking at a blackbird are 12 too many for someone who still believes that facts are born not made, and that differences of perception reduce to differences of opinion. That they do not so reduce is apparent from a recent series of rather desperate attempts to get a sociological hold on the contemporary Maghreb – i.e., western North Africa – a part of the world which, resembling everything but itself (when Tocqueville first saw Algiers it reminded him of Cincinnati), has an unusual capacity for inviting the application of standard notions about how societies work, and then defeating them. (Geertz 1971)

In 1969, photographer Paul Hyman spent over four months in the Sefrou region of Morocco at the invitation of Paul Rabinow. Hyman and Rabinow had first met in kindergarten in Sunnyside, Queens, New York City. Together in Queens they attended Public School 150 and Junior High School 125 before heading to Manhattan's Stuyvesant High School. Hyman majored in French literature at Columbia University, then embarked on a career as a professional photojournalist and fashion photographer, while Rabinow went off to the University of Chicago to study anthropology. In 1968, Rabinow left Chicago to conduct fieldwork in Sidi Lahcen Lyusi in the Middle Atlas Mountains, his Moroccan experiences and local interactions yielding two books, *Symbolic domination: cultural form and historical change in Morocco* (Rabinow 1975) and the landmark work, *Reflections on fieldwork in Morocco* (Rabinow 1977).

Both of Rabinow's books on Morocco include Hyman's photographs. Eleven appear in *Symbolic domination*. Twelve more are scattered throughout *Reflections*, including one of Rabinow in the field – literally in a field, taking tea with his Moroccan friends (Figure 1). Although Hyman produced hundreds of images in both black-and-white print and colour slide formats during his Sefrou sojourn, only 64 black-and-white photos (including some overlap with Hyman's images in Rabinow's books) appeared in a third major anthropological work about the Sefrou region, the 1979 publication authored by Clifford Geertz, Hildred Geertz, and Lawrence Rosen, titled *Meaning and order in Moroccan society: three essays in cultural analysis*.[1] As noted in the Introduction to this volume, the essays by Geertz, Geertz, and Rosen were 'not closely integrated' (Geertz, Geertz and Rosen 1979, p. 6), although each was based on fieldwork conducted between 1965 and 1971 in Sefrou: 'a single small-city-and-dependent-environs of north central Morocco' (p. 2). Hyman's images were inserted following Lawrence Rosen and Clifford Geertz's essays and preceding that of Hildred Geertz, an undigested yet powerful visual mid-section that was an example – to borrow Margaret Mead's expression – of 'a visual anthropology in a discipline of words' (Mead 1975). In fact, Hyman's photos were almost excised from the final publication, as he recounts:

> Ten years after we got back, we had this meeting at Cambridge University Press, at a 25-foot-long, 250-year-old conference table. So Geertz introduces us, Hilly was there – they were coveted authors – the gist of it was they introduced me, This is Paul Hyman, a photographer from New York, he worked with us and we would like to publish some of his pictures. So Walter Lippincott says, Oh fine. Geertz says, We have a 72-page chapter we would like to publish of his pictures. And Walter Lippincott almost fell off his chair. He said, We can't do that, it's impossible, this is 1,500 copies, we cannot do it, this, that, and the other, all kinds of excuses, it's prohibitive, the

Figure 1. Tea with Moroccan friends, Sidi Lahcen Lyusi (Paul Hyman)

cost. Geertz listens to all that and he said, Well, we want to do it. So [Walter] said, in a last ditch effort to sabotage the photographs, This chapter might fall in the middle of one of your chapters unannounced, hoping their ego might be offended. Geertz, said, Oh, that's OK, and so here we have it.[2]

Hyman recalls that when Clifford Geertz heard that a photographer friend of Rabinow's was arriving for a visit to Sefrou, Hyman was urged to buy extra film with the understanding that the Geertzes would provide support and introductions to the people of Sefrou, which they did:

> I couldn't have done it without the Geertzes and Rabinow. They gave me credibility. They introduced me around town and they walked with me everywhere. First I took Polaroids and I gave them away. If there were two people in the picture I tore it down the middle.

Hyman's photographs – unlike texts by anthropologists – were of immediate value to their recipients. The photographer's generous acts of giving his Polaroids away created artifacts of friendship and obligation. Hyman recounts that he walked around Sefrou with his camera, not hiding what he was doing, even though initially few locals were acquainted with him or his project. He employed the celebrated Nikon F 35-mm single-lens reflex (SLR) camera, a best-selling Japanese camera launched in 1959 that heralded its superseding Germany's Leica, a dominance that persists to this day. Hyman describes his technique:

> So I was very public and people would come up to me and say, Why are you taking my picture? And so I learned how to respond in Moroccan: Because you're nice, I like you, and because we're doing a book. Oh, you're doing a book, when is it coming out? And so this little constant conversation helped me out and [established] my identity. Had I studied Arabic at Harvard I would not have known the phrase: Why are you taking my picture?

Once settled into Geertz's former place in the medina of Sefrou, Hyman became acquainted with his neighbours and discovered that there would be moments when not wanting to be photographed became part of the picture. Figure 2, originally a colour slide, is filled with blur and movement: a man grabs a woman, her colourful green-and-red patterned dress whips about as he tries unsuccessfully to turn her face for a photographic portrait. They are both laughing. The blurred image conveys forceful action. We see what photography curator Mia Fineman (2000) calls 'the traces of a classic slapstick struggle between human and machine,' one that is further complicated by the frame of an anthropological photo project conducted in a foreign place where men hold control over picture-taking events, if not the camera itself. Unintended by the photographer (or perhaps he is in on the joke), the playfulness of the man trying to hold the woman motionless is clearly erotic. Hyman comments:

> Everybody thought you couldn't take photographs of Moroccans – Koranic interdictions and so on. And you had to stand on the roof and take pictures from a distance. People loved to photograph Arabs because they're photogenic, but from a mile away. But photography is all about the encounter with another person.

How people presented themselves to the camera suggests the ways in which surrender to the authority of the photographer is enacted. At least while in Sefrou, Geertz famously shared this distaste for becoming the subject of a photograph. Hyman's rare picture of Clifford Geertz is Figure 3, a small, blurred square never printed beyond the contact sheet. Geertz is seated while photographed at close range. He is framed without any Sefrou context, although he is within the context of the contact sheet that also features Hyman's multiple visual studies of the *fqih*, a teacher in Sefrou (Figure 4). Viewers note Geertz's irate dismissive expression as well as any blurriness occasioned by an arm waved deliberately in front of the camera in

Figure 2. Man grabbing a women to present her for the photographic portrait (colour slide, Paul Hyman)

Figure 3. Clifford Geertz (black and white contact sheet, Paul Hyman)

Figure 4. Fqih of Sefrou (Paul Hyman)

order to ruin the picture, a gesture that remains cross-culturally the ideal strategy for avoiding capture of the self on film.

History of photography in Morocco

Hyman's previous quote (above) points to the absurdity of looking to Qur'anic interdictions on image-making as the primary reason why Moroccans might not want to be photographed. Recent colonial history and economics are more informative. During the 1960s, being photographed and owning an image of oneself was a luxury, except for Morocco's obligatory national system of the identification card that bears a portrait of each citizen. North African regimes possess an extensive administrative infrastructure to unambiguously regulate the identity of each and every one of their subjects. Morocco inherited from the French Protectorate a 19th-century European 'culture of identification' in which the personal name and the photograph are essential components of the modern state system of identification: in France, laws governing personal names (for example, the law of 1 April 1803, repealed only in 1993) restricted the French to names duly registered at birth (Caplan 2001).[3] France extended the notion of standardised names to its Arab subjects in North Africa beginning with Algeria, the first North African country invaded in 1830 and colonized. The law of 23 March 1882 on the civil status of Muslim natives in Algeria imposed the combined French systems of identity cards and patronymic surnames on all Algerian heads of households. In cases of Arab refusal to choose a fixed surname, Article 5 states that French civil servants may create one of their own devising.[4] The apparatus of French state control over the individual was preceded historically by registration controls for the French family, embodied in the family passbook (in French, *livret d'identité et d'état civil*; in Moroccan Arabic, *kunnash al-ta'rif wa al-hala al-madaniya*). Laws creating family documentation papers for a couple and their offspring are said to have been enacted after fires set during the 1871 Paris Commune, an uprising that burned registers of civil status in the Paris region. Demonstrators targeted official buildings for destruction, such as the Palais de Justice and the Hôtel de Ville which housed birth, marriage, and death certificates. For a time, Parisians could fabricate false documents and create new identities. By 1875, however, residents of greater Paris in the Seine prefecture carried family passbooks.[5]

French laws presuming a fixed patronymic surname and establishing identity registration for Morocco, a protectorate headed nominally by the Moroccan sultan, appeared much later than similar laws in Algeria, incorporated into metropolitan France as provinces. In 1914, two years after the protectorate was installed, the decree of 4 September established the administrative means to register only French nationals. In contrast, full and obligatory documentation of 'native' Moroccans was not uniformly enacted until 1950, six years before independence.[6] Over decades, identification documents were nonetheless issued in piecemeal fashion, with the earliest ones of 1925 optional and readily available only to Moroccan workers and employees in French factories and establishments.[7] That the police were in charge of issuing identity cards apparently contributed to their unpopularity and to the lack of compliance, as did the two required photographs in profile and full face, as if the bearer were a wanted criminal (Decroux 1952). Identification – in France, a civil and legal practice to establish citizenship – was placed under police control in Morocco, emphasising its role as a criminological practice foisted on tractable colonies to circumscribe identity without granting full citizenship.

Two other factors contributed to Moroccan resistance to French-inspired identification laws. The fear among the populace was that identity documents were a prelude to mass conscription. More important was the fierce opposition by the Moroccan sultan to foreign systems of registering births, marriages, and deaths; these were perceived as intrusions on Islamic control over family law (Filizzola 1958, p. 23). The formation of a centralised, authoritarian Moroccan state after independence in 1956 owes much to continuities with the bureaucratic French colonial state. Family passbooks and identity cards remain constituent elements of Moroccan sovereignty even as they are administrative formalities of civil identification that extend control over the population, a surveillance that was at its most efficient and rigorous in large urban settings. The capacity to identify criminality through records and photographs is salient to comprehending attitudes towards photography in Morocco.

Anthropology and photography

When Hyman first met the Geertzes, he told Clifford Geertz that he 'wanted to photograph Allah' (God). Thus, they two attended 'Id l-Kebir, the Muslim Feast of the Sacrifice celebrated inside Sefriwi homes. According to Hyman, if you look at his image of the freshly butchered lamb upside down (Figure 5), the animal and its blood spell 'Allah' in Arabic letters – 'it came out that way, three hands and the eye and the fingers.' Certainly without Clifford Geertz, notes Hyman, pictures of Sefrou interiors – courtyards, schools, and life conducted indoors – would never have been possible, as in the picture of the schoolteacher of Sefrou, the Fqih Sahraoui[8] (Figure 6):

> Cliff knocked on the door and he knew this fqih and he opened the door and I don't even think I took a Polaroid. [The fqih] was there with the kids, and I took two or three shots, and he closed the door

Figure 5. Freshly butchered lamb, upside down (Paul Hyman)

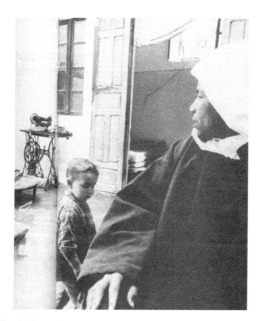

Figure 6. Fqih Sahraoui (Paul Hyman)

and good-bye. So as I was walking away with Cliff I said, Well, you know we got some good stuff but I'm going to try to come back anyway, maybe we can get something more beautiful, you know what I mean? And Cliff said, No.

Hyman was in search of God's image on earth, the divine in the pictorial, or at least beauty as he understood it and would create it. Geertz tangentially considered aesthetic aspects of Hyman's visual project when he penned this unsigned, one-page Introduction to Hyman's photograph essay in *Meaning and order*:

> Most photographs in anthropological works are intended to illustrate something, to prove something, or to beautify something. These are not. They are intended to say something. They are a view and a comment, visual notations of Sefroui life.

> Paul Hyman, a professional photographer, took these pictures over a period of four months in 1969 at our invitation, mainly as a kind of experiment to see what someone innocent of academic social science who approaches the world through a lens rather than a typewriter would see. We anthropologists who were in the field at that time – Clifford and Hildred Geertz and Paul Rabinow – discussed our work and that of the study as a whole with him, but offered him no thesis to document nor findings to illustrate. We just introduced him to our acquaintants. Hyman learned enough conversational Arabic to become welcome in their homes on his own. We were impressed by his ability to gain access and to mingle freely.

> The selection of the photographs presented here was a difficult task. We wanted to provide examples from a wide range of Sefroui activities, to include all of the major social groups, and still remain true to Hyman's own visual sensibilities – to allow the larger, ordered view of life in Sefrou that he found to stand forth.

> The nature of that view is best known through an unimpeded study of the pictures themselves and so the captions we have provided at the end of this section are merely description, designed only to connect the images to our written texts.

> This is what, to a mindful eye, Sefrou looks like.[9]

Provocative phrases stand out. Geertz writes of 'visual notations'; the photographer as 'innocent of academic social science who approaches the world through a lens rather than a typewriter'; the photographer with 'visual sensibilities'; the emphasis on Hyman as 'a professional photographer rather than an anthropologist' who catches 'the look of the place, its people, and its life' (Geertz 1979, p. 4); finally, the photographer who is most emphatically not an anthropologist yet the possessor of 'a mindful eye' – a beautiful Geertzian paradoxical compound phrase.

But what does Geertz mean? David MacDougall's wide-ranging explorations of visual anthropology (MacDougall 1994, 1998) suggest numerous possibilities for understanding these Geertzian phrases about Hyman's images. Historically, anthropology had already produced several important intertwined ethnographic and photographic projects. Alfred Cort Haddon (1855–1940) and his eight-month-long expedition to the Torres Straits in 1888–1889 are considered among the earliest to deploy cameras in a sustained manner. Other important photographic and fieldwork projects were Bronislaw Malinowski's New Guinea photos in the early decades of the 20th century, and the 1936–1939 collaboration between Margaret Mead and Gregory Bateson in Bali which yielded extensive visual documentation.[10] With hindsight, we use terms such as 'visual ethnography' or 'ethnographic photography' to describe what Hyman accomplished in Sefrou. Certainly, Hyman's visual project shares aspects of Jay Ruby's canonical definition:

> Ethnographic photography is a practice without a well-articulated theory or method. . ... The primary function of photographs taken in the field is as an aide-mémoire, similar to written field notes. . ...

Some images become illustrations for publications, slides for lectures, or, occasionally, the basis for an exhibition. Once the fieldwork is written up, the photographs are deposited either in a museum or in the author's personal archive along with written field notes and are usually forgotten. (Ruby 1996, p. 1346)

Approaches to picture-taking during fieldwork have gone through a variety of re-thinking (re-visioning if you will), comparable to inquiries into ethnographic authority and text-making. In *Reflections*, Rabinow offered key questions relevant to Hyman's project:

If the discipline of anthropology depended on participant-observation or ethnographic fieldwork, then why was it that so little attention had ever been explicitly paid to the nature and experience of fieldwork? And what exactly was fieldwork supposed to contribute to a practice of critical thinking?' (Rabinow 2007, pp. xi–xii)

If the word 'photography' is added to 'fieldwork' in Rabinow's formulation, the question becomes: 'And what exactly was 'fieldwork photography' or 'ethnographic photography' supposed to contribute to a practice of critical thinking?' Researchers scrutinising anthropologists' books and subjecting them to critiques about hidden literary and rhetorical tropes have advanced a parallel vocabulary to encompass critiques of unreflective visual representations of fieldwork. Malinowski's early photographs, republished in 1998, were subjected to these newer critical approaches: Malinowski's picture-taking techniques are said to mirror his fieldwork, a methodology characterised as the 'straight-on middle distance viewpoint,' presumably reflecting Malinowski's interactions with informants – with or without his camera:

The only plausible explanation is that [Malinowski's] marked preference for the middle distance was methodologically driven, albeit of an inarticulate nature. The implication is that Malinowski invariably felt obliged to capture a background, a setting, a situation, a social context. He sought to inscribe visual clues to what he was later to define in a theoretical contribution to linguistics as 'context of situation.' (Young 1998, p. 18)

Two decades after Malinowski's photographs, Margaret Mead in Bali articulated a similar vision, hers evoking Malinowski's approach in which context is everything: 'the investigator is minimally present, effaces himself or his camera as much as possible, and records the surrounding context of behaviour as well as the actual behavior' (Mead 1946, p. 678).

In contrast, so many of Hyman's images are in-your-face close-up portraits that they also inform us about the subjects' reactions to Hyman's presence, to this *darija*-speaking American photographer-*flaneur* sampling Sefrou's treasures with his apparatus in full view. Hyman is rarely the Malinowskian middle-distance photographer. Frequently he is the unseen present interlocutor directly addressed by Moroccans appearing within his photographs. In Figure 7, he is a valued contributor to an intense conversation; in Figure 8, a Berber-speaking country woman visiting the city beams an incandescent smile at him; and in Figure 9, Hyman and Rabinow are barely outside the picture's frame. Both are the honored guests and recipients of Moroccan tea hospitality, a social practice adaptable to any venue since Hyman's image informs that even a roof terrace in the remote and beautiful Sefrou foothills is graced by the unexpected appearance of the tea service.

Allowing oneself to be a subject photographed in intimate close-up or, its opposite, refusing to be photographed at all, are two extreme responses to the camera that intersect in fascinating ways with the practices of ethnographic text-making. Some individuals possess a seemingly blanket aversion to being photographed. In contrast and coexisting with a nearby person who shares the space of the picture frame is the delight of another person who enjoys being photographed (and may seek out opportunities to appear in pictures). For example, Figure 10 presents

Figure 7. Contributor to the conversation (Paul Hyman)

Figure 8. Berber countrywoman (Paul Hyman)

Figure 9. Moroccan tea hospitality, Sidi Lahcen Lyusi (colour slide, Paul Hyman)

Figure 10. Seated women, Sidi Ali Bousserghine shrine steps (colour slide, Paul Hyman)

a vivid image of four women seated on the steps of Sefrou's Sidi Ali Bousserghine shrine that captures an array of possible emotions when faced with Hyman's camera: one woman covers her face, another looks away indifferently, and some smile happily for him.

The omnipresent aversion to being photographed leads to my consideration of the cover image of Rabinow's *Reflections* (Figure 11). Hyman's black-and-white photo lends itself to theorising and speculation, as it has for me ever since I first set eyes on it during my first year at UC Berkeley graduate school in 1977, the year Rabinow's book was published.[11] Hyman, the photographer, is physically close to his two subjects, as if approaching directly head-on to thrust his camera in the face of a clothing merchant in his store in the Sefrou *suq*. In the background are items for sale displayed in boxes while a prominent middle-ground feature is the filmy night-dresses hanging full-length from the ceiling. A potential customer for the nightdresses is the young woman who stands even closer to the viewer than the shop owner; she is on the viewer's left and appears in three-quarter profile. Her thick dark hair is partly covered, although wavy tendrils and a curl stylishly escape from her patterned headscarf. She wears a creamy white *jellaba* that picks up and reflects much of the light. Her arms akimbo, she stares at us provocatively, a smile hovering on her lips, asking the photographer, perhaps daring us to come toward her and the highly illuminated whiteness and brilliance of her robe. In contrast, the man on our right stands slightly further back, situated in a darker receding plane of vision. Hyman's image captures his movement – the shop keeper seems to suddenly lunge forward across his wooden counter, his face grimacing in anger and his left hand gesturing, on the viewer's right, as if to contradict or counter-balance the woman's welcoming gaze. He conveys the opposite message, one reminiscent of Geertz waving away Hyman: Go away, photographer, anthropologist, *imshi*

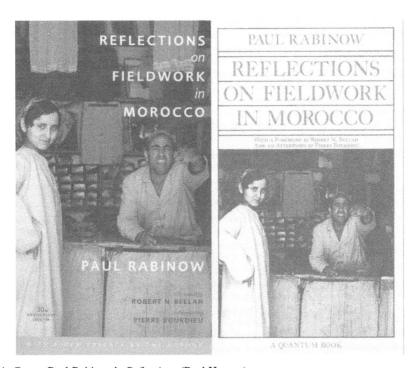

Figure 11. Cover, Paul Rabinow's *Reflections* (Paul Hyman)

Westerner, and interloper. Our eyes are constantly drawn to the blurred left hand of the merchant as he waves urgently, the hand that seems to achieve an impossible three-dimensionality of reaching out and grabbing the onlooker's space in order to exacerbate a sense of imminent confrontation and distaste. The hand's blurriness contrasts with the usual sharply delineated black-and-white focus of Hyman's image; it speaks of agitation at worst, peremptory annoyance at best: buzz off, don't take my picture, you don't have my permission, I hope I ruined your image-making enterprise.

What are the ways in which Rabinow's cover photo exemplifies complex relations between textual and visual authority? Hyman's images are featured textually and referentially in Rabinow's books just as Hyman's invited presence as the Sefrou photographer is warmly acknowledged by the Geertzes and Rabinow, best exemplified by Rabinow's heartfelt book dedication: 'Most of all I wish to thank Paul Hyman, for his stunning and perceptive pictures, his acute and unique insights, and his friendship' (Rabinow 1977, p. v). Textual references by anthropologists to photographs extend the meanings of these photos: Hyman's images produce visual, perhaps subliminal analogies to the experience of the ethnographic 'being-there-ness.' They carry out the task of offering glimpses into historical and social representations of fieldwork in Morocco by Americans. Hyman's photos speak to aspects of the inquiry into ethnography research methods – an inquiry Rabinow acknowledges in his 2007 Preface to the 30th anniversary edition when he refers to his book's initial reception in the 1970s. Rabinow notes that *Reflections* was described as a shocking, annoying book, its contents too personal, too sexual, overburdened with the young anthropologist's unwelcome descriptions of his inner states and his conflicts and everyday annoyances with his surroundings.

> I had gone into anthropology in search of Otherness. Meeting it on an experiential level was a shock which caused me to begin fundamental reconceptualisation about social and cultural categories. Presumably this was the sort of thing I had come to Morocco to find, yet every time these breaks occurred they were upsetting. (Rabinow 1977, p. 29)

In addition to framing the cover photograph of Rabinow's *Reflections* as the problematic intersection of fraught relationships between men and women, Moroccan and Westerner, anthropologist and subjects, nuanced and layered memories and meanings emerged as I interviewed Hyman in 2007. It is also possible to read the photograph in terms of Hyman's own experiences in Sefrou, where he was constantly followed by *drari*, the entourage of mischievous children that heralds the movements of foreigners, certainly in Sefrou in that decade. The shop owner was irritated by the crowd of little boys and gestured that they, the children, should depart, not the photographer. A different reading and triangulation of relationships occurs, one that places sexual knowledge and adulthood on one side of the counter, aligns the photographer, shop owner, and female customer in complicity, and establishes relationships through potential economic exchanges. Thus, the three adults (shop owner and female customer visibly, photographer implicitly present) are in opposition to the wild and willful taunting young boys whose energy and movement Hyman captures so well in Figure 12.

Indeed, the placement of two images facing each other in the Geertz, Geertz, and Rosen volume (Figure 13) encourages my highly speculative reading, if one takes the imaginative route rather than the arbitrary stance on how and where the photos fall into sequence. I read meaning into the order of these images: on the left page reproduced here (no. 53 in *Meaning and order*) are the adults who perceive the Western visitor as a potential customer and financial resource, welcomed and protected from the imprecations of the young. This is visually balanced and emphasised by the choice and placement of the right facing image (no. 54), in which the

Figure 12. Wild and willful marauding youngsters (Paul Hyman)

Figure 13. Facing pages, two images from Geertz, Geertz, and Rosen, *Meaning and Order*, nos. 53–54 (Paul Hyman)

butcher welcomes Hyman. Therefore, we can assume that both the shopkeeper and the butcher might easily be shooing away Hyman's entourage of children.

Captions

Another way to explore the power of these photos by Hyman as well as other images in anthropological texts emerges from Geertz's own lengthy analysis of photography in anthropology, specifically when he discusses the ways in which photographs relate to their texts in terms of whether images are or are not captioned. Consider Geertz's critique of E. E. Evans-Pritchard's considerable corpus of monographs, photographs, drawings, and kinship charts on the Nuer, the Nilotic nomads of Sudan, a subject to which Geertz devotes an entire chapter in his *Works and lives* (Geertz 1988). Geertz comments on 'the intensely visual quality of Evans-Pritchard's style... so apparent to anyone who has read much of him that a few allusions to particular images is sufficient to call up entire books of his' (p. 64), all of which characterises an optical style that signals to Geertz a passionate sense of Evans-Pritchard's 'being there' (p. 65). Geertz sees Evans-Pritchard's ethnographic snapshots as

> not so much illustrative as emblematical. Frankly, even ostentatiously posed, so that they seem almost like still lifes, objects arranged for ruminant viewing... or when that is not possible, meticulously composed..., the photographs stand irregularly among the word paintings, unreferred to, barely captioned... and for the most part singly, making points of their own. (Geertz 1988, pp. 66–67)

Thus, Geertz's main criticism of photographs deployed within *The Nuer* can be summarised in his own words as images made to 'stand irregularly among the word paintings, unreferred to, barely captioned.'

Captions serve to steer viewers to an appropriate emotional response: not merely how to look at a picture but what to feel when looking at a picture. In *Regarding the pain of others*, critic Susan Sontag highlights the acts of captioning images, the ways in which texts surrounding pictures are didactic: 'all photographs wait to be explained or falsified by their captions' (Sontag 2003, p. 10). Sontag's example is James Agee's eloquent prose accompanying Walker Evans's images in *Let us now praise famous men*, whose aim was 'to deepen the reader's empathy with the sharecroppers' lives (Sontag 1977, p. 72). While most agree that an image is open to multiple interpretations, in contrast, Sontag seems to say that captions close in to constrain and disambiguate meanings. Christopher Morton, an anthropologist at Oxford University's Pitt Rivers Museum, insists that 'textual references to the plates can be considered extended captions that operate to both narrow and open out the potential range of meanings within the image'[12] – those texts so often composed, as Geertz notes, of emblematic not illustrative messages.

Brief captioning is currently marked as the characteristic writing method to 'essentialise' if not 'Orientalise' people. Prime examples are the vast numbers of Algerian postcards produced and mailed back home to the metropole by French colonizers and settlers. In the corpus of postcards analysed by Malek Alloula in his book, *The colonial harem*, he focuses on terse captioning techniques – the recurrent 'types' and 'scenes' (likewise in French, *types et scènes*) that both encapsulate and eroticise a people photographed, i.e., the Kabyle maiden, the Saharan, the Moorish woman. Alloula published nude versions of Algerian female 'types' that reflected the pseudo-scientific preoccupations of the omnivorous colonial 'ethnographic survey' (Alloula 1986, p. 28) best found in repetitive catalogs of body and breast types on display in varying degrees of undress and diaphanous dress. For Alloula, staged images – recognised as studio performances enacted by Algerian prostitutes for the benefit of French male viewers – represented neither Algeria nor the Algerian woman, but rather French phantasms about the Oriental female, inaccessible behind the veil yet revealed in naked splendour despite being hidden in the forbidden harem (Harlow in Alloula 1986, p. xiv).

In contrast to Alloula's documented history of the French colonial photographic tradition about the Algerian native, if we follow Geertzian concerns about the proper deployment of ethnographic photographs in anthropological texts, the framing device of copious captions is necessary because they intertextually cross-reference images to written texts, thereby embedding photography in the words and arguments of the anthropologist's description and analysis. Despite Geertz designating Evans-Pritchard on the Nuer as the counter-example, captions for the photos in *Meaning and order* are minimal, perhaps more a testament to the last-minute insertion described by Hyman into an already remarkable but purposefully fragmented three-authored tome – or four authors if you count Hyman. The captions were composed by Paul Hyman with important input from Hildred Geertz, who also winnowed down Hyman's large number of photos for publication.[13] Unlike the presentation in *Meaning and order*, the people depicted in Hyman's images are deeply embedded in Rabinow's narratives, certainly in *Reflections*: photos are tagged with brief but evocatively personal, sometimes humorous captions always cross-referenced to the text. Furthermore, rich, layered readings do become part of the captions (or lack of captioning) when viewers see the same Hyman photo appearing in Geertz, Geertz, and Rosen and Rabinow's respective works.

Afterlives

Visual anthropology assumes that its importance derives from the fact that photographs objectively preserve fading and dying cultures, places, and people of the past for future analysis (Edwards 2001, Edwards and Hart 2004a, b). Although this type of 'salvage' ethnographic recording was of no interest to Hyman, there are nevertheless obvious re-uses of his photographs through projects of re-photography intimately linked to witnessing a changed Sefrou. Re-photography, also termed 'repeat photography,' is a method used to monitor physical changes to places and people. It calls for no less than two images placed side by side in visual counterpoint: a historically prior image is placed on the page next to and against a set of deliberate re-takes. The first image, 'original' in time, records an historical truth in rich ethnographic detail, exemplified by Hyman's Sefrou photographs of 1969, which is simultaneously an historic vision, an archival image, a postcard, and an art photo. Comparisons between the 'original' and the contemporary 'repeat' photographs shot in the same location and at the same angle some 40 years later create an afterlife with which to trace Sefrou's visual landmarks since altered or disappeared (even as they possess yet another afterlife by being displayed on the walls of UCLA's Fowler Museum). Places in Sefrou are made new through prior visual anthropological documentation. When I returned to the exact location where Hyman photographed in the medina, sometimes selective aspects of the façade of the walled city were altered; for example, in my photo of a street wired with satellite dishes and telephone lines and dotted with internet cafés that were not present or even imagined in 1969 Morocco (Figure 14). A more striking example of change is Hyman's photo taken at the shrine of Sidi Bousserghine, then surrounded by verdant park land, placed constructively next to mine showing the same land paved over, with an overlook, promenade, and parking (Figures 15 and 16).

Another afterlife occurs in photos of Sefrou individuals never anonymous to their fellow Sefriwis – at least not in the way that ethnographic texts are capable of creating composite subjects or pseudonymous characters that inhabit anthropologists' written accounts.[14] Hyman's

Figure 14. Sefrou medina (Susan Slyomovics, June 2007)

Figure 15. Sidi Bousserghine, 1969 (Paul Hyman), and 2007 (Susan Slyomovics)

Figure 16. Sidi Bousserghine, 2007 (Susan Slyomovics)

1969 photograph on the cover of Rabinow's *Reflections* (Figure 11) depicts a shop owner who might be shooing away – pick your object – the viewer, the photographer, or perhaps Sefrou's pack of children. To the people of Sefrou the shopkeeper is readily identifiable as a Soussi merchant, a Berber from Morocco's High Atlas regions, part of the rural in-migration to urban Sefrou. I was told his name is Dassi Kacem. The young woman who appears in the picture next to him was identified as Khadija Boussougua of the Ait Youssi tribe from the nearby village of Kouchata. At the time Hyman photographed them together, Khadija was affianced to Dassi Kacem. Hyman captured flirtatious pre-nuptial moments in the couple's life before they two would marry and move to Meknes where Dassi Kacem and his wife are retired as of this writing.

Hyman's photographs possess a visual afterlife because to this day they give viewing pleasure to Sefriwis who revel in the formerly youthful faces of the town's inhabitants: Dassi Kacem and Khadija (Figure 11); Mohammed Alaoui, then the Pasha of Sefrou (Geertz, Geertz, and Rosen 1979, Hyman's photo no. 12); and Khadija, maid to the Geertzes (photo no. 22, briefly captioned 'Woman shopping in medina'). Hyman's photos continue to circulate in Sefrou. While walking in the suq of Sefrou in the summer of 2007, I recognised a Hyman photo (no. 48) taped to the window of a store owned by Merouane Mimet. It was Hyman's image, now captioned briefly as the '*majdoub*' – literally the 'possessed,' a kind of a gentle madman (Figure 17). Merouane identified him as Mamas Charaf. When I asked why the picture was on display, he replied that the people of Sefrou liked and missed Mamas, who had died around 1971 before Merouane was born. Merouane maintains that the image is a way to remember and collect stories about Mamas, Sefrou's majdoub, because the image brings pleasurable memories to passers-by. Consequently, the domain of the brief caption about Sefrou as published in the works of Hyman, Rabinow, Rosen, and the Geertzes expands to include a name, a history, and knowledge about the town's affection for its departed son. When I asked to photograph Merouane next to the

Figure 17. Merouane Mimet and the *majdoub* (Susan Slyomovics, June 2007)

photo of Mamas, he chose to pose holding a bound photocopy of *Meaning and order*, as if to attach himself to the latest exchange of images circulating across generations and between Moroccans and Americans. He does a brisk business scanning and photocopying books and articles about Sefrou, specialising in works by American anthropologists that are not widely available in Morocco and much in demand by university students.[15] If anthropologists in Sefrou employed pseudonyms to mask and protect Moroccan identities, then Hyman's project resembles benign aspects of the Moroccan national identity card photographs in that his photos reveal the faces of actual Moroccans, instantly recognisable and named during my June–July 2007 visit to Sefrou. Photographic portraits are not easily rendered anonymous; they possess and proclaim their own and their subjects' biography and autobiography.

Notes

1. Other works that feature Hyman's Sefrou photographs are Saltman 1973, as well as his photos from Geertz, Geertz, and Rosen 1979, separately reproduced and bound in a limited edition of 300 by Halliday Lithograph Corporation, West Hanover, MA, 1979.
2. All Paul Hyman quotes are from interviews with the author in New York City, 24–25 June 2007.
3. This section on colonial photography in Morocco is excerpted from my work on *The performance of human rights in Morocco*, chapter four on the 1981 Casablanca uprising (Slyomovics 2005, pp. 101–131).
4. The decree is in Estoublon and Lefébure 1896, 500. Article 5 appears on p. 574.
5. On the chaos of identity brought about by the burning of city records, see Bertillon 1883, 5. On the family passbook, see 'Historique du livret de famille,' available at http://pagesperso-orange.fr/paysdaigre/genea/textes/questions/lelivretdefamille.htm.
6. On the history and law of family names, see Chafi 1989, 1999.
7. See the *dahir* of 14 February 1925, published in Vuillet 1936, 22–24.

8. According to Hafid Ouchchak, elected president (i.e. mayor) of the municipality of Sefrou, if Hyman's picture had been taken in 1963 rather than 1969, he would have been among the children photographed (Ouchchak, personal communication, Sefrou, June 2007).

9. Geertz, Geertz, and Rosen 1979, n.p. Hildred Geertz confirmed Clifford Geertz's authorship when she attended the 10–13 November 2006 Park Avenue Armory show of Hyman's photographs and informed Hyman.

10. On early histories, see Jacknis 1984, 1988.

11. In the interest of full disclosure, I too was among the legions of intrepid trekkers and throngs sipping mint tea in the 'Soco Chico' cafés within the walls of Tangier. In 1969 at the age of 18, I escaped from my summer school programme near Barcelona, hitchhiked through Andalusia, and on a whim (the impulse that reroutes a life), I boarded the ferry from Malaga to Tangier. The key destinations at the time were the vibrant walled city squares of Tangier, Marrakesh, and Fez, and the beaches of Essaouira where the experimental troupe, 'The Living Theater,' had set up its 1969 summer quarters. Now in our 50s, my Moroccan friends and I continue to reflect on our respective and retrospective exchanges about 1960s Morocco. They tell me of their parents' shock at the 60s wave of foreigners, and contrast their own urban-based generation of post-independence Moroccans who believed they too belonged to a worldwide 60s youth culture. We shared similar aspirations and passions for innovative cinema, fashion, leftist movements, the culture of *tiers-mondisme*, and the revolutionary sexual politics that swept post-1968 Paris, New York, and Prague no less than their own country, and its legacy of the 23 May 1965 Casablanca student protests.

12. Anthropologist Barbara Wolpert strongly disagrees with Geertz's description of Evans-Pritchard. She notes that Evans-Pritchard refers repeatedly to photographs within the text, emphasising the close cross-referencing mechanisms between the visual and the textual (Wolpert 2000). For extended commentary and discussion, see Morton 2000.

13. The visual section of *Meaning and order*, titled 'People of Sefrou and the Middle Atlas,' was designed by Bea Feitler, a friend of Hyman, then the well known art director at *Harper's Bazaar* and later at *Ms. Magazine*, *Rolling Stone*, *Self*, and *Vanity Fair*.

14. Paul Rabinow writes (email communication, 13 January 2008) that his use of pseudonyms was 'not to protect the Moroccans. The gendarmes who regularly visited the village as well as every other official knew who I was talking to. The pseudonyms were another bit of anthropological "ethics" and imposed on me.'

15. Merouane Mimet requests that American anthropologists forward our reproducible materials for recirculation in Morocco via underground channels. He will videotape and interview you when you arrive in Sefrou. He is of another generation of visual and textual historians in Sefrou.

References

Alloula, M., 1986. *The colonial harem*. Minneapolis: University of Minnesota Press.

Bertillon, A., 1883. *L'identité des récidivistes et la loi de relégation*. Paris: G. Masson.

Caplan, J., 2001. 'This or that particular person': protocols of identification in nineteenth-century Europe. *In*: Jane Caplan and John Torpey, eds. *Documenting individual identity: the development of state practices in the modern world*. Princeton, NJ: Princeton University Press, 49–66.

Chafi, M., 1989. Le nom de famille au Maroc. *Revue juridique et politique*, 1, 3–17.

Chafi, M., 1999. *Al-Ism al-'a'ili bi al-Maghrib*. Marrakesh: Dar Walili.

Decroux, P., 1952. L'état civil et les Marocains. *Revue juridique et politique de l'union française*, 6, 1–18.

Edwards, E., 2001. Material beings: objecthood and ethnographic photographs. *Visual studies*, 12, 67–75.

Edwards, E. and Hart, J., 2004a. Introduction. *In*: Elizabeth Edwards and Janice Hart, eds. *Photographs objects histories: on the materiality of images*. London: Routledge, 1–15.

Edwards, E. and Hart, J., 2004b. Mixed box: the cultural biography of a box of 'ethnographic photographs.'. *In*: Elizabeth Edwards and Janice Hart, eds. *Photographs objects histories: on the materiality of images*. London: Routledge, 47–61.

Estoublon, R. and Lefébure, A., 1896. *Code de l'Algérie annoté: Recueil chronologique des lois, ordonnances, décrets, arrêtés, circulaires, etc., formant la législation algérienne actuellement en vigueur, avec les travaux préparatoires et l'indication de la jurisprudence*. Algiers: A. Jourdan.

Family Passbook, *Historique du livret de famille*. Available from: http://pagesperso-orange.fr/paysdaigre/genea/textes/questions/lelivretdefamille.htm. [Accessed 30 September 2008].

Filizzola, S., 1958. *L'organisation de l'état civil au Maroc*. Rabat: Librairie Générale de Droit et de Jurisprudence.

Fineman, M., 2000. *Other pictures: anonymous photographs from the Thomas Walther collection*. Santa Fe, NM: Twin Palms.

Geertz, C., 1971. In search of North Africa. *New York review of books*, 16 (7), 22–24.

Geertz, C., 1988. Slide show: Evans-Pritchard's African transparencies. *In*: Clifford Geertz, ed. *Works and lives: the anthropologist as author*. Stanford, CA: Stanford University Press, 49–72.

Geertz, C., Geertz, H., and Rosen, L., 1979. *Meaning and order in Moroccan society: three essays in cultural analysis. With a photographic essay by Paul Hyman*. New York: Cambridge University Press.

Jacknis, I., 1984. Franz Boas and photography. *Studies in visual communication*, 10 (1), 2–60.

Jacknis, I., 1988. Margaret Mead and Gregory Bateson in Bali: their use of photography and film. *Cultural anthropology*, 3 (2), 160–177.

MacDougall, D., 1994. Whose story is it? *In*: Lucien Taylor, ed. *Visualizing theory: selected essays from V.A.R., 1990–1994*. New York: Routledge, 27–36.

MacDougall, D., 1998. Visual anthropology and the ways of knowing. *In*: David MacDougall, ed. *Transcultural cinema*, ed. Lucien Taylor. Princeton, NJ: Princeton University Press, 61–92.

Mead, M., 1946. Research on primitive children. *In*: Leonard Carmichael, ed. *Manual of child psychology*. New York: John Wiley & Sons, 667–706.

Mead, M., 1975. Visual anthropology in a discipline of words. *In*: Paul Hockings, ed. *Principles of visual anthropology*. The Hague: Mouton.

Morton, C., 2000. Commentary: the anthropologist as photographer: reading the monograph and reading the archive. *Visual anthropology*, 13, 389–400.

Rabinow, P., 1975. *Symbolic domination: cultural form and historical change in Morocco*. Chicago: University of Chicago Press.

Rabinow, P., 1977. *Reflections on fieldwork in Morocco*. Berkeley: University of California Press.

Rabinow, P., 2007. *Reflections on fieldwork in Morocco*, Thirtieth anniversary ed. Berkeley: University of California Press.

Ruby, J., 1996. Visual anthropology. *In*: David Levinson and Melvin Ember, eds. *Encyclopedia of cultural anthropology*. New York: Henry Holt, vol. 4, 1345–51.

Saltman, D., 1973. *The Marrakech Express: a train of thought*. New York: Links.

Slyomovics, S., 2005. *The performance of human rights in Morocco*. Philadelphia: University of Pennsylvania Press.

Sontag, S., 1977. *On photography*. New York: Farrar, Straus and Giroux.

Sontag, S., 2003. *Regarding the pain of others*. New York: Farrar, Straus and Giroux.

Vuillet, P., 1936. *Code marocain du travail*. Rabat: Publications Juridiques Marocaines.

Wolpert, B., 2000. The anthropologist as photographer: the visual construction of ethnographic authority. *Visual anthropology*, 13, 321–343.

Young, M., 1998. *Malinowski's Kiriwina: fieldwork photography, 1915–1918*. Chicago: University of Chicago Press.

Chicken or glass: in the vicinity of Clifford Geertz and Paul Hyman

Paul Rabinow

Department of Anthropology, University of California, Berkeley, CA, USA

Paul Hyman's photographs disrupt the narrative of American anthropology in Sefrou, Morocco in 1969. How the fashion photographer in fringe pants met Moroccans and photographed them, how he captured the contingent, the fleeting, the ordinary, the local, and the singular, is refracted in Paul Rabinow's reflections on some of the aims, assumptions, methods, and results of ethnography and photography.

The unexpected, born-again renaissance of Paul Hyman's trove of unsettling beauty and idiosyn-cratically engaged witnessing through the efforts and insights of Susan Slyomovics deserves our most sincere gratitude. Hers is an act of simple audacity and perceptivity. Audacity may seem too grand a word given the riveting work she has done on human rights abuses in Morocco (Slyomovics 2005). Not to downplay the significance and power of that work or those long-standing horrific practices in any way, nonetheless by the early 21st century there exists a genre of narration and performance concerning torture and its horrors, its tragedy, and its disturbing banalities. In fact, Slyomovics' book powerfully documents this state of affairs in its mode of cool chronicle, thereby producing the devastating effects of a clear-sighted and anti-maudlin presentation of a terrible reality long since known and long since submerged. Her organisation of a conference featuring Hyman's photographs is perceptive because she seized their singularity, and audacious because so many others had ignored them. There were things to see, and to say, and to learn, and to discuss, beyond the discursive and the conceptual.

A critical disturbance

Ce qui vient au monde pour ne rien troubler ne mérite ni égards ni patience. (René Char, *Fureur et mystère*)[1]

Slyomovics' simple but decisive act of recognition of Hyman's photographic oeuvre as well as his presence in Morocco functions as a disruptor (to use Gilles Deleuze's term) of the parade of appropriately nostalgic eulogies (is there any other kind?) that have followed Clifford Geertz's death. We can rest assured that the patina of pious affect and unconcealed sentimentality ever accumulating as Geertz's heritage will not lack for care-keepers and guardians. Let us be clear: this state of affairs is perfectly normal. Its unimpeded continuance, however, is also normalising in the sense that the repetition of one narrative line (with its minor variations) lays out a field of what counts as true and right in this history and therein lies the rub. The history is more complex, as is what counts as true and right. Any true thinker would feel betrayed by this lack of critique: loyalty worth its salt must include honesty.

Other contributions in this collection attest to the aesthetic power and reflect on the cultural significance of Hyman's photographic contributions per se. However, less attention has been paid to the arrival and brief stay of Paul Hyman in Morocco. This arrival turned out to be a minor disturbance to the scripted flow of things at the time as well as their representations in the future perfect that had been orchestrated by the maestro himself and his supporting cast. Cliff, Hilly and Larry ('I am Cliff's man in the grey flannel suit') Rosen were nothing if not serious about their project. Although seriousness in one's work, diligence in respecting one's hosts, and commitment to bringing facts and insights to bear in a volatile state of affairs, are virtues, as Jean-Paul Sartre often observed of the *esprit de sérieux*, the prescriptive attitude of the bourgeoisie to reality and to those different from themselves, their air of self-importance, for Sartre demanded criticism.

Today, criticism is a charged term that is taken to be (often appropriately) a trope of denunciation. Criticism, however, takes its modern meaning from Kant and his three Critiques where the term means the establishment of legitimate limits. Thus, the *Critique of pure reason* (Kant 1950) is not an attack on reason but an attempt to demonstrate its limits, forms, and powers. Kant had intended to write a fourth Critique (in addition to Pure Reason, Judgment, and Practical Reason), a Critique of Historical Reason. That Critique would have addressed the limits of historical conditions, their contingency, and their relative importance. In effect, over the last 200 years, the modern human sciences, while not dallying in the arrogant and the comic travesties of what they took to be the natural sciences, have done little else. Or, more accurately when done well they continue to pursue the goal of understanding and practising the pursuit of historical understanding: the appropriate mode of comprehension of the contingent, the fleeting, the ordinary, the local, and the singular.

Chicken or glass

The above remarks are no doubt outsized words for the small anecdotes that follow. Yet anthropologists, the miniature painters of the social sciences, as Geertz put it, borrowing from Claude Lévi-Strauss, are attuned to small events, minor processes, petty breakdowns, and the like, as places to pause and inquire as to what is happening in front of us. These are not quite the petty, grey details that the Nietzschean genealogists seek out as the sites of malicious struggles over the real, covered over by grand words, but perhaps they are not so far distant from those sites of contestation over meaning and respect, for the self and for others. Regardless, here are a few minor incidents and some untimely observations on their significance.

Paul Hyman happens to be extremely gifted at languages. He was a musician (and a mathematician) and had that gift of recognising and reproducing tone, timbre, and pattern that most of us lack. Hyman had been a French major at Columbia. A professor of French nationality told his French conversation class that he could teach them to speak French quickly but only if they spoke English quickly. Although trivial as an insight, the claim was a critical one. It was a critical one in the sense that it indicated a legitimate limit. Of course, the university world is full of language professors who are not natives and who perform their duties more or less satisfactorily. That being said, for some, and Hyman was one of those souls, taking up a pursuit in which one would feel oneself to be judged as constantly inadequate and about which one could do little to remedy the situation, was, when added to myriad other obstacles, enough to make him move on to different vocational pursuits, in particular, photography.

One of the essential aspects of speaking Arabic in Morocco in the provincial setting of Sefrou and its hinterlands, was the centrality – not the totality – of what Jean Duvignaud in his classic *Change at Shebika: report from a North African village* (Duvignaud 1970), incisively called the palaver of daily life. There was almost always, as the American idiom has it, time to kill, or better, to fill: there was ample unemployment and under-employment, there was a culture of indirectness and alert redirecting of questions, there was a vast reservoir of salutations and verbal adornment, and there was a joy in the rather baroque ornamentation of phrase and counterphrase that, in some imaginary quantitative analysis of speech acts at the time, would have had to hold a place of prominence. Certainly, this genre of performance, of palavering, was much practised and socially esteemed. Not being able to engage in this palaver or simply refusing to do so, whether for reasons of temperament or out of an ingrained dispositional *esprit de sérieux*, constituted a critical limitation for those attempting to participate in, to respect, and ultimately, in subtle but significant ways, even to understand what was going on.

Hyman, who had time to fill, was dispositionally primed to adopt and enjoy this form of Moroccan palaver. The fact that Hyman mastered the skill's basics is striking because it is not actually a skill he excels at in English (or French). One indication of this observation is that with insistence in the years following our time in Morocco, and even today decades later, there is a range of talk that we use our no doubt comical Arabic to enact. Even in email of late these greetings and relationship-affirming seeming non sequiturs serve that purpose. They are a salutary counterbalance to the 'Hi' of email, not to mention the regressive telegraphy of text messaging. In a word, Hyman quickly learned a certain cut of Arabic just as many Moroccan youths at the time learned a cut of English or Swedish or German that was at one and the same time utterly fluent and distinctively and massively partial. I remember a conversation with a young Moroccan about Jimi Hendrix (about whom he had more superlatives to display than I did); when asked about the Moroccan school system, he lacked even the most basic vocabulary to continue the discussion. No one had ever asked him such questions before. This was a matter of demand, not ability.

In like manner, Hyman had nothing to say about parallel cousin marriage (in any language, it is true) but could fill hours over tea bantering about what appeared to be very little. Serious work in Arabic with its extraordinary beauty and complexity was not what Paul had come to master: no grammar books, no educated tutors, no formal lessons. Equally, that whole range of seriousness, the array of command language, that could not have failed to be associated with the curt rationality of colonialism, was absent from Hyman's linguistic arsenal. Whoever this guy was, he was not a willing representative of dominance. Whatever else this rather exceptional foreigner with his fringed pants possessed, it seemed with all the time in the world, he was no colonist, technocrat, or even Peace Corps worker there to improve the Moroccans' lot. In sum, Hyman was not in Morocco to till and sow the field of normalisation, to capture the culture's deep meaning, or to put the boys in the café on the world map. It was no surprise therefore, that his Arabic was both fluent and limited, precise and thin: this guy was no threat and, from the start, wittingly and unwittingly, he established trust.

In that available light, Clifford Geertz's performative limitations in Arabic are critical. Geertz had all the requisite dictionaries, tutors in Chicago and Sefrou, a familiarity with the scholarly literature on Arabic, and extensive theoretical reflections on the relations between language and culture. That his accent was horrific was of minimal importance; that he was constitutionally allergic to chatter and impervious to palaver (no doubt in any language) constituted a telling diacritic of who he was, how he was perceived, as well as what he himself was able to perceive. Perception, here as elsewhere, it is worth remembering, is not the same thing as conceptualisation or narration, abilities Geertz possessed in abundance.

Early on in Hyman's stay, Geertz wandered down from his villa in the adjacent hillside (formerly the French quarter) to observe some kind of procession that was underway in honor of a saint. He invited Hyman to join him. They caught up with the group meandering on a pathway at the edge of town. Hyman asked Geertz, 'What is going on?' Geertz shuffled over to a young boy in the procession and entered into a brief verbal exchange. He returned to Hyman and said in his gruff, rapid-fire delivery, 'Chicken or glass.' Hyman, nonplussed, responded to the effect of 'Oh?' Geertz rapidly glossed his cryptic claim by explaining that the Moroccan words for chicken and glass sounded alike and he did not know for certain which one was being used. For years later, Hyman and I would introduce the speech act 'chicken or glass?' into our conversations, often, no doubt, to the utter consternation of those with whom we happened to be mingling, especially as it was usually accompanied by peals of laughter and a hearty '*eh-way a Sidi?*' The point is not the cheap one that Geertz was not very skilled in Arabic, especially spoken Arabic. Rather, it is that had Geertz been attuned to banter and chatter rather than direct questioning, he would have found out not only whether it was chicken or glass but what was going on, and how the participants felt about it, the famous 'ethos' of anthropology.

Although this is not the place to enter into a more scholarly discussion of the importance of the anthropologist and command of language, let us just remember that Vincent Crapanzano – who did not learn Arabic but worked closely with an informant and translator with whom he established a complex rapport – and Geertz made fluency a point of controversy, a critical touchstone of how anthropology ought to be practised (Crapanzano 1980). Speaking 'the language,' Geertz held, was the ethical and epistemological diacritic of the discipline. That being said, Hyman's presence and the insights his minor disruptions occasioned, demonstrated that whatever conclusions learned professors may arrive at on the above matter, one had to acknowledge that language was a practice and that practice was composed of diverse dimensions as a performative art; (relative) mastery was more than grammar, more than vocabulary, more than accent. Finally, Hyman's presence also showed that making no attempt to demonstrate the aforementioned mastery, while hanging out in an attentive manner as a keen urban observer of the human comedy, could show us many things about those observed as well as those authorised to observe them.

Concave or convex

If grasping the centrality of daily life and its zones of lack of deep meaning can be a problem for the cultivated anthropologist, so too can arenas held to be overly saturated with significance. One of those arenas is sexuality. It is worth remembering that we are talking about events taking place in 1969. Although Hyman and I at least had been beneficiaries of the sexual energy of the time and of our generation, the scholarly literature on Morocco and/or Islam of the day languished in its own self-imposed discursive prudery. Studies of parallel and cross-cousin marriage not to mention segmentary lineages abounded, but the sex and sexuality of the people strategising in all those diagrams was passed over in silence and perhaps shame.

To his credit, Geertz was interested in sexuality in Morocco. He was, however, too bashful to broach the topic with his informants who had just traipsed up the hill and sat in his study informing him of how things were in the land below. So he seized the occasion, however awkwardly, of Hyman's presence – the guy was a New York fashion photographer, after all – to see if Paul would be willing to do some informal fieldwork. Geertz assumed that Paul's Arabic was insufficient and furthermore that opening such an inquiry in Sefrou would be risky (*sic*, a Geertzian pun awaits); when he heard that Hyman and I planned a short trip to Tangier, and knowing that we both spoke French, Geertz seized the day, broached the topic, and underscored both its casual interest to him and its potential importance for the ethnographic record. What was the difference, for example, between homosexuality, homoeroticism, and male friendship? Sketchy references to the Greeks were provided. All very serious but not yet freighted with decades of scholarship and political correctness. A naïve time.

Off we went to Tangier (Figure 1). Sex was not hard to locate, only to avoid. Sexuality, to accept Foucault's famous distinction some years later, the discourse of the thing, was harder to find. As it turned out, when Hyman and I had lived together in Paris (during 1965–66), he had befriended a cosmopolitan Jewish homosexual. Through him (?) we contacted some of his friends in Tangier or through Hyman's friendship with George some of the customs and habits of that age-set were already familiar. A conversation with one of George's Tangier cohort cleared things up fairly quickly. What was the difference between homosexuality, homoeroticism, and male friendship, Hyman asked the aging queen. The response was elegant and eloquent: 'Concave and convex.' What counted was who was penetrating and who was penetrated. All the rest was secondary. However, it became clear that there was one further distinction that several young men who made a living from engaging in sex with the older male tourists

Figure 1. Paul Hyman and Paul Rabinow, 1969, Tangier (unknown street photographer)

insisted on: if the penetrator was not a Muslim, there was no shame, who cared what they wanted and what they did, as long as they paid. Any other questions?

Before the politically correct among our contemporaries get all huffy, of course, more research would reveal that this claim, like most such claims, was a bit more complicated. So be it. Remarkable as it may be, nowhere in this discussion did the topic of *nisba* come up.[2] Moroccan identity had more axes than one marketplace could reveal; other arenas of commerce, it turns out, would have provided other lessons.

Patrons and clients

Fundamentally Cliff Geertz was an awkward human being who learned to use that awkwardness to his own continuing advantage. What in others would be taken as rudeness or abruptness in social interaction was more frequently than not attributed to the man's genius and forgiven or at least forgotten. In the Morocco fieldwork years, I had no particular gripe with his distance, curtness, and general 'away-ness.' He was rarely available, infrequently had anything to say when we did meet, yet he continued during that time to write captivating essays and many of his mumbled offhand remarks proved to be fertile suggestions for things to follow up on. By and large, this arrangement suited me fine since it left me alone to do what I thought needed to be done. When I was sick in Morocco, the Geertzes' maid brought me soup. Not a bad arrangement, all things considered.

In 1969, instead of returning to the University of Chicago to write my thesis, I decided to move back to New York. Renting an apartment on St. Mark's Place, down the block from W.H. Auden whom I never met, the East Village in those days was inexpensive and full of nourishing Jewish and Ukrainian cafés and restaurants. I wrote my thesis, 'A History of Power in a Moroccan Village.' Geertz read a draft, said, 'There is a thesis in there somewhere, keep going.' I kept going. Spending a good deal of time with Hyman at Max's Kansas City, just off Union Square, a hangout for part of the fashion world. I rewrote the thesis. I received my degree. I was offered two jobs at different branches of the City University of New York and accepted one at Richmond College, then an experimental upper-division college. The first book I taught was *Village in the Vaucluse*, a book about a French village where small things, and palaver, held great import and were the site of wise insights about things French.

With some prodding, Geertz agreed to have me as his assistant at the Institute for Advanced Study during the fateful year of 1972–1973. The year was fateful in a number of ways. For me, the fact that Pierre Bourdieu was at the Institute and initially did not speak much English was a gift, as it meant I got to spend a great deal of time with him in the early months. He hated the Institute for its smugness and attributed or misattributed a set of spiritualist motives to Geertz. Bourdieu held a clear and well articulated position that, with his appointment as the first social scientist at the Institute for Advanced Study, Geertz had a unique responsibility to the human sciences. Bourdieu thought, and said, that Geertz should take the opportunity to form a programme of interpretive social science and, if not establish a school, at least make the Institute's vast resources, both symbolic and material, the foundation for a larger project. Geertz would have none of it. 'I am not a cruise director,' he pronounced on one occasion. Of course, no one would ever have considered that he was, nor was that the role that Bourdieu was proposing. Exercising the prerogatives of power and privilege that were now securely his, Geertz felt he did not have to answer to anybody and acted accordingly. Bourdieu explained to me, on the basis of a detailed sociological analysis of the French academic scene that he would later publish in a different version under the title *Homo academicus*, how he would be nominated for and voted into the Collège de France. He would start a journal, build alliances, and gradually advance his vision of the social sciences. He had elaborate justifications about the impersonality of these strategies. He took things seriously, very seriously.

Equally, the year was a fateful one because the nomination of Robert Bellah as a member of the nascent School of Social Sciences at the Institute was rejected in a nasty academic manner. Around the time of the decision, the Bellahs lost one of their daughters. Although I did not spend much time with Bellah that year, nor was I privy to the Institute's politics, three years later I participated in a National Institute for the Humanities Seminar for College Teachers at Berkeley during the academic year 1975–1976 that Bellah directed. During that year, I met William Sullivan with whom I edited two books, and Hubert Dreyfus with whom I became fast friends of a philosophic sort and with whom I would write a book on Michel Foucault several years later.

Bellah, it is a pleasure to add, saved my career. By his accepting me in his NIH seminar, I was able to connect with Sullivan and Dreyfus as well as learn a great deal from Bellah himself about an interpretive social science that was morally committed. Although I did not agree with all of his positions, I remain deeply impressed with Bellah's clear sense of right and wrong and his profound loyalty to those he valued. By this point, I had written the manuscript of *Reflections on fieldwork in Morocco* (1977), but was basically ready to abandon it as it had been rejected by four or five presses. The editor at the University of Chicago Press told me to put it in a drawer and take it out when I was famous. Geertz told me it would ruin my career. Bellah tactfully intimated that it might be wise to stop asking Geertz for recommendations. Bellah talked to the University of California Press and now, thirty years later, the book is still in print. It did not ruin my career.

During this period, the Geertz team was giving shape to what eventually became *Meaning and order in Moroccan society*. I was invited to contribute a chapter but was told it had to be on a set of specific topics none of which interested me (irrigation systems, etc.). I wrote what was no doubt an uninteresting and flat essay and sent it to Hildred. I never heard anything about it. When Hyman mentioned that the book was going to press, I inquired about the status of my essay: Cliff told me to talk to Hilly; Hilly said that she had sent me a letter explaining why they were not going to include my essay in the book. Having never received the letter, I asked to see a copy. I never heard from her again. Basically I was relieved, as I did not share their view of fieldwork, anthropology, or this particular book. I do not doubt that my essay was poor. That being said, I was disgusted by the lack of the most minimal courtesy or human consideration. But by this point in my career I was beginning to learn enough about academic life that it was no longer a shock to encounter such inconsideration and assumed lack of accountability. These people took themselves very seriously. I saw very little of the Geertzes in the decades that followed; we exchanged extremely brief greetings at anthropology meetings from time to time. Aside from an extremely uncomfortable Wenner-Gren conference in Fez where Geertz, Marshall Sahlins, and Edmund Leech exchanged verbal insults and performed mutual contempt, that was that.

Although I did not fully share Bourdieu's attacks on Geertz nor admire the unbridled ambition they both were invested with, I did agree that something more should have been done with the opportunities presented by the Institute. The contrast with Bellah, who became a committed public intellectual and devoted the next part of his life to his group of young scholars collaboratively attempting to influence the moral direction of the American polity, could not be more striking. One can only wonder if Geertz's refusal to collaborate with others or articulate and defend a common cause, intellectual or otherwise, was not ultimately his own burden, his own Achilles' heel. In my opinion, his refusal to engage in the 'theory' or 'Writing Culture' debates and skirmishes of the 1980s and 1990s seems related to the ever more involuted prose, devastatingly reviewed as a *soufflé* that deflates if you stick a fork in it. Whatever personal demons the man struggled with, his retreat from larger engagement, from challenging collaboration, from accepting the responsibility of the construction of a new venue for the human sciences in America, was a loss for the larger polity of scholars and thinkers.

And I think it is fair to say that this refusal of collaboration was a loss for Geertz as well. Although being your own patron is a well known practice, one we all practise to one degree or another, and although being a Big Man carries with it incessant obligations and annoyances – as the villagers used to say, '*Les grosses têtes, jamais labes*' – systematically refusing responsibilities and relationships – 'I am not a cruise director' – may leave one without debts but also, as Bourdieu has analysed so keenly, outside of the circle of exchange in which the cycles of gift and counter-gift are endlessly deferred and never completed so as to solidify and fortify social relations.[3] Said more simply, as the Moroccans put it when describing one of the locals who wandered back and forth without accruing debts or credit, without tying himself to family or locale, '*Za et msha*,' 'he came and went.' The phrase is not a compliment, only an observation of someone considered to be more or less mad. The tone was tolerant, even affectionate, but always tinged with a certain comic pathos. Obviously the analogy is far from exact but it is not exquisitely imperfect either.

Poses

Before and after his stint in Morocco, Paul Hyman worked as a fashion photographer in New York, having apprenticed in his trade, albeit in an amateur mode, in a similar milieu in Paris. Hence it was fashion that uneasily defined the orientation, practice, vision, and values of what was seen, taken, captured, or lost. At the typical fashion photographer's studio, the pulsing constellation of people and energy centered on the director. Moving closer to the director, practising the techniques and nuances of his style, aiding his overall production, were among the necessities and challenges of apprenticeship. The promised rewards of money, fame, glamour, sex, drugs, and rock and roll were omnipresent in their luster, while being all too frequently elusive in the quotidian reality. In this world, aging was the great demon, the gates through which only a very few managed to pass (for example, Richard Avedon). Although age and their looks were both the haunting demons and the hovering angels for the models, in a less obvious but still compelling way, so too did this inevitable specter haunt the photographers. No one needed to be reminded, having played the role themselves, that in this scene, there were always younger, less marked, more ardent aspirants ready to work, play, deal more vigorously and decisively, than those just a little older. Not surprisingly, in conversations late at night or mid-morning caffeine exchanges, there was a leitmotif, wistful and bitter, of art, vision, and real photography shadowed by the acute awareness of the banality and exploitative character of what was actually on display. Pointing out this contradiction, this structure and its affect, easy for the anthropologist, harder for the friend, occasioned diverse but always riven responses. So much talent, so much bullshit.

Hyman's voyage to Morocco, his mission under-specified and under-compensated, had nonetheless the allure of a moment for him to shoot much more freely. It became a tacit test, an *épreuve*, as the French say, of character and desire. This anthropological photo opportunity would not be anything like the fashion shoots in Marrakesh (taking shape even then), but who knew what it would be? A turn into the unknown: definitely not toward the exotic but an unmarked exploration of the talent and imagination of the observer, the photographer. How good was he? Was all that lamenting at Max's Kansas City anything more than the dawn of the days of wine and roses? Who knew? Who knew how to gauge the answer?

***

Roland Barthes, in his *Chambre claire: note sur la photographie* (Barthes 1980), at least re-read today in 2007, provides some benchmarks that clarify the question of judging, of gauging these matters. As with all Barthes' work, this book-length essay attempts to balance, often unsuccessfully, and from time to time with stunning clarity, his own hyper-refined subjectivism with his standard device of deploying concepts and principles from would-be sciences (structuralism, discourse theory, semantics, psychoanalysis, etc.). Barthes used this checks-and-balances approach as a rhetorical check aiding him to discipline, to counter, to remand his own wayward consciousness to the prison house of the real.

More than halfway through the book, Barthes announces with a declarative joy and relief, apparently having just discovered it, a principle guiding his philosophical meditations (and sporadic psychoanalytical ruminations) concerning the nature of photography:

> Je m'étais fixé au début un principe: ne jamais réduire le sujet que j'étais, face à certaines photos, au *socius* désincarné, désaffecté, dont s'occupe la science. (Barthes 1980, p. 115)

Hyman did not require any elaborate self-policing in order to fix this principle, the principle of refusing to picture anything, above all the Moroccans, as bloodless, immaterial, hygienised things that Barthes declaims as the normative object of a science of the social. In this instance such a temptation had never structured Hyman's subjectivity; so, when the Geertzes proposed that he photograph parallel cousin marriage, or unproductive agricultural fields, Hyman had no trouble refusing the request to capture a social science concept, not only on the object side but, of course, on the subject side as well (*ne jamais réduire le sujet que j'étais*).

And yet, Hyman's photos are at an infinity of aesthetic and ethical distance from the Orientalist blather that the photo shoots in Marrakesh continue to disseminate. Barthes' *Mythologies* (1957, 1972) had demolished the semantic underpinnings of this insidious fantasy-world long before Edward Said. Hyman's photos show us something specific, particular, and singular. And here, acutely, Barthes provides the means to establish a bridge from fashion photography to Photography, capital P. What underpins the nature of Photography, Barthes writes,

> c'est la pose [. . .] une chose réelle s'est trouvé immobile devant l'oeil. Je reverse l'immobilité de la photo présente sur la prise passée, et c'est cet arrêt qui constitue la pose. (Barthes 1980, p. 122)

If there is anything that springs out from Hyman's photographs as a persistent leitmotif, it is that they are posed. This posing if often quite formal. I believe that there is a strong ethical component to his poses. With Hyman there is no surreptitious attempt to 'capture the moment' *à la* Henri Cartier-Bresson who shot his photos with his camera cocked at his waist; just as there is no elaborate studio set-up requiring professional lighting equipment, make-up and hair stylists, as well as the requisite elaborate darkroom work of a Richard Avedon. And yet, Hyman's photos are posed and they consistently mark that posing for the viewer. This form seems ethical to me, as an anthropologist, because Hyman always engaged those he was photographing; he wanted them to be aware of what he was doing. He wanted their attention. He wanted them to pose naturally or perhaps culturally, but in any case, as they saw fit. The pose was not imposed. This claim, of course, does not mean that all the photographer had to do was arrange people and things and then click. Rather, again Barthes seems on the mark when he observes that,

Figure 2. Paul Hyman, Sidi Lahcen, 1969 (Photographer unknown)

'la vraie photographie totale,' elle accomplit la confusion inouïe de la réalité (*'Cela a été'*) et de la vérité (*'C'est ça!'*); elle devient à la fois constative et exclamative. . .. (Barthes 1980, p. 176)

Barthes is making two claims here: the first, which for him is central, is the capturing of a being's existing at a moment in time – *cela a été*. By itself, however, any snapshot will do that much. The second claim – *c'est ça!* – is a truth claim of a very particular sort. Specifying that particular sort requires Barthes to make several more distinctions. We know that the truth claim will not be of the ascepticised kind. We also know it will have strictly nothing directly to do with thick description or deep play. The reason Barthes gives is the alchemy of unexpected confusion of reality and truth that 'la vraie photographie totale' yields. But this talk is getting murkier and murkier, far beyond the intentions of Hyman.

The talk of a distinction between reality and truth and then their unexpected confusion through the truth of total photography indicates that Barthes has lost his way. His theory will not enable him to tell us from the object side what is going on in the photographs that move him. As usual, he is surer when it comes to his own feelings. And here we arrive at the distinction for which Barthes has received the most critical attention: between *studium* and *punctum*. *Studium* might be translated as a 'study,' but that is too academic, too reserved, too reflected. Rather, subjectively, Barthes uses the term to point to a kind of documentary capacity that photography is well suited to produce and by which millions of consumers or spectators are by now well disposed to receive. The *studium*, Barthes writes, returning to the home ground of his own taste and reactions, is

le champ très vaste du désir nonchalant, de l'intérêt divers, du goût inconséquent. (Barthes 1980, p. 50)

The taken-for-granted (because learned and practised and disseminated) disposes both photographer and audience to the picking out of an image, 'sans acuité particulière' (Barthes 1980, p. 48). This is the aspect of seizing some bit of stereotyped reality that Pierre Bourdieu claimed as the defining characteristic of photography in his sociological study of photography, *Un art moyen* (Bourdieu *et al.* 1965, 1990). Clearly, however, Barthes is not doing sociology but rather is seeking to understand why certain pictures, especially those of his mother, move him so strongly.

And this embrace of his own taste and reactions brings him to the other learned term, the counterpunch to the banality, the ordinariness affectively and substantively, of the *studium*: the *punctum*. The latter term shares its Latin roots with the term 'to punctuate,' as in the marking, the underscoring, of something made. Barthes performs a reversal here; in emphasising punctuation as the diacritic of true photography, it would seem to be the subject who performs the defining act. But for Barthes, the *punctum* is an objective quality; it comes, like an arrow, from the photo, to pierce the viewer's consciousness.

> Le *punctum* d'une photo, c'est ce hasard qui, en elle, *me point*. . . . (Barthes 1980, p. 49)

Although it is plausible that some parallel tension between the marking of time, cultural expectation, and this small, affective piercing (Barthes calls it a fly bite – *émouchèment* – at one point) may exist in other forms of photography, its particular acuity in Hyman's photos comes, it seems to me, from his transformation of the sociological study into the marking of a singular moment, as well as from the deft equipoise with which these scenes of vulnerability, tenderness, and energy in a troubled world have been composed.

Notes

1. Char cited in Caws 1976, p. 2.
2. Geertz made the Moroccan word *nisba* the centerpiece of his long article on the market and the key to Moroccan identity (Geertz 1979). On the Amazon webpage, the publisher has not supplied the cover image.
3. The expression is a mix of Moroccan and French argot: 'Big men are never at ease.' On exchange, see Bourdieu 1975, 1977.

References

Barthes, R., 1957. *Mythologies*. Paris: Le Seuil.
Barthes, R., 1972. *Mythologies*. New York: Hill and Wang.
Barthes, R., 1980. *La chambre claire: Note sur la photographie*. Paris: L'Étoile, Gallimard, Le Seuil.
Bourdieu, P., 1975. *Esquisse d'une théorie de la pratique précédé de trois études d'ethnologie Kabyle*. Geneva: Droz.
Bourdieu, P., 1977. *Outline of a theory of practice*. Cambridge, UK: Cambridge University Press.
Bourdieu, P., et al., 1965. *Un art moyen: Essai sur les usages sociaux de la photographie*. Paris: Minuit.
Bourdieu, P., et al., 1990. *Photography: a middle-brow art*. Stanford, CA: Stanford University Press.
Caws, M.A., 1976. *The presence of René Char*. Princeton, NJ: Princeton University Press.
Crapanzano, V., 1980. *Tuhami: portrait of a Moroccan*. Chicago: University of Chicago Press.
Duvignaud, J., 1970. *Change at Shebika: report from a North African village*. New York: Pantheon.
Geertz, C., 1979. Suq: the bazaar economy in Sefrou. *In*: Clifford Geertz, Hildred Geertz and Lawrence Rosen, eds. *Meaning and order in Morocco: three essays in cultural analysis*. Cambridge, UK: Cambridge University Press, 123–313.
Kant, I., 1950. *Critique of pure reason*. New York: E.P. Dutton.
Rabinow, P., 1977. *Reflections on fieldwork in Morocco*. Berkeley: University of California Press.
Slyomovics, S., 2005. *The performance of human rights in Morocco*. Bloomington: Indiana University Press.

Of time and the city: Clifford Geertz on urban history

Susan Gilson Miller

Department of History, University of California at Davis, Davis, CA, USA

This paper explores Clifford Geertz's thinking about cities and modernity in the Moroccan context. From the historian's perspective, Geertz made important contributions to the study of Moroccan urbanism. In his writing on Sefrou between the 1960s and the mid-1980s, he mapped out how material changes in the city accompanied an emerging sense of a localised urban consciousness. By asking the eternal question, 'For whom is the city made?' he showed that even in provincial Sefrou, the built environment could unexpectedly serve as a site for ideological and social confrontation and the working out of one group's desire for political domination over others. On the more theoretical level, his work on Sefrou also demonstrates how architects and builders could play roles as agents of change, while the buildings they created served as representations for wider shifts in the cultural and historical fields.

Introduction

Clifford Geertz's work on cities is embedded in larger projects not directly concerned with describing processes of urban change in the Maghreb. Yet his various writings about Sefrou over the course of four decades profoundly influenced the ways in which historians of the North African city think about their craft. He introduced concepts into the study of the city that have fundamentally altered the way we 'read' the changing urban form both as text and as experience. He was a historian's anthropologist, in that he provided theoretical inspiration to those of us who easily become lost in a welter of facts. At the same time, he was an anthropologist with a sense of history, who visualised cities by looking backwards over the *longue durée*. Fully absorbed by the ethnographical practice of closely analysing social behaviour, he also paid attention to the temporal practice of creating setting, trajectory, and context. Moreover, his approach was relatively free of the staple dogmas of his era. He was wary of the reductive idea of the 'Islamic city' at a time when others adopted it as a given, and his early work on Sefrou in the 1960s was largely devoid of Orientalist imaginings. It was only later, when he revisited Sefrou in the late 1980s, that he entered into this prickly debate, and then only half-heartedly.

Here I would like to follow some of Geertz's evolving reflections on the Moroccan city, locating them within the current of ideas relating to Moroccan historical urbanism more broadly. For writing about cities is a rich and ongoing tradition in Moroccan historiography, and Geertz's contributions to this discussion are more than relevant. His work on cities is a fully accredited yet missing link in what Janet Abu-Lughod (1987) has famously called the 'isnad' of writing about Muslim cities. The questions he dealt with are central to discourses of urbanism, such as: What are the contours of urban identity and how is it manifested? How does a connection to place bring order into a society? To what extent does the close analysis of urban institutions shed light on the stringent ties that hold a city together? His Moroccan ethnographies serve as textual evidence for an unfolding sense of a localised urban consciousness. In this discussion I shall pay special attention to those elements in his writing that contributed to the concept of an 'urban identity' that appeared in various guises over time, but always with the function of articulating a symbolic social order that lent definition to the changing cityscape.

The colonial urban legacy

By the mid-1960s, when Geertz and his students arrived in Sefrou, there was already a long-standing and well-established colonial tradition of writing about Moroccan cities that loosely informed their fieldwork. French social scientists of the early 20th century had carefully gone about the task of constructing the unique difference of the Moroccan city, by casting it in sharp relief against the backdrop of the modernising and increasingly denatured cities of Europe. In Morocco, French urbanists discovered an 'authenticity' that was missing at home, along with intimations of a refined social life conducted behind closed doors, in private places beyond their reach. Countless traveller accounts and guidebooks bear witness to the 'otherness' of the native town, with its blank walls, aimlessly wandering streets, and mysteriously abrupt transitions that eventually achieved tropical status in colonial thinking about the Moroccan city (de Kerdec Chény 1888). By the 1930s, a more serious body of colonial literature had begun to appear, rooted in detailed *in situ* studies of Morocco's major cities, such as Le Tourneau's articles on Fez, later to become the substance of his grand work on that same city, and Michaux-Bellaire's study of Tangier. Each of these accounts is impressive for its scholarship, but flawed because of a lack of contextualisation, so that the Fez of 1930 easily became the source book for Fez of the 15th century.[1] As the brothers Tharaud (2002) wrote, 'in Fez there is only one age and one style: that of yesterday, today, and tomorrow.'[2]

As time went on, terms like 'la société citadine' began to appear in French texts, as knowledge about the urban social order became more sophisticated and social distinctions became more evident. Georges Hardy, influential advisor to Résident-Général Lyautey and deft observer of local forms, used this phrase to specify the urban elite, thereby reinforcing already nascent ideas about Moroccan urban society as strictly divided into distinct castes. He believed that this elite was composed 'of an oligarchy of birth, intelligence, and fortune,' and made up of people who could trace their ancestry to al-Andalus. This select group could be found in only a handful of cities – Rabat-Salé, Tetuan, and Fez – but nowhere else (Naciri 1986, p. 257). Proud of their ancestry and culture, disdaining political authority, they provided a true and enduring cultural model onto which the structure of urban life could be transposed. They contributed the moral glue that held the city together, providing continuity over space and time and from one era to the next. Dense with factual data, these later colonial texts still suffered from a limiting optic that emphasised the 'otherness' of the Moroccan medina, regarding it through the lens of a doubly hierarchical urban order that split the traditional from the modern and the Moroccan from the European, in a manner that reinforced the absolute difference between two modes of city living.

This difference was further inscribed in the colonial approach to planning and managing native society. The old city was to be left alone, according to this perspective; it could be minimally updated and refurbished, but never changed in its substance. Lyautey, the grand architect of protectorate Morocco, put it this way:

> The Arab and the Jewish quarters, I will not touch them. I shall clean them up, restore them, supply them with running water and electricity, and remove the waste, but that is all. . ... And out in the bled, I shall build another town. . ... (Rivet 1988:3, p. 147 n 716)

In terms of urban design, Lyautey administered 'a despotic interventionism' at every level of planning and construction of the new town, regulating the height of buildings, the décor and colour of their facades, the volumes of the rooms, even the type of plumbing that was used (Rivet 1988:3, p. 155). Inspired by the Norman architecture of Sicily, he built Morocco's new cities for the ages, imposing a modernist vocabulary that had selectively absorbed the elements of a sober yet elegant traditional native style (Hardy 1949, pp. 288–290). His was an architecture of morality, expressive of enduring cultural qualities in Moroccan society that could serve as a link between the past and future.

The separation between old and new towns in Morocco was later construed by some observers as 'apartheid,' but this is an incorrect reading of reality; rather, it was based on a 'sociology of conservatism,' as Daniel Rivet has put it, derived from the belief that if Europeans were allowed to invade the native town, they would corrupt it beyond repair. Equally so, if the native moved to the European town, he would become decivilised, just as the French country peasant had lost his soul in the big cities of France.[3] Both faces of the city were deeply hierarchised and controlled; the new quarter had its precise zones for living and working, carefully segregated by function and by socioeconomic status, while the old town was left to its own devices, kept silent and immobile while held in the grip of a co-opted native patrician class.

During the early years of the protectorate, this complete separation between the old town and the new was justified in terms of ethnicity – the idea that Moroccans and Europeans could never mix; after 1930, the discourse changed from one of ethnic division to a difference of values, evidenced by the fact that wealthy Jews as well as Muslims began to leave the old town for the *ville nouvelle* (the 'new city' built by the French alongside the preexisting medina) in order to take advantage of its more modern amenities. The discourse of opposites formerly couched in terms of ethnicity now gave way to one reflecting dichotomies relating to social class (Rivet 1988:3, p. 159).

But nothing ever remains the same in cities, generally acknowledged to be among the most fluid of entities. Already in the 1920s, according to Jacques Berque, new neighbourhoods were growing up on the fringes of the big Moroccan cities, in open spaces and empty lots between more permanent settlements (Berque 1967, pp. 185–187).[4] These ugly shantytowns were an unwanted development and a visual reproach to the elites on both sides. To the French planners, they demonstrated the inadequacies of their exercises in urban planning; for the Moroccan elite, they represented a dangerous breakdown of native society in which some people no longer lived or worked in any formal framework. The new settlements challenged the idea of the bifocal city by creating a third, indeterminate space that conformed to the exigencies of neither side. French norms of rational planning, proper sanitation, and good design were clearly not operating in the *bidonville*, nor were native paradigms of connectedness and respect for privacy. The colonial urban system was beginning to break down and reconfigure itself, with the issue no longer one of half the city standing in sharp juxtaposition to the other, but rather neighbourhoods contesting neighbourhoods, laid along two intersecting axes: one aesthetic, and the other of social class.

Finding meaning and order in Sefrou

When Clifford Geertz arrived in Sefrou, this evolution was already well under way, evidenced not only by the growth of clandestine housing on the fringes of the town, but also by the movement of old, wealthier Sefroui families into the newer parts of the city. By the mid-1960s, Moroccans had thoroughly conquered the *ville nouvelle.*[5] Meanwhile, migrants from the countryside had begun to infiltrate the medina, absorbing vacant spaces left behind by the departed. These new city-dwellers had very little to do with their older prototypes, according to social geographer Mohamed Naciri: 'The new urbanism is exactly the opposite of the old,' he wrote; 'instead of assuring integration, it enables solitude in the crowd...' (Naciri 1986, p. 260). If the ground was shifting beneath their feet, if the human component of Sefrou was in transition, Clifford Geertz and his colleagues took little interest in it. Instead, they concentrated on finding the continuities that lay beneath the surface flux. True, the Jews were leaving and Berbers were moving in. 'But for all that,' we read in the Introduction to *Meaning and order*,

> the institutions of social life and the categories of persons and relationships employed remain common among the various generations and segments of the Sefrou population, and it is in the flexible application of these concepts and institutions that the shared distinctiveness of the region is to be found. (Geertz, Geertz, and Rosen 1979, p. 16)

The closely narrated ethnographies that were the fruit of the Sefrou research are brilliant exercises in uncovering those underlying verities, laying the basis for an understanding of the complex systems of exchange and interaction – in the bazaar, in the *qadi*'s courts, in family relationships – that were distinctively 'Sefroui.' At the same time, and perhaps inadvertently, they offered a baseline for measuring how individual Sefrouis connected to urban space, and how that connection might evolve over time.

The contours of local identity seemed to reside in three different spatial and conceptual locations. First, there was the bazaar itself, a landscape that Geertz came to know like the back of his hand. Mapped, lived in, and absorbed, it was Sefrou writ in miniature, a simulacrum of the city itself. Then there were the people of the bazaar that Geertz came to know with a startling intimacy, their names, provenances, types of work, families, and personhoods, in all the immense variety that was particular to that time and place. And finally there were the urban institutions implicated in the workings of the bazaar, such as the *habus*, which lent a distinctive shape and quality to the city. Each of these sectors – space, human relations, and social institutions – was rich in information that defined the cultural specificity of the town.

I would like to stop for a moment to consider Geertz's comments on the *habus* of Sefrou, because the research here was especially remarkable (Miller 2005, p. 276). The *habus* is a devilishly difficult institution to study on the ground, mainly because the documentation is so obscure. Until the rise of the modern nation-state, *habus* archives were kept at the local level, and suffered for it; sometimes they were destroyed or carried off by dishonest administrators fearing punishment for their misdeeds, at other times they were ruined by fire or flood. *Habus* archives usually consist of bits of writing strung together in notebooks of a fragile nature, which collectively make up what is called the archives of the *habus*. Exploiting their value as a written source is always a challenge, because they do not follow a 'normal' narrative style and they lack the qualities of continuity and legibility that historians look for. To truly understand them, the reader must have an intimate knowledge of the layout of the town and its important personalities, both historically and in the present. Perhaps for this reason, *habus* records are sadly understudied and our lack of knowledge about them is one of the glaring gaps in our understanding of Moroccan urban history.[6]

Yet there is no doubt about the centrality of the institution to both the premodern and the modernising Moroccan city. Geertz understood the importance of the *habus* and made it a subject of inquiry. In the absence of a formal municipality on the European model, the *habus* traditionally acted as a *de facto* framework of governance. Its administrators made important decisions about rents, the purchase and sale of properties, and improvements to existing structures. Geertz says that it was the largest holder of property within the medina 'by far.' While its responsibilities changed over time, it was (and still is) a central urban institution, its decisions constituting an essential element in the functioning of the city (Geertz 1979, p. 151).

It is Geertz the anthropologist, who elaborates the historical reality of the *habus* by showing how its long tentacles reached out into the urban fabric. Through careful observation and inquiry, Geertz demonstrates how hundreds of Sefrouis were affected by this occulted mechanism of transfer and exchange. It is thanks to his meticulous study of Sefrou's 'bazaar economy' that the *habus* emerges into the light as a pivotal urban institution (Geertz 1979, p. 153). Yet by construing the *habus* as an expression of 'normative Islam,' and by recasting it as the linchpin that bound the economic with the religious in the bazaar, Geertz was emphasising only one aspect of its work. In fact, the *habus* was a complete system for the transfer of money, property, people, and goods that knit together the body politic in one continuous web of activity and interdependency, on a scale that included the bazaar but also went far beyond it.

As Geertz's study of the *habus* suggests, Sefrou of the 1960s was a reasonably stable urban conglomerate that functioned according to its own particular set of inherited norms and practices that, once uncovered, permitted entry into a unique social world. The political climate of Morocco in the 1960s, as heated as it was, was not evoked in *Meaning and order*, perhaps because it was a distraction from more important goals of research. But when Clifford Geertz returned to Sefrou in the late 1980s, it was no longer possible to ignore what was going on in a troubled and transformed political scene, in which left, right, and center fiercely contended for dominance on the national plane. The tremors that Geertz may have felt and ignored 20 years earlier were no longer avoidable, and Sefrou was in a state of upheaval.

Toutes directions

An article Clifford Geertz wrote in 1987, titled 'Toutes directions: changing signs in the urban sprawl,' is both a lament at the passing of 'old' Sefrou and cry of dismay at what was happening in the new. A return to Sefrou in 1986 exposed the differences between Geertz's recollections of the place and a wildly chaotic new order. In the midst of flux, he strove to understand the sweeping changes he witnessed by means of abstractions and metaphors that captured the effects of a rising modernity that introduced new expressions of personal identity. The complicated strands produced by change came together in this memorable essay, which has received little attention but is an important contribution to understanding Geertz's thinking about urban form, the nature of historical evolution, and the impact of transformation on the minds of those who are witness to it (Geertz 1989).

What were the shifts that created such disequilibrium? The decade of the 1970s was an explosive one in Morocco which completely changed the rules of the game, moving the position of the monarchy from one of a ruling institution tentative about its use of authority, to one that manipulated the reins of power with audacious contempt for its rivals. The attempted coups of 1971 and 1972, the Green March of 1975 to recover the 'lost' territories of the Sahara, the violent border confrontations with Algeria, the beginning of the sinister repression of the Moroccan far left and the onset of the 'years of lead' were milestones in a pattern of increasingly authoritarian and unpopular rule. Meanwhile, a growing economic crisis prompted a policy of privatisation that was badly managed, creating great inequalities in an already fractured body politic. The 1980s ushered in even more crises: a severe drought in the countryside between 1980 and 1983 accelerated migration to the cities, while a paralysed state, suffering from its own economic woes, stood idly by. In Casablanca, where fully 25% of the population lived in illegal housing of one form or the other, bread riots in 1981 and again in 1984 raised the specter of a population in full revolt. In the midst of all these troubles, Clifford Geertz returned to Sefrou.[7]

'Toutes directions' begins with a vignette. In February 1986, the municipal council of Sefrou issued a decree: henceforth, all buildings in the city were to be uniform in colour (*crème*, in French, *qehwi*, or coffee-coloured, in Arabic). Particularly targeted by the decree were the brightly coloured houses with variegated facades in certain sections of the city, examples of what Geertz jokingly calls 'masterpieces of design bravura.' Practically overnight, these dwellings were ordered to shed their colourful fronts for a less interesting beige. Behind this decree was a more complex story having broad ramifications for political, social, and cultural matters, as viewed from the urban perspective. The question on the table, according to Geertz, is the following: What should the 'proper' Islamic city look like? Here he is being more than a little disingenuous, for Geertz was surely aware that the phrase 'Islamic city' was already a troublesome one, under attack by urbanists, historians, sociologists, and other assorted intellectual gadflies. So he does not ask the question directly himself, but rather puts it in the mouth of a Sefroui; theoretical issues aside, he says, ordinary people in Sefrou have 'a certain idea of the city' which is increasingly difficult to see 'in the disordered sprawl of modern life' (Geertz 1989, pp. 291–292).

Expressed more elegantly, this notion of 'a certain idea of the city' can be summed up by the notion of *citadinité*, or *mudaniyya* in Arabic, a word that Geertz, quoting Naciri, translates as 'belonging *to* and *in* a city' (p. 291).[8] Here we are in the presence of a notional archetype of the sort that Geertz often used to encapsulate the disparate and often confusing manifestations of change over the *longue durée*.[9] By deploying this turn of phrase operating on several levels at once – historical, cultural, and individual – he is able to bind together a set of divergent ideas into a single conceptual field. He uses the phrase to bridge the temporal gap between past and present, thereby creating a framework for comparing cityscapes that will say something about change in the wider world. With roots allegedly deep in the Moroccan past, the concept of *citadinité* provides the link between what was and what is; it proposes the notion of a more perfect urban order that stands in the background of the messy reality that has overcome Sefrou and other Moroccan towns. In other words, we are on rich terrain in which Geertz's consummate skills as a cultural anthropologist – having the ability to read and interpret what historian Natalie Zemon Davis calls 'repeated forms of telling behaviour' (Davis 2005, p. 38) – will become manifest.

To return to Sefrou, the causes of the crisis of 1986 are clear to Geertz because of his long familiarity with the town. Behind the drama is the fact that the population of Sefrou has radically changed. Not only are the Jews gone, but the Muslims too have become more diverse, now separated into 'old' or 'real' Sefrouis, long-time residents, and 'outsiders,' mostly Berbers newly arrived from the countryside who lack those qualities that constitute *citadinité*. They live on 'remittances... casual labour, casual trade,' and in Geertz's words, 'to an uncertain extent, casual crime' (Geertz 1989, p. 295). Not surprisingly, the field between these two groups becomes one of contestation, where all those unspoken areas of rivalry that prevail in 'this masculinist, power-candid world' come into play (p. 295). Moreover, this agonistic relationship is anchored in space. Old Sefrouis live mostly in the *ville nouvelle*, in well designed villas abandoned by the departing French, while the dwellings of the newcomers on the urban periphery are devoid of architectural merit and painted in outlandish colours, a poke in the eye, as it were, to good taste. Geertz reads these house fronts semiotically, as a sign of the new-comers' desire to make Sefrou's 'coloured peripheries, not its decayed core, its defining feature' (p. 300). Moreover, the political ramifications of this confrontation run deep and parallel to the architectural ones. The newcomers voted socialist, unlike old Sefrouis who were royalists, and for seven years they took over the city council in an interregnum that inserted 'a populist moment in a paternalist system' (p. 297). Geertz argues that by forcing the issue of their inte-gration through political means, they challenged the notion of *citadinité* upon which the urban compact rested. Not only a political revolution ensued, but a social one as well, in which the newcomers turned the urban order both upside down and inside out.

At the end of the day, Geertz felt that the argument about the colour of walls was not simply about the colour of walls, but a representation of a profound cultural shift taking place in Sefrou that was complex, multilayered, and irreversible. We are not talking here merely about house painting, he says, we are in the midst of a battle over politics and power, and the effort to under-stand this conflict presents an opportunity. By looking closely at the urban landscape, by reading architecture as a semiotic system, we come closer to understanding what exactly is going on – to discern what Geertz calls 'the web of perceptions we weakly call "experience"' (p. 293).

It is not difficult to tell where Geertz comes down in this argument. Sefrou, once 'a chiseled jewel set in a paradisian garden,' was now 'a sprawling, disorganised, anything but jewel-like *bourg*' (p. 296). Something has gone out of the town, some ineffable quality of tranquility, coherence, and rationality that gave 'meaning and order' to Sefroui society. Faced with this deficit, Geertz frankly struggles to place these disturbing facts into a larger framework of under-standing. While the political difficulties are easy to sort out, the cultural ones are more resistant. 'What sort of a place should Sefrou be, and who decides?' is the question left hanging in the air. In 'Toutes directions,' Geertz leaves us with a feeling of anxiety that reflects the upheavals in his own soul: What is the relationship between meaning and materiality, and where do we find a sense of the city amidst the confusing signposts and garish facades that the cityscape impresses upon us? A Sefrou transformed and disarticulated is now a metaphor, not only for Clifford Geertz's own personal sense of cultural loss, but also for the state of confusion that Morocco of the late 1980s seemed to impose.

Hassan the builder

The conflict in Sefrou was a bit of micro-history enfolded in a much larger historical frame rela-ting to the question of power in Morocco of the 1980s. In the context of a contested monarchy seeking to remake itself, even the colour of the houses in Sefrou could be viewed as a token of political currency and a manifestation of political will. In the background was a speech made by King Hassan II at the Royal Palace in Marrakesh on 14 January 1986 to a group of architects on the subject of Moroccan urbanism, in which he singled out Sefrou for special criticism. Noting that his predecessors had 'always accorded a great importance to construction and urbanism,' the king remarked that, at the same time, Moroccans were not mired in the past but were open to innovation in building. Despite these advantages, something had gone wrong. Known abroad as 'Hassan le bâtisseur,' he saw only ugliness when he cast his eye about at home. New construction everywhere suffered from a lack of aesthetic appeal and an absence of both 'authenticity' and 'homogeneity.' 'If you were blindfolded and parachuted from a helicopter into a Moroccan city,' said the king, 'you would be hard pressed to tell exactly where you were.'[10]

The reason for this deplorable state of affairs, according to Hassan II, was that architects and urban planners had failed in their responsibility. Instead of limiting themselves to problems of construction, they should be devoting themselves to turning building projects into statements of a 'philosophy of life' attentive to preserving 'the beauty' of Morocco. The specific example the king chose to demonstrate this loss of aesthetic appeal was Sefrou, 'the city we once knew as lovely has since become quite ugly.' It was an example of the neglect that mainly affected rural towns, where few city-based architects set foot to practice their craft. Never one to overlook a political opportunity, the king announced that henceforth, he would promulgate an architecture for the masses: 'Every Moroccan, no matter who he is, has the right to a home' (*Tout marocain, quel qu'il soit, doit disposer d'une maison*). His solution to the architectural problem was a truly bureaucratic one – to constitute a 'corps' of architects, just like other professional groups that could be closely watched, monitored, and directed toward building projects outside the big cities. 'Be assured,' he said, 'when you have created your own [organisation], we will be able to follow your activities and you will be able to contact us more easily and more often.'[11]

Unspoken yet present in the speech is the king's disdain not only for a failed urban policy, but also for a hyper-modern architectural style that had abandoned forms expressive of the 'unique personality' of Morocco. Behind this development was a building boom at mid-century that aimed for modularity, functionality, and a rigorous, even brutal adherence to simple forms. Led by Michel Ecochard, the Moroccan disciples of the 'School of Athens' abandoned the cities of the interior and concentrated instead on the 'Atlantic axis,' the coastal strip between Casablanca and Kenitra where the majority of the population was now moving (Dethier 1973, pp. 213–221). Fez, for example, was in a colossal state of disrepair, and the great monuments that had once served as unmistakable symbols of the power of the ruling dynasty were now threatened with collapse. In January 1986, the king had hosted the foreign ministers of the Islamic Conference in Fez, and in the course of the meetings, the decrepit state of the city's architectural patrimony emerged as a deep source of embarrassment.[12] Hassan II – always sensitive to the judgment of history – may have read the condition of Fez as symptomatic of the status of his own rule. Sefrou was only one small part of a much larger problem in which architectural representations and their relationship to power were very much in the forefront of royal image-making.

If politics both high and low animated the king's discourse of 14 January 1986, for the Sefroui 'old guard,' the speech carried a message that reached closer to home about the status of their city as measured against other Moroccan cities. Hence the order to repaint the facades and to upgrade Sefrou to conform to some nebulous yet potent idea of what it meant to 'be Moroccan.' The conjuncture of historical events in this story was too alluring to dismiss. Morocco was indeed changing, and here was one of those luminous moments when everyone from the king down to the average householder, and including the visiting anthropologist, could pause and contemplate what that change meant to each of them and how they should respond to it.

After the fact

Geertz returned to Sefrou one more time in his writing, in his second from last book, *After the fact* (Geertz 1995), a meditation on his long life in anthropology. The story of repainting of the houses of Sefrou comes at the end of the book, in a chapter titled 'Modernities.' Here the incidents surrounding the house fronts take on their final form, at last settling into an intellectual framework consistent with a life spent observing and interpreting. In this retelling, remarkably consistent with the previous one except for a few minor points, Geertz's Sefrou is no longer just Sefrou, no longer a stand-in for the exploding metropolis; it has ceased being the symbol of a society in disarray. Picking up where the earlier version left off, Sefrou's house fronts are now evidence of a cacophonous modernity wandering in every direction. Moreover, Geertz says, the wheel has not yet turned, it is still too early to tell where matters are heading, and we cannot make any real progress on understanding the confusing norms that now govern urban life in Morocco, or anywhere else, for that matter. Nor can he readily predict what the next stage will bring.[13] The best we can do, he says, in true Geertzian manner, is to continue to read the signs in the hope that some clarity will eventually emerge. His resolution to this problem is deeply personal and significant for his own work and life, and constitutes a sound reflection on the meaning of the anthropological endeavor: 'We may not be able to trace the track of modernity before it is laid down,' he says, 'but once it is we shall have explanations enough... for the course it has taken' (Geertz 1995, p. 167).

Are there solid conclusions we may draw from Geertz's thoughts on the Moroccan city? Is there something here more than signposts pointing nowhere? Indeed there is. First of all, we should take note of the extent to which Geertz's idea of urban change as sensitive node for understanding larger issues of development in Morocco continues to be true. Cities in Morocco and elsewhere remain the prism through which the problems of contemporary life are most clearly visualised. The size and scale of the expansion of cities around the globe in the past century have impacted above all on poor and middle-income countries like Morocco, and there is no end in sight. While metropolises such as Casablanca have felt it most, small and medium-sized towns like Sefrou continue to swell in size, with many inhabitants living in slums or substandard housing. Bad taste in design is now the least of the problems of these poorer quarters; more pressing are matters such as inadequate sanitation, violent crime, and political volatility.[14] It has become a platitude that the *bidonvilles* are breeding grounds for extremism and anti-state activity. Yet recent research has shown that their inhabitants are not without hope. On the contrary, many belong to local activist organisations, join together in microfinance groups, vote in elections, and express strong feelings of attachment to their neighbourhood, despite its downtrodden appearance. In short, they have become politically and economically engaged and it is no longer possible to ignore them (Zaki, n.d.). They and other associational groups that have come together voluntarily over the past two decades in Morocco pose a major challenge to an autocratic monarchy seeking to institutionalise itself at the risk of its own undoing. In their actions they limn the larger trends that are roiling Moroccan society today, and serve as the sort of reflective mirror to which social scientists of the more imaginative sort are drawn.

Moreover, those who study cities and their forms are aware that these poorer citizens and their varied housing solutions now cover a far greater range of typologies than ever before. Some still live in slums and temporary housing, but others are clearly on their way to integration by living in neighbourhoods that have become formalised and accepted by the municipality.[15] While better-off citizens still harbour intense feelings of scorn for the inhabitants of slum quarters, the definition of who is a *citadin* is no longer so clear-cut as it was 25 years ago. The rapid expansion of spatial and social categories in recent years is not only indicative of a more sophisticated social analysis; it also speaks of more complex forms of self-representation and more varied capacities to negotiate situations of conflict on the part of disadvantaged city-dwellers themselves.

Finally, it must be acknowledged that, in fundamental ways, Clifford Geertz changed the way historians of Morocco go about their work. He gave us a sense that there were lines between the lines in our precious texts that intimate the existence of a more richly diverse social life than the actual words allowed us imagine. He encouraged us to wander in the city and look for experiential examples of a sensibility only dimly hinted at in the written word. He advised us that the city of the past is present in the city of today, even if in a much altered form. At the same time, he warned us that those past cities must not be mistaken as models for eternity. He insisted that Moroccans have a certain idea of city life – call it *citadinité* – that shapes and informs their comportment and approach in the urban setting, but this quality is not solely the province of the elite, and it can be learned and adapted to modern life. Thanks to him, historians of Morocco appreciate the inimitable gift of Moroccans to recreate themselves in new and different guises, to fit into new modernities, while retaining something of the old. Whether this process will eventually exhaust itself or reach a point of no return, one never knows.

It is true that Moroccan cities are no longer what they once were. It is also true that new urban populations – made up of undisciplined youth, savvy technocrats, professional women, and other life forms not mentioned in Geertz's writing about the city – are coming to the foreground and reshaping our sense of what city life is today. New forms of membership are taking shape that are dynamic, anti-authoritarian, non-hierarchical, and the inverse of that quality of mind that regarded 'belonging in the city' as the property of a closed caste of patrician elites. All in all, 'the idea of the city' is too capacious a category to be left alone; it offers a space for all sorts of yearnings, including an identity with place that fulfills one's need for inclusion in something beyond oneself (Holston and Appadurai 1996, p. 189). Even though Morocco's cities are 'losing definition,' as Geertz put it, perhaps even more today than ever before, they may be 'gaining energy.' If that is indeed true, we can expect countless sequels to 'Toutes directions,' and many new iterations of what *citadinité* might mean.

Notes

1. Le Tourneau 1949, Deverdun 1959, and Michaux-Bellaire 1921 are principal book-length studies of cities and city life; there are also many monographs and shorter articles.
2. All translations are mine unless otherwise indicated.
3. See Lyautey 1995, speech of 10 December 1926.
4. His chapter titled 'Quarters' is vintage Berque, packed with the minute details of lived experience. As a snapshot of life in the neighbourhoods of the Maghreb in the 1930s, it is incomparable (Berque 1967, pp. 185–212).
5. The recuperation of colonial housing during and after the War of Independence is dramatically recounted in Leila Abouzeid's novel, *Year of the Elephant* (1989).
6. There are very few studies of the Moroccan *habus*. Among the most significant are Michaux-Bellaire 1911, 1914, Gaillard 1916, Milliot 1918, and Luccioni 1942, 1982.
7. The most informative sources for this period are Monjib 1992, Vermeren 2002, and Daoud 2007.
8. Emphases in the original. Among Naciri's several articles that deal with the concept is 'Le rôle de la citadinité dans l'évolution des villes arabo-islamiques' (Naciri 1997).
9. This theme profoundly informed his work and engaged him in the practice of history. See Davis 2005.
10. The king's speech was widely reported in the Moroccan press. It appears in its entirety in 'Hassan II le bâtisseur' (Hassan II the Builder), *Le Matin du Sahara*, 15 January 1986. An Arabic version appears in *Khutab wa nadawat, sahib al-jalala al-malik al-Hassan al-thani* (Speeches and seminars of King Hassan II), vol. 9 (Rabat: Ministry of Information, n.d.), 12–16. Geertz's interpretation, which he avows was not based on a

transcript but rather 'a paraphrase of a paraphrase' gleaned from 'Sefroui informants,' is a rather fanciful rendering of the king's actual words.

11. Ibid.

12. See *Le Matin du Sahara*, 5 January 1986, and subsequent articles on the problems besetting Fez as a 'national and universal patrimony.'

13. It is important to note that *After the fact* was written before the death of Hassan II, and before the changes that came with the investiture of Mohammed VI in 1999, some of which are attributable to the policies of the new king, while others are due to a liberalisation begun under his father.

14. 'The world goes to town: a special report on cities,' *The Economist*, 5 May 2007, 3–18.

15. The so-called 'clandestine housing' that was initially considered illegal but gradually became absorbed into the urban system, as described by Navez-Bouchanine 2003, 8–9, 21.

References

Abouzeid, L., 1989. *Year of the elephant: a Moroccan woman's journey toward independence, and other stories.* Austin, TX: Center for Middle Eastern Studies, University of Texas at Austin.

Abu-Lughod, J.L., 1987. The Islamic city: historic myth, Islamic essence, and contemporary relevance. *International Journal of Middle East Studies*, 19 (2), 155–176.

Berque, J., 1967. *French North Africa: the Maghrib between two world wars.* London: Faber.

Daoud, Z., 2007. *Maroc: les années de plomb, 1958–1988; chroniques d'une résistance.* Houilles: Manucius.

Davis, N.Z., 2005. Clifford Geertz on time and change. *In*: Richard A. Shweder and Byron Good, eds. *Clifford Geertz by his colleagues.* Chicago: University of Chicago Press, 38–44.

de Kerdec Chény, A., 1888. *Guide du voyageur au Maroc et guide du touriste.* Tanger: G. T. Abrines.

Dethier, J., 1973. Evolution of concepts of housing, urbanism, and country planning in a developing country: Morocco, 1900–1972. *In*: L. Carl Brown, ed. *From Madina to metropolis: heritage and change in the Near Eastern city.* Princeton, NJ: Darwin Press, 197–243.

Deverdun, G., 1959. *Marrakech des origines à 1912.* 2. vol. Rabat: Éds. Techniques Nord-Africaines.

Gaillard, H., 1916. *La réorganisation du gouvernement marocain.* Paris: Comité de l'Afrique Française.

Geertz, C., 1979. Suq: the bazaar economy in Sefrou. *In*: C. Geertz, H. Geertz, L. Rosen. *Meaning and order in Moroccan society.* Cambridge, UK: Cambridge University Press, 123–313.

Geertz, C., 1989. Toutes directions: reading the signs in an urban sprawl. *International Journal of Middle East Studies*, 21 (3), 291–306.

Geertz, C., 1995. *After the fact: two countries, four decades, one anthropologist.* Cambridge, MA: Harvard University Press.

Geertz, C., Geertz, H., and Rosen, L., 1979. *Meaning and order in Moroccan society.* Cambridge, UK: Cambridge University Press.

Hardy, G., 1949. *Portrait de Lyautey.* Paris: Bloud & Gay.

Holston, J. and Appadurai, A., 1996. Cities and citizenship. *Public Culture*, 8 (2), 187–204.

Khutab wa nadawat, sahib al-jalala al-malik al-Hassan al-thani [Speeches and seminars of King Hassan II] n.d. Rabat: Ministry of Information, 9, 12–16.

Le Matin du Sahara, 1986. S.M. Hassan II le bâtisseur [Hassan II the Builder]. *Le Matin du Sahara*, 15 January.

Le Tourneau, R., 1949. *Fès avant le protectorat: étude économique et sociale d'une ville de l'occident musulman.* Casablanca: SMLE.

Luccioni, J., 1942. *Le Habous ou wakf: rites malékite et hanéfite.* Casablanca: Impr. Réunies de la Vigie Marocaine et du Petit Marocain.

Luccioni, J., 1982. *Les fondations pieuses 'habous' au Maroc: depuis les origines jusqu'à 1956*, n.p.

Lyautey, L.H.G., 1995. *Paroles d'action.* Paris: Imprimerie nationale.

Michaux-Bellaire, E., 1911. La guelsa et le gza. *Revue du monde musulman*, 13, 197–248.

Michaux-Bellaire, E., 1921. *Tanger et sa zone.* Paris: Ernest Leroux.

Michaux-Bellaire, E., ed., 1914. *Les Habous de Tanger: registre officiel d'actes et de documents, part 2. Analyses et extraits.* Paris: Ernest Leroux.

Miller, S.G., 2005. Finding order in the Moroccan city: the *hubûs* of the great mosque of Tangier as an agent of urban change. *Muqarnas*, 22, 265–283.

Milliot, L., 1918. *Démembrements du Habous: Menfa'â, Gzâ, Guelsâ, Zînâ, Istighrâq.* Paris: Ernest Leroux.

Monjib, M., 1992. *La monarchie marocaine et la lutte pour le pouvoir: Hassan II face à l'opposition nationale, de l'indépendence à l'état d'exception.* Paris: L'Harmattan.

Naciri, M., 1986. Regard sur l'évolution de la citadinité au Maroc. *In:* Kenneth Brown, et al., eds. *Middle Eastern cities in comparative perspective: points de vue sur les villes du Maghreb et du Machrek; Franco-British Symposium, London, 10–14 May 1984*. London: Ithaca Press, 249–270.

Naciri, M., 1997. Le rôle de la citadinité dans l'évolution des villes arabo-islamiques. *In:* Mohamed Naciri and André Raymond, eds. *Sciences sociales et phénomènes urbains dans le Monde Arabe: actes du colloque de l'Association de Liaison entre les Centres de Recherches et Documentations sur le Monde Arabe (ALMA), Casablanca, 30 novembre–2 décembre 1994*. Casablanca: Fondation du Roi Abdul-Aziz al Saoud pour les Études Islamiques et les Sciences Humaines, 131–148.

Navez-Bouchanine, F., 2003. The case of Rabat-Salé, Morocco. City Global Report, UNHSP/DPU, University College of London. Available at: http://www.ucl.ac.uk/dpu-projects/Global_Report/pdfs/Rabat.pdf. [Accessed 25 August 2008].

Rivet, D., 1988. *Lyautey et l'institution du Protectorat français au Maroc, 1912–1925*. 3. vol. Paris: L'Harmattan.

Souleimani, M. Pourquoi la sauvegarde de la ville de Fès [Why preserve the city of Fez] 1986. *Le Matin du Sahara*, 5 January.

Tharaud, J. and Tharaud, J., 2002. *Fès, ou, les bourgeois de l'Islam*. Rabat: Marsam.

The Economist, 2007. The world goes to town: a special report on cities. *The Economist*, 5 May. 3–18.

Vermeren, P., 2002. *Histoire du Maroc depuis l'indépendence*. Paris: La Découverte.

Zaki, L., 2005. Pratiques politiques au bidonville, Casablanca (2000–2005). Thesis (PhD). Institut d'études politiques, Paris

Zaki, L., n.d. Après le bidonville: Le deuil d'une 'identité difficile'? Entre déni et nostalgie, les relogés de Lahjajma (Casablanca). Available at: http://www.unil.ch/webdav/site/iepi/users/cplatel/public/atelier_4/Zaki.pdf [Accessed 23 August 2008].

Observing *Islam observed*: the family resemblance and the pun

Lawrence Rosen

Department of Anthropology, Princeton University, NJ, USA

Clifford Geertz's Moroccan work was of a piece with his overall project of understanding how cultural categories are formed and reformed in the context of such institutions as the marketplace and religious settings. His study of the Moroccan market was therefore really as much a study of religion as of economic structures. He sought to uncover the everyday morality that informs that domain and to show how that morality represents and incorporates concepts that are deeply embedded in Islamic thought. Far from romanticising or judging Moroccan social life, he sought to use his comparative work in Indonesia to highlight the distinctiveness of Moroccan local knowledge.

Clifford Geertz always said that context matters, and his own work on Islam proved no exception. Geertz's interest in Moroccan Islam came about as he sought a place through which he could pursue his comparison of cultures, a comparison he felt was indispensable to understanding both the range of cultural variation and the guiding processes through which the benefits of comparison itself could be grasped. Having worked in Java, Sumatra, and Bali, he looked for a place that shared some features with Indonesia but whose contrasts would stimulate ideas about the relation of cultural patterns to local circumstance. He had thought for a while about working in Pakistan, but with his children still quite young, he and his wife Hildred decided that might prove too difficult. Instead, he went to the other end of the Muslim world, and found in Morocco the congeniality and the challenge of a Muslim culture that also appeared to be profoundly different from that of the Indonesian archipelago. He was still in the early stages of his main fieldwork when he was called upon to summarise his approach to Islam, a summary that, as it turned out, was to be his most explicit but, as we shall see, by no means his only substantial analysis of Moroccan Islam.[1]

It was in 1966, just as he turned 40, that Geertz was asked to deliver the Terry Lectures at Yale. In less than a decade of publishing he had already produced many of the essays that were soon to be collected in *The interpretation of cultures* (Geertz 1973a), essays that immediately established him as a new and brilliant voice in the social sciences. Having concentrated for the preceding dozen years on Indonesia, he had only arrived a few months before to initiate sustained fieldwork in Morocco.[2] Whether it was because he had just made contact with the village and descendants of the Moroccan saint, Sidi Lahcen Lyusi, or because the commission prompted him to recall the Indonesian saintly figure, Sunan Kalidjaga, the challenge of the Terry Lectures brought together several elements that had clearly been emerging in Geertz's work.

In two essays written in the early 1960s, Geertz reminded readers that what is distinctive to our species is that we developed the capacity for culture – the ability to create the categories of our own experience – before, not after, we achieved our present speciation. Moreover, he emphasised that thought is essentially extrinsic: rather than lurking in some 'secret grotto of the mind,' it is worked upon in public, through shared symbols, concepts, acts, and orienting events which, proliferated across multiple domains of life, give the appearance to their adherents of being both common-sensical and real.[3] From this baseline Geertz was now able to elaborate, in a variety of additional essays, his thinking about religion and social ideologies.

In 'Religion as a cultural system' (1966), Geertz formulated a working definition of religion that focused on how people cast up, through the symbols he called 'the material vehicles of thought,' their associated emotions, and the sense of order they bespeak – those orientations and concepts that appear to their adherents to partake of the very nature of reality. In 'Ideology as a cultural system' (1964), he articulated the view that, as it becomes part of an ideational structure through which the process of encountering a changing world is grasped, religion takes on challenges to common sense that render problematic its coherence and capacity to guide social life. In each of these essays, Geertz's formulations stood in marked contrast to those accepted by many of his intellectual predecessors. Well into the mid-20th century, comparison in religious studies had been focused on universals and essentials – mysticism, spiritual experience, 'ultimate beliefs.' But Geertz's own theoretical orientation, worked out in his comparative studies in Indonesia, had instead led him to concentrate on 'family resemblances,' where similarities and differences form amalgams that are not reducible to a single circumscribed feature. And, no less importantly, Geertz had been finding his own literary style, a style that (as he was later to say) was as integral to the capacity to convince as it was to suiting the mode of analysis to its point.[4] Having discovered that his favourite form of expression was the extended essay, he was now able to marshal substance and style to the task of rethinking religious studies as a form of comparative social inquiry.

In his Indonesian work Geertz had explored the ways in which a Weberian ethos suffuses both the marketplace and the ideologies that inform a wide range of social acts. Approaching Morocco in a similar vein, he was struck by the contrasting ways in which Islam was incorporated into the culture of the early postcolonial experience. Where the Indonesians played up the image of the state as a ritual centre around which political and religious life acquired shape, the Moroccan experience suggested that the governing ethos included a sense of activated spiritual power and collective moral temper that was at once intensely personal and contestably institutionalised. How, in such contrasting environments, was one to understand the differential role of Islam? Indeed, given this contrast, how was one to describe the experience of ordinary people as the state and the market, the mosque and the home all became venues through which people had to learn *how* to believe in a world in which *what* they believed was becoming increasingly contingent on outside forces?[5]

Geertz loved a richly textured story, one that cried out for deep interpretation. He thus found, both stylistically and intellectually, that it was far wiser to begin by telling a story – whether of a contested funeral, as in one of his first articles (Geertz 1957), or a riotous cockfight, as in his most famous article (Geertz 1972b) – and then to unpack its mysteries and its implications. So, in the stories of two saintly figures he found the turning point for his analysis. For not only would each appear out of place in the other's context, but each becomes the embodiment of just those forces that are at work in their people's ways of comprehending everyday experience.

Arguing that 'there is no ascent to truth without descent to cases,' he demonstrated one of his enduring talents: the capacity to encapsulate an entire ethos in a pregnant phrase. He could say that the Indonesian pattern 'is essentially aesthetic; it portrays its ideal,' or characterise the Moroccan cultural pattern as one of 'ecstatic moral intensity.' He could note 'the solemn self-deception' of both, or remark that, for each, 'naturalness seems increasingly difficult actually to attain.' Whether in pointing out the Moroccan 'talent for forcing things together which really do not go together' or the 'Koranic moralism' of the marketplace, the specifically Moroccan approach to the sacred as 'an endowment of particular individuals' or the more general proposition that 'nothing alters like the unalterable,' his characterisations never reduced a culture to some professed essential but raised each to a level of graspable complexity.[6]

Given this orientation, Geertz was reluctant to speak about 'Islam' in the abstract, or (perhaps as much for its infelicitous sound as for its air of collective essentialising) of Islam*s*. As a result, he was notably critical of much of the work that had been done by Western scholars on the subject. Some of these reservations, together with his broader way of thinking about Islam, come out in the reviews he published of others' work on the topic, as well as in his occasional remarks about the contemporary politics of Islam. A closer look at these remarks may, therefore, help place his overall orientation in context.

In his extensive, two-part essay in the 'New York review of books' in 2003 (for whose title he chose the caption of a famous *New Yorker* cartoon depicting a driver lost at a desert crossroad: 'Which way to Mecca?'), Geertz reviewed more than a dozen books – chosen, he said, after surveying literally dozens more – and divided Western studies of Islam into four broad categories: the 'civilizational' studies that compare 'East' and 'West'; the contrastive studies that try to pick out 'good' Islam from 'bad,' 'authentic' from 'inauthentic,' and 'tolerant' from 'terrorist'; the studies that attempt to reconcile the Islamic and the non-Islamic through a shared 'Abrahamic' or philosophical base; and those that emphasise the local distinctiveness of Islamic cultures, and to some extent their family resemblance, rather than their unitary identity. With each he found fault. The civilizational approach (most notably represented by Bernard Lewis) is, he argued, simultaneously judgmental and non-specific; the contrastive approach glosses over differences in a vain attempt to sort matters into self-satisfying categories; the 'Abrahamic,' which by trying to claim that we are all really the same under the surface, produces anodyne approaches to vastly more complex situations; and the localists seldom come to grips with what it is that is varying and in response to what forces. When 'Islam' is made the direct concern, most writers, Geertz implied, simply bore the reader with their endless repetition of the pillars of faith, their moralising tone, their characterisation of Muslim societies as static and subject to inevitable forces, and their account of wars, invasions, and fungible dynasties as 'a temporal unfolding out of [Islam's] 'primitive,' revelatory moment' (Geertz 2003, pp. 1, 27).

Not surprisingly, Geertz – always delighting in the particular, the *un*-inevitable, the changeable, the contingent – was particularly intrigued by the opinion surveys reported by Riaz Hassan (2002), concluding that:

> Any notion of Islam as a bloc universe, everywhere the same in content and outlook, can hardly survive such findings. The sense that everywhere Islam is moving on, if in varying directions, and not just setting its face against 'modernity,' the West, and internal change, comes out very strongly. (Geertz 2003, p. 2)

On those rare occasions when he did generalise, Geertz would imply caution with scare quotes, as when he wrote (following a discussion of architecture in Sefrou and education in the Javanese town he studied) that what is happening 'is what is happening both in those places and elsewhere to "Islam" as such. It is losing definition and gaining energy' (Geertz 1995, p. 165). And when he did speak about Moroccan or Indonesian Islam it was always in the context of place, as when he wrote of the former: 'Islam in Morocco is sustained by personages, by a vast, inconstant crowd of severely independent, grand and middling, middling and petty, religious notables. . . like the society generally, an irregular network of irregular figures, constantly adjusting their plans and allegiances' (Geertz 1995, pp. 58–9).

Curiously, Geertz did not praise any general work on Islam under review. But then neither did he mention any of those particularistic studies he obviously commended, perhaps thinking them too narrow for the general readership of the 'New York review'. Yet the choice of what to include and exclude can also be seen as a statement about his approach to Islamic studies more generally. Three features in particular suggest themselves in this regard: that Islam reveals itself less in abstract propositions than in its enactment in the rough and tumble of political, economic, and familial life; that focusing on this emplacement is not only true to the orientation of most Muslims but restrains the analyst from the very generalisations Geertz found insupportable in many of the books he critiqued; and that (following the lead of various pragmatist thinkers) one could indeed compare incomparables and still resist the allure of essentialising.[7] Each of these propositions is worth considering in a bit more detail.

Geertz, as we have seen, was always concerned to see the domains in which religion is enacted in everyday life – not in some rarefied domain of spiritual intensity – and for this his favored venue (no doubt following Weber's lead) was the marketplace. Whether in *Peddlers and princes* (Geertz 1963b) or in his most extended essay on Morocco, the analysis of the Sefrou *suq* (Geertz 1979), Geertz followed the idea that religion is a system through which people orient their actions in multiple domains of life.[8] It was not that he ignored the emotional or the 'experiential.' In his William James Lecture in 1998 he had expressed his reservations about James' emphasis on disembodied religiosity and the uselessness of mysticism and spiritualism as categories for comparison. Noting that people nowadays often do not know how they are supposed to feel, Geertz nevertheless concluded that, ''Experience," pushed out the door as a radically subjective, individualized "faith state," returns through the window as the communal sensibility of a religiously assertive social actor' (Geertz 2000b, p. 178). And in the many anecdotes he included in his analytic essays, the experiential was certainly an important component of the overall picture he sought to convey.[9] Indeed, bringing matters up to the time of his *Islam observed* lectures, Geertz could write:

> The bulk of our two populations still considers either an inward search for psychic equilibrium or a moral intensification of personal presence the most natural mode of spiritual expression. The problem is that these days naturalness seems increasingly difficult actually to attain. [. . .] The transformation of religious symbols from imagistic revelations of the divine, evidences of God, to ideological assertions of the divine's importance, badges of piety, has been in each country, though in different ways, the common reaction to this disheartening discovery. (Geertz 1968, pp. 61–62)

Geertz's aversion to generalising, whether about Islam or any other social phenomenon, was, as we have noted, displaced by his propensity to think of Islam as a set of variations that bore a 'family resemblance' to one another. This analogy was characterised by Geertz himself in the following terms: '[A] very great deal, in my opinion, rests on family resemblances, the oblique similarities that arise as specific histories take form against the background of persisting ideas' (Geertz 1982).[10] Geertz had borrowed this concept from Wittgenstein, and had earlier written:

> We think we see striking resemblances between different generations of a family but, as Wittgenstein pointed out, we may find that there is no one feature common to them; the resemblance may come from many different features 'overlapping and crisscrossing.' This sort of approach seems more promising than one that sees the history of Islam... as an extended struggle of a gentle pietism to escape from an arid legalism. A picture of the Islamic venture derived from 'overlaps' and 'criss-crosses' would be less ordered and less continuous, a matter of oblique connections and glancing contrasts, and general conclusions would be harder to come by. (Geertz 1975, p. 18ff)[11]

All this might seem to skirt the question of how comparison is possible were it not that Geertz saw in such family resemblances the impetus for returning to individual cases with greater insight about what features vary in relation to different contexts such that a coherent entity, one to which people can attach meaning, may result. But he was not unmindful of the temptations of such an approach:

> The resolution I have taken... not to describe either of my cases [Morocco or Indonesia] as a reduced version of the other, the bane of a great deal of comparative analysis in the human sciences – Spain lacked Holland's Calvinism; China, Japan's feudality – becomes particularly hard to sustain when you look... at Islam in North Africa immediately after looking at it in Southeast Asia. (Geertz 1995, p. 57)

And though he followed this by referring to his comparison as 'an instructive example of the heuristic uses of belatedly appreciated commotion and muddle' (Geertz 1995, p. 63), he does not suggest that, as a result, nothing can be said but, quite the contrary, that only in this way can one say something about something, that one can only speak of specific instances and not of 'Islam' in so abstract a fashion that it cannot be brought down to cases. One does not, in Geertz's borrowed phrasing, have language but *some* language, and one does not have religion but *some* religion – indeed, some particular, culturally embedded version of that religion.

It is here, too, that Geertz's problems with Orientalism also become relevant. In his 1978 book, titled *Orientalism*, Edward Said cited Geertz as one of the few scholars of whose work he greatly approved:

> Thus interesting work is most likely to be produced by scholars whose allegiance is to a discipline defined intellectually and not to a 'field' like Orientalism. An excellent recent instance is the anthropology of Clifford Geertz, whose interest in Islam is discrete and concrete enough to be animated by the specific societies and problems he studies and not by the rituals, preconceptions, and doctrines of Orientalism. (Said 1978, p. 326)

This opinion took a quick turn, however, when Geertz criticised Said's later book on media coverage of the Middle East, characterising Said's as 'grain-of-truth arguments' involving a 'tone of high panic' that 'leave us with a bad taste in the mind, a sense of having been held by the lapels and screamed at by someone reckless to persuade.'[12] Thereafter Said spoke of the 'standard disciplinary rationalisations and self-congratulatory clichés about hermeneutical circles offered by Clifford Geertz' (Said 1985, p. 5). He wrote of Geertz's 'trivial arguments against me,' how Geertz thinks of him as 'an intemperate left-wing non-Orientalist Christian Palestinian,' and stated that, by not also referring to the background of others whose work he reviewed, Geertz 'merely underlines the racist Orientalist habit of reducing the intellectual positions of wogs to their ethnic genealogy' (Said 1982).[13]

There were other criticisms of Geertz's work that came from some historians, even ones who were deeply sympathetic to his approach. Geertz has thus been praised and vilified for seeming to pay too much attention to a slice-of-time, synchronistic view of culture, rather than changes that occur over time, and for his concentration on what is shared rather than what is contested by various groupings within a culture. Some, like historian William H. Sewell, Jr., have sought to have the former critique both ways: he characterises Geertz's work as overly synchronic but then says that 'it is more important for a historian to know how to suspend time than to know how to recount its passage' (Sewell 1997, p. 41). Sewell also notes that Geertz's formulation of cultures as 'models of' and 'models for' tends to gloss over the discrepancies between the two, as analysts make their representations of the world less varied and less susceptible to change than is really the case (p. 47). Others, emphasising disagreement *within* a culture, criticised Geertz for ignoring the views of women or other subordinate groupings.[14]

All of this is relevant for an understanding of Geertz's approach to Islam. First, it is clear that few of the critics have read Geertz's entire corpus. Like the blind men surveying the elephant, each comes at Geertz's work, as their limited citations reveal, using him for the purposes that most readily suit their own pursuits. Sewell, like many Europeanists, seems never to have read *Agricultural involution* (Geertz 1963a), the essay on the suq in *Meaning and order in Moroccan society* (Geertz 1979), *The social history of an Indonesian town* (Geertz 1965), or *Peddlers and princes* (Geertz 1963b) – each of which is extremely diachronic in approach. And those who say he ignored 'subalterns' never cite *Kinship in Bali* (Geertz and Geertz 1975), his Afterword (Geertz 972a) in the volume edited by Claire Holt, or various essays in *After the fact* (1995). Like Weber, Geertz's individual essays have to be read as chapters of a single, overarching oeuvre, and failure to see that he did not replicate the same data or issues in every separable part of that overall comparativist project is to gravely misread particular parts of it.[15] Second, it is true that the high-water period of Geertz's work – the 1960s at Chicago – was one in which the idea of culture as shared symbols was preeminent, but that attention was focused more on the symbols part of the equation than on the extent and modes by which symbols are shared. It is a mistake, however, to think that the issue of internal cultural disagreement was simply ignored. Geertz, like the others at Chicago in those days, did not see in culture the proof of ineluctable forces or reducible patterns of historic necessity, nor did the Chicago scholars fail to consider the highly contested nature of the politics of the developing nations. Reading, for example, the essays in *Old societies and new states* would show critics that Geertz viewed culture as something constantly subject to creative alteration rather than mechanical replication even as he focused on how the family resemblance among diverse approaches to a shared set of symbols could hold a society together (Geertz 1963).

With these points in mind we can begin to see how central both the shared and the disputed were to Geertz's thinking about Islamic societies. In Javanese culture, for example, Islam was differentially absorbed by the Hinduized *priyayi*, the animist *abangan*, and the scripturalist *santri*, yet all could, in very significant ways, orient their actions to one another sufficiently so that their shared identity as Muslims could render the formation of a national identity possible. And the intense, even centrifugal individualism of Moroccans could still contribute to a common nation-state when the precepts by which alliances are forged were themselves rendered within a framework of Islamic legitimisation. In each case internal variation and contestation, as well as the use of diachronic change alongside an assessment of structural forms, were central to Geertz's understanding of Islam's malleable place within each society and time.

Indeed, as Segal points out, Geertz's view of meaning in religion always necessitates that action be taken in terms of one's orientations: neither intent nor attachment to unenacted propositions is sufficient to render a belief system socially and culturally viable.[16] Thus, as Geertz sought to understand the Moroccan and Indonesian experiences of Islam over the 40 years he studied them, he looked for the places where they were given life, the areas where they were enacted and where they created realities – the marketplace, the political arena, the household, the ritual – firmly convinced that one cannot participate in a cultural system without the categories generated by experience receiving some enlivening form. Moreover, just as Aristotle had said that the wise man does not attribute greater specificity to a matter than is appropriate to its nature, Geertz resisted characterising the events he observed as having a greater precision than seemed to accord with both the actions and the statements he encountered. Just as he argued that Islam did not have some pristine form that occurred at a given moment in Islamic history, only to suffer a scattering out, much less diminution, over the course of time, so, too, he stuck to his theory of culture as centered on the publicly worked nature of symboling behaviour that is integral to the highly fluctuating and variable ways people create a common heritage of categories and meanings. From his first major article about an Islamic funeral that went awry in Java because of the different meanings Muslim groupings attached to their identity, right up to his last iteration of Islam in the Introduction he wrote to the Hebrew translation of *Islam observed* (2007a, pp. 11–17), Geertz sought to point out the poignant, and not necessarily successful, attempts to settle views that, as the acts and utterances of his informants revealed, were by no means static or beyond analytic grasp.

It is here, then, that one can see how the essay on the market in Sefrou was, in no small way, an elaborate essay on Islam. For if, to paraphrase Geertz's characterisation of the work of Malinowski and Victor Turner, the Balinese rituals are in large part engines of status, the Moroccan marketplace is a forum for moral action.[17] This morality is neither abstract nor unlinked to Islam. Quite the contrary, it *is* Islam – its bespoken manifestation in a world where workable relationships among men are central to the retention of a community of believers, its expression of a world in which chaos is to be averted by the hurly-burly of interpersonal engagement, and its enactment in a realm where the idea of what it is to be a Muslim receives one of its most characteristic, if variant, manifestations. In this regard Geertz attended very carefully to the specifically Islamic institutions of the marketplace – the *habus* (mortmain), the *zawiya* (brotherhood), and the *shari‘a* (Islamic law). But he also explored the relation of these institutions and the broader culture of integrative orientations, appreciating that, 'in a country notorious for a clamorous sort of piety,' a good deal of the effect of Islam

> is diffuse, a general colouring of style and attitude in commercial relationships that only extended ethnographic description could capture, and then but obliquely. Some of it, also, is only skin deep – quranic prohibitions against interest taking, gambling, or trafficking in gold that seem to exist mainly to be circumvented. But some of it is both precise and powerful, built into specific institutional forms whose impact on commercial life is as readily visible as that of transport, taxation, or the rhythm of the seasons. Among the world religions, Islam has been notable for its ability to sort its utopian and its pragmatic aspects into distinct and only partially communicating spheres – the former left as ideals to be affirmed, explicated, codified, and taught; the latter cast into ingenious pieces of social machinery regulating the detailed processes of community life. (Geertz 1979, pp. 150–151)

For Moroccans to say, therefore, that 'it is by the Grace of God that contentiousness is put between the buyer and the seller' is only to demonstrate how much Islam always is what Muslims do and say, and how much it is part of the Arabo-Berber version of Islam that the market should be a key venue for demonstrating that religion and moral action are inseparable.[18]

Three things, then, came together in Geertz's work on Islam: that local meanings, which may once have been more defined by social group attachments, had, in the period of his own observations, increasingly become loosened from those groupings and rendered more capable of being moved, synthesised, rearranged, or ignored by individual personalities acting independently of the places or collectivities within which such meanings had once been implanted; that the capacity to orient one's actions toward others on the basis of knowledge drawn from social origins, kinship, or territorial base had shifted with migration, population growth, patterns of gender employment, and colonial contact, but that the emotional attachment to finding one's footing in these changing circumstances through some rationale that could properly be called Islamic remains very intense; and that the human propulsion to constantly recreate the categories of our experience is just as likely to produce highly localised orientations, rather than simply 'globalised' patterns, as has been the case at many other moments in our cultural histories. Thus among the most significant changes he saw occurring in the Muslim world are: 1) 'the progressive disentanglement. . . of the major religions. . . from the places, peoples, and social formations, the sites and civilizations, within which and in terms of which they were historically formed;' and 2) 'the emergence of religious persuasion, inherited or self-ascribed, thinned-out or reinforced, as a broadly negotiable, mobile and fungible, instrument of public identity – a portable persona' (Geertz 2007a, Introduction).[19]

Islam observed, Geertz said, was a pun – in the dual sense of examining Islam and attending to it as a *participant*-observer. In any event, he said, people didn't get the pun. Yet the punning exercise was not without its own value: it underscored that without some *comparative* examination one may assume that things must be the way they appear in any given situation because of some inherent necessity, whereas comparisons show the variability of every cultural feature. Indeed, without some circumstantial involvement, the actual meaning of an enterprise may lack traction altogether. Notwithstanding some criticisms that largely missed the point, Geertz's definition of religion, for example, not only holds up well under comparison but continues to refocus attention on the specifics of culturally distinctive manifestations of Islamic commonalities. His 'definition' of religion thus creates not a rigid dictionary bounding of religion but a proper emphasis on how religion connects with numerous other domains in the life of an adherent.[20]

Indeed, 40 years on, Geertz's insights continue to be of enormous value to our present understanding of the world. It remains quite true, as he said, that the wider a religion becomes the more precarious it becomes, that we ignore the local at our peril, that turmoil is internal however much it is externally stimulated, and that 'scripturalism seems likely to remain in the position of cheering on a modernism whose every advance undermines its own position.' As one confronts a world in which the temptation of the universal can seduce even the well intended interventionist into self-deluding acts, Geertz's prescient reminder that people will seek local meanings for their local lives should give pause to those who think that events must unfold in a predetermined way. In the end, Geertz's quest was always for that 'social history of the imagination' in which 'the real is as imagined as the imaginary.' For if the members of the two Muslim cultures to whose comprehension he devoted his lifelong efforts teach us anything, he seems to be saying, their 'struggle for the real,' their encapsulation of their religious life as 'a materialised idea,' deeply suffuses the structure of their interpersonal orientations – and with them the ways in which we who share a world with them must also struggle to comprehend their meaning and the trajectory of our entangled lives.

Acknowledgement

Several passages in the present essay previously appeared in my Introduction to the Hebrew translation of Clifford Geertz, *Islam observed*: *Ayonim b'Islam* (Rosen 2007).

Notes

1. One reason why *Islam observed* may have been his most explicit account of Moroccan Islam relates to the initial plan for the volume, *Meaning and order in Moroccan society* (Geertz, Geertz, and Rosen 1979). It was to have consisted of eight chapters, two each by Clifford Geertz, Hildred Geertz, Lawrence Rosen, and Paul Rabinow. Clifford Geertz was to write on the market and on political culture, while Rabinow was to write one essay on Moroccan Islam and another on the village of Sidi Lahcen Lyusi. It was my task as coordinator of the project to see to it that each author had copies of the relevant portions of each other's complete fieldnotes. In the event, Rabinow did not contribute to the volume. Geertz's own essay on the suq had also grown to monograph length, and Hildred Geertz had done an extensive analysis of the census data. As a result, it was decided to publish the volume instead as three signed essays by the remaining authors. Perhaps because of this history Geertz himself never returned to write a sustained essay that portrayed itself as being specifically about Moroccan Islam, a subject that did, however, continue to be addressed by several of his students. It will be argued below, however, that the essay on the market is very much an essay on Islam.

2. Geertz had made several trips to Morocco before settling in Sefrou. He had lived for some months in Rabat and had surveyed a number of towns before choosing the Sefrou area as his main site. For a brief account of his search for a field site in Morocco, see his *After the fact* (1995, pp. 67–70). Perhaps uniquely among Third World towns, Sefrou was later to hold a conference and publish a book in honour of his work: *Sefrou: Mémoire, territoires et terroirs... Hommage à Clifford Geertz* (Jennan and Zerhouni 2000). For his work in Indonesia he received that nation's highest civilian award.

3. Geertz here relies, in part, on Galanter and Gerstenhaber (1956).

4. On Geertz's style, see Boon 2005, Shweder 2005 and Geertz's response (2005a). The volume in which these essays appear (Shweder and Good 2005) also contains a complete bibliography of Geertz's work through 2003. Geertz died on 30 October 2006. For Geertz's comparative analysis of how writing style relates to inclusion in the anthropological canon, see his *Works and lives* (1988).

5. 'On the spiritual level, the big change between the days of [the 18th-century Indonesian kingdom of] Mataram and [the contemporaneous sultan of Morocco] Mulay Ismail and today is that the primary question has shifted from "What shall I believe?" to "How shall I believe it?"' (Geertz 1968, p. 61). In his review of *Islam observed*, Raymond Firth phrased it this way: 'Increasingly, people hold religious views rather than are held by them; there is a difference between being religious-minded and being religious' (Firth 1969, p. 909). One is also reminded of the words of Zayd ibn 'Amr, one of the early followers of monotheism, standing beside the Kabaa before he was driven out of Mecca for criticising the pagan gods, who broke off his criticism and cried, 'Oh Allah! If I knew how you wished to be worshipped, I would so worship you; but I do not know.' Quoted from Ibn Ishaq, *Sirat Rasul Allah*, 145, in A. Guillaume, *The Life of Muhammad: A Translation of Ishaq's Sirat Rasul Allah* (London, 1955), as cited in Armstrong (2006, pp. 44–45).

6. The quotations in this paragraph are from *Islam observed* (1968), pp. 22, 30, 33, 17, 61–62, 76, 42, 44, and 56 respectively.

7. See Geertz 2000b. See also Boon 2005 and Rosen 2005.

8. See also Cefaï 2003.

9. See, e.g., the story of the Jewish merchant in 'Thick description' (Geertz 1973b, pp. 7–9), and the story of the Indonesian man being driven crazy by the law in *Local knowledge* (Geertz 1983, pp. 175–181).

10. Geertz employed the idea of the family resemblance in his essay about the Sefrou suq when he commented that 'the great social formations of the Maghreb do bear a family resemblance to one another that the suq, as one of the most formidable and most distinctive of them, can, when properly understood, throw into more exact relief' (Geertz 1979, p. 235).

11. Compare Geertz's use of Wittgenstein's concept of family resemblances with its usage in Needham 1972.

12. Geertz 1982, reviewing, among other books, Said 1981.

13. Said, in his anger, goes so far as to say of Geertz's work on the marketplace in Morocco that Geertz gives 'no proof that he knows the spoken or written language of that market place,' thus demonstrating how his own ignorance and invective undermine his own scholarly credentials. On Geertz's command of colloquial Moroccan Arabic, see n. 14 infra.

14. Other totally fallacious charges were also leveled at Geertz, specifically relating to his fieldwork in Morocco and Indonesia. Thus Varisco (2005, p. 143) falsely states that Geertz had 'no more than a smattering of colloquial Arabic,' when in fact he had an excellent command of Moroccan colloquial Arabic (*darija*), something Varisco should at least have had reason to inquire about given Geertz's clear account in *After the fact* (1995, pp. 45–46) of his studying the language, an account that was published well before Varisco's own book appeared. Varisco

also accuses Geertz of having a thin ethnographic base for his analyses, an absurd statement easily refuted by anyone who wishes to review Geertz's voluminous fieldnotes that are archived at the University of Chicago's Regenstein Library. Varisco, who understands neither Geertz's theory of culture nor the nature of such an analytic enterprise, illogically claims that Geertz's views are not supported by reference to natives' own words, thus confusing source material with its explication. The cowardly and slanderous obituary by Lionel Tiger (2006) simply represents an example of ancient jealousy that reflects far more on the character of the writer than his subject. And those who think Geertz ignored women need to read such works as *The religion of Java* (1960) and *Kinship in Bali* (co-authored with Hildred Geertz 1975). They also need to place their own unfounded claims – as Biddick (1994) wrongly asserts, that Geertz engaged in 'rhetorical collusion' with dominant males – in the context of his research topics, the division of labour among the members of the Modjokuto (Java) project, developing interests among anthropologists since the 1950s, and the difficulties attendant on a male anthropologist working with women in both Indonesia and North Africa. Many of the issues relating to women in the joint fieldwork conducted by Clifford and Hildred Geertz were contained in her publications, including *The Javanese family* (1989 [1961]) and 'The meaning of family ties' (1979).

15. Indeed, Geertz's original impetus for the book that became *Meaning and order in Moroccan society* was to place great quantities of the data collected by those working with him in and around Sefrou within a single volume so that each would be freer to go about writing shorter, interpretive essays without having to constantly repeat the background data. This idea may have arisen from the critiques by some readers of his briefer works on Indonesia that he did not supply data to back up his assertions, even though they never bothered to read such circumstantial accounts as *The religion of Java* (1960), *The social history of an Indonesian town* (1965), or *Negara: the theatre state in nineteenth-century Bali* (1980), which laid out such raw information in enormous detail.

16. Segal contrasts Weber and Geertz in the following terms: 'For Geertz, the payoff of belief is behaviour. Belief is a guide to behaviour. Culture requires belief so that behaviour will make sense, but culture is behaviour foremost. For Weber, the payoff of behaviour is belief. Behaviour is the justification for belief. Religion prescribes behaviour not merely because adherents need to know how to act but also because their behaviour validates their belief. ... Where for Geertz one needs to know what to believe in order to know how to behave, for Weber one needs to know how to behave in order to know what to believe' (Segal 1999, pp. 70–71).

17. Speaking of the ritual exchange mechanism described by Malinowski and the liminal *mukanda* ritual of the Ndembu, Geertz says, 'If kula magic is an engine of action, mukanda is a school for passion' (2007b, p. 219).

18. 'The orthodox impulse is activist; it does not reject intellectualism but subordinates it to the end of moral dynamism. The philosophers' reality is an immobile eternal truth; the orthodoxy's ultimate reality is also eternal truth, but being primarily a moral truth, it must result in moral action. The orthodox conception of truth is therefore not of something which merely is but essentially of something which "commands"' (Rahman 1958, p. 110).

19. The phrase 'a portable persona' was used in both Geertz's Frazer Lecture, 'Shifting aims, moving targets' (2005b), and in his Introduction to the Hebrew translation of *Islam observed* (2007a).

20. See, in regard to Geertz's characterisation of religion, the misplaced critique by Varisco (2005). For a more balanced appraisal, see Inglis (2000).

References

Armstrong, K., 2006. *Muhammad: a prophet for our time*. New York: Harper Collins.

Biddick, K., 1994. Bede's blush: postcards from Bali, Bombay, and Palo Alto. *In*: John Van Engen, ed. *The past and future of medieval studies*. Notre Dame, IN: University of Notre Dame Press, 16–44.

Boon, J.A., 2005. Geertz's style: a moral matter. *In*: Geertz. *In*: R.A. Shweder, and B. Good. ed. *Clifford Geertz by his colleagues*. Chicago: University of Chicago Press, 28–37.

Cefaï, D., 2003. Introduction. *In*: Clifford Geertz. ed. *Le souk de Sefrou: sur l'économie de bazar*, Daniel Cefaï, trans. Saint-Denis: Bouchène.

Firth, R., 1969. Review of *Islam observed*. *Journal of Asian studies*, 28 (4), 909–910.

Galanter, E. and Gerstenhaber, M., 1956. On thought, the extrinsic theory. *Psychological review*, 63 (4), 218–227.

Geertz, C., 1957. Ritual and social change: a Javanese example. *American anthropologist*, 59, 32–54. Reprinted in Geertz 1973a, 142–169.

Geertz, C., 1960. *The religion of Java*. Glencoe: Free Press.

Geertz, C., 1963a. *Agricultural involution*. Berkeley: University of California Press.

Geertz, C., 1963b. *Peddlers and princes: social development and economic modernization in two Indonesian towns*. Chicago: University of Chicago Press.

Geertz, C., 1964. Ideology as a cultural system. *In*: David Apter, ed. *Ideology and discontent*. New York: Free Press, 47–76. Reprinted in Geertz 1973a, 193–233.

Geertz, C., 1965. *The social history of an Indonesian town*. Cambridge, MA: M.I.T. Press.

Geertz, C., 1966. Religion as a cultural system. *In*: Michael Banton, ed. *Anthropological approaches to the study of religion*. London: Tavistock, 1–46. Reprinted in Geertz 1973a, 87–125.

Geertz, C., 1968. *Islam observed: religious development in Morocco and Indonesia*. New Haven, CT: Yale University Press.

Geertz, C., 1972a. Afterword: the politics of meaning. *In*: Claire Holt, ed. *Culture and politics in Indonesia*. Ithaca, NY: Cornell University Press, 319–35. , Reprinted in Geertz 1973a, 311–26.

Geertz, C., 1972b. Deep play: notes on the Balinese cockfight. *Daedalus*, 101, 1–37, Reprinted in Geertz 1973a, 412–453.

Geertz, C., 1973a. *The Interpretation of cultures*. New York: Basic Books.

Geertz, C., 1973b. Thick description: toward an interpretive theory of culture. *In*: Clifford Geertz. ed. *The Interpretation of cultures*. New York: Basic Books, 3–30.

Geertz, C., 1975. Mysteries of Islam. *New York review of books*, 22 (20), 18–25.

Geertz, C., 1979. Suq: the bazaar economy in Sefrou. *In*: C. Geertz, H. Geertz, L. Rosen. ed. *Meaning and order in Moroccan society: three essays in cultural analysis*. Cambridge, UK: Cambridge University Press, 123–313.

Geertz, C., 1980. *Negara: the theatre state in nineteenth-century Bali*. Princeton, NJ: Princeton University Press.

Geertz, C., 1982. Conjuring with Islam. *New York review of books*, 29 (9), 25–28.

Geertz, C., 1983. *Local knowledge*. New York: Basic Books.

Geertz, C., 1988. *Works and lives: the anthropologist as author*. Stanford: Stanford University Press.

Geertz, C., 1995. *After the fact: two countries, four decades, one anthropologist*. Cambridge, MA: Harvard University Press.

Geertz, C., 2000a. *Available light: anthropological reflections on philosophical topics*. Princeton, NJ: Princeton University Press.

Geertz, C., 2000b. The pinch of destiny: religion as experience, meaning, identity, power. *In*: Clifford Geertz. ed. *Available light: anthropological reflections on philosophical topics*. Princeton, NJ: Princeton University Press, 167–186.

Geertz, C., 2003. Which way to Mecca? Parts 1–2. *New York review of books*, 50 (10), 27–29, 50 (11), 36–39.

Geertz, C., 2005a. Commentary. *In*: Geertz. *In*: R.A. Shweder, and B. Good. *Clifford Geertz by his colleagues*. Chicago: University of Chicago Press, 108–124.

Geertz, C., 2005b. Shifting aims, moving targets: on the anthropology of religion. *Journal of the Royal Anthropological Institute*, 11 (1), 1–15.

Geertz, C., 2007a. *Islam observed: Ayonim b'Islam*. Noam Rachmilevitch, trans. Tel Aviv: Resling.

Geertz, C., 2007b. 'To exist is to have confidence in one's way of being': Rituals as model systems. *In*: Angela N.H. Creager, Elizabeth Lunbek and M.Norton Wise, eds. *Science without laws: model systems, cases, exemplary narratives*. Durham, NC: Duke University Press, 212–224.

Geertz, C., ed., 1963. *Old societies and new states: the quest for modernity in Asia and Africa*. New York: Free Press.

Geertz, C. and Geertz, H., 1975. *Kinship in Bali*. Chicago: University of Chicago Press.

Geertz, C., Geertz, H., and Rosen, L., 1979. *Meaning and order in Moroccan society: three essays in cultural analysis*. Cambridge, UK: Cambridge University Press.

Geertz, H., 1979. The meaning of family ties. *In*: C. Geertz, H. Geertz, L. Rosen. ed. *Meaning and order in Moroccan society: three essays in cultural analysis*. Cambridge, UK: Cambridge University Press, 315–391.

Geertz, H., 1989 [1961]. *The Javanese family: a study of kinship and socialization*. Prospect Heights, IL: Waveland Press.

Hassan, R., 2002. *Faithlines: Muslim conceptions of Islam and society*. Oxford, UK: Oxford University Press.

Inglis, F., 2000. *Clifford Geertz: culture, custom, and ethics*. Cambridge, UK: Polity Press.

Jennan, L. and Zerhouni, M., eds., 2000. *Sefrou: Mémoire, territoires et terroirs des moments, des lieux et des hommes (récits et témoignages); Hommage à Clifford Geertz. XIIème Colloque de Sefrou*. [Fez]: Commission Culturelle.

Needham, R., 1972. *Belief, language, and experience*. Oxford, UK: Blackwell.

Rahman, F., 1958. *Prophecy in Islam: philosophy and orthodoxy*. London: George Allen and Unwin.

Rosen, L., 2005. Passing judgment: interpretation, morality, and cultural assessment in the work of Clifford Geertz. *In*: Geertz. *In*: R.A. Shweder, and B. Good. ed. *Clifford Geertz by his colleagues*. Chicago: University of Chicago Press, 10–19.

Rosen, L., 2007. Introduction. *In*: C. Geertz. ed. *Islam observed: Ayonim b'Islam*. Noam Rachmilevitch, trans. Tel Aviv: Resling, 7–10.

Said, E., 1978. *Orientalism*. New York: Pantheon.

Said, E., 1981. *Covering Islam: how the media and the experts determine how we see the world*. New York: Pantheon.

Said, E., 1982. Orientalism: an exchange. *New York review of books*, 29 (13), 44–46.

Said, E., 1985. Orientalism reconsidered. *Race & class*, 27 (2), 1–15.

Segal, R.A., 1999. Weber and Geertz on the meaning of religion. *Religion*, 29 (1), 61–71.

Sewell, W.H. Jr., 1997. Geertz, cultural systems, and history: from synchrony to transformation. *Representations*, 59, 35–55.

Shweder, R.A., 2005. Cliff notes: the pluralisms of Clifford Geertz. *In*: R.A. Shweder, and B. Good. ed. *Clifford Geertz by his colleagues*. Chicago: University of Chicago Press, 1–9.

Shweder, R.A. and Good, B., 2005. *Clifford Geertz by his colleagues*. Chicago: University of Chicago Press.

Tiger, L., 2006. Fuzz, fuzz... it was covered in fuzz. *Wall Street journal*, 7 November, A.12.

Varisco, D.M., 2005. *Islam obscured: the rhetoric of anthropological representation*. New York: Palgrave Macmillan.

Sidi Lahcen blues

Aziz Abbassi

Global Linguists Solutions, Washington, DC, USA

This story is one of seven biofictional pieces written over a three-year period in the mid-1990s. The choice of seven pieces is consistent with the proverbial mystique of the number 7, as in the oft-implored *sab'atu rijal* (Seven Saints), a leitmotif popularised in Morocco through a cult that originated with the 17th-century Sufi scholar al-Hassan al-Youssi, the subject of work by both Jacques Berque and Clifford Geertz. The stories depict scenes from the author's childhood in Sefrou, *chef-lieu* of a historical region of Morocco whose history was neglected by native scholars until a certain *nasrani* researcher by the name of Clifford Geertz put it back on the map. The first story in this series, 'Theft in Broad Daylight,' originally commissioned by Elizabeth Fernea for an edited collection, *Remembering childhood in the Middle East* (Fernea 2002), subsequently opened a cathartic cascade of long pent-up emotions that led to more descriptions and story-weaving around Sefrou's corn fields, cherry orchards, mountains, rivers, marketplace, narrow streets, city walls, cemeteries, and saints and spirits, among them Aisha Qandisha and Sidi Lahcen. The former haunted the author's tender childhood; the latter became his story number 3, 'Sidi Lahcen Blues.' It tells of a walk by child and father from Sefrou to Sidi Lahcen, the township of the shrine of al-Hassan al-Youssi. The trip becomes a mindwalk and a detour to life in Sefrou before and shortly after Independence, and the social interactions among the town's traditional elements: Arabs, Amazigh, and Jews, and their relationships with the French.

Weep eye of mine, weep
(for) you are estranged in the land of other folks
Weep eye of mine, weep
(for) I am a vanquished soul with severed hopes
(Al-M'chaheb 1980s)

'Well, are you excited at all about the outing, son?' said my father as we walked across the Beni Medrek Bridge.

'I certainly am,' I answered in a tone that sounded both boastful and unsure at the same time, 'and I can't wait to get on the Sidi Lahcen bus.'

'Good for you,' continued my father.

'But where do we actually catch it, father? Is it one of Laghzaoui's buses, like those we take at Bab al-Mqaam to go to my uncle's in Fez?'

'No, this is one of Daoui's buses, it leaves from Bab al-Mrabba' Garage.'

'But this is not the way we usually take to Bab al-Mrabba'.'

'That's because we don't have to go all the way to Daoui's Garage, we'll wait for the bus by the roadside in front of the city jail; all of Daoui's drivers know me and they'll stop for us.'

Beni Medrek, across the bridge from the Great Mosque, was one of the oldest sections of Sefrou. It stood like a small fortress, a real Casbah, with an archway and an old gate, Bab Beni Medrek, which seemed to serve no functional purpose any longer. The archway led up to a winding path which in turn soon forked into several narrower cobblestone alleys that dead-ended at the south wall of the city. At the north side wall, the roofs and windows of the houses looked out on the River. This river's claim to fame ironically came from its infamous annual floods, one of which, the Big Flood of 1950, had taken numerous human lives, destroyed most of the districts adjoining the riverbed, and since become a time-marker in Sefrou's history.

The houses along the alleys of this *derb* were occupied by several generations of families belonging to the Beni Medrek tribes. My memories of typical scenes from this Casbah were like snapshots, going back to the few times I had ventured there when 'Arsat Dar had played Beni Medrek in a seasonal game of marbles: a great-grandfather crouched down to the side of a wooden door, swatting flies while waiting for the next prayer-call; a mother standing at a doorway nursing an infant and calling out to another child playing outside; a great-grandchild crawling after a turtle in the house courtyard. Another one, out in the street holding a piece of barley bread in one hand and trying to touch the tail of the garbage man's donkey with the other. A man behind a donkey blowing his horn to announce to the whole neighbourhood that it was time to bring out their garbage. Three veiled women slowly walking up an alley followed by several bored-looking children.

I woke up at dawn that morning, not even needing someone to come up and get me out of bed. I had barely gotten any sleep the night before; I must have counted every tick made by the old clock downstairs, chuckling at the loud dreams of my younger siblings who slept in the same room. With confirmation coming from both the nearby muezzin calling the Dawn Prayer and the shrieking crows of the rooster who seemed oblivious to the prospect of being served as a tagine the following day, I knew it was time to rise and get ready. I had been looking forward to that day for a while; since my father had promised, as a recompense for my accepting to accompany him to the mosque from time to time, to take me along on one of his out-of-town missions, to let me explore some relatives' farm, and even to make me a hunting rifle. That Sunday, in response to an invitation by some of my mother's *cousinage* from Sidi Lahcen, he was to go out and mediate amongst the heirs in an inheritance dispute and propose an amicable settlement to them.

***

Around the year of the Big Flood, and for about two decades prior to that, my father, though not directly working for the government, was, in an adjunctive capacity, in the service of various tribal chieftains, *caids*, who had been coerced into working with the local French administration. Because of his Arabic literacy, his command of Berber, his knowledge of Islamic jurisprudence and of religious matters in general, he held several advisory positions among the Ait Youssi, the Ait Serghouchen, and the Beni Yazgha tribes of the Middle Atlas. He also served as an interpreter for those non-literate *caids* who could not read or write Arabic but had to settle customary law matters in the Berber language. In return for his services, he was paid, like most in his profession, rather modestly in cash but quite generously in kind. I can remember the weekly procession into our alley on 'Arsat Dar of several porters and their overloaded donkeys, bringing in sacks of wheat, of chickpeas, of lentils, of olives in season, baskets of fruits and vegetables and other staples all of which, much to my mother's chagrin, arrived under the envious eyes of neighbouring onlookers. The women of the house always pleaded with my father to send the caravan of porters after dark, if not from fear of the omnipresent evil eye, perhaps so as not to show off what others could not afford to buy.

The nature of my father's profession also meant that he had to be away from home several days a week. Outside of his regular work with the chieftains and with the courts, and if he had not lost himself in prayers at the mosque, he would often be summoned somewhere to advise and mediate among some remote relatives or family friends. That was why I jumped at the opportunity when he offered to take me along on the outing, even if it meant having to compromise. I had agreed that I would start frequenting the mosque with him, which in practical terms meant less playtime.

***

The streets were almost deserted that Sunday morning. It was too early to witness the usual signs of traditional town life. The absence of the typical noises created by the daytime hustle and bustle – the frenetic human commotion, the occasional clash of donkeys with wind-horses (bicycles), the maze of traffic jams caused by all three together – gave the place an eerie feeling. Had it not been for the reassuring crows of roosters coming from the roofs and the occasional snores coming from open windows, one would have thought the town had been abandoned following some natural disaster or that its inhabitants had been exterminated by the passage of some unspeakable plague.

'Hurry up a little, we might miss the bus if we follow your pace,' said my father, noticing that I was slowing down his pace as we passed under the arch of Bab al-Miter.

'I'm coming, father, I'll even run if you want, we won't miss that bus,' I responded with a sense of self-assurance and determination.

Out in Derb al-Miter, the streets had begun to show some life. The faithful who had visited the mosque for the Dawn Prayer were going back home; some men were returning from the hammam, towels wrapped around their necks and bath-bags in their hands. A few de rigueur *salamu-alikum*s were exchanged between the passers-by, thus breaking the early morning silence; then a choral '*Arra Zid Arra*' and some clicks of tongue from a group of sharecroppers who were coaxing their mules, on which they were riding side-saddle, to trot faster. Soon we were outside of Derb al-Miter on the road to El Menzel and, standing on the right-hand-side pavement near the city jail's main gate, we waited.

A man carrying a large straw basket that had been carefully covered with a wet burlap bag walked behind his donkey which was loaded with two paniers of fresh mint. He was coming from the direction of the fields and must have been on his way to the Bab al-Mrabba' market-place. As he went past us, the fragrances of the spearmint and of whatever else his basket was hiding sent a cool feeling into my eyes and nostrils. My father, being an expert tea-maker, soon confirmed that the aromas emanating from the straw container were wormwood (absinthe) and other mint-like herbs that usually complement a tea session during springtime. From the opposite direction, a young girl passed holding two steaming strings of *shfenj* donuts, enough breakfast for a family of ten. Minutes later, a deep voice, like that of a smoker, drew my father's attention.

'Good morning sir,' said a man who rode his bicycle with his left hand while carrying a long ladder over his right shoulder with a supporting right hand to keep it from falling.

'Good morning Ya'qob, and where are you going this early in the day?'

'Well, I promised al-Haj Boubker the tailor to finish painting his house today,' answered Ya'qob who, out of politeness and despite the balancing act he had to perform, decided to dismount for a while.

'And when are you coming to whitewash our roof? You said you would attend to it as soon as Pessakh was over, didn't you?' asked my father.

'I did sir, I did, and you will be next, I swear to my God,' answered an embarrassed Ya'qob.

'Well, now we'll see.'

'Believe me, soon insha'allah,' said Ya'qob as he tried to steal a handshake, then remounted his bicycle and rode away.

A sharp squeak made by the jail's metal gate opening behind us suddenly redirected our attention. A guard holding a machine gun to his side appeared first, then about a dozen of shaven-headed prisoners filed out one by one, each carrying either a shovel or a pickaxe over his shoulder. They were being taken to do gardening work at the private residences of the French officials in the Ville Nouvelle, my father informed me. Across the street, an old man, bent from a lifetime of harsh labour, was caught in a coughing fit leaning against a tree as his young girl-companion waited patiently by. Then came more people on either side of the road; then more bicycles with their annoying bell-ringers; and more donkeys announcing their passage with loud and unabashed brays. Sefrou was alive again.

Daoui's buses to El Menzel, heartland of the Beni Yazgha tribes, were supposed to leave Bab al-Mrabba' station about seven in the morning, but in fact they left whenever all the seats were sold out, or else when the bus driver and his greaser-assistant would find out, from other incoming bus drivers or truckers, that there were potential paying ride-seekers waiting at one of the major crossroads between Sefrou, Azzaba, and El Menzel. It was not quite seven that morning, so we waited. Every time I heard the loud acceleration of a choking diesel engine coming down Hospital Hill, I got all excited and started to look out. But after waiting for what seemed like an hour or more, my father suggested that we start walking along the roadside and maybe later hail the bus, instead of just nervously pacing. So we walked and walked until my unprepared feet, tightly squeezed inside a pair of unbroken black shoes bought especially for the occasion, began to hurt. My father, noticing my limping and huffing, decided to stop and let me rest a while. We each sat on one of those large boulders skirting the road shoulder – undoubtedly stacked up together and whitewashed by the Department of Public Works to serve as a natural railing to prevent dozing drivers from rolling down some steep hill or running into a strawberry field.

Not far from where the shrine of Sidi Boumedienne was hiding among olive trees, I noticed the manicured looks of everything along the road. A stream that had meandered around for a while began to divide into smaller tributaries which created an intricate crisscrossing of waterways, the magical *saqia*s that brought life to all things they touched. I saw a small field of half-grown fava beans side by side with that of some precociously full-sized cardoons. Then there was an apple grove in full foliage but with no visible fruit yet next to an orchard of cherry trees in full blossom. Further up, there was a green and yellow patch of *slawiya* squash, the club-shaped but somewhat curved vegetable whose climbing and over-protective vines were rumoured to have miraculously concealed the Prophet Mohammed inside his meditation cave from his ill-meaning pursuers. For that reason, my grandmother called it the 'Noble Squash.' Across from it, there was a small field of chickpeas whose rounded and bushy foliage reminded me of my head of hair before visiting the barber. In the distance, all you could see were the bright green wheat fields that seemed to have no end, far away in the horizon.

After a short rest, we started walking again, stopping only when my father needed to rid one of his *balgha* slippers of the tiny pebbles that would lodge themselves under his bare feet or between his toes.

'Let us walk just a bit further, the bus should be passing by any time now,' my father kept saying as the morning went by.

As we walked up Azzaba Hill, I could hear the sounds of morning in the countryside: the twitter of turtledoves; the monotonous shrills of some early cicadas; the faint bleats of a few lost baby sheep begging their guardian to locate their mothers; the turbaned shepherd boy entertaining his herd with a high-pitched melody of which I could only make out, '*Awaa maytaanit ah, awaa maytaanit ah*' (Oh! how are you, oh! how are you), a Berber greeting that my grandmother had explained to me after I had heard it used so often by my father's illustrious guests.

Still, there was no sign of a bus. In fact, with the exception of the sound of the tractor belonging to M'sieur Michel, the French colon; the open jeep of the local gendarmes; and the black low-riding Citroen belonging to the *contrôleur civil*, passing a few minutes apart, there was very little motorised activity that morning.

***

Everything motorised at the time – from cars to buses to trains to boats and to any machine with a motor – spelled 'French' and seemed synonymous with the name France. The French were really Nazarenes to us, at least until I started public school at Bab al-Miter Primary and I was corrected by Mme Samson, my first French *maîtresse*. My grandmother had said so many times; and even my parents used that term when referring to those 'strangers who had come from far away to usurp our land and force our Sultan into exile.' Those strangers who were neither Muslim nor Jewish and who chose to live separately from both. Their big houses looked lonely without any adjoining ones. They looked empty and frightfully quiet. Even an industrious, inquisitive, and daring child could not catch a glimpse of the inside. They had inside walls and outside walls with barbed wire all around for protection against the *indigènes*.

At least on 'Arsat Dar, from our rooftop I was able to satisfy my curiosity about how our Jewish neighbours lived. I saw them eat and I heard them talk, or rather, just like in our own home, I heard loud voices bouncing in all directions, very lively, or perhaps desperately trying to assert their existence through some yet-to-be divined cogito: 'I shout, ergo I exist.' On the south side, I saw Hannah give a final touch to the freshly kneaded bread-dough by slapping the typical egg-and-saffron mixture on top of the round loaves. On the west side, I saw Pinhas lying on a banquette and calling out to his wife Saada to bring him some *mahia*, a special water – water-of-life, they called it – that apparently gave the Jews in Sefrou more 'liveliness.' I never saw such water in our own house. Our adjoining roofs also gave me a perfect opportunity to observe their celebrations and festivities. I always wondered why, once a year, those neighbours would leave the downstairs of their homes empty and come up to the roofs to eat and sleep in small huts made of reed. My grandmother would of course explain that those were Jewish festivals not unlike our own annual Sacrifice Festival left to us by the Prophet Abraham or our traditional annual fast during the month of Ramadan.

As for the French, they were both strangers and strange indeed. They kept large, fierce-looking and mean-sounding dogs not only in their front gardens, but even in the inner sanctums of their homes. They also let perfectly edible fruit rot on their trees. For us, it was sinful to let it go to waste; consequently, my friends and I would spend many a leisure hour climbing the garden walls trying to reach the outward-leaning branches that bore ruby-red persimmons, dark-gold medlars, green mountain apples or succulent black mulberries. When we were not eating those forbidden fruits, we would watch the children of the Nazarenes play. They always played among themselves. Their parents must have insisted on that so they would not catch 'nati-vitis,' that communicable but very rare humane condition whose visible symptoms can be a frequent and uncontrollable urge to get close to the natives, and a markedly elevated warmth of the heart often followed by fair shakes, given and taken, with a possibility of simultaneously losing oneself and regaining conscience, all of which very conceivably leading, in severe cases, to xenophobia-death. The children of the Nazarenes played with real rubber balls. We played with makeshift rag ones we made out of old underclothes which we then tied with string. When the French children spoke to each other, we could not understand them, maybe because their speech was nothing like what Madame Samson had taught us at school, or maybe because only their puckered lips seemed to move, as if they had been caught outside in a mid-Atlas winter snowstorm.

Why did the Nazarenes come to our land? As a child, I was content with the simple answers. Then, of course, I realised. They came to teach us how to pucker up, like their own children, as we struggled with their twisted tongue and adopted their crooked ways. They came to build a few bridges, but then erected walls everywhere. They came to teach us not how to 'love thy neighbours' but how to laugh at and despise them. They told the Berbers that they were the free and noble ones of the land. They told the Arabs that they alone deserved precedence and privilege. They told the Jews that they were more civilized than both. And the teaching went on. They came to show us how to build lonely houses away from relatives and friends. How to remain aloof as we lost our colorful core and began to bleach our identity. How to wean one from the group. How to pull our love and affection out of the 'liver' and into the 'heart.' How to think that closeness was less civilized and distance more refined. How to denigrate the old and reject the roots. How to let the meek and the weak inherit nothing but the wind. And how to accept all this humiliation with a perverted sense of admiration for them.

***

'Look, I think that your mother's cousins are waiting for us over there,' said my father with a noticeable sigh of relief in his voice, pointing to two men who were standing in the distance with several mules by their side. At a crossroad up the hill, Uncle Hashem and Cousin Lemfeddel, who often showed up for lunch on Thursdays, our market day, had brought in transport for the second half of the trip. What my father had not told me was that even if Daoui's bus had indeed come by, it would have only taken us to that crossroad. There, the one good road continued to El Menzel and the one to Sidi Lahcen became a mere beaten path. As we approached them, the two men rushed in turn to greet us. They both tried to kiss my father's hand, but he modestly withdrew it. I of course had to kiss theirs to prove my good manners. Our 'rescue team' then helped us mount what looked like the biggest but most subdued of the mules. My father sat in the front so I could sit and hold on to him from behind. After they mounted their own animals, we all started to ride single file with Uncle Hashem ahead, Cousin Lemfeddel at the back, and my father and I in the middle.

The ride on mule-back was exciting despite the suspenseful moments when the trail took us straight into a swamp. 'Ain Taragrag, a spring that seemed to have been too shy to pour all its heart out and run down the plateau to form a river in the outlying plain, had submerged all the lush vegetation around it and formed a swamp-like pond which, at the time, looked like a lake to me.

All we could hear were the incessant croaks of the loud but prudently invisible frogs. A sudden flutter that came from one of the partly submerged bushes to the left of the small caravan sent my heart racing and my arms tighter around my father's waist.

'It's all right, son, don't be scared, they are only wild ducks fearing for their lives,' said my father in a reassuring tone. 'The Nazarenes come to shoot them down during the hunting season.'

I remembered the hunting season. How, on Sunday evenings when the local Frenchmen would drive back through town from such exclusive expeditions, those poor ducks, quails, and doves would be hanging down the blood-stained doors of their jeeps or station wagons in strings of five or six pieces. That was about when I started to ask my father if I could go hunting and, if not, if I could at least carry a plastic toy rifle across my back and parade it in front of my friends.

'Well, are you going to make me a rifle today like you promised?' I asked my father, nudging him with my chin, as our mountain caravan safely filed out of 'Ain Taragrag.

'At Sidi Lahcen perhaps,' he simply replied; then he went back to whispering something to himself. But in fact, I seemed to have interrupted one of his interminable liturgical recitations from which he seldom resurfaced without a truly pressing reason. Then, I thought to myself, what if those recitations were not always intended for liturgy alone? I never really saw my father thinking or worrying about a problem silently, like my mother often did when she would sit in a corner, crosslegged with one hand over her face. What if he actually recited his verses, repeated his liturgy, and thumbed his rosary simply as a way to ponder and reflect over earthly matters while still scoring points with his creator? In that case, he may not have really heard my request. And as if I in turn had not heard his response the first time, or perhaps just in order to confirm his positive response to my stubborn ears, I repeated the question,

'Ba! Ba, will you still make me a hunting rifle?' this time pressing his abdomen with my clenched hands to draw his attention. Visibly annoyed by my persistent questioning and my intrusion upon his empty stomach, he nudged me back with a sharp elbow to indicate that I should cease interrupting him, then mumbled three words in the middle of the whispering: 'At Sidi Lahcen.'

***

Qaïd Lahcen was a very familiar name to me. This chieftain of the Ait Yousi tribes from in and around Sefrou would, according to my mother, regularly visit our house during the 20-year tenure my father had spent as his assistant. He and his children developed an addiction to the delicate seasonal salads, the spring tagines, the steamed lamb ribs, and the seared marinated kebabs of the Ben Seddiq family. He would rather eat at our modest house on 'Arsat Dar than feast at his estate in Sidi Ahmed Attadli. Al-Yousi, the appellation by which he was better known in our household, would simply drop by whenever my father extended a socially de rigueur, albeit passing, invitation. He considered our home his home, although, from the sound of grandmother's gossip with relatives who envied us, the reverse was not necessarily true.

Qaïd Lahcen al-Yousi was a very powerful Middle Atlas tribal chief with a strong allegiance to the country's sultan, a fact that ultimately brought upon him the ire of the French colonial authorities and his subsequent political demise which led to my father's sudden loss of livelihood. A few years later, after Sultan Mohammed Ben Youssef returned from exile to become King Mohammed V of independent Morocco, Qaïd Lahcen became one of the crown ministers, but his good fortune did not translate into the same for my father who, after an interlude of ill health and forced leisure, had neither independent means nor a proper job with which to crown his long and often illustrious career.

'When did Qaïd Lahcen al-Yousi become Sidi Lahcen al-Yousi, is he not still alive?' I asked my father, not without some apprehension, fearing a nudge with the other elbow, because I was interrupting again and because the question may have sounded altogether impertinent as I was assuming he had been inside my head following my train of thought. But my father's calm and lengthy answer was a pleasant surprise. I must have caught him having already resolved the thorny inheritance problem for which we were traveling to Sidi Lahcen that day, or else I was lucky and had touched on a favourite topic of his.

'Well, son, simply because there are two 'Lahcen al-Yousi': the first one had the power of the word, the second had the might of the sword, if you wish,' he replied in the usual metaphoric language of the adults.

'Qaïd Lahcen with whom I worked for so long,' my father went on, 'is a chieftain who ruled through the customary law of his tribe, including the law of the stick; but the one whose shrine is near the village we're visiting today was a great mind, a sea of religious scholarship and a mystic who lived about 300 years ago, spending his time enlightening others across our land and beyond – they say he even reached Egypt, teaching and interpreting the laws of God and of his Messenger, may Peace be on Him. After his death, the knowing al-Yousi was buried near your maternal ancestors' land; then those who appreciated his knowledge and knew his worth later built a small shrine for him and that's how he came to be known as Sidi Lahcen al-Yousi, or simply 'Sidi Lahcen' for the locals.'

'Then is he like Sefrou's own Sidi Ali Bousserghine, Sidi Ahmed Attadli, Sidi Boumedienne, and Sitti Messaouda?' I asked, having thus far heard most stories and explanations through the mouths of women.

'Something like that; but the truth of God, son, is that they were all simple men and women during their lives, different from others only by virtue of their good deeds toward their fellow humans and by how much faith they had in their Creator. After their death, I agree, they should be well remembered but not immortalised, venerated but not idolised.'

I understood what he said, or at least I knew to what and to whom he was referring. I had heard him repeat the same pronouncements to the women in our household many times in the past, when he accidentally discovered that they were going to, or had just come back from visiting, some holy man's shrine. He strongly criticised all those who sought a dead man's help in solving their earthly problems. He considered them heathens and miscreants 'liable for Allah's wrath on the Day of Reckoning.' He also bemoaned and decried all the money and the material goods that people took as offerings each time they went to a shrine:

'You could feed the poor and the beggars from here to Baghdad with all those roosters, he-goats, and calves that are slaughtered, and you could illuminate the Sahara from Marrakesh to Timbuktu with all those candles lit and wasted, all in the name of some holy person,' my father would say in utter desperation.

Unfortunately, ordinary folks, including my grandmother, my mother, my mother's aunts, cousins, neighbours, and the rest often found themselves helplessly at impasses, without answers or remedies to the one thousand and one problems and ills they encountered in their daily lives. There were those who wanted children but could not have them. Those who could have them but could not feed them without begging door-to-door. Those who begged for their children's return from the far-away lands to which they had exiled themselves, and those children who had gone nowhere and had remained children. There were those with incurable illnesses and those with imaginary ones. There were those with unknown ailments and those with known ones they found insufferable. There were the love-stricken ones, like 'Qaïss and Leila,' whose condition was blamed on dementia, and there were the simply demented ones. There were the deaf who were still hoping to hear some day; the blind who had heard too much already and wanted to see; and finally the mute who were only asking for a chance to be heard. When their own prayers would not suffice and their humanly limited means became exhausted, they resorted to a higher authority. Realising that their records with the Higher

Being might not have been perfect ones, they sought the intercession of a mediator, someone with a better and more acceptable record, a saint of sorts.

Sidi Ali Bousserghine, the region's patron saint, majestically sat on top of the highest Middle Atlas foothill around Sefrou, visible to the incoming visitor from the distance and overlooking the entire city and its environs. It was there that my mother dragged me whenever I suffered from a persistent abscess that her own home application of hot onion-layers would not cure, or when her own migraine headaches would not subside after several Aspros, or when my sister recovered from typhoid fever and the women wanted to give Him thanks.

The main mausoleum was a white structure with a green-tiled pyramidal roof to indicate its distinguished character. At the entrance, a throng of visitors waited their turn to be allowed in by the shrine keeper, some holding batches of giant hand-dyed candles, others the sacrificial roosters they brought as offerings, others large brass incense-burners that sent off aromatic clouds of smoke in the air, others carrying the invalid or the sick on their backs, while others surreptitiously rubbed a few fingers of henna paste on the side wall as a part of some auspicious ritual. Access to the inside of the shrine strictly required bare feet and of course being a believer with a cleansed body and a clean mind. The inner sanctum was a large room at the center of which the holy man's marble tomb had been cordoned off, between four pillars, by a wrought-iron railing from which hung a hotchpotch of headscarves, lace, and cloth-wrapped talismans, traditionally left behind along with secret wishes by the women visitors. The rest of the floor was covered by layers of tribal rugs and wool blankets on which the daily visitors and the long-term pilgrims sat or slept. On either side of the main building, there were two smaller shrines with white domes, each believed to house the tombs of family members or disciples of the saint.

From where he stood, Sidi Ali Bousserghine could, as it were, see the whole low-lying area and be seen by all from any direction. It was as if the townspeople had in fact intended to erect a shrine for a guardian who, even from underneath the earth and the marble, would keep a watchful eye on their city and protect them from all evil, be it the evil eye of some envious neighbours or the evil intentions of outsiders.

**

When the French arrived, they found in Sefrou a perfect geographical point from which to control the only alternate route through the Middle Atlas to the South during the snow season, and to launch their campaigns to 'pacify' the mountain populations. They also found it to be a perfect logistical centre from which to manage the administrative affairs of the sur-rounding Berber tribes, not to mention its ideal soil and climate that made it the breadbasket for a wide region. They then set out to establish the military apparatus, the juridical system, and the spiritual cover to implement their scheme. They chose to build their military camps at two strategic elevations, one on top of a hill alongside the southbound road that the country's sultans once took on their annual visits to their native Tafilalet, and one catty-corner from Sidi Ali Bousserghine. Outside the gate of this camp sat two decorative cannons aimed straight in the direction of the shrine. The French then imposed their laws so that the prescriptions of Mohammed, the Shari'a law, and those of Moses, the Talmudic law, became subordinated to the imperialistic Code of Napoleon. Then came the Nazarene priests to erect a church one hill away from the patron saint and to start a proselytising campaign.

Ever since, poor Sidi Ali Bousserghine seemed to have lost his powers of guardianship and protection to the French-mandated protectorate over the land. He could not even help himself, let alone his Sefrou protégés. How could he protect al-Qal'a, Nas 'Adloun, Beni

Medrek, al-Qasbah, 'Arsat Dar, al-Mellah, al-Mgaz, Habbouna, or Slaoui, when the new outsi-ders, in the name of their 'mission civilisatrice,' or rather their Pax Napoleona, were wreaking wanton havoc on people, places, and spirits? His name had been defiled. Those barracks that housed thousands of ill-meaning forces, hundreds of destructive tanks, and tons of deadly ammu-nition became known as Camp Sidi Ali Bousserghine. Not far away from the immediate proxi-mity of the shrine, the earth was always littered with pieces of tin and metal, bullet shells, and grenades left after the frequent manoeuvres performed by the local battalion. I still remember the story of the poor boy who had strayed from his pilgrim mother to go digging for wild hearts of palm, and was maimed by a live grenade. Even Sidi Bousserghine could not help – his space and his spirit had been desecrated. The retaining walls below his mausoleum were turned into 'pis-soirs' for inebriated French officers. Instead of the pleasant aromas of sandalwood, musk, and amber filling the air, the stench of dry urine suffocated the unwary visitor. Nearby, some dark mountainside caves, once used by wandering ascetics for meditation, were turned into 'caves-de-passe' for illicit fornication with itinerant prostitutes servicing sex-starved regulars among the French, the Senegalese, and the native soldiers.

Sidi Ali Bousserghine could not provide protection against the outsiders even after they sup-posedly vacated the land. In 1956, and just months after the declaration of the country's indepen-dence and the return of the king from a long exile, they deliberately and blatantly commandeered, over Morocco's airspace, the airplane that was taking Algeria's resistance leaders to an inter-national peace conference. The subsequent arrest of the Algerian leader Ben Bella and his com-panions sparked an unexpected reaction and sent millions of newly liberated, slogan-enriched, and still euphoric Moroccans into the streets to protest the odious act. I don't think I ever experi-enced the feeling of a large crowd like I did on that day, when the streets of Sefrou seemed to suddenly turn into an ocean of human motion, now calm, now roaring, the white turbans of the elders looking like undulating foam, with the black hair of the youth like some churned up algae. When it roared, eight words were chanted; eight words that you could hear; eight words that gave you gooseflesh; eight words that moved even the nine-year-olds like myself who were tagging along two-by-two as instructed by their schoolmasters:

'Guy Mollet au poteau! Ben Bella au château!'

On the radio, they later announced that similar marches in the larger cities had been not only moving but in fact tragic, as many people had been crushed to death or injured in the process.

Tragedy was barely avoided in Sefrou on that day, perhaps thanks to a miraculous recovery of Sidi Ali Bousserghine's powers of intercession after decades of impotence. Or was it the miracle of people suddenly taking charge of their own destiny? The students at the Collège Musulman de Sefrou, the only secondary institution in town and the only boarding school to house youths from the remote villages, wanted to join a peaceful demonstration as a show of solidarity with their Algerian brethren. Those from Sefrou proper boycotted classes, but none of the boarders could leave. The headmaster, a Frenchman who may not have known that Napoleon was very much dead, refused to let them out. A group of student representatives, led by my older brother who was then a budding Istiqlal Party member, went to negotiate with him. When they pleaded with him in the name of independence and in the spirit of the new era between the two countries, M'sieur Toraval's response was reportedly less than civil. 'Moi, je m'en fiche pas mal de votre Ben Bella et je me contre-fiche de votre indépendance,' he told them. Then, as if to further prove his words and add insult to injury, he grabbed a red-with-green-star flag from the hands of one of the students and was about to tear it up or step on it. Outraged by the rude and arrogant response and by what was going to happen to the new symbol of the country's national identity, my brother, some friends later recounted, jumped over to reclaim the flag at which point Toraval opened his desk drawer, pulled out a revolver and pointed it at my brother's head. From that point on, the rest of the story took on folkloric dimensions. Apparently, after it became obvious that negotiations had reached a deadlock, the leaders of the local chapter of the Istiqlal Party, some former resistants who had suffered greatly under French torture, were alerted and briefed about the situation. They came prepared for the worst but fortunately succeeded in diffusing the crisis by persuading M'sieur Toraval. The incident, however, became an opportunity for the city to collectively and retroactively protest the nefarious schemes and actions of France during four decades. For all those who had repressed their feelings about colonialism before, or had felt cowardly and too afraid to join in overt resistance, it was a kind of catharsis. Thousands poured outside the city gates of Bab al-Miter, Bab al-Mrabba', Bab Sitti Messaouda, and Bab al-Mqaam into the Ville Nouvelle, where many French people still lived, and into the municipal stadium, shouting anti-France slogans interspersed with chants of,

'Long live Morocco! Long live the King! Long live the Istiqlal Party!'
'Long live Algeria, long live Ben Bella, long live the Liberation Front!'

***

'Ba, Ba, is that the dome of Sidi Lahcen over there?' I asked my father when I noticed in the distance a white dome with a green flag on top adorning the only white building amongst several tan-colored ones scattered all around.

'It is indeed, little one,' replied Uncle Hashem who, before my father could interrupt his own reveries, seemed to want to take charge, and added, 'but we won't be going that far, you see our village Lahmari starts here and goes almost half way back to 'Ain Taragrag; Sidi Lahcen starts over to the right, up there,' pointing with the hand that was not holding the reins.

'Will you take me there later, Uncle Hashem?' I asked.

'I know your father would not like it or we'd gladly take you for a visit, right, al-Fqih?'

'You are right about that, Hashem, your cousin [my mother] has already filled this boy's head with a lot of antiquated flaky tales about saints, let's not encourage that anymore,' said my father with a not-so-subtle reference to my mother's tales of her experiences at the shrines she always visited.

When Cousin Lemfeddel uttered a few 'Ooh! shaa' to the mules, our small caravan came to a halt in front of a gathering of single-level houses whose tan-coloured walls were made of a mixture of mud, clay, and dry straw. A line of tall trees stood behind the walls to provide both privacy and shade. That was finally Lahmari, I thought to myself, and I was about to have a field day, literally of course, but I hoped figuratively as well. Lahmari, the land my mother always talked about to relatives and friends. It was there that her paternal grandfather, or great grandfather – she never said, or maybe she never knew herself – decided to settle after migrating from the Jbala region, the plateaux immediately below the Rif mountains. Later, her father, who was a religious scholar and a man of letters, came to Sefrou to teach and counsel, and to marry a woman, my grandmother, who descended from the Beni Mtir of the Middle Atlas and whose ancestors had moved to Sefrou a few hundred years earlier. My mother's uncle and his family chose to remain at Lahmari and work on their land. After his death, his children built additional sections in the village to accommodate their own growing families but decided to postpone division of the property and other inheritance matters until it was deemed necessary. Such necessity somehow became pressing when on the Thursday prior to the visit, the three brothers, Uncle Hashem, Uncle Driss and Uncle Si Mohammed all came to our house to plead with my father to 'enter as a white thread among them,' as he often did during similar disputes, and help them resolve a situation that 'would only fester with time if left pending.'

While Lemfeddel was helping both my father and me dismount and with the synchronised barking of a greeting party of dogs in the background, the rest of the male *cousinage* was already out by the gate waiting their turn to greet us, exchange hand-kisses, and invite us in.

'Welcome to the *fqih* and to the son of the *fqih*, come in please, this is a big day for us and you brought us *baraka* with you,' they each repeated as we walked inside. After going past a log-gate barely high enough to keep the cattle and the dogs out, we were ushered into a courtyard, then through a corridor of what looked like the first residential unit. I clearly noticed that the shape and style of their houses differed from our own back in Sefrou. We walked through a second inner courtyard where some women were busy preparing lunch. I could tell from the pleasant whiffs that had already invaded my nostrils at the entrance. The brass couscousier was steaming up in a corner, filling the air with the mouth-watering aromas of meat, spices, vegetables, legumes, and semolina that make up couscous. Just like at 'Arsat Dar, the bottom pot and the upper steamer had been carefully belted up at the waist with a yellow saffron-stained cloth to keep steam from leaking out. Closely by, one of the women sat in front of a clay oven slapping handfuls of dough together and placing them inside to bake some *matloo'* bread. A younger woman was churning milk in a goatskin container that was strung to a lemon tree on one side and a giant grapevine on the other. That meant pure, undiluted buttermilk was also on the menu that day. In the centre, two other women were squatting over a large pail of hot water, plucking and cleaning a few chickens that one of the cousins must have killed earlier, judging from the fresh bloodstains that had not yet been cleaned off the front courtyard.

As soon as they took note of our presence, all those otherwise busy women stopped their chores and rushed to greet us one by one, eyes down out of respect for my father, as they queried us about each and everyone's health back home. I noticed that as he responded to each 'how is so-and-so' with a '*labas al-hamdullah*,' my father was also looking to the side, away from them to avoid eye contact, *pudeur oblige*. After the never-ending greetings temporarily subsided, we were ushered into a large living area. Before we entered, we took our shoes off at the door and neatly tucked them against a corridor wall. The room's main furnishings were old mountain rugs covering a cement floor, four long wool-stuffed mattresses arranged in a rectangular fashion, and piles of blue-velvet–covered cushions leaning against the walls. Décorwise, the place looked rather stark, with the exception of three dust-covered pictures that had been nailed directly to the center wall. I had seen similar pictures before, either hanging on the whitewashed walls of other homes or displayed flush with the ground in Bab al-Mrabba' plaza at a Thursday market. The biggest and most prominent of the three posters represented the name 'Allah' in Kufic calligraphy. The other two were sketches, almost caricature-like, that popularised through imaginary recreations the ancient Islamic events, battles, legendary tales, and especially the larger-than-life heroes. One sketch was titled 'Ali and Ghoul-Head.' It represented Ali, the Prophet's son-in-law and famous defender of the faith, sitting on his beautiful Arabian horse brandishing his special 'split' saber and facing Ghoul-Head, the legendary pagan king, who was seated on an ugly-looking and almost deformed horse, holding a sword in one hand and in the other a cut-off leg that was still dripping blood. As the blind storyteller with the melodious voice at Bab al-Mqaam plaza would recount to the alternating beat of his tambourine, Ghoul-Head, the evil-minded, hideous-looking Yemenite king, was

Ali's nemesis for a long time. Ghoul-Head would always challenge Ali to duels by means of blasphemous provocations, and as the two would face each other sword-on-sword, Ali, the Valiant

Knight of early Islam, would always prevail and Ghoul-Head would flee in shame. Then, when Ali caught up with him in the end and had to face him for a last duel, Ghoul-Head would not die easily. He lost the first leg and he used it as a shield; then he lost the second leg and he kept on fighting. They say that even after losing all his limbs, his main body kept struggling, and when Ali finally dealt him the coup de grâce across the neck, the severed head lay on the ground giggling with eyes wide open for a long while.

The third of the sketches, nailed to the left of the 'Allah' calligraphy, was titled 'Antar and Abla,' and showed the African-Arabian poet-warrior, Antarah Ibn Shaddad al-Absi, famed throughout the Islamic world for his proverbial courage and bravery and for his legendary romance with his cousin Abla. Antar and Abla's love was already legendary during their lifetimes, but centuries later it took on Sheherazadesque dimensions. Antar, the 'Father of Cavaliers,' as he was referred to by his admirers, was sitting on his famous horse Abjar with a solemn look on his face and with his hands beseechingly raised in the direction of Abla who was facing him seated inside her camel-borne see-through palanquin. Antar's verses seemed to ring out and flow in between them as if inside a heart-shaped cartoon caption:

> Oh Abla, say when spears are locked in combat, Antar used
> to guard the palanquins.
> When every disaster befell, Antar used to fear a battle's outcome
> but he had no fear of foe.
> Oh Abla, take care on the march for now I cannot challenge heroes.
> Oh shooter of the arrow so slender, you slew me by treachery,
> your arrow was not the betrayer. . ..
> Oh Abla, weep for a knight of courage who goes into battle
> and fears not the spear point.
> A hero who tumbles the armour-clad with a blow.
> How many a youth is a partner from his thrust.
> He fears not death in the battle.
> He rises aloft to the rings of Saturn.
> Wail, oh Abla, and mourn. Mourn for the lion of battle
> as one sad, mad with love, and stricken dumb. . ..
> How good a soul. One noble and mighty, hospitable and a conqueror. . ..

***

'Well, please sit or lie down, as you wish, and rest up your feet awhile, the trip must have been exhausting for the two of you with all the uphill walking you did,' said Uncle Hashem. Then, as if to dramatise to his brothers and their families the sacrifice made by my father in coming out to help them on that day, he said,

'Did you know that they had to walk all the way from home to the Sidi Lahcen crossroad, because the bus never came by?'

'It is too much for them, by God!' replied Uncle Si Mohammed, Uncle Hashem's older brother, 'and of all the days Daoui's bus does not run; someone must have died in his family, or maybe the driver is very sick, who knows?'

'Or maybe the bus is broken down at the station, or the gendarmes are penalising Daoui for carrying too many passengers on the roof of the bus, who knows?' said Uncle Driss, the middle brother, who then added, trying to close one chapter and move on to another, 'In any case, God alone shall, from His Goodness, reward this generous man here and shall protect his children and protect the woman for whose sake he has always benevolently helped us during difficult times.'

'Amen,' said the audience in unison, touching their foreheads with the tips of their right-hand fingers, then kissing them.

'Now, before we start talking about our problem, how about a bowl of fresh buttermilk to quench your thirst? Hnia has perhaps finished churning by now,' said Tahra, Uncle Si Mohammed's wife.

'Well, woman, just bring them some, don't ask them,' said her husband in a teasing tone.

Soon, two children about my age, carrying a low-legged round table laden with bowls of buttermilk, entered the room, slipped off their tire-soled sandals at the door, put the table down in the middle, and started handing out bowls that were filled to the brim. It was a minor miracle that those children did not spill a drop of the white liquid; with our entry, the loose tribal rugs had folded slightly to create tiny obstacles here and there. The thought of an impending disaster had for a second crossed my mind and set my wild imagination in motion as I pictured someone stumbling, falling, and sending off small tidal waves of buttermilk all over our laps and faces. The buttermilk was fresh, but the realisation that it was not dripping elsewhere was even more refreshing.

'*Uuuh! Al-hamdullah!*' belched Uncle Si Mohammed with a sound that expressed his deep appreciation for the thick beverage. Soon, several other belches resounded in the room, concurring with the first belcher's opinion, and complemented with a series of '*al-hamdu li-llah!*'

'Now, in order that I may listen and talk to you in peace without interruptions from this child, let me go and make him something that will keep him busy for a while,' said my father as he stood up, motioning to me to follow him out.

'Look, al-Houssayn and al-Mahdi here will take him around the farm and show him things; they'll keep him busy,' said Uncle Hashem, patting one of the children who was sitting next to him.

We put our shoes back on and went out the same route we had taken coming in. As we passed the women in the courtyard, I overheard Tahra instructing the rest of them:

'Yallah, yallah, make your hands go faster, we must not serve lunch too late, our guests would laugh at us.'

Outside, my father started down a pathway toward a nearby stream; the two children and I followed behind. There, he leaned over some aquatic bushes that looked like thin but malleable reeds, and started to pull them out by the handful. He collected a batch and took out a small folding knife from the leather purse that always hung around his waist, and started to smooth out the edges of the reed-like stalks. When he had a handful of them ready, he took out some string and tightly bound them at several points. He skillfully folded one end of the flexible stalks in the shape of an obtuse triangle which he also tied together, so that the resulting object looked like the long barrel and the shoulder support of a rifle. He made three of them, gave each of us one and smilingly told us to go hunting:

'Well, here is what I promised you in Sefrou. Go play with your cousins, go hunting if you wish, but be good and do not fight with each other, yallah! And don't be late for lunch, come back when you hear the call to prayer.'

'We will insha'allah, Ba…. I promise, and I'll bring some wild fowl too,' I told him as he turned to go back to the house. There was not much time to waste. Judging from the sun's position in the sky, the early afternoon prayer call would soon be heard from nearby Sidi Lahcen. Abusing my privilege as a guest, and perhaps the very reason for our being out there and not at home doing some dull chores, I instructed the cousins to hurry so that we could make the most of the little time we had. They listened and quietly complied.

The hunting expedition began. We roamed around Lahmari looking for the elusive game, my companions still somewhat perplexed by the whole exercise. They did not know anything about this 'hunting game,' nor what to do with the makeshift weapons my father had made them; neither did I really. They giggled as they flung them above their heads, flaunted them around, played the flute with them, dueled with them and did everything that crossed their minds at the time. I wanted so much to do the same things they did, had it not been for my mind being set on fulfilling my fantasy. But what was the fantasy, I asked myself: to shoot some wild ducks, some wild pigeons, some quails, and some turtledoves like the French did at 'Ain Taragrag, Lake Aoua, and Lake Ifreh? Even if those creatures had come to pose right in front of my eyes, I would not have known what to do with them. Yet I was determined to take something back to show my father. So I looked about in all directions, raised my head toward the sky, ducked under a tree, and aimed whenever I heard something in the air. I did everything I remembered from the few films my father had taken me to see at the Cinema Lynx – when he was in an exceptionally good mood – but all to no avail. Suddenly a voice from afar came to interrupt our adventure:

'God is Great! God is Great!'

The muezzin was calling the early afternoon prayer, and that meant that it was already lunchtime and the end of playtime. As we started walking back toward the house, I suddenly noticed, along the bank of the stream from which my father had extracted his raw material for our rifles, what looked like a tribe of chickens. At the head of the file were the roosters and the hens, then followed dozens and dozens of chicks.

'This is it, brothers,' I told my two companions, 'there go my birds of prey.'

I then ducked, with my rifle in the proper position, aimed at the fowl population and sounded out 'boom boom!' Of course nothing happened. My cousins burst into laughter. They must have enjoyed all my clowning around, or else they were making fun of the fact that I had not landed any real game. So, I set out to correct them. I started to chase the frightened and hurrying chickens, the parents being able to fly some but the little ones barely walking. Then the play-rifle turned into a deadly weapon indeed when I waved it with my hand and took a first swipe at the helpless chicks, then another one and another. Before long, three of them lay dead in front of our eyes.

First, nothing was said, undoubtedly out of collective disbelief that the fantasy was quickly turning into a somber reality. Then, to brush off what had just happened as part of the whole hunting game and to try to whitewash it with humour, macabre as it may have rung in their heads and in my own, I told my cousins al-Houssayn and al-Mahdi,

'Let us collect our game for today and take it home for lunch.'

But the two were not tickled and this time they weren't laughing. In fact, they were not in the least interested in carrying on with the game. They made it clear that they wanted no part of it and that I would have to pick up the dead chicks myself. Al-Mahdi, the more outspoken of the two, said to me,

'Yallah! brother, let us go home now, leave those poor things there and come along, God will forgive, and hopefully our parents won't find out about this.'

'I am coming along with you, of course, but I must take these birds to show my father. After all, he did send me hunting, didn't he?'

'Well, in that case, it's your business to explain this incident. You have wasted these chicks because they cannot be eaten now, they are dead and you must know, being the son of a *fqih*, that we do not eat a dead animal.'

'Yes, but these are not sheep, cows, or roosters, they are only birds,' I answered, partly to candidly confess my ignorance of the subject and partly to try and evade the real issue.

'They must be properly hunted, then if they don't die on the spot, they have to be salvaged through the ritual throat-slitting,' al-Mahdi went on.

'Listen, we country boys know much more about these things than you city brats,' stepped in al-Houssayn, who had thus far contented himself with occasional head-nodding or head-shaking to indicate his concurrence or his disagreement. Then he added, with a cynical look on his face, 'You see, we grow up faster here, we do tough jobs sooner, we become men earlier, and we even marry earlier than you do.'

I could not believe my ears. First, because he sounded like an adult in his affirmations, and secondly, that he sounded anything at all. All morning long, I had thought him to be a timid and quiet fellow incapable of conversation. But he most appropriately confirmed and illustrated for me the popular proverb that the older people used now and then:

Proceed (safely) over a roaring river
but tread not over a quiet one

***

The Aggay River, born as a spring up in the Atlas foothills west of Sefrou, roared down the steep cascades, but ran quietly and limpidly on flat land. It was an ideal river course for adventurous children seeking thrills and escapades, for diving, swimming, wading, and water-splashing. To some, like me, it was also a place to learn and practice 'shirt-fishing.' That was when we would quietly stand in the running river in pairs, and each person would tightly hold one side of a white linen shirt. We would dip the shirt under water against the current for a few minutes and then take it out. Sometimes it would contain a few tadpoles that made you dizzy with their fast and erratic swimming until they got thrown back in the water. Sometimes it would even have some minnows which were placed into a waiting jar full of water. Often, however, it only had a few pebbles and some sand that our feet would have propelled upward. As a child, I disliked eating fish, so even when my team was successful in catching some, I would donate my share to another less lucky pair.

When it hit the city, Aggay turned into the River. There, it became more than a recreation for youths. It generously gave all the people its goodness. While the main course continued down through the middle of town and out into the fields and groves which it plentifully fed through small meandering tributaries, part of it was diverted and canalised somewhere above al-Qal'a. This traditional canalisation system, though old-fashioned in conception, was very intricate and efficient. It reached every house in Sefrou and poured into its water-rooms an unlimited volume of water that people used for washing and cleaning, while the drinking water was piped in through a different water supply available, for a small fee, to those who could afford it. Those Sefrouis with modest means had free access to the neighbourhood fountains which poured out the precious liquid day and night.

The River's waters were so tranquil and so innocuous most of the time that they gave Sefrou's unconcerned inhabitants a false sense of safety and tranquility. The small wood bridges that connected the north side to the south served their casual purpose for a while, but were in fact too old, too low, and too flimsily built to withstand serious challenge. On several occasions, the River did roar and challenge all that came in its path. The year that came to be known as the Year of the Flood, it roared very loudly following some torrential rains. From the Aggay hills it dragged down with its murky waters large chunks of earth, rocks of all sizes imaginable, and whole trees that had been uprooted in the process. Nothing could stop nature's wrath and its powerful forces which some naively mistook for the Final Deluge, especially when they realised that the disaster had been foretold out loud in the streets by Mulay Driss Ben al-Alem, Sefrou's mystical and most revered *majdoub*.

The town's swimming pool, which during part of the year would retain some of the River's flow to the delight of many a happy bather, filled up in a flash with mud and stones. The rest of the traveling debris broke the retaining wall on impact and went on to cause the heaviest human and property toll in the city's recorded history. The first to get washed away were the 'feet-stumpers' who used to gather at Ghaddiwa, where the overflow from the pool created small waterfalls, to wash their clients' wool blankets and heavy outerwear. Apparently, even down-stream the waters spared neither humans nor animals. Fortunately for most, however, the news of the flooding river spread almost as fast as its sudden onslaught and people began to take evasive measures at once. At our own house on 'Arsat Dar, it was no different. I still remem-ber – though I was barely three then – my father, my teen-age brother, and our nanny stacking up cement blocks on top of sand bags at the entrance to the narrow alleyway leading to the door of our house. Inside, my mother was shouting something about blocking all the openings in the water-room that might bring in flood waters. Then we were instructed to all file upstairs and remain there until further notice. The next day, it was the voice of the public crier outside which momentarily reassured the frightened Sefrouis:

'Oh! Servants of God, you will hear nothing but good news insha'allah, the flood waters have receded and you may leave your homes now.'

Nobody was really reassured, however, until a deeper waterway was dug, higher cement retaining walls were erected, and bigger and sturdier bridges were built.

***

When my cousins and I arrived back at the house in Lahmari, we stood at the door of the main living room for a few minutes while our respective fathers and the other men were at their final 'bow-and-kneel' in prayer. It looked just like a little mosque in there, with my father leading the prayer in the front and the rest of them behind. There was an '*Allahu akbar*' followed by a bow and some whispering, then another '*Allahu akbar*' followed by a kneeling and some more whispering, then my father's voice leading the closure with a solemn '*Assalaamu 'alaykum*,' as he turned his head to the right, then to the left, followed by everyone else's closing greeting and head gestures. They had barely regained their lounging areas when I walked into the middle of the room with my play-rifle in hand and the three dead chicks tied onto it, boasting to my father and to whomever was likely to be impressed,

'Look, I am just as good as Mme Samson's husband when he returns from his hunts, right?'

I was not really sure what everybody's reaction was going to be, especially my father's. My young cousins' earlier displeasure with my deliberate killing of three potential egg-layers, or a Friday lunch's main course, could very likely have had a magnified echo in my father's eyes and strict judgment. For a few seconds there was a silence with all the tension and suspense that I alone could fathom. Then, without word or comment, Uncle Driss burst into laughter, followed by his two brothers and, much to my great surprise, by my father who first tried to muffle a laugh but then let out a refreshing one that sent his shoulders into an irresistible up-and-down boun-cing. He who often associated laughing with profanity had just revealed his humanity. And humane he was, too, when he decided to make the best of the situation and went on to embellish the farce by adding his own humour:

'Did you at least mention Allah's name as you were hunting them? Because that would have still made them *halal* and perfect for some *bastilla* stuffing.'

My response was to cast my eyes evasively downward, not fully grasping the intent of his statement. My father turned to his hosts, embarrassed nonetheless by what had happened.

'You must really forgive him and blame me, it was my fault. I promised him a toy rifle when we got to Lahmari and I told him to go hunting, thinking he would use his imagination only.'

'It is quite all right, sir! God will replace them with more. Besides, we have plenty of them running around as it is,' replied Uncle Hashem.

As the profusion of apologies and the exchange of niceties proceeded in one corner of the room, more children walked in, kissed adult hands, and sat down. Uncle Mohammed asked the oldest of the newcomers,

'Are we going to eat any time soon? Our guests must be starving by now with all that talk about chicks and fowl, and I hope we'll have some today, otherwise we shall all develop some craving-pimples on our tongues.'

At that very moment, Hnia, one of the daughters in the household, came to the door and handed al-Houssayn a brass basin-and-kettle, indicating that he was to take it around the room for the pre-meal hand-washing. Relieved by that sight, the men sat up from their half-reclining positions and, in turn, extended their hands over the basin as the kettle holder, going from right to left, stood in front of each and poured water, then handed him a towel. When al-Houssayn stood in front of me and water began to trickle down my soiled hands, I could not help thinking again of the proverb about him and the quiet river. I looked up and just smiled.

The festive lunch was plentiful, but from my selfish viewpoint somewhat rushed. With several cooked salads placed here and there along the rim of the short-legged table around which only the men were seated, three main courses were paraded over, one at a time. But just because we all used three fingers of our right hand to eat from a collective dish in the middle, it did not mean we all ate the same amounts. Some of us were faster, or had longer fingers, or swallowed without chewing. Since my mother had always taught us never to show bad table manners, eat a lot, or be the first or the last to help ourselves, especially in the company of others, I found myself losing what appeared like a fingers-to-mouth race. The children were too hungry following their outing and the older people were eager to resume their twice-interrupted discussions, once by a call to the soul and once by a growl from the stomach. Every now and then, Hnia would come in and inspect the state of the table, then her father would ask, 'Well, is there anything else or what?' At which point she would take the still half-full dish back to the courtyard and would soon come back with the next course.

First they served us a tagine of lamb with prunes, roasted almonds, and sesame seeds. Then they served a tagine of four whole chickens with olives and preserved lemons. With both courses, we sampled the *matloo'* bread that one of the women was baking in the yard when we came in. Finally, they brought in the much-awaited couscous dish shaped like a mountain, with several assorted vegetables, raisins, and chickpeas sliding down the side of steamed semolina. Buried inside were chunks of lamb that 'melted in the fingers.' As soon as the hand-to-mouth exercise – in which couscous balls skillfully rolled by the fingers inside the palm of the right hand were placed in the mouth – finally ceased, Hnia came back, took away everything that was on the table, and started cleaning. She then brought back the brass basin-and-kettle and handed them to al-Mahdi who was sitting closest to the door. After the mouths were rinsed, the hands washed and dried, and a few belches sounded in a guttural chorus, the children, with the exception of myself, walked out and the men scattered around the room.

'*Al-hamdu li-llah*, and may God replace your generosity,' said my father as he rested his left arm over two pillows and reclined his satisfied body over one of the mattresses. Some of the hosts followed suit, others sat up to make their upcoming arguments more convincing. On my father's advice, I too positioned myself on one of the mattresses and lay down.

As he started to speak, preacher-like, to his avid listeners who were finally nearing a settlement of a long neglected or postponed issue, my father had taken on an earnest tone:

'If you do not want your father perpetually tormented in his grave, it behooves you to come to an equitable division, for his own sake, if not for yours.'

'That's what I have been telling them myself,' added Uncle Driss.

'Yes, but there were the younger female siblings to think about,' said Uncle Hashem. 'We wanted to wait until they came of age so they could get what God had allocated for them.'

'Well, for the sake of God, let bygones be bygones and let us find you a solution here and now.'

'You are right, Lafqih, and we are all ears from now on, may God have mercy on your parents' souls,' responded one of them.

I could not tell at that point, my eyes had already begun to close under the influence of fatigue and the bloating sensation from the hastily ingested meal. The voices seemed farther and farther from my ears, as if I had started to levitate away from the stage where things were happening, or something strong was pulling me down to and beneath the earth. To where everything was solidly rooted, the green vegetables in the fields, the fruit trees in the orchards, the reed in 'Ain Taragrag, the oak in the forest, the ducks and the deer in the wild, the sheep and the cows in the meadows, the chicks in their open space, the River in Sefrou, the children in their families, the people in their land, and Sidi Lahcen in time.

How life is hard: visceral notes on meaning, order, and Morocco

David Crawford

Department of Sociology and Anthropology, Fairfield University, CT, USA

This essay explores Clifford Geertz's injunction to attend to the 'hard surfaces of life' in cultural analysis, and the importance of how such surfaces are experienced, how they feel, in conveying their significance. Reflecting on his personal experiences in Morocco, the author examines how the corporal concerns of the researcher relate to the material dilemmas recognised among his Moroccan interlocutors, and how these change over time. The article concludes that anthropologists have tended to outline a disembodied 'culture' at the expense of 'hard surfaces,' and that scholars have had special difficulty expressing visceral understandings, especially of being poor in Morocco.

Introduction

In one of the most influential essays in the history of anthropology, Clifford Geertz wrote,

> The danger that cultural analysis... will lose touch with the hard surfaces of life – with the political, economic, stratificatory realities within which [people] are everywhere contained – is an ever-present one. The only defense against it, and against, thus, turning cultural analysis into a kind of sociological aestheticism, is to train such analysis on such realities and such necessities in the first place. (Geertz 1973, p. 30)

The ethnographic vignette included with this admonition involved rural Berber tribesmen, a Jewish peddler, and a bumbling Protectorate that came nowhere close to appreciating the 'thickness' involved in this multiple murder and robbery, and the transaction of sheep that followed. The French, it seems, could see only twitches while the Moroccans were winking at winks.

Rural Morocco has no shortage of hard surfaces, thus no shortage of opportunities to focus cultural analysis on them. The word for 'hard' (*ishqa* in Tashelhit) is a sombre refrain and key explanatory framework in formal interviews and everyday conversation in the mountains south of Marrakesh, where I work. People are 'hard' when they are ruthless or unkind; steep trails, drought, and cold winters are hard; the government can be hard. Most centrally, people tell me, life is hard. *How* life is hard is not a purely existential question, however. It is not something that is stable through individual lives or broader history, nor can it be neatly summarised by an algebra of lack ('poverty') or division of labour ('patriarchy').

What is clear is that hardness is something experienced, something *felt* more than seen. Anthropology has been much better at unveiling concepts than sensation, and attempts to illuminate sentiment or suffering generally devolve into ideas about them. We are intellectuals, after all, and our tendency has been to engage the intellects of our interlocutors far more than their bodies. The fact that we think of these as separate is telling in itself, and there is a hierarchy to the terms. Descartes suggests that he 'is' *because* he thinks, and Paul Rabinow begins his *Reflections on fieldwork in Morocco* (1977), a watershed text about the experience of fieldwork, with comments about the books he had recently been reading (Thomas Kuhn and Lévi-Strauss, it turns out). The whole point of *Reflections*, Rabinow tells us in the 30th anniversary edition (2007), was to 'retell Hegel's chapter on sensory experience,' but despite this ambition the attempt to 'situate' ethnography never quite situates it in bodies.

To get at the hard surfaces of life in rural Morocco requires attention to bodies, their corporality and transformation. What Searle (2004) calls the 'first person ontology' of consciousness is in this case consciousness of poverty: heat, cold, and drudgery, the exigencies of lack (of things you need) or excess (of things you don't). Such experience is undertaken by integrated mindful bodies/embodied minds. But human bodies are inextricably social, too, and some attention is due to the way suffering bodies are built through, and incorporated into, larger social bodies. Our own bodies can be obstacles (they drive us to do things, they crave, they fail) and vehicles for (more elevated?) desires. Likewise social bodies – households, families, even the state – can simultaneously function as the means of dealing with the difficulties of everyday life and be 'stratificatory realities' in themselves. Patriarchy can hurt like dentistry without anesthetic, and for some Moroccans the inability to find work, marry, and have children is a sharp, enervating starvation. The complexly hard world in which and through which Moroccans make their lives demands *cultural* analysis because no human body is merely a body, and no idea ever came from anywhere else.

Key to analysis of hard surfaces, then, is an explanation of how we feel (and thus feel for others), and key to this is providing some record of how we bring our fleshy selves to the ethnographic encounter. How each of us is calibrated as an anthropologist (and before that, as a person) has much to do with what we are able to measure, how we interpret, what we can grasp. There has been a great deal of work on how social position impacts what we *see*, how social relations of domination provide us with perspective, a place from which to see. The visual metaphor is revealing, and it has allowed anthropology to remain scientifically sanitary, observant of but not part of the travails of our subjects. But precept, affect, and concept live together in growing (and thus suffering, dying) persons. Our individual incorporation (our being-in-a-body that is constituted through a social body) has much to do with how we learn to feel, and thus how we come to empathise.

This essay mostly involves reflection (impressions, sensations, visceral understandings) from nearly two decades of moving through Morocco, two decades during which Morocco and I have changed. This venture is obviously inspired by Rabinow's *Reflections*, but I intend to extend the ethnographic moment and try to show my own objectifying body as a process, too. Through slow moving change (of myself and the Moroccans who teach me), I hope to focus attention on the enduringly hard surfaces I have found in North Africa, surfaces Geertz long ago suggested might save philosophically informed ethnography from 'sociological aestheticism.'

The first time

I arrived in North Africa via Marrakesh in 1988, alone with $150 and no credit card. I landed in the dark and made the quick trip downtown apprehensive and silent. I gave the address of some place right on the square, the old CTM building, but moved down the alleyways looking for something cheaper, or beyond that, very cheap. I landed in a room that was 25 dirhams a night, about two dollars and change in those days, with a toilet two floors below me and a single cold shower if I dared. Each morning I purchased two boiled eggs from the *hanut* up the alley, four to six loaves of bread from women selling them out of baskets, and a pile of oranges.

It was January and it rained a lot. I drank two pots of tea each day while sitting around the shabbiest cafés, one in the a.m. and one after my lunchtime bread. I read used paperbacks, wrote poems about swallows and prostitutes, and fended off suggestions that I have sex, pay boys for sex, or let them take me to girls for sex. It became apparent that young male Europeans must go to Marrakesh for sex, as that is what many people assumed I was doing. I had one month before my flight would take me back to Paris, and about five dollars a day to spend. I had a passport, of course, and could escape Morocco willingly, thus the strategic difficulties of my poverty amounted to a kind of game. For Moroccans it is no game, of course, and it does not involve a month alone so much as a lifetime entangled in family and economy and a struggle for making sense that is inevitably a struggle to stay alive. But we will come to that later.

For dinner each night I had *harrira* at a stand in the Jemaa al-Fna, two bowls or three. It was only a dirham or two. In those days there was no electricity in the square, no straight lines or numbered stalls, and the propane lanterns rendered the scene unearthly. That was its allure. It was here that I rescued a young boy (maybe six? eight years old?) beaten savagely by his begging peers for some crime against the gang. He became my official guide, and I his protector. The Lords of the Flies were not anxious to tangle with tourists, or not anxious to tangle with *tourisme*, and my sidekick stayed 15 feet away from me for at least a week, heckling my hecklers while remaining distant enough to avoid trouble with the police. It was illegal for him to talk to me, he said.

I milled about, read a lot, and met some bored guys my own age, early 20s, who wanted desperately to figure out what I was doing, and plied me with revolting homemade booze to find out. They packed it beneath their shirts in Coke bottles secured with rubber bands and cellophane. I was not at all sure that its intoxicating force did not come from gasoline. We choked it down, burning even with orange soda, but their method failed because I had no idea what I was doing and so no way to explain. I was avoiding Paris and all the trouble I had started there. My answers were unsatisfying.

I soon came to smell like the overflowing sewer in my street, the animals, sweat, my own clothes, so I learned to use the public *hammam*. This was harder than it sounds because I lacked the requisite undergarments and had to use a loaner Speedo reserved for country bumpkins and other idiots too stupid to show up with their own underwear. It turns out Moroccan men, like Americans, are deeply suspicious of the human body and do not bathe naked even though they bathe together. Wearing somebody else's cold, wet Speedo – many sizes too small, I am large for a peasant – was my initiation into the arcane rules of public bathing. I never got very good at it.

During the days and evenings I got pickpocketed frequently, or evaded pickpockets mostly, and then was robbed in a drug buy I agreed to conduct for a paranoid Dutch traveler in my hotel. This was humiliating as the Dutch guy had been bugging me for a week, asking, 'Why is all the Moroccan hash in Holland?' So when somebody offered me something, I followed him into the spice souk and with a frightening, furtive exchange came away with a chunk of a nut wrapped in plastic. I could only apologise to the Dutchman for losing his money and decided to get out of Marrakesh.

I bought a seat on the cheapest bus for Agadir at some ridiculous hour of the morning. The bus circled the station, revving its engine and honking the horn, plying for more customers. None came despite the bombast and with the sun high in the sky we began the slow crawl over the mountains to the small station at the north side of Agadir. From there I wandered around the city looking for the local bus to Taghazoute, a little coastal village now filled with condos and surf shops. In those days, in January, the place would be deserted, which was exactly what I wanted. An offer of help finding the bus made me suspicious, but not enough to refuse. My new Agadir guide took me from bus stop to bus stop, querying the passing drivers, but the right bus never seemed to come. He told me a story of the city changing the bus lines so we eventually gave up and went to the main hub. There he insisted on buying me tea, then insisted on guiding me physically on to the correct bus and finding me a seat. He then conscripted the guy in the next seat to be my new guide, and to my utter amazement he left without accepting a tip. He worked at the fish market, he said, he had to go, just wanted to make sure that I found what I was looking for. In Morocco everybody is excruciatingly kind, whether they are taking your money or refusing to take it.

My new best friend on the bus had a six-pack of beer hidden in a bag. He cradled it like a baby, patting the bag and winking at me. The bus disgorged us at the end of the line and he walked me out to Ankar Point to watch Danes and Australians surf. He offered me a beer. I was again suspicious. Having been calibrated in Los Angeles, Paris, and now Marrakesh, I knew that too-good-to-be-true was nearly always bad. A single beer cost more than my hotel room, though at that point in my self-inflicted isolation I was ready to choose alcohol over lodging. But I didn't have to pay. He gave me two of his six beers and, delirious, I watched the boys in thick wetsuits slip down the reeling, right-hand barrels one after another after another until it was too dark to see. The beer angel had to go. He gathered up his Stork bottles, said goodbye, and that was that.

The next day I was lying on the beach bundled against the wind, my bag of bread, two boiled eggs, and oranges next to me in a black *mica*. Two guys came my way, directly at me from across the sand in a manner that suggested I was the object of a plot. But my LA frame of reference again turned out wrong as the pair aimed at the big house just off the beach behind me. The big house was shut down for the winter, as it turned out, and Lahcen worked as a gardener and caretaker for the governor of the province (who owned the house). To augment his salary, Lahcen subleased floor space in his cement shed out back to the two other guys, one in the army and the other studying religion. Lahcen himself had a degree in engineering, but could not find a job other than as caretaker of this empty mansion. The shed was gray cement, about 15 feet long, ten wide, with a bright metal door and no windows.

I shared my oranges; they dug up some carrots, potatoes and other vegetables from the garden. They cooked and we ate. For the rest of my month I came back every day. We had fantastic, slow conversations in three languages. I could only do French. The army guy spoke *darija*, the religion student spoke Tashelhit, and so Lahcen had to translate everything for everybody.

Lahcen's own themes revolved around unemployment, the pointlessness of higher education in Morocco, unfairness, inequality, corruption. He was obviously bright and overtly frustrated, but his gentle nature made him less militant than contemplative. The army guy lived for one thing and one thing only: sex with German women. He awaited the season when they would return like migrating flamingos. Licking his lips, losing himself in a reverie of misty-eyed memories, he could inject something into any conversation about the virtues and virtuosity of German sex bombs. His underlying refrain was that Germans were 'not racist' like the French, by which he meant that French women would not fuck him. He was also a big fan of Ronald Reagan, who evidently had supplied the Moroccans with helicopter gunships and night-vision goggles to hunt down dissidents in the extreme south, the means to kill Sahrawis as they ran blindly in the dark.

The religion student was not so much embarrassed by these graphic descriptions of military slaughter and Teutonic breasts, as anxious to convey to me deeper beauties: the transcendent poetry of the Qur'an. He would pray rhythmically beneath the olive trees in the dappled light of the garden, then come and repeat verses to me, and beg Lahcen to explain. The student focused on the excruciating elegance of the prose. He chose sura after sura about gardens and heaven and virtue and goodness and I tried to seem interested. He insisted I *listen* as he recited, and I did; the sensual thrill was in the flow of the words, he said, the sublime susurrus of God that breathes peace into your heart if only your heart remains open to it.

The roommates were not always there, but every day Lahcen and I would meet for lunch and a slow afternoon of talk. He occasionally managed to get fresh sardines from the port, which he would crank through a grinder, then roll into balls with cumin seeds, parsley, and other tidbits from the garden. We'd fry these in the argan oil his family would send him from the mountains and it was the best thing I had ever eaten. Mostly we dined on oranges, eggs, and bread, though. Lahcen made tea and plucked things from the earth and I provided the bread. At the end of my time I said a goodbye, gave Lahcen my Sony Walkman, and promised I would come back.

Returning to Marrakesh, I had to last one more day. I was hungry and broke and it did not look promising. I milled about the square in the dark, inhaling the cooking smells, and counted the hours until the plane left the next day. Irritatingly, one of the team that had robbed me in the drug deal (the initial contact, not the actual perpetrator) kept trying to rob me again. I explained over and over that they had already taken my money, that I didn't want any dope, but he didn't recognise me and didn't understand what I was saying. Finally, I robbed him, dragging the poor guy into an alley and stealing his stash when he took it out for me to see. It was all very polite by American standards. I explained that in my country we are responsible for the misbehaviour of our relatives, and this got his attention. Now he remembered, he said; he was sorry; his brother could not always be trusted, but what could he do? It disturbed him that his brother was a thief, he said, and I felt bad. Then he complained that his brother had only robbed me for half as much as I had robbed him, so I split the chunk of hash, gave half back, and walked away. I sold my chunk to an Irish guy because the Dutchman had already departed. This provided dinner, breakfast, and the money to get the bus to the airport, so I only had to walk the last bit from the main road to the terminal.

I only thing I had ever read about Morocco at that point was Clifford Geertz. It had been assigned in a class on cultural theory and it did nothing to help make sense of the struggles of everyday Moroccans I had come to know. I had several more arrivals after this first one, but the idea that Moroccans lived a long way from American ethnography about Morocco was already taking hold.

Second coming

I rode south from Madrid in early summer 1995 along with thousands of Moroccans carrying their wages home. On the bus I befriended a woman who lived in Spain cleaning toilets. She was on her yearly trip to see her children. She helped me figure out how to board the ferry in Algeciras, then shepherded me through the vicious throng on the Tangier side of the strait, where she and her kids, some strikingly young, were reunited in great sobbing bursts of joy. I moved away, embarrassed by all the emotion, and got ripped off trying to change money, and was then swindled again at my hotel. I didn't care, though. I was in the country and set to head south to find Lahcen, to find someplace to spend my time and money and begin what I hoped would be a 'career.' I had just turned 30 and it seemed time to have a career. I had quit my job as a 'Kelly girl,' answering phones in a doctor's office, gotten myself accepted to grad school (somehow, with no background at all in anthropology and no idea what I was doing), and was now looking for a research project by which I could become something... legitimate.

In the south everything had changed. The Jemaa al-Fna was tidied up, though they had not yet completely tamed it. The old cheap hotel was more expensive and less friendly. The bus to Agadir was orderly and they charged money to put your baggage on the roof, and then again to take it off. When I finally found Taghazoute it was utterly transformed. The beach had been colonised by millions of *baidawi* families, sprawled out over the sand like birds in the nesting season. Soccer balls shot like fireworks, music blared, huge, heaving women lumbered like mastodons after scurrying children, and skinny boys drunk on their own laughter staggered in circles, throwing sand, groping each other, falling in the surf. It was hell and it was hot. A terrible drought gripped the nation and Lahcen was gone, of course, back to his home village somewhere in the hills, explained the new *gardien*. So I made my way sadly back to the bus terminal and kept pushing south, to Tiznit then Tafraoute.

The bus out of Tiznit was a rickety castoff from some defunct European public transportation system, and it ground noisily through the mountains to Tafraoute. It was stifling in the terrible heat and I was quietly terrified by the narrowness of the road. Poor farmers in dirty *jellaba*s wiped snot on the window curtains, and great arguments broke out about whether to open the windows for air or close them against the heat. I was sitting in the back, and could not track the angry debate until the guy behind me, another Lahcen, offered to translate. This Lahcen was retuning to his home village – like everybody, it seemed. He had been in Moscow studying for his doctorate in mathematics. Naturally, he asked me to stay with him at his mother's house, and naturally I accepted. The bus made it to the town centre. We bought kilos of meat wrapped in bloody paper, put it into black plastic bags, and started walking south.

This, I thought, could be my research site if it were not so awfully hot. It was a modern village, built beyond the valley of Tafraoute on a small plain below an ancient, fortified hamlet. The French had bombed these villagers out of their hilltop redoubt in the early 20th century, and almost the entire male population had migrated. They now used European money to build an empty, idyllic village of cement, with little water towers and solar-power panels, garages for the cars. Some women remained, especially the old ones, and a very few young children were installed to incorporate the values of village life. Great black Mercedes cars arrived with German license plates and tall women with $400 shoes peeking out beneath their voluminous folds of inky cloth. All the women here wrapped in black, and they would rarely talk to Lahcen, much less me, especially the women who actually worked in the fields, the permanent residents. If Lahcen and I approached, they stopped all activity, turned away from us, pulled their expanse of black sheet into a seamless shroud around them and made muffled replies to our questions until we went away.

What a place! This was a homemade Moroccan Disneyland Main Street, but alive and public and amenable to building. The two most successful men were fuelling a housing boom, constructing competing Moroccan McMansions on opposite sides of the road, including whole separate floors for men and women and huge stables for sheep that could never possibly graze on the desiccated hills that surrounded us. These were Moroccan dreams materialising in the heat, dreams that could be visited maybe once every two years, but real enough to sustain men working somewhere in the far green and white north, in the cold among the Christians who did not seem to have dreams at all.

But I couldn't stand the heat. Even Lahcen had a hard time, probably because he'd adjusted to Moscow, and we agreed to take a trip to the high mountains in hope the altitude would provide some relief. Lahcen knew his village, Casablanca, Paris, and Moscow. That was it. He had never seen any of the rest of the country. I agreed to pay his way if he would help me find mine. We set off for Taroudant, which we saw as the gateway to the High Atlas and cooler climes. On the way I explicated the various ethnographies I had packed along, but when I saw how upsetting they were to him, I let anthropological matters drop. Lahcen was serious about his religion and his studies, and these strange cults, tribes, and issues of representation had nothing whatsoever to do with the practice of proper Islam, or what he saw as the reality of Morocco. The real issue in his country involved jobs, he made clear, good jobs that would save people from being forced from home, forced to live far from the soul-sustaining networks of kin and friends that made life worth living. Lack of jobs led to lack of morality. If you want to talk about Islam, he said, forget about *marabout*s and *moussem*s and make it possible to worship *and* pay rent, to marry and raise a family amongst your own family.

Lahcen and I arrived in Taroudant just after market day, or after the particular market day when the trucks would come from the high mountains. We could wait a week, or develop another plan to get out of the valley, and I chose another plan. We'd take the main road by the daily bus, up and over the Tizi n Test, then get off at the first place where the road crossed a sizable river. We only had the Michelin map, so only major rivers were listed. It looked like some place called Ijoukak would be our destination; it sat on the intersection of the road and the Agoundis River. We left before dawn and arrived at midday. The local residents could not figure out why we stayed off the bus – buses commonly stopped in Ijoukak to let the passengers eat, pee, and pray, but nobody actually stays when the bus goes. We left the heaviest items in my pack with a shopkeeper (no need to carry *all* of my library up the hill), bought some canned sardines and a few loaves of bread, and started upstream.

From the asphalt road at Ijoukak, a nondescript dirt track leads east along an alley of olive trees on the bank of the Agoundis River. The walls of the canyon grow steeper and begin to envelope you; the cover of oak and juniper becomes denser. Thickets of blackberries line the route and are punctuated by an occasional wild rose bush and clumps of bamboo. Ancient walnuts and almonds flourish in the riverbed and on terraces where there is more sun. Irrigation ditches are etched into the slope above, invisible in the overgrowth. The perennially leaking water inspires a chorus of birds and frogs. It was meltingly beautiful after the drought and heat in the rest of the country.

Then the road begins to rise above the level of the river, tracking its bends, and edging higher on the slope. We reached a fork and chose the branch that went north, up into the high country. This quickly went from a road to a path, though men were working with dynamite and jackhammers to etch out a proper road. We continued up the path until dark, then went down to the river and slept. Lahcen chose a spot on the sand. I took a large, flat rock in the middle of the river. We only found out later that people died this way from flash floods.

In the morning I awoke to find myself carefully observed by some ragged local boys. Torn clothes, dirty hair, black nails, skinny. They looked at us with wide curious eyes and I wrote in my journal something about feral animals. I found a rusty can and, while Lahcen slept, the boys and I invented a game throwing rocks into it. This was a new Morocco for me, under the great cool walnut trees with these boys who seemed to live in the earth rather than just on it.

Lahcen and I kept moving upstream, and found our way up the precarious terraces to the path again and into the sun. We had no idea where we were or where we were going. This was a vast blank area on our map, and we were already running out of food. We met a man sitting in the shade selling candy and warm Cokes. We bought Cokes and he invited us to stay, but we declined. It was too early in the day. I got his name – Abdurrahman – and the name of the village, and told him I would be back. Three years later, I was. This became the village I lived in and have written about for the last ten years.

We passed through one dilapidated hamlet after another with clumps of wan women and sick children wearing rags and begging for money, for medicine, for anything. Lahcen clearly found this embarrassing, especially the questions from the women, the beseeching. In Lahcen's village in the far south, women were silent and shrouded in black; in Taroudant they were standoffish and covered in blue. Here the women were brightly dressed in the most uproarious colours, sequins, and spangles, and were every bit as forward as anyplace else I have been. Women, alone or in groups, would stop us dead in the trail and pepper us (or Lahcen, really) with questions and demands. He'd stammer and shuffle his feet, staring at the ground. He could not make eye contact and was reluctant to translate. Their propositions were not things he would put into French.

Every village was clotted with trash, with old tea boxes and scraps of plastic, the petrified feces of goats, donkeys, chickens, and people, shards of pots and swatches of frayed cloth. Men would pass us sweating with huge bags of manure hoisted on their shoulders; women staggered by with loads of firewood or babies, or firewood *and* babies. Everybody who was not gawking was busy, moving things up or down the mountains. They would stop when we came into sight, but the general bustle resumed in our wake. Here was a very different face of poverty than I was used to in the city, one characterised by a superabundance of labour rather than a lack of meaningful work.

Lahcen and I nearly died climbing over the pass to the Marrakesh side of the mountains, he of hypothermia and me of altitude sickness. We parted at the French hiking refuge below Toubkal. I gave him his fare home and he zipped quickly down the mountain; I trod more slowly with my huge pack, still carrying a few of the ethnographies Lahcen hated. I got a ride to Marrakesh by befriending two Korean mountain climbers who could not speak French. They had been paying 100 times the normal rates for taxis, and were appreciative that I did the bargaining for them.

In Marrakesh I began searching for a map so I could find out where I had been, but before I could lay my hands on one I was flattened by microbes. It remained unbearably hot. I vomited into the sink when I wasn't squatting over the toilet, and tried to drink from the taps to keep hydrated, but the taps only flowed periodically and the water made me sicker still. I could keep nothing in my body, not even water. I was alone and terrified and wrote a kind of will in my notebook as my insides emptied out, a letter to my mother. I lay panting, face on the cool tile floor, and mercifully slipped into unconsciousness. But I did not die, and upon waking gobbled handfuls of Imodium and traveled north to Fez, then tried to recuperate in the cooler climes of Chefchaouen, living off vegetable broth and yogurt. Finally I gave up, swallowed more stomach-paralysing Imodium, and aimed to meet my girlfriend in Ceuta, Spanish territory. She put me in the hospital as soon as she saw me. I emerged a week later, having had no food or water, only an IV and the antics of my neighbours to sustain me: Fouad (an immigrant who believed the Spanish doctors were trying to kill him, and so only pretended to take his medicine) and Juan (a Spaniard who had Alzheimer's and deafness but no other reason to be in a hospital). I left for mainland Spain, weak and thin, alive and happy. I could see there was much to write about Morocco. That had become all I cared to do.

Third return

In the late summer of 1997 I made it back with a purpose beyond sampling the 'intense' experience long ago promised by my *Let's go!* guidebook. I was studying Arabic in Fez part-time, living down in the old medina, and beginning to find my feet in the country. In one sense this was easy – Moroccans are friendly people, and the demographic pyramid is so flat you could mistake it for a speed bump. There are *lots* of young people to talk to, and lots who talk to you. Making sense of what they're saying is not always easy.

There were whispers. An acquaintance stealthily flashed me a picture of himself praying at what he said was an underground Christian church. There are thousands of these around, he assured me, the countryside is full of Christians hiding from the government, Berber Christians who never succumbed to Islam, apostates and converts. There are secret churches in the city, too, he said. When I related this to other friends in the café, everyone laughed, called it insane, and some muttered darkly that this was the government testing me, checking to see if I was really doing what I said I was doing. What *are* you doing, Daoud? What is anybody *really* doing?

Stories circulated. The hotel on the hill had been burned down because it was owned by the royal family. Riots followed a hike in the price of bread, and Fez was not favoured by the ruling elite, was falling behind, the young were leaving for Casablanca, and the Fassi *cultural* elite (as they saw themselves) were being undermined by the crass bourgeoisie. Then there were protests at the university. We were never able to find out exactly what happened, there was little in the news and the gossip contradicted it. Three students had been shot, one student had been shot, seven students had been shot, they had been shot at a demonstration, it had been after the demonstration, they were not even students, but students had run from the army into a neighbourhood where random people, unaware of what was going on, were shot dead in front of their houses. The demonstration led to a fight between socialists and Islamists, the army had invaded a girls' dorm, a Leftist student had entered the dorm and the Islamists and the young women protested and it spawned a fight that the police had to put down.... Who knows? Who knew?

Two women studying with me were robbed – young men ran past them and grabbed their necklaces. That might have been the end of it, but one woman protested and one robber wheeled around and attacked her with a pipe. The women went off to the police and the police took them along on a raid, presumably to demonstrate their commitment to solving the crime.

The police vans raced through the night and pulled up to a group of youths with screeching tires. Young men ran, the cops grabbing and beating whomever they could, then throwing them into the back of the van – *with* the original victims, which we expatriates all found portentous. Off to the police station, some men silent, some begging – literally begging the women – to tell the cops that they were not the perpetrators. They didn't know anything! They cried, sobbed in fear.

At the station everyone was dragged before the everyday instruments of coercion – benches, rope, buckets of water. One young man was shaking uncontrollably, weeping, and literally shits his pants as the cops threaten and bluster. These unlucky boys had better come up with some information about this crime, and had better come up with it soon. The police beam proudly at the women. The young women were traumatised, trying to make sense. Was this about their proposed Ph.D. research in politics? A local power show? A royal example?

I was comfortable down in the old medina. I had a large dilapidated old house, empty but for swallows and my bed in one room. I spent time with the owner of a hardware store, Abdelhai, who sold nails and other whatnot from what amounted to a small closet. He would teach me Arabic, we'd watch soccer on a small TV, and play chess. Abdelhai usually won, but not always. The merchant across the road sold beauty products for women, and he seemed far less interested in selling anything than in keeping as many women as possible standing in front of his store for as long as possible. Abdelhai and I appreciated this. I would climb in and take Abdelhai's seat when he would slink off to smoke cigarettes. Despite being in his mid-30s, he was furtive, trying to ensure that his older brothers and father did not ever see him. This would be terrible, he assured me, you could never smoke in front of a father or an older brother, so I was instructed in how to lie convincingly if any family member came by looking for Abdelhai while I was watching the shop. I was a poor salesman of hardware as I never learned all the words for different gadgets, straightened nails, and other bric-a-brac that people wanted to buy. I learned to say, 'Wait, Abdelhai will be back soon.' I kept people's hands out of the till.

I was a lacklustre student of formal Arabic at the school up in the *ville*. I had research money now, and knew I would need to know Tashelhit rather than Arabic to pursue it, but I was discouraged from taking lessons in Berber. Others had been arrested, someone had heard, we would have to ask the mayor, though one should never go see the mayor, but one should always see the mayor.... Better to stick with the Arabic. Abdelhai wanted to teach me proper Arabic, but never really used it himself, and he and his friends found it incomprehensible that I would want to learn Berber. They openly mocked the one Soussi merchant down the *talaa*, but Abdelhai did introduce me to the guy and attempt to explain my plan. I spent long days on my roof, reading and sleeping in the sun, enjoying the privacy and the quiet. I came to love the call to prayer, the rising chorus that built to a crescendo in the city, as if the walls themselves were speaking. It would be the end of my peaceful time in Morocco, however. It was time to get on with research.

Rural return

I staggered into Tagharghist in bad shape. It was July of 1998. I was a nervous PhD candidate with a backpack crammed with the paraphernalia of fieldwork, from cooking pots and a tape recorder to a camera, water filter, antibiotics and a sleeping pad. The village now boasted a Peace Corps volunteer, and a few tourists wandered around, so I was not the novelty I had been when Lahcen and I came through and bought cokes. There was a dirt road now, but I was still walking. The backpack weighed more than me, or seemed to, and I had been traveling since well before dawn by bus, crowded group taxis, and then on foot. I was growing older, less physically fit. Graduate school had softened me and the hike was a bother rather than an adventure. It was nearly dark at the final incline below the village. I doffed my pack, collapsed by the side of the road, and prayed for a mule, a truck, a miracle.

Instead, to my horror, a group of women rounded the bend below me, chattering and laughing. When they came nearer I saw they were not just returning from the fields but were traveling resplendent in their best clothes with sequins, bangles, and scarves of every hue from luminous lime green and yellow to crimson, purple, gold, and orange. They wore jangling tin jewellery, beads, and twittered all at once, musically, singing and joking. Their hands and feet were stained the burnt-rust colour of henna. They appeared to me like a flock of tropical birds, or bright reef fish. I thought I might be hallucinating.

The women were coming from a *moussem*, they said, and they gathered in a circle to examine me. At first only the older women would speak, but my obvious helplessness and their festive mood soon had everyone peppering me with questions. I could not understand most of them, especially with the younger girls giggling hysterically, literally crying with laughter behind the skirts of their elders. They wanted to know where I was going, if I meant to go to Tagharghist, if I was looking for Abdurrahman (since I was obviously going to Tagharghist, and he was the only one likely to know foreigners), and, most of all, what in God's name was in that huge pack.

My Tashelhit was worse than shaky – I'd only studied a week. I said, 'I'm tired,' which sent them into paroxysms of laughter. 'My pack is big' also sent them into convulsions, and inspired one brazen woman to lift it with the wave of one hand and declare languidly that it was not heavy at all. She sauntered off with the pack slung over one shoulder like nothing more than a parasol and I was forced to stumble after her to take up my ridiculous parcel myself. Thus humiliated, shaking my head confusedly to the questions that kept coming, I shouldered my load and dragged myself up the road, prodded by the women like a decrepit mule.

Thus I arrived at Abdurrahman's door, the man who had invited me three years before. It was the first door of the first house next to the road, at the base of the village. By this point the women ran silent, melted into the village pathways, slid inside houses and disappeared into stables, their ebullience muffled by the weight of village propriety. I was bidden to enter Abdurrahman's small, irregular door and passed into a dark hallway, then through a second door, then a third. I dropped my pack to the floor. Abdurrahman laid thick carpets on top of the plastic *tagertilt*, a red one, an orange one, and a striped white and black blanket too. I writhed out of my boots and collapsed. He asked, 'Would you like some tea?'

It only took a day for Abdurrahman to get me set up with a house (rented from somebody who had migrated to the city), but it was much tougher to arrange eating and shitting. There were no toilets and the customary rules of who goes where and when were not immediately obvious. Worse, it seemed everybody wanted to feed me and I had no idea how I would reciprocate all this generosity. It took weeks – and some hurt feelings – to get it all straight, but finally I managed to make it customary that I eat with only three families, one relatively rich (Abdurrahman's) and two poor. These three families would receive equal parcels of meat and other rarities from me every market day, whether or not I ate with them the previous week. Thus I avoided a quid pro quo that would disturb the nature of a gift, but managed to keep from further impoverishing people living on the very edge of subsistence. The children did not need any calories subtracted from their diet. I would send the parcels via children, usually, or furtively pass them to women, or leave them subtly behind like a forgotten trifle as I departed after tea. Thus families fed me with food I partly provided. They remained generous hosts, and I remained a grateful guest for the entirety of my stay.

I quickly came to see that the main point everybody wanted to make was that life was hard. They used this exact phrase again and again: life in the mountains is hard. As it turned out, I did not need any special anthropological training to understand it, or any subtle linguistic preparation. I only had to listen. *Life. Here. Is. Hard.* Men would gather my hands in theirs, stare into my eyes, and repeat it slowly enough that they were assured I could not miss the message. Women would stop me on the trail, and between marriage proposals and rebuffs of whatever gossip they assumed I had heard from somebody else, they would remind me that life was hard in the mountains. My objective, then, became detailing how life was hard. The presumption of equality and the general horrific poverty masked striking differences between households. Villagers were very focused on the diversity amongst themselves, not just their position in the larger political economy.

I began by building a kinship chart – standard old-school anthropology I was now glad I had learned – and the old men loved this. They would quiz me on this or that long-dead relative, and I would be able to tell them who his brother was, who his sister married. They pronounced me 'smart.' I did a census, counting the household members of different ages as well as the number of migrants and other information like ownership of cattle. I mapped each of the 1,400 odd fields and assessed their ownership, whether or not they were irrigated, and whether the field was used for crops or fodder. I counted each almond, walnut, pomegranate, and carob tree owned by the villagers, and determined who owned which of them, a project that was complicated by various types of communal ownership in some areas. I mapped the canals and determined water rights and irrigation rotations on all of them, and computed the comparative amount of time households owned on each canal.

While I worked to determine the shape of each household's material substrate, and how households were linked together, I also tried to understand the positions within households, the way individuals experienced their tight social world. To this end I conducted a few taped interviews about life in the mountains. These were transcribed into Tashelhit written in Arabic characters, then translated into English by Latifa Asseffar, a friend in Taroudant. The first interview I did was with Abdurrahman, my primary host and emerging friend. The second interview was with my neighbour Fatima Id Baj. Fatima was so stunningly eloquent that every subsequent interview seemed flat. Her version of the difficulties of mountain life has become iconic for me, a consolidation of everything I tried to specify with numbers and pie charts and tedious observation. She constructed it for me with some care, I think. It did not seem extemporaneous.

What time necessitates

Fatima had a quick wit and an unfailingly cheerful disposition; she was one of my favourite people in the village, and remains one of my favourite people today. It was not easy for us to spend much time together – she is a married woman in a small Berber village and I was an unmarried *rumi* there on a mysterious mission that involved writing things down. But we managed short conversations nearly every day, and I asked if she would 'make a cassette' for me, that is, let me tape her life story. She enthusiastically agreed, and a couple of days later appeared at my door and insisted I come to her house. We will do it *now*.

Fatima's house was just below the mosque, which has the advantage of being very central and thus an unlikely location for a tryst or other misbehaviour. The door was short, about five feet high, and the entrance hall no higher. We had a running joke where Fatima would tell me to keep my head down and I would pretend to knock myself unconscious. This was funny because two or three times I nearly did knock myself unconscious. When we reached the cramped living room I was surprised to find that Belaid, her husband, was not home, nor were the children. 'Start the machine,' Fatima said tersely. She poured me tea and I worried about how this would look to the old men observing from the window of the mosque antechamber, or how it would look to her husband. We tested the microphone, played back the test to make sure it worked, then started.

> *David:* Do you want to talk about women's lives?
> *Fatima:* You are asking about *my* life. I was born in Tagharghist and after Tagharghist I married to Imaouen. I stayed there for six years. I left two children there. One is named Mustafa, and one named Rbia. After that, I came back to my father's house and I stayed there for a while. And then I married Belaid.

Here Fatima pauses for the significance of this to sink in. I had not known that she was married before; this was her way of telling me. Her first two children live with their father 21 kilometres away at the weekly market, where her father's brother had long ago moved to make a living as a merchant. Fatima had been married to her patrilateral parallel cousin, but he smoked and was abusive and she came home. She wanted this to be known before she went on, and she wanted it entered into the record while her current husband was not in the room. She missed her children terribly, and only saw them on rare occasions. Missing her two oldest children is a central agony in Fatima's life, but she never mentions it in normal conversation. Stoicism, patience, a resolute endurance is a central feminine ideal in the mountains. She continues.

I carry bundles [of grass and wood] and I weave. I grind barley and I grind corn. I gather wood. I bring fodder for the cows. After that I wash clothes. . . .. I come back to make food for the children and after I eat dinner, I go to bed. I only sleep a little. When I wake up, I make coffee and *askeef* [barley flour soup]. I go out to the fields and cut fodder for the cows and come back and feed the cows. I take the broom [a bundle of branches] and sweep the house, I change the clothes on the children, I serve breakfast and we eat it. We eat breakfast.

After breakfast I bring wood from the mountains, I come back and I work on the loom. The loom right here in the room [she points]. We only make the loom in the summer, in winter we do not because in winter work is very hard. Because we have to go to the forest, we bring lots of wood, always when it's cold. When it does not rain a lot, we leave early in the morning. If there is rain, we do not leave early in the morning, we will stay until after breakfast, after we have tea and bread. After we eat, we bring wood. When we come back from gathering the wood, make lunch. We eat and go again to the fields. I went to the fields and brought fodder for the cows. I give it to the cows. I fetch water for them with a bucket. I water them in the stable. I close them there and then I come back to prepare dinner. I prepare the oven [build a fire], knead the dough, I make the *tajine*. I make the bread [literally, press the dough directly against the inside of the oven]. I serve the children their dinner so that they can go to bed.
David: Do you eat the same food in winter as in summer?
Fatima: Oh no. It's different in winter when it's very cold. When it's very cold we eat lentils and beans. In summer we grow squash and potatoes, we do not eat lentils and beans. Summer no. We eat vegetables.

At this point Fatima's husband, Belaid, comes in with their two small boys. He is trying to be quiet, but the room is so cramped that he has to step over Fatima while she is talking. The children are talking, too, and Belaid is trying to quiet them, holding them in his lap. Brahim, Fatima's oldest child in the village, says, 'In Ramadan we have *sahoor*,' and Fatima shushes him and keeps talking.

After summer we sow barley. We water it until it is grown. We harvest it and carry it on our backs to the place where we thresh it. We leave it there for three months. Uh. . . no, before we store it we have to thresh it. We take some to the house. And then we plant maize and care for it. It takes six months to be ready [grow and dry]. When it's ready, we break off the cobs one at a time and leave the stalks in the fields. We women carry the stalks on our backs and store it. We do not give it to the animals, we store it until it's very cold. Until December. Then we give it to them little by little. Because at that time there is no more fodder in the fields. The grass is gone, all gone. Do you understand? It's all gone.
David: Yes.
Fatima: There is no fodder. And then we bring *aori* [a local shrub?] and add it to the stalks we have. This is winter. And then we go back to summer. The work never stops, it goes on. . . .. When we finish with the maize, we take the manure from the stables to each plot. We plow with mules. They sow it in rows. Today they finish the rows in one plot, tomorrow they go to another, tomorrow another. Every day another one. Because it's hard, and the fields are far. When they finish all of them, they come and stay and work their turns on the canals. The first day they work on Targa n Issreran, one day they work on Targa n Taforikht, one day Targa Ijaneten [these are names of canals and their associated fields], one day they go up to Agouni and work the dam there [the shepherds' huts and fields above the village], one day they go up to the mountains. After that they can irrigate the barley. The barley stays nine months in the fields before it's ready. They always irrigate it with their *tamadirt* [short-handled hoe]. And when it's ready, we harvest it with a sickle. After the harvest, we irrigate the plots in order to sow corn. Once we harvest a plot, we take it away in order to irrigate. The plot we irrigated yesterday, we will sow it. The one we irrigate tomorrow, will be sown the day after. When we finish all of them, then we sow the corn. When the maize sprouts, we water it. After fifteen days, we water it. After eight days, they water it again, then they thin them [pull some of

them out] because there are really a lot of them. They reduce them. They *sousint* [thin them, pull some of them out]. And so then the corn grows. After *sousint* we water it, always. Before *sousint* they water it. They sometimes water in the morning, sometimes at night. They take candles and lanterns and they go to the fields until they have irrigated. For the far canals, they take lanterns and stay there from eight until one in the morning. At one, they come back and go to sleep. They sleep from one until four, when they get up and go to the mountains.

David: Is your work the same as everyone's work?

Fatima: Yes, everyone. Just the same. When men sow, women go there [to the fields] and gather fodder. Do you understand? When they gather fodder and bring it and put it down. Then they light the oven. All the work is the same, summer and winter. Same for men, same for women.

David: What is the difference between men and women?

Fatima: Between men and women? [She makes a face, looks at Belaid, who starts laughing. Then, indicating her son and changing the subject, she says, 'He is doing sports.' Her son Brahim is jumping around.]

David: Well, I know the difference between men and women. What's the difference between men's work and women's work?

Fatima: [suppressing laughter] The difference between men and women is that men do not *taougat* [haul things on their backs]. Men don't carry a hundred kilos on their backs. Men, no, they will only take their *tamadirt* [irrigation hoe] and a *terialit* [sack]. He will not take a broom and clean the house, or wash clothes for the children. A woman will wash for children and feed them. She brings wood on her back, and fodder. A man cannot do [or is not able to do] women's work. There is specific men's work and women's work. There is a difference.

David: Which one is harder?

Fatima: Women's is harder. [Belaid nods, agrees.]

David: Do you like your work?

Fatima: Yes, it's difficult, because women work from seven in the morning until midnight or twelve-thirty. Then she sleeps. She never sits down, she's hurrying at night and during the day. A man, him, no. A man, if he works from seven until seven in the evening, then he goes to pray, enough. He changes his clothes. His work clothes, he takes them off and throws them there [she points to where Belaid has piled his work clothes]. And he takes others he will pray in. Enough, he goes where he will pray [the mosque]. Enough, he rests at night. A woman, no. [laughter] A woman she is rushing around, she doesn't sit down. Even if she is pregnant she still carries loads on her back. She is still rushing. If she has an infant, she straps him to her back and the load [of wood or fodder] goes here [she points]. She doesn't rest because 'what time necessitates be done must be done.' Even if it's raining, she carries her baby and her load of fodder or wood on her back. What she needs, she must bring it, whether it rains or not. Everything is outside. Because there is nothing here in the house that replaces it.

In winter there are differences. Winter is really hard. Summer no. In summer we only get wood when people are harvesting walnuts [and branches break off]. We bring some and cook the food with it. It's the same concerning fodder. We don't go to the mountains to bring *aouri*, just to the fields to get *tooga* [fodder, grass grown in fields too shady for other crops] and corn [she means the leaves from the corn]. Winter, no. There is no *tooga* in the fields, there is nothing to bring from them. In the winter, after breakfast you go to the mountains to bring food for the cows. You feed them, and then you feed the children. When you eat breakfast, you take the broom and clean the house. You straighten things, because the house looks like a threshing floor. [laughter]

At this point it is obvious that Fatima is discussing the details of her work, but I am missing the specific verbs for all the tasks. I am anxious to change the subject somewhat. Another neighbour who was very pregnant has disappeared from public view and I am trying to figure out what happened to her, and how childbirth is managed in the village.

David: Where do you give birth to children? In your house?

Fatima: Yes, they are born here. All of them. . ..

David: Where, in the stable or up here?

Fatima: No, right here they are born [indignantly she points to the carpet we are sitting on]. If you want to give birth to a baby you have do it in a room. Because if a woman feels she will give birth to a new baby, she must not go outside, she must stay in her room until she gives birth.

Fatima and I then discuss the case of the neighbour who has just had a baby and why I have not seen her. Evidently this family has a storeroom built under the house beside the stable, and this is where the woman has gone to give birth. Belaid is coughing, Brahim is causing some sort of problem. We turn off the tape recorder and eat dinner, discussing marriage and other aspects of how life is transacted in the mountains. Later we continue the interview. Fatima has an agenda for our taping that she has not yet exhausted and she is anxious to complete her statement.

David: Have you said everything you want. . ..?
Fatima: No, I want to speak about giving birth for new couples. When a child is born, he lives for two months. He dies. Another one is born. He lives for one month, he dies. Sometimes four or five die and then she has one that lives. The other ones are dead. And then time passes, she has another one that dies. Then another time there is again one that lives. Then women advise her to *qeed* her head [blister the scalp with a red-hot iron]. May God protect us, they call this *tezdait* [bad luck]. And so if God finishes [fulfills] what she wants, she will have children. If not, they will continue dying. Until every child in her stomach is finished [she reaches menopause]. Until she finishes all the children that are in her life. All she has given birth to dies. They die when they are still very little, still very new. Still very little, they die. There are those who have nine who die.
David: Nine children?
Fatima: Nine children, *wa Allah* [I swear to God]. There are those who have five who die. Everyone has children who die, everyone has a different number. These die when they are still babies.

The anthropology of mundane suffering

For nearly 20 years now I have been traveling to Morocco, originally as a tourist and later with professional ambitions. I began in the cities and worked my way into a particular village of people in the mountains. I was unmarried for most of this time, but more recently I returned with a family. With help from a Fulbright grant, my wife, toddler son, and infant daughter moved with me to Tagharghist in the summer of 2004. Our very first afternoon in our new home, we heard frantic whelping and discovered a group of boys torturing a puppy below our balcony. It had stolen eggs, we were told, and deserved its fate. I walked down and suggested that a quick death rather than protracted agony might be more in line with the values of the Prophet, Peace be upon Him, but I was dismissed by the boys who extended the process glee-fully. They eventually flung the dog off a cliff and stoned it to silence. It might have been a portent.

Days later I was working on updating my village census and heard commotion outside in exactly the same spot. There in the dirt, ankle swollen, one of my neighbours writhed in pain from a snakebite. People argued about whether to apply honey, whether to give her tea. Women were beating their heads, and some of the toughest grandmothers I knew flashed frightened eyes and involuntarily covered their mouths with their hands. We sent a young man to fetch a truck from a few villages up, and I slipped Abdurrahman some money to pay the driver, to pay the hospital. People asked me what to do – I was the 'doctor,' after all – but I did not know. Her ankle was the size of a volleyball and the fang marks were clotted black with dry blood so we could not suck the poison out. Fatima o Hussein might be saved if we could get her to the clinic at the base of the valley, and if they had medicine. Eventually, painfully slowly, we got her there via the truck, but the clinic was empty and so the truck con-tinued on to the district hospital. They could do nothing there, either, so transferred her to an ambulance which set off to Marrakesh. She died along the way. Abdurrahman had accompanied the ambulance, and when he returned I asked careful questions about the precise spot along the road where Fatima left this world. I do not know why this mattered to me.

This seems an infuriating, straightforward case of 'structural violence.' My neighbour died in searing pain because she was *poor*, in the final instance, because there was no immediate transport, because she could not access a simple injection of antivenin that did not cost more than a cheap tin teapot. The saving *tesmi* that should have been in the clinic had been sold on the black market, some alleged; Fatima had died from the greed of others. But it mattered little. Fatima o Hussein was dead and as the story further unfolded it grew more confounding and, for me, more gruesome.

Fatima o Hussein was bitten on her way *down* to the fields, it seems. She did not return to the village immediately, but continued to finish her work. A girl had seen it happen, another of my neighbours, and did not say anything to anybody back in the village, assuming that Fatima would do what Fatima needed to do. In fact, with her ankle blackening, and swollen and bleeding, the puff adder's poison searing in her veins, *Fatima went to work in the fields*. She stayed more than an hour, maybe two hours some said, and only when she could no longer work did she begin her staggering, swooning death march back to the village. That's why she collapsed in the road below my window. This, everyone agreed, showed just what a good woman she was. A great woman. A great woman *endures*, after all, she is patient. *Sber*. It might be extreme to kill yourself this way, but men shook their heads muttering that Fatima indeed was one good woman. She had incorporated values, embodied them, that cost her life.

Only weeks later my wife Hillary was stricken with dysentery and I did not want her to die a good woman. She became dehydrated enough to hallucinate, she thought she was in Santa Barbara having a baby, was verbally incoherent, telling me that I should cook cauliflower for her PhD advisor. She was too weak to drink any liquid, even from a baby bottle, and I was terrified and pretending not to be. I was being officious, making decisions, trying to stay calm. Our babies were sleeping and it was quiet except for Hillary moaning. I woke one of the nannies to help me think, and before long most of the household was up. We debated what to do.

Just before dawn I tried to get Hillary in the truck to the market, but they would not take her. No white woman was going to die in his truck, the driver said, so I got in to try and find an ambulance in the district capital, some way to get Hillary out. The other men stood while I sat in the back with my face pressed against my knees, angry, scared, not wanting to cry openly. At the souk I managed to locate and wake the ambulance driver with difficulty, then fought with him when he insisted on stopping for a coffee in the café and a quick cigarette. He asked incredulously whether I really expected him to drive up *that* road without a coffee, while I burned with the rage of Rosaldo's headhunters (1989). Abdurrahman calmed me, pulled me away, held my hand, took me outside, and we managed to return to the village with the driver in the Land Rover, a dingy mattress in back.

Soon we bounced down the road with Hillary and the nursing baby, our daughter Lula, and arrived at the clinic that Fatima had visited, but again there was no medicine, nothing really they could do. It was an empty building. We continued to the district hospital. The doctor saw us ahead of dozens of waiting and very sick country folk, and we were not about to pass up white privilege. They put us in a bed in the back next to a woman with a wet new baby, and gave us oral antibiotics and suggested we try to get fluids to stay. The woman wanted Hillary to bless her baby, and while Hillary protested weakly that she was too sick to hold a newborn, the fluids would not stay. There was a clotted pool of afterbirth and blood on the floor before the pit toilet and we had to wade through it. There was no IV. I contracted another ambulance to take us to Marrakesh. I rode in the back with Hillary mumbling weakly and our baby gently cooing for her mother's milk. Abdurrahman rode in the front with the driver.

In Gueliz, in a sleek modern clinic with televisions and intravenous antibiotics, everything was fine. It was fine almost instantly and it cost about $150 – so little that I did not even bother filling out the paperwork for the insurance reimbursement. I spent the night to make sure all was well, then went back to the village to retrieve my son, our nannies, as well as a visiting anthropologist friend. I rented a car. No more buses. No more waiting. We have never as a family gone back to Tagharghist.

I returned in 2006–07, however. A Spanish friend accompanied me for the *'Id*, and as usual, everything had changed. New houses were being built, others had been abandoned; old people had died and new households were formed, property was reassembled amongst the new generation. Villages seem to be stolid places, but in an important sense this is not so. Life and death is transacted rapidly here, bodies are born and die at a pace that makes those of us sensitised elsewhere weak in the knees, sick to our proverbial stomachs.

When I asked, Fatima Id Baj told me her daughter Sumaiya had died just after I left in 2004, probably of dehydration; she had had a new boy after that, Hisham, and now a tiny baby daughter, Salma. Salma looked sickly to me, white, goggle-eyed, and unresponsive. I felt a chill when Fatima opened her swaddling to show the skeletal baby to me. Fatima wanted to ask about my family, though, about Hillary and whether she had fully recovered, whether my children were OK, whether they would ever come back. Fatima's brother had lost a baby since I had seen him, too, and as I started to ask around it was clear that, as Fatima had told me years ago, everybody has children who die, everybody has a different number. This statement hit me differently in 2007 than it had in 1998. I thought of my own babies far away in Connecticut in the snow. My four-year-old boy had a terrible flu when I left (he was supposed to have come with me) and I did not know how he was doing, whether he was OK. My throat constricted; my eyes burned. I wanted to hug Fatima and weep for her lost baby and all lost babies, but I could not and did not. She continued making small talk, lightly detailing the comings and goings of village bodies since my previous visit, and all I could hear was a high whine in my ears and the throb of my own blood pumping.

In 2008 I returned again. Salma had indeed died, Fatima told me, but she was about to give birth again. She prayed and prayed that God would send her a daughter, and I prayed Fatima would survive another birth. Only a few days passed. I was in Marrakesh trying to get the solar hot water fixed in the mosque and Fatima's baby was born, alive. Fatima was fine, but weak. I left some baby clothes and a little money and went to America before anyone had chanced to give the new girl a name.

If my early impressions of the hard surfaces of life in Morocco involved the difficulties of young urban people – fathers all powerful and too strict, no jobs, no ability to marry, no way to have sex, to migrate, to escape boredom – I was now a parent. I was focused on the new tragedies that had become visceral to me, and how these intersected the exigencies specific to rural life. Abdurrahman had lost two boys, but for him this was not so bad. After all, he told me with some pride, 'We used to lose about three babies in ten, and now we barely lose one.' *One in ten babies dead....* This sanguine health statistic results in a rising population, of course, more babies living, and thus more children sent down to the city to work, a whole new set of hard surfaces to deal with. It is an excruciating world villagers endure.

***

Morocco has always seemed hard to me, and contradictory; it involves arresting beauty, kindness, and warmth, but more ugliness than I care to see, fear I do not want to acknowledge, and pain that should not be. What is hard about Morocco has changed over time, and it changes in different parts of the country, with differently situated people, among different classes, in rural and urban milieux. I cannot arrange the 'stratificatory realities' of Morocco in a sensible architecture because the hardness does not align in strata so much as coagulate in clots. Tough situations are built of confused amalgamations, distressing amplifications of misfortune without unilinear precedents or simple responses. We tend to think of 'power structures' and 'relations of inequality' in clean graphical terms, but Morocco's problems *feel* like great sticky piles of bad luck, skewed odds, and misshapen dilemmas. It is hard to know where to start.

This is hard to portray, too, hard to put into text, because the anthropology of mundane struggle is about the experiential, and it must be understood experientially. Hard surfaces are *felt* rather than observed, as I have emphasised. They can be documented in some ways, calculated, and I have tried to do this in at least one village, but documentation lacks visceral meaning, what Searle calls the 'first person ontology' that stymies inquiry into the *experience* of consciousness. Human consciousness has a feeling to it, in other words, a sense of itself, and is not simply an idea or an arena for ideas.

This has been one of the central difficulties of the Geertzian notion of culture, as Unni Wikan (1990) and others have pointed out. We know that our lives are thoroughly cultural, that our bodies incorporate culture and are understood in cultural terms, but even Wikan is unable to explain how bodies speak back, what part they play in the dialectic of growth and history. We are rightfully dismissive of mute biological determinism, but this has left us poorly equipped to explain bodies as anything other than empty receptacles for culture, as containers that for some reason do not shape their contents. And this has left us sputtering in the face of our own everyday experience. My children crawl into bed with me virtually every night, for instance, their little bodies seeking the warmth of others, or maybe just following some primal directive to disrupt my marriage. I put them back in their own beds virtually every night, too; I attempt to install the discipline of my alienated society, impress upon them the importance of being alone, in your own space. Eventually my message is bound to penetrate, they will embody my culture, but it is very clear to me that my exogenous instructions are in dialogue with something else, with my children's own corporal directives. My son even explains it this way. He says, 'My body wants to be in your bed,' or when he behaves badly he tries to avoid responsibility by claiming that his heart wanted to do it, or his tummy. It is not 'him' but his body – not exterior cultural forces. He has on his own decided that his *'aql* is underdeveloped, in other words, he lacks a body that has had reason built into it. My argument is that the development I seek for my son is the inculcation of a *feeling*, a bodily preference for private space more than an idea about it.

For meanings to be meaningful they must be more than culturally logical, they must be *feelingful*, to borrow terminology from Robertson (2001, p. 94). Thus when Geertz says dismissively that we need not come half-way round the world to count the cats in Zanzibar, or when Rabinow asserts that it is not necessary to come to Morocco to learn that Moroccans are poor, they are only partly right. To learn *that* life is hard is relatively straightforward, but to learn how it feels requires significantly more. The question of everyday struggle demands more than material tabulation, but it also begs for something beyond an abstracted cultural schematisation. Not only must theoretical assertions 'hover low' over interpretations (Geertz 1973, p. 25), but interpretations themselves should at least hover low over – if not try to actually grasp – the bodies they reference.

We have developed a rich catalogue of concepts in Morocco, a range of sophisticated ways of thinking about what anthropology is and does, but I am not sure we have well evoked suffering, at least of the rural poor, the specific suffering by which growing, working, dying farmers maintain their cultural worlds. It has not been for lack of trying. Following Geertz, and reacting against him, anglophone anthropology has developed a canon that is elaborate and conceptually elegant, philosophically sophisticated and deeply informed. The Moroccan canon has a number of ethnographic gems, masterpieces of the genre, but as a body it strikes me as too seemly, too Apollonian. Disembodied anthropological intellects are poorly equipped to engage the corporality of everyday struggle, and thus we have left the question of how life is hard –how it *feels* – for artists to evoke and development workers to ameliorate. This has had consequences far beyond North Africa.

References

Geertz, C., 1973. Thick description: toward an interpretive theory of culture. *In*: Clifford Geertz, ed. *The interpretation of cultures*. New York: Basic Books, 3–30.

Rabinow, P., 1977, 2007. *Reflections on fieldwork in Morocco*. Chicago: University of Chicago Press.

Robertson, A.F., 2001. *Greed: gut feelings, growth, and history*. Cambridge, UK: Polity Press.

Rosaldo, R., 1989. Grief and a headhunter's rage. *In*: R.I. Rosaldo, ed. *Culture and truth*. Boston: Beacon Press.

Searle, J., 2004. *Mind*. Oxford, UK: Oxford University Press.

Wikan, U., 1990. *Managing turbulent hearts: a Balinese formula for living*. Chicago: University of Chicago Press.

Are we there yet? Geertz, Morocco, and modernization

Thomas Dichter

International Development Consultant

This paper explores Clifford Geertz as a teacher, fieldworker in Morocco, writer, and observer of 'new nations.' Beginning with a patchwork of personal reminiscences of Geertz and his influence on the author's fieldwork in Morocco four decades ago, the paper explores the creative tension in Geertz between cultural anthropology (especially the practice of fieldwork) as 'art' and as 'science,' and the relevance of anthropology (and that tension) for economic development interventions as undertaken by development agencies like the World Bank. To illustrate the latter, the author describes, in the second part of the paper, a recent World Bank intervention in Morocco in which he participated.

In the shadow of Geertz at Chicago and in the field in Morocco

Geertz and my introduction to anthropology

Index finger held to her lips, Hildred Geertz stage-whispered 'SHHH!!' as she opened the door. 'He's with an informant!'

It was the late fall of 1965. On the advice of a fellow Peace Corps volunteer, I had taken a taxi 20 miles out to Sefrou from where I was living, in Fez. I was eight months away from the end of my two-year Peace Corps assignment, and reluctantly I began to face the thought of what to do next. I could have extended my stay in Morocco, as a few Peace Corps volunteers chose to do. But I had notions of getting on with an adult life. Not knowing what that might be, graduate school seemed like a bridge to it, but in what? My Peace Corps acquaintance was facing similar dilemmas and, as we sat around one penetratingly cold grey day in my house in the Fez medina, he said, 'Hey, what about anthropology? There's a guy doing it in Sefrou. Maybe you should go talk to him. I think his name is Geertz.'

With the confidence of the ignorant, I found and knocked on Clifford and Hildred Geertz's door in Sefrou, in the middle of a weekday afternoon, with no appointment, no idea of who they were, or what anthropology was. 'He's with an informant' should have been my first clue. 'Informant' conjured for me a snitch, a tattletale, and I guessed that anthropologists were not police detectives (only later did I learn that my initial sense contained some truth). Moreover, the hyper-urgent way Hildred said 'SHHH!!' – I had not opened my mouth even to say good afternoon – and especially the dual sacredness that seemed to be assigned to Him and to the Act of being with an informant, made me think that this 'anthropology' was perhaps more serious, more mysterious, and much more important than I had guessed.

I whispered to Mrs. Geertz who I was, and what I thought I wanted – to talk about going to graduate school in anthropology. She told me to sit and wait.

Stripped of the awe that comes from knowing about someone's celebrity, I saw a slight man with a salt-and-pepper beard come out of the room with his 'informant,' say something in awkward Moroccan Arabic as he walked him to the door, and then come toward me. I rose to shake hands and introduced myself. He seemed at first sight shy and uncomfortable, but he spoke fast and asked me what I wanted. I explained. He asked me what I had done in Morocco. I explained that I was a Peace Corps English teacher and had spent my first year in a traditional Islamic university in Marrakesh, where the idea of teaching English seemed absurd, and so I had spent my time learning Arabic and talking to my students about their lives. Now I was teaching in Fez and spending my spare time hanging around woodworkers in the medina trying to learn how to operate a traditional foot lathe.

I hadn't been there long when he began to seem impatient. 'Look, why don't you come to Chicago?' 'OK,' I said, 'but can I ask you a few questions?' 'Like what?' 'Well, what exactly is the difference between anthropology and sociology?' 'Good question,' he said, and ushered me to the door.

In the fall of 1966 I was standing in a corner of Ida Noyes Hall having 'soch tea' (social science tea) and nervously looking around at my fellow classmates (I had since learned what a rising star Geertz was and how prestigious the University of Chicago's department was considered), some 25 or 30 people in their 20s, an assortment, I now see, that reflected the bell curve of talent, ambition, and life chances – some, perhaps six or seven, destined to become more or less well known names in the discipline (Rabinow, Eickelman, Ortner, Foner, Dwyer, Fabian, Fischer, et al.), some, perhaps another third, who would either drop off the anthropology planet altogether or have 'small-c' careers as journeymen, and another third who would become respectable professionals in the pastures of academe, grazing here and there on grants, chairmanships, editorships, publications, and trips to their field. Did Susan Sontag's description of the anthropologist as hero fit the group in Ida Noyes Hall?

> [A]nthropology reconciles a number of divergent personal claims. It is one of the rare intellectual vocations that do not demand a sacrifice of one's manhood. Courage, love of adventure, and physical hardiness – as well as brains – are called upon. It also offers a solution to that distressing by-product of intelligence, alienation. Anthropology conquers the estranging function of the intellect by institutionalising it.... The anthropologist is not simply a neutral observer. He is a man in control of, and even consciously exploiting, his own intellectual alienation. (Sontag 1970, p. 189)

I was definitely alienated and estranged, but also quite marginal even amongst the other aliens. Anthropology as an institution certainly did not conquer my estrangement; even social tea and its small rituals provided no, even temporary, 'at homeness.' And the last thing I was, was in control, and certainly not of my intellect, which during those first weeks I was hard put to locate. Befuddled, bewildered, I wrestled with the labels: functionalism, structuralism, structural-functional, Parsonian, emic, etic (now which one is which again?). Even words I knew, one-syllable ones, like thick and thin, became laden with significance that my classmates seemed to nod to so easily.

But I learned to nod. I learned – by accident really – that silence and a knitted brow could often be mistaken for intelligent seminar participation. And I practiced – in secret – a well lubricated ease with terms like 'reify.'

For several months in the fall and winter of 1966–1967, I went with others of a small group of Morocco-bound or Morocco-interested students to Cliff and Hilly's condo where we talked about Morocco, and where what Geertz later referred to as the 'Moroccan project' took shape. His idea was to replicate, in 'chain-link' fashion (a succession of anthropologists studying one town), the Indonesian Pare study in which he, Hilly, and others had participated in the early 1950s (Geertz 1995, p. 119).

Time, courses, and papers went by, and though I recall the three Chicago years as an uncomfortable experience, it probably wasn't all that bad. In any case – those were the days – by 1969 I had an NIMH grant to do my fieldwork, an MA in hand, and my thesis proposal accepted.

Fieldwork: Sefrou, Morocco, September 1969

Geertz had now left Chicago, having moved to the Institute for Advanced Study at Princeton where he could lead the life of the mind. We corresponded sporadically. He was not really in a position to guide my fieldwork, though he felt still responsible for me, and I was probably just as glad to be left alone.

How to do fieldwork? Well, they didn't teach us that, and though we had read Malinowski and had some notional guidelines, advice was restricted mostly to what equipment to buy. We were on our own, the rite of passage aspect being pretty clear. But even that path to anthropological manhood was quickly thwarted. For while the Geertzes, Lawrence Rosen, and Paul Rabinow had come and gone from Sefrou, their ghosts hung around, and as a result I didn't have to look for my first informant. Rabinow's dour 'Malik,' aka 'the *fqi*,' showed up at my door soon after I had unpacked (see his photo in Rabinow 1977, p. 160). He had worked with Paul, who had left no more than a month before I arrived, and understood what I was about, or so he said, and wanted to work with me too.

I was grateful, because though my part of the Geertz Sefrou project was fairly clear – I was going to study the schools of Sefrou and try to get at how they played a role in culture change – I did not know what I was doing. 'Malik,' who re-packaged Rabinow's method and fed it back to me, gave me some months of illusion that I too was an anthropologist.

Like Malinowski, once I had my own first 'informant,' I often found myself impatient, wished he'd go away, found him and his Moroccan habits annoying, and had other 'impure thoughts.' But unlike Malinowski, my reactions and my diversions were not just something that I put away in my diary, they were, for much of the time I was there, my fieldwork.

Everything that could get in the way of getting on with it, did. I spent months trying to get permission for what I was already doing, making trips back and forth to Rabat, secretly grateful that the whole process was so bureaucratically insane, since it meant that I could not get on with it fully. I spent much time perfecting my Arabic, and did many other things to 'prepare' for getting on with it. I felt compelled to do something quantitative because the 'qualitative' work I was doing seemed so shapeless and impressionistic. 'Scientistic,' a word Geertz liked, now began to make sense. My need to do quantification was not a need to be scientific, but merely scientistic.

In any case, I had devised a questionnaire that could be coded by hand, and found in Fez a marvelous wooden wheel about three inches round with ten rubber numbers on the edges, so that with a stamp pad, one could stamp any number on any place on the page.

The longer I did other kinds of fieldwork – chatting with folks in my car, wandering the souks, interviewing teachers, going back and forth between Sefrou and Sidi Lahcen Lyusi – the more the scientific ideal pressed on me, to borrow a phrase from Mary Louise Pratt:

> Evans-Pritchard and Maybury-Lewis are the heirs of the scientific, professional ethnography Malinowski invented. The scientific ideal seems to press on them acutely, calling for codified field methodology, professional detachment, a systematic write-up. Whatever about the other culture impedes these tasks is an ethnographic obstacle, as well as an ethnographic fact. Both writers complain, for instance, about the impossibility of having private conversations with informants, as if private conversation, once baptised as a field method, ought to be culturally possible everywhere. As methodology gets increasingly codified, the clash between 'objective and subjective practices' becomes increasingly acute. (Pratt 1986, p. 41)

I did not have a problem between objective and subjective, didn't even faintly hear a clash. If I gave it much thought, which I did not, it seemed to me obvious that any attempt on my part as an outsider to penetrate completely 'their' frame of reference, the way and the why of their construction of meaning, would be problematic; that the dialectic would usually be out of balance; and that all was distortion 'from the git-go,' more or less. If I was aware of anything, it was of how impossible communication was (but I knew that already from my relationship with my wife). Self and Other? Sounded like reification to me.

But as I said, I didn't think much about it. And that is perhaps because I didn't have a codified methodology. My method was a combination of hanging around and bopping around. The former I did on foot, or on my haunches, and the latter in my white VW bus which, in those days, when the average Moroccan did not own a car, had become a source of much informal informant information, as like Rabinow before me, I was constantly pestered for transportation. I would repeatedly blur the line between ethnographic obstacle and fact. And though I didn't put it this way at the time, everything was grist for the mill, and the less well organised, the better. I went to the Ministry of Education in Rabat and waited. I wrote letters. I stopped and picked up hitchhikers daily. I ate at small roadside stands, I went south to buy dates for a week in October, I interviewed students and their families, sat in classrooms, and walked in the hills around Sefrou. I couldn't resist my old fascination with woodworking and briefly 'apprenticed' myself to a 13-year-old foot-lathe operator who told me I was hopeless. I spent more time in the weekly markets than I cared to admit, since I never really figured out much about them. It was all inchoate grist for my mill – the anthropologist as tourist, the tourist as anthropologist, ethnography as futzing around – I had no method, no professional detachment, and when I finally did write my thesis, only I seemed to notice its disorganisation.

Besides just my own quirks (which must bear most of the responsibility for my approach), I believed I had absorbed something Geertzian in my fieldwork in Sefrou. Geertz had given me tacit permission to do anthropology in the way I did, or more accurately, I had chosen to interpret Geertz's emphasis on 'guesswork' in a way that was convenient for me. Clearly, he would never have allowed himself to be as casual as I was.

For Geertz, even though he talked about 'guesswork' fairly early on – he says in his essay on thick description: 'Cultural analysis is (or should be) guessing at meanings, assessing the guesses, and drawing explanatory conclusions from the better guesses...' (Geertz 1973, p. 20) – the scientific ideal pressed on him with considerable strength, if not acutely. While he seemed able to live with the tension between science and guessing – maybe even by viewing his way of guessing as scientific – much of his fieldwork was as scientific as it could be; a formal proposition based on carefully and systematically gathered evidenced, tightly wound in hypotheses and their testing. For all his occasional protestations that he would really have liked to become a great novelist, this Balzac manqué was, 'au fond,' a thorough scholar and leave-no-stone-unturned systematic investigator – a real social scientist. When he chose a subject, Indonesia, Morocco, he fully immersed himself in it, investing huge energy and time in reading ethnography, geography, colonial and economic history, quaint travelers' accounts, and so forth, much of the time in dusty archives in the Netherlands, the UK, the USA, and France. He studied languages intensively. The values of academia after the Second World War – discipline, precision, and erudition – especially perhaps at places like Harvard where he did his graduate work, were deeply instilled in him. He could not escape them, nor did he want to.

It was only much later in his life that Geertz was seemingly able to let go of science more completely:

> It is necessary then, to be satisfied with swirls, confluxions, and inconstant connections; clouds collecting, clouds dispersing. There is no general story to be told, no synoptic picture to be had. Or if there is, no one, certainly no one wandering into the middle of them like Fabrice at Waterloo, is in a position to construct them, neither at the time nor later. What we can construct, if we keep notes and survive, are hindsight accounts of the connectedness of things that seem to have happened: pieced-together patternings, after the fact. (Geertz 1995, p. 2)

Then, in the next paragraph, with his classic mix of one part bewilderment and nine parts sure-footedness, he asks 'Where has all the science gone?'

Being less disciplined and erudite than Geertz – basically lazy is what I was – I was inherently comfortable with an artful approach to fieldwork, an approach informal, loose, and flexible, prepared for the chance encounter, for the predictable unpredictableness of it all, in short, fieldwork as going with the flow; understanding coming at you, if and when it does, when you least expect it, from left field. (Was I ahead of my time?)

I claim – and this too is of course another convenience – that if forced, I could give a respectable name to my fieldwork: participant observation. And though I was not a Moroccan even for a day, I was standing and even at times swimming in the stream of Moroccan culture, letting it wash around and over me, while it and they, the Moroccans and their systems, made me think, made me laugh, and made me mad.

Fieldwork was also therapy, and why I spent much time, too much time from a professional standpoint, just taking in the light, the sounds, and especially the smells and tastes of food, and the density of life in the medina or in the weekly souk.

Perhaps this was because, like Geertz 25 years later, I had no intention of developing a synoptic picture; despite my thesis proposal, I did not really have a large question to bring to the field; modernity, tradition, colonialism, neocolonialism, dominance-submission, alienation. If such big questions are like soaring eagles one tries to capture and tame, my little questions were more like fleas whose itch made me want to scratch. Why, for example, was nothing ever done in a 'straight-line' way? If I would approach a taxi driver – in the days before I had a car – and say I want to go to El Menzel, he'd say get in. I'd say are you going there? Yes, get in. I need to leave now. Are you leaving now? Yes, I get in. And ten minutes later, I ask why aren't we leaving. We are. We leave finally, and then we turn down a road that I know doesn't lead to El Menzel. You said we are going to El Menzel. We are. But this is not the road to El Menzel. I know.

So I'd sit back, suspend my annoyance, and scratch my head. The French teachers I knew when I had been a Peace Corps English teacher would say that's how they are. Yeah, but *why* are they that way? Well, it's their culture. Well, yeah, OK, but I mean, *what* made them that way? I don't know, that's just how they are.

Rabinow, who describes several incidents of similar exasperation in his fieldwork, talks about a cycle of 'testing thrusts,' to see who comes out on top, and that this 'brinkmanship' is repeated in almost every encounter – 'a culture which thrives on the agonistic clash of wills, where assertions of character and denials of those assertions are the fabric of social life...' (Rabinow 1977, pp. 48–49, 77). OK, but why do that with a customer in a taxi? Why do that with a foreigner, who in a sense doesn't count, and thus isn't worth playing the game with, or even for? He doesn't even know me, and besides I'm paying him.

Then there is the short-form history explanation. Moroccans have a turbulent history, *bled es-siba*, *bled el-makhzen*, etc., and so they have learned to dissimulate. Yeah, OK, but everyone has had a turbulent history. . ...

OK, well how about humility in the face of God's perfection? Only God can do things in a straight line and thus if the taxi driver does so, he is arrogantly competing with God, therefore, we do not take the short route to El Menzel.

I continued to scratch my head. And just as during my two years in Morocco as an English teacher, the more I learned the less I understood and the more mysterious things became, the only comfort I had was the realisation that there was always another layer, and it was likely to be a surprise.

The truth is, I basically gave up repeatedly, and repeatedly kept going back, or so I told myself, to 'collect more data.' But what I was really doing was going back to 'the flow.' I'd hang around with the kids in the college, and I was struck by their enthusiasm to perform and the way they seemed to play with language; their exuberant and athletic trying out of English – as in the incessant 'helloo meester!!' – the jostling, the jumping up and down, the rambunctiousness, aware that it might have been for my benefit, but also intrigued that it might have been far more so for their own. But alongside it, or behind it or above it were all sorts of traditional, it seemed to me 'authentic,' forms embedded in a dour formalism, coming out as sincerity, generosity, and hospitality.

And so went my fieldwork, zig-zaggy, try this, then try that, go here, then go there.

Then one day in February 1971, my wife ran off with a Japanese tourist, leaving me with two kids. Was my fieldwork finished? I didn't know, or rather I knew it wasn't but I couldn't see when or how it might ever be. But I was finished, and after a frenetic month selling things, nego- tiating myself out of the lease on my house, and putting my notes in a box, I and my two little kids left Morocco.

Changes, cultural and otherwise

It was only three years later, away from Morocco and its dissonances, that I felt free to search for a framing idea, a metaphor, that would work, and I knew I needed it to work just long enough to finish my thesis. Geertz was again by my side, or at least the version of Geertz I interpreted – giving me tacit permission.

Re-reading Geertz and uncovering subtleties I had not seen the first time around, I began noti- cing a fairly constant thread of what I took to be intellectual humility, even though I later saw that it was probably the opposite. When Geertz, in what is a quintessential element of his style, uses several qualifying clauses in one inevitably longish sentence, it suggests, subtextually of course, that he is hedging, and in two ways: in the sense of trying to be accurate, and also in the sense of being not quite as committal as he might be. Another writer might say, for example, 'God only knows,' but Geertz is compelled to say, 'God, as they say, only knows' (Geertz 1968, p. 89). Or consider the regular use of the word 'anyway,' as in, '. . .and, so it is claimed anyway. . ..' This is classic Geertz, and so is the all-inclusive 'we' which, after a professorial sentence or two of firm conviction, jars the reader with its unexpected dose of humanism and humility:

> Religion must be viewed against the background of the insufficiency, or anyway the felt insuffi-ciency, of common sense as a total orientation toward life; and it must also be viewed in terms of its formative impact upon common sense, the way in which, by questioning the unquestionable, it shapes our apprehension of the quotidian world of 'what there is' in which, whatever different drummers we may or may not hear, we are all obliged to live. (Geertz 1968, p. 95)

And so I felt somewhat free to listen to my particular drummer.

Many Moroccans during the 1960s and early 1970s were playing with their identity as actors rehearse a new play on a stage. I was not looking for any kind of deep structure that could explain the relationships between people and institutions, or about myths and laws. I was trying to under-stand why Moroccans struck me, more often than not, as somewhat melodramatic, even at times as inauthentic. I saw, of course, that this was likely *my* problem, but it also seemed as good a way to frame a thesis as any I could think of, and so I pushed the idea. Where was my evidence? Since I didn't worry about my anthropology being science, and fully accepted that it couldn't be (even what is true can be proven, said Oscar Wilde), I was free to be the anthropologist as spinner of plausible tales, of 'pieced-together patternings.'

What I 'saw' were Moroccans trying out roles daily and I saw this especially at the intersec-tion of languages in the schools, as Moroccan kids learned to be fluent in French and English and began to mix them up with Arabic. Simple enough and hardly surprising. I went on to embellish here and there about how Moroccans intermediated between these languages and cultures, picking and choosing, sometimes fully cathecting the alien form, or in contrast, doing a poor job in the role, and everything in between; a floating crap game in which the dice were identities, with, of course, conveniently for me, no rules or not much structure, the game itself being about no rules and not much structure.

Despite the self-consciousness some of us may have (or have had) about art and science, about hedging our descriptions and interpretations, we couldn't help, in the end, falling into the trap of saying some things about Morocco that seemed definitive, whether Moroccan culture as an agon-istic clash of wills (Rabinow), or Moroccans as the greatest bunch of rugged individualists the world has seen (Geertz), or me saying it's all theatre. Our statements were definitive because we had to say something, and if you are going to say something you ought to say it with some degree of authority, or there is no point in writing. We are all aware, or have been trained to be so, that you cannot get away with sounding like an idiot. It doesn't cut it to say, 'I was there, I spoke to hundreds of people, I lived their lives as much as I could, I observed this and that, and yet I haven't a clue. . ..'

How much the trap of definitiveness catches us is only clear with hindsight. For all of us – and Geertz captures this eloquently in *After the fact* – Morocco today is of course a changed place. Some of the insights we had in the 1960s and 1970s seem ludicrously off the mark now. Others still work, but not very well. And even when certain places look the same now as they did in 1969, the experience is utterly different.

To start with, the place then was far, now it is near. It was sparsely populated (12 million or so in the mid-1960s, now approaching 34 million). Then, Fez ended right before turning onto the road to Sefrou, and Sefrou did not begin until you got there. Now Fez and Sefrou seem connected by an endless suburb.

On the last pages of *Islam observed*, Geertz describes a young Moroccan on a plane to New York, his first trip away from home, with the Qur'an in one hand and a glass of Scotch in the other. Geertz calls him an anxious traveller and the description is apt. Geertz wonders aloud about what is a useful strategy in the struggle for the real. Is the young Moroccan's moral double-bookkeeping a 'desperate holding action?' Geertz was on to something, as usual, but the surprise today is that the young man on the plane is no longer possible. That ambivalence, the being on the cusp of one world and another, the tension between 'the forms of religious life and the substance of secular life' (1968, p. 81), has, in some pretty evident ways, gone from the lives of individuals. The shift has been to put the tension into society as a whole, where the struggle with, or on behalf of, Geertz's four horsemen of modernity – secularism, nationalism, rationalism, globalization – takes place. The need for a desperate holding action, more poignant and urgent than ever, now manifests itself at the level of society.

As for the individual, it is the Scotch *or* the Qur'an, not both at once. Though the young man with the Scotch may kick off his shoes and put on his babouches when he gets home at night, have a *halal* couscous waiting for him and invoke Allah before eating, these are less likely markers of his religious 'culture' or identity than they are a kind of residue – surface-level symbols with about as much deep meaning for him as calling himself 'Italian American' might have for an American named Campobasso whose grandparents were born in the US. In short, if the secular Scotch and the religious couscous don't jar each other, it may be because neither is necessarily substance; both are possibly forms.

As for the other Moroccan who has the Qur'an in his hand and no glass of Scotch, it is a strong possibility that for him his religion is somehow less than a way to make sense out of life. It is a refuge, to be sure, but one thinly cast.

So, in addition to asking where all the science has gone, might we also ask whether we can still talk about thick description, about a 'stratified hierarchy of meaningful structures' (Geertz 1973, p. 7), or are we back to thin? Is thin perhaps all we've got today?

In any case, things have clearly changed, and unpredictably, as we ought to have predicted. Recall that 40 years ago Geertz called Sefrou a 'small, ancient walled city in the interior' (1968, p. vi). Perhaps he meant to invoke the romantic imagery of remoteness cultivated by 19th-century explorers. And recall also how relatively stable and slowly changing life was then in Morocco, and in the developing world in general.

But Sefrou today is anything but a small, ancient walled city in the interior. And Morocco, the 'far west' of the Islamic world, as its full Arabic name implies, is not at all remote today. Yves St. Laurent & Co. are ensconced in Marrakesh, Moroccan condo ads appear in the *Wall Street Journal*, and Moroccan food is commonplace not only in Paris, but in Chicago and Portland, Oregon. Labor migration and tourism have become not only huge sources of income, but of 'foreign contexts,' bringing them inside Morocco's borders. In 2004, according to OECD statistics, of $12.5 billion in externally sourced revenue for Morocco, 37% came from tourism, 33.8% from remittance transfers (money sent home by Moroccans working abroad), 23.5% from Direct Foreign Investment, and 5.6% from foreign aid for development.

What has happened to the 'will to be modern' and to the institutionalised efforts to make modernisation happen?

The development industry

Economic development, the field I ended up in after leaving academia, is, unlike anthropology, not about understanding changes such as those noted above, but rather about engineering change, or in the kinder, gentler version, 'fostering' it. Between the 1970s and now, I ended up working in just about every kind of organisation in what I came to see as the 'development business,' from the Peace Corps to the non-governmental organisation (NGO) sector, to the world of international foundations, to the World Bank and the United Nations Development Program (UNDP). During those decades, though I was not always conscious of it, I remained a Geertzian. I too saw the urge (and the accompanying institutional efforts) to bring the 'developing' nations 'up to speed' as 'developmentalism,' and the institutions involved in the effort as increasingly 'economistic.' As Geertz put the project of modernisation, with his usual acuity,

> A good deal of what had to be done was obviously economic. Infrastructure must be laid down, agriculture reformed, industrialism begun, trade encouraged. But it soon became apparent to even the most economistic, the most thoroughly convinced that material progress was but a matter of settled determination, reliable numbers, and proper theory, that political forms, social institutions, religious beliefs, moral practices, even psychological mind-sets would also have to be turned around. Rather a task – obscure, dubious, towering, and disquieting. (Geertz 1995, p. 139)

The problem is (and Geertz would have seen this had he too worked inside the development business) that this towering task – taking into account culture and society, politics and psychology – was marginalised from the beginning. And though lip service began to be paid to the social side of things (to use a shorthand form) in the 1980s, in practice the task continued to be ignored. Indeed, given the nature of the development industry, it could not have been otherwise. The institutions of the industry had to be responsive not only to the close-the-gap notions of fostering modernisation, but also, from the 1970s on, to the moral subtext that resulted from the realisation that poverty wasn't going away just because airports, bridges, and industries were built. Something *had* to be done. Action, which is what developmentalism had been all about in its airport-building days, was now called for on the poverty front too, and even when intelligent analysis might indicate a postponement of action, or even in some cases inaction, maintaining the appearance of action was imperative. Each development organisation, be it an NGO, e.g. Save the Children, Oxfam, ActionAid (UK), CARE International, or a bilateral agency like United States Agency for International Development (USAID), or a multilateral agency like the Food and Agriculture Organisation of the United Nations (FAO) or International Fund for Agricultural Development (IFAD) or the World Bank, exists in the end to act; to mobilise and to use funds.

Looking into political forms, social institutions, religious beliefs, moral practices, and psychological mind-sets is not what these organisations were set up to do. Yet one would think that the need to do this kind of homework, or, to put it more in the Geertzian vernacular, the need to find out what is going on and what it is folks think they are up to, would be self-evident. But no. For to look into these things would mean to take some time, to acknowledge the degree to which context and local peculiarity, history, and all the rest might influence projects or programmes. Indeed, the development industry could do little more than pay lip service to such a task precisely because it is so disquieting – one might not like what one learns, reality would likely turn out to be too complex, local contexts might mean an end to grand schemes and their 'replicability,' and all in all the result would be that action might have to be postponed or otherwise compromised – an unacceptable risk.

> [The analysis of culture is] not an experimental science in search of law, but an interpretive one in search of meaning. (Geertz 1973, p. 5)

And so the art-versus-science dilemma persists. It has gone from a somewhat personal one for me and my fieldwork – a matter of little consequence – to, I believe, a central dilemma for a whole domain of institutions whose mission is to assist the development process, with significant consequences for them and for the intended beneficiaries of their annual expenditure (these days) of over $100 billion.

Doing development artfully – 'picking one's way' through the 'piled-up structures of inference and implication,' as Geertz puts the interpretation of cultures (1973, p. 7) – rather than as science, has turned out not really to be possible. The World Bank in the late 1990s, led by some of its in-house anthropologists, tried in vain to integrate what it called 'social analysis' with project planning (I was involved in that effort). Most professionals at the World Bank, several hundred of whom are anthropologists, in the end get caught up in developmentalism and the economistic. For a while under James Wolfensohn, there were attempts at 'cross-ferti-lisation' between disciplines, one hope being that economists and engineers would learn to talk and think like anthropologists. What happened was that the anthropologists learned to sound like economists. Matrices and 'logical frameworks,' PowerPoint presentations laden with numbers and quantities – Geertz captures it all in the word 'graphs' – continued to dominate.

The case of the World Bank's Morocco Housing Sector project

The last project I worked on as a consultant to the World Bank was in 2005, a $50 million dollar Housing Sector Development Policy Loan. The money was to go to the Moroccan Ministry of Housing and Urbanism, and the aim of the project was 'to establish a market-based institutional and regulatory environment for the housing sector, including better access to and greater affordability of housing finance and housing services for the urban poor.' The effort was to be connected to a newly mandated programme, arising out of a speech given by King Mohammed VI in August 2001 in which he made housing a national priority, and given greater urgency after the 16 May 2003 Casablanca bombings. The new government programme, approved in July 2004, was called Villes sans Bidonvilles (VSB) and called for the elimination of bidonvilles in 70 urban centers in Morocco by 2010 – a massive slum eradication effort.

Partly influenced by the completion of a set of procedures for 'social analysis' (in the form of a 'manual') and also by the growing external pressures to do things in a less heavy-handed way, the World Bank had added a new requirement to an already long checklist of things to do in the project preparation process – to conduct a Poverty and Social Impact Assessment (PSIA) before new projects were finalised, the goal of which was to 'assess the poverty alleviation and distributional impacts of policy,' in other words, to establish, before the loan was made, whether or not the impact of the policy would be the one desired. Again, a good idea to which lip service was given. In the case of the Morocco Housing Sector Assessment (the PSIA), it was launched *after* commitments had already been made by the Bank to the Government of Morocco to go ahead with the project in full; it was given little time to do its work and was under-staffed.

Some background to the housing problem in Morocco. . ..

The French word *bidonville* for slum or shantytown appears first to have been used in Casablanca sometime in the first quarter of the 20th century, and referred to the habit of poor squatters putting up shelter made out of flattened tin drums (*bidons*). Tin shack slums have been part of the urban landscape in Morocco from as early as 1907, and by 2005 there were about 1.4 million people in them, or over 4% of the population. And this is just the bottom layer of the roughly 5 million people who are considered to live in substandard housing (*habitat non-réglementaire*).

Public sector efforts to do something about slums go back to 1941 with the creation of the Ain Chok housing project in Casablanca. Other efforts in the 1950s and 1960s resembled what had become standard fare for slums almost everywhere – either total or partial bulldozing, consolidation, or transfer of slum dwellers to zones in the urban periphery with basic services. The first five-year plan for substandard housing arose in 1972 with the creation of the Moroccan Ministry of Housing (later to be called the Ministry of Housing and Urbanism). The subsequent history is complex and detailed but the long view makes it clear that the slum housing situation was not contained, much less eliminated.

One of the reasons, as researchers began to uncover, was that while slums may look stable and even permanent, their populations can be dynamic, and even in a sense, upwardly mobile.

There are slums almost everywhere in the world and they differ in aspect and quality, from living in the open air on bits of cardboard in the streets of Mumbai, to the tin and cardboard shacks in Nairobi's Mathare Valley, to squatting in abandoned apartment buildings in the Bronx. And while there are people whose whole lives are passed in them, they also function, for many, as a transition point – from rural to urban, from temporarily up to more permanently down, from almost up to temporarily down, and so on.

Urban policy experts and municipal governments want to see, over time, the number of people leaving a slum becoming less than the number who arrive, and actively work to reduce slums, by various means, including bulldozing them away. Social scientists are a bit more subtle, and see the slums as complexly layered social environments, with equally complex dynamics, as this case shows. And the case illustrates also how ill adapted development institutions are to the kind of analysis and interpretation anthropologists might provide, and as such how the art versus science dilemma is manifest in the effort to make modernity happen.

In Morocco in the last 20 years, despite government efforts to do something about them, slums have grown at a rate of about 4% per year. In the bidonvilles of Agadir, in southern Morocco, for example, a government survey in the late 1990s showed about 12,000 shacks in the bidonvilles. Six thousand of these were successfully removed over a period of three years (their population was provided either with new subsidised housing, or with plots of land and assistance in building their own house). A couple of years later, a survey was done in the original slum area and came up with a total of 13,000 shacks. Politicians in Agadir sardonically refer to this as the 'new math' – 12 minus 6 equals 13.

What happened is complex, but amounts to this: the government's effort to solve slum pro-liferation in itself became a stimulus for slum proliferation. The more people got wind of the possibility that a slum might be the beneficiary of government effort, the more they wanted in on the future action, and the more the slum became attractive. A slum version of a real estate speculation industry developed. The selling and buying of tin shacks benefited local politicians, middle-class speculators, moneylenders, as well as the poor and the less poor. Families with little money would borrow (often from a third party or from members of their extended family) as much as (the equivalent of) $4,000 or $5,000 to buy a 350-square-foot shack that had no legal existence. These sales were done in cash, without any paper or title being transferred. The local authority would take a cut and look the other way, the move would often take place at midnight, and the new 'resident' would then claim to be in line for whatever 'rehousing' programme the government had in the works, so strong is the urge for legitimacy on the part of the residents.

Local governors, mayors, and other officials, disturbed by this trend, began to do more rigor-ous counting, deciding not to count households or people, or even shacks, but numbers of doors. Soon people began subdividing their shacks, selling off or leasing parts of them, and putting in more doors, thus increasing perceived future value. Once the authorities caught on to that, they began painting numbers on the doors so that a new door would be noticed. But so strong was the hope for a government programme to legitimise the poor as real property owners, that the practice of shack expansion, adding doors, and buying and selling putative 'rights to be rehoused' continued.

The World Bank, working with the government, had by 2004 become convinced that to solve the problem reforms in housing policy were needed. Land was to be provided by the state, loan guarantee funds were to be provided by the state to the banks to encourage housing loans to the poor, incentives were to be provided by the state to private contractors, and infrastructure standards were to be lowered in order to drop the cost of housing for poor people and thus entice building contractors to do low-cost housing. Finally, work was initiated on rationalising the land titling system. Almost all of these reforms involved money. The government imposed a tax on cement in order to raise more money for slum eradication and the World Bank got ready to put $50 million more in the kitty.

But in fact, money is not / was not the answer here, or at least not the amounts being spoken of. Nor are such thoughtful manipulations of the system as necessary as the government and the World Bank believed.

In the three-week study I led in six slum areas in Morocco, I met with scores of officials including governors, and scores of slum dwellers. Virtually all the officials were aware of and understood the problem of the 'new math' and its causes. A key regional figure in the Ministry of Housing and Urbanism, after giving me his official story about all he and his people were doing, paused and then said he would now like to comment, not as an official, but as himself. His personal view was completely different. He said that the only sensible thing was a policy of benign neglect; in effect, to make some improvements in the slums to benefit the truly destitute, and leave the rest of the situation alone. He felt that in undertaking this highly visible, complex, and radical VSB slum eradication programme, 'We are feeding this monster, but if we want it to die, we have to stop feeding it.' A similar view was openly expressed by several other officials. But since the culture of the development industry is a culture of action and engineering, benign neglect was not an option.

As I noted earlier, the World Bank, a huge institution with 10,000 employees, cannot really help but approach a project like this in any way but within the preconditioned framework of money and policy engineering. The institutional imperative, getting the money out the door and 'managing the tasks' that go along with it, dominates. The Bank cannot be heuristic, it cannot do thick description. It cannot operate in a reflexive way. It is caught in its own habitus.

And so increasingly is the Moroccan government. The one hope for a more interpretive approach to the VSB effort was the creation of the tiny Social Development Agency (SDA), the only structure formally charged with understanding what is going on inside the bidonvilles. Nominally a sub-unit of the Ministry of Housing and Urbanism, the SDA was undermanned and sidelined within the traditional structure of the government ministries (tellingly, it had no authority to allocate resources). And while it was marginalised within the government structure, ironically, it soon became overwhelmed by demands from outside the structure, from foreign donors, all wishing to better 'understand' the social context. And so other donors came knocking to ask, 'Can you be a partner in our project? Can you help us figure out what to do with this project and that project?' The SDA basically said yes to everyone and soon became a kind of reactive consultancy spread so thinly that it could do little other than superficially.

The slum eradication effort in general began to reflect this tendency to do things superficially. The galvanisation of the response to the king's call (and commitment) to *do* something seems to have created a rush to be seen as on board the train. The stakes had become even higher after the incidents of 16 May 2003 in Casablanca.

This urgency took away the possibility of preparing the VSB program carefully. Moreover, because the King's imprimatur was on the programme, a paradoxical inertia began to set in once things got underway – an inertia that was in proportion to the visibility of the players. Thus the incentive became to appear to act, but in fact to do very little out of fear of taking a wrong step. Numbers and technicity, public works engineers and flow charts took over – graphs again.

The administrative evolution of Moroccan officialdom (a large subject of study all by itself) seems, since Independence, to have been a history not only of greater and greater control – all is now *bled el-makhzen* – but of greater and greater institutional sedimentation; adding new departments, divisions, and agencies and never eliminating the resulting redundancy. To tack on the new without letting go of the old was perhaps another response to the desire to be modern.

The VSB program epitomises the pattern. The Ministry of Housing and Urbanism, with its multiple directorates and divisions, is now tied (within the VSB plan) to the Ministry of Interior (and the king's *walis*), the Ministry of Territory and Water, the Ministry of Social Development (not to be confused with the Social Development Agency), and the Ministry of Finance. In addition, there are the newly created privatised or semi-privatised parastatal organisations, as well as the key private sector partners such as the major banks. Woven into this plan for the 'coordination' of the VSB effort is the old structure of the *caïds* and *moqaddems*. The result: many meetings, new webs of influence and control, much watch-dogging, and little real coordination.

If there was a common thread to be noted in this institutional confusion, it was the fluency with which most of the parties used the almost universal modern vocabulary of governance: accountability, transparency, sustainability, participatory, inclusion, consultative, decentralisation, partnership with the voluntary sector, pro-poor policies, etc.

Given the unwieldy layering of authorities and agencies, it is perhaps not surprising that what was left was room only for words and impression management; any possibility of taking an artful approach to the problem was crowded out. Certainly an alternative, such as a do-less approach, not to mention a do-nothing approach, was out of the question.

The wise applied anthropologist, seeing the rules of the game in these two institutions (the Moroccan ministry and the World Bank), does not have much choice but to throw up his hands and concede, 'They gotta do what they gotta do.'

Geertz's views on modernity re-observed

In the early 1960s, as modernisation theory was reaching its height, Geertz thought and wrote a fair amount about the theory and its application in the development institutions (see e.g. Geertz 1963). We could still talk then of 'traditional society' and modernisation theory with its notions of stages, transition, 'social change'; it seemed worth thinking about seriously and thus also criticising seriously, for example, as neo-imperialist and ethnocentric. The institutions involved in working in development were also subject to criticism, then as now, but in a more constructive and hopeful vein. A surprising example of this hopefulness is Geertz in 1962 at the end of a short chapter on 'Social change and modernisation in two Indonesian towns' (which later became the expanded *Peddlers and princes*):

> [P]erhaps this sort of community-study approach to economic growth will help to turn planning in
> underdeveloped countries away from the rigid, a priori, hypertheoretical, almost dogmatic approach
> which has often been characteristic of it toward a more pragmatic, concrete, and realistic approach –
> one which uses general principles, economic or sociological, not as axioms from which policies are

to be logically deduced but as guides to the interpretation of particular cases upon which policies are to be based. (Geertz 1962, p. 407)

Geertz, not at all an insider in the development business, understood, almost a half-century ago, the deepest tendencies of the business, and yet he hoped they could be overcome; that someday 'interpretation of particular cases' might be the starting point for deciding what ought to be done.

Also somewhat hopefully, Geertz talked in the same chapter about social change in the two towns he studied, as the result partially of exposure to a wider world, a dynamic he saw early on, and one which is now near universal.

In prewar Modjokuto the town's traders were a self-contained, set-apart, rather despised group; today they are becoming integrated into a broad and generalised middle class within an uncertainly urbanising structure. In prewar Tabanan the aristocrats were the unquestioned political and cultural elite of the region; today their position is increasingly threatened by the growth of a universalistic civil bureaucracy and the populist sentiments of nationalist ideology. It is thus neither upward nor downward class mobility or a blockage of these which is necessarily crucial but any kind of decisive change in intergroup relations which, by throwing accepted status demarcations into disarray, stimulates active efforts to anchor social positions to new moorings. (Geertz 1962, p. 406)

The hopefulness comes through in the twin metaphors of anchors and moorings, as if human culture really *has* to have such solid points of connection (both anchors and moorings are made of iron and steel). Thus when one loses a traditional anchor, or comes un-hooked from a traditional mooring, we (human beings) move naturally to find another equally solid one.

Later, Geertz seems to have let go of that kind of equation as he and the world moved on, e.g., in 1988:

The world has its compartments still, but the passages between them are much more numerous and much less well secured. (Geertz 1988, p. 132)

But still, he remained somewhat hopeful:

The next necessary thing (so at least it seems to me) is neither the construction of a universal Esperanto-like culture, the culture of airports and motor hotels, nor the invention of some vast technology of human management. It is to enlarge the possibility of intelligible discourse between people quite different from one another in interest, outlook, wealth, and power, and yet contained in a world where, tumbled as they are into endless connection, it is increasingly difficult to get out of each other's way. (Geertz 1988, p. 147)

In 1995 he tries again to talk about modernisation. Trying to define it, he throws up his hands, deliberately disingenuously:

Whatever [modernity] is, it is pervasive, as either a presence or a lack, an achievement or a failure, a liberation or a burden. Whatever it is. (Geertz 1995, pp. 136–137)

And goes on to say something surprisingly anodyne:

One thing it may be is a process, a sequence of occurrences that transforms a traditional form of life, stable and self-contained, into a venturous one, adaptive and continuously changing.... (p. 137)

But what if, as I suggested earlier in the case of the 'anxious traveller' with the Scotch in his hand, modernisation is perhaps no longer a 'process' with its implications of transformation, of slow and fairly deep absorption of new ways, of learning and adaptation, but instead, a rapid, 20 minutes or so, taking-on of mere trappings?

Of Geertz's four horsemen of modernity, the one that counts today is globalisation, and the troika that pulls it: communication, technology, and the accompanying spread of capitalism. These may well have, in only the last decade or so, reduced the 'process' of modernisation to a universal will simply to be moder*nistic*; to take on, or better yet, buy the symbols of the modern. And the fact that 'traditional forms of life' which were probably never all that stable and self-contained to begin with, often get reduced to a remnant, albeit meaningful for those who hold on to it, does not necessarily mean that we went through a sequence of transformative occurrences, other than perhaps shopping.

Are we there yet? Yes, we are.

References

Geertz, C., 1962. Social change and economic modernisation in two Indonesian towns: a case in point. *In*: Everett E. Hagen, ed. *On the theory of social change: how economic growth begins*. Homewood, IL: Dorsey Press, 385–407.

Geertz, C., ed., 1963. *Old societies and new states: the quest for modernity in Asia and Africa*. New York: The Free Press of Glencoe.

Geertz, C., 1968. *Islam observed*. New Haven, CT: Yale University Press.

Geertz, C., 1973. Thick description: toward an interpretive theory of culture. *In*: Clifford Geertz, ed. *The interpretation of cultures*. New York: Basic Books, 3–30.

Geertz, C., 1988. *Works and lives: the anthropologist as author*. Stanford, CA: Stanford University Press.

Geertz, C., 1995. *After the fact: two countries, four decades, one anthropologist*. Cambridge, MA: Harvard University Press.

Pratt, M.L., 1986. Fieldwork in common places. *In*: James Clifford and George E. Marcus, eds. *Writing culture: the poetics and politics of ethnography*. Berkeley: University of California Press, 27–50.

Rabinow, P., 1977. *Reflections on fieldwork in Morocco*. Berkeley: University of California Press.

Sontag, S., 1970. The anthropologist as hero. *In*: E.Nelson Hayes and Tanya Hayes, eds. *Claude Lévi-Strauss: the anthropologist as hero*. Cambridge, MA: M.I.T. Press, 184–196.

Welcome message from the Mayor of Sefrou

Hafid Ouchchak

President of the City Council of Sefrou, Sefrou, Morrocco

Hafid Ouchchak, President of the City Council of Sefrou, offered this message of welcome to participants in the conference, 'Islam re-observed: Clifford Geertz in Morocco,' at the University of California, Los Angeles, 6–9 December 2007.

On behalf of the City Council and the residents of Sefrou, and speaking for myself as well, I would like to thank those at UCLA responsible for the praiseworthy initiative of organising this major scientific conference.

It is a great pleasure to express my gratitude to all of you, and particularly to Susan Slyomovics, Kamal Oudrhiri, Lahouari Addi, Peter Szanton, and to all those here and abroad, who contributed to the successful realisation of this scientific and cultural event. Allow me, dear friends and honourable members of the audience, to acknowledge the presence of the members of the Moroccan delegation who have travelled here all the way from our country. Their presence is a measure of the honour given to the city of Sefrou, and also to Morocco which, for numerous reasons including its sociocultural characteristics, has always been a preferred field of study for some of the most renowned American and European researchers, including the late Clifford Geertz, Rémy Leveau, John Waterbury, Paul Rabinow, Thomas Dichter, Lawrence Rosen, Susan Slyomovics, and many others.

I take this opportunity to express my sincere gratitude to the Consul General of the United States at Casablanca and to all of his colleagues, and to Mr. Charles Cole, cultural attaché at 'Dar America,' for the particular care and attention they gave to this event and for the many services they provided in facilitating its organisation through the consulate.

Ladies and gentlemen, it is with great pride that I emphasise the significance of this conference, not only because of its chosen theme, but also because of the rich cultural programme that is part of it, and above all because of the quality of the participants. It is a great honour for us, as representatives of the city of Sefrou, to find ourselves in the company of the eminent researchers who have come from far and wide to discuss and debate a subject of such burning importance, and above all to give homage to the late Professor Geertz, a great man whom we all respect and love for his person, his wisdom, and his ideas.

It is an honour for the name of our city to be linked to that of the eminent anthropologist through his work, the fruit of his research and study and of his sojourn with us from 1965 to 1971, work that undoubtedly constitutes an essential reference in the field of anthropology. During that productive sojourn, Geertz was able to rub shoulders with the people of Sefrou, share their daily life, and thereby meet people and develop friendships. His time with us is always spoken of with a great deal of feeling and nostalgia by those who knew him.

Based on his thorough knowledge of the terrain and his deep analysis of the Sefroui way of life, Geertz's work on the souk of Sefrou shed light on many aspects of the city's economic, religious, and cultural life. Nevertheless, there are still aspects that remain to be discovered, and I would invite researchers to further the study of this city, its history, and its recent evolution.

Ladies and gentlemen, as you know, Geertz's work on Sefrou was a milestone in the history of anthropology, and for this reason it contributed to the international influence of our city, to the extent that his work is widely known and admired throughout the world. In recognition of Geertz's choice of Sefrou as a field of research, the city devoted its 12th Cultural Conference to paying tribute to this great man and his scientific contribution.

That conference, which was honoured by the presence of Professor Geertz, took place on 3–6 May 2000 and was organised around the theme of 'Sefrou: Mémoire, territoires et terroirs des moments, des lieux et des hommes... Hommage à Clifford Geertz,' in collaboration with Princeton University's Institute for the Transregional Study of the Contemporary Middle East, North Africa and Central Asia, as well as the Princeton University Center of International Studies, and with the assistance and support of the King Abdul-Aziz al-Saud Foundation in Casablanca.

Thanks to the efforts and attention of Professor Abdellah Hammoudi, to whom we express our sincere gratitude for kindly having headed the scientific committee, the international gathering in Sefrou brought together participants from many different countries, notably from the United States, Europe, Israel, and the Maghreb, to discuss the themes that were set for the conference, to wit: small towns and metropolises (coexistence, identities, multiculturalisms); cultures and cultural practices (comparison and expression of differences); history, memory, and space in the construction of modern and contemporary Maghrebi societies; and discourses and practices of change, transformation, and past and present utopias (what are the frameworks for future lives?).

Around these axes and through some 15 presentations, the conference in Sefrou was an occasion for specialists in various disciplines in the social sciences to 'exchange ideas and reflect on the contribution of anthropology to knowledge of Maghrebi societies, using Morocco as an example.' Those discussions of high quality, conducted at a high scientific level, were crowned by the comments of Professor Geertz.

Beyond its scientific aspect, the 12th Cultural Conference at Sefrou was the occasion for meetings and reunions of researchers, notably those whose studies focused on the city of Sefrou in particular and on Morocco in general. There were a number of touching moments, full of good feeling, when the late Professor Geertz was able to reunite with certain companions he had known in Morocco, such as the late Professor Rémy Leveau, as well as old friends from Sefrou whose daily lives he had shared.

One question in particular arises for specialists as well as for non-specialists: Why did a great researcher like Geertz (and others) take an interest in studying a little town like Sefrou? This is a difficult question, but the late Geertz, and certainly his wife Hildred Geertz, and his companions Paul Rabinow, Thomas Dichter, Lawrence Rosen, and others interested in his work and his ideas, were and are possessed of the scientific basis to provide a response. But one thing is certain, and that is that Sefrou offers a number of characteristics that merit the scientific curiosity of researchers (like that which drew Geertz to the city more than 42 years ago), and the simple curiosity of discovery.

Given its location at the foot of the central Middle Atlas, as an important stage on the ancient caravan trade route (Tariq as-Sultan), Sefrou throughout its long history has been a point of transit, a crossroads, and a human gathering place. These factors, combined with the diversity of its resources, provided Sefrou with significant possibilities for human integration and development. Sefrou thereby attracted a population of diverse ethnic, tribal, and religious origins (including Muslims, Jews, and Christians), which made it a center of coexistence and cohabitation where a secular urban tradition based on openness and tolerance was able to develop.

Sefrou is also representative of the traditional small Moroccan city which, with its ancient medina serving as an important commercial focus and a living memory, offers an important material historical patrimony (with its ramparts, gates, bastions, and religious edifices including mosques, synagogues, and *zawiyas*, its homes of historical and architectural value, and traditional socioeconomic establishments such as *funduqs*), as well as an immaterial historical patrimony (including its traditions, music, cuisine, and savoir-faire), all of which is the fruit of a thousand-year history and a constructive human symbiosis.

It is true that Sefrou has experienced profound changes over the past half-century and more, the most important of which relates to its human composition, altered through the emigration of certain old-line Muslim families and the departure of the Jewish community, on the one hand, and, on the other, the massive arrival of mostly rural immigrants. This human mobility has certainly had an impact on various aspects of the city's cultural, economic, and socio-spatial life.

Nevertheless, despite the loss of a not insignificant part of the city's vital substance (its traditions and savoir-faire), its memory still survives through representative and expressive material and immaterial testimonials. The value of this memory calls for an expanded awareness of the importance of preserving, actualising, and mobilising it in the service of local development.

It was in recognition of its millennial history, so deserving of special interest and attention, that the city of Sefrou organised its 16th Cultural Conference on 14–15 December 2005, with the support of the US Agency for International Development (USAID), around the theme of 'Sefrou: City of Coexistence.' That conference was the occasion for the public and for specialists of all kinds to recall Sefrou's rich patrimony and to discuss its current situation and explore the best ways to perpetuate its patrimony.

This initiative was all the more relevant in a context characterised by religious and intercommunal intolerance in certain regions of the world, and, in certain countries, by indifference to the common historical heritage that bears our universal human values.

It was this spirit that animated the work of the 16th Cultural Conference in 2005, which was articulated around two primary axes, firstly, the concept and the actuality of coexistence. One part of this axis dealt with the concept of coexistence from various angles. In this discussion, the city of Sefrou was offered as one example among others, since it has been a place of mutual understanding and dialogue between the communities that have coexisted there. A second part of this axis allowed participants to look back over the course of Sefrou's history and find earlier manifestations of coexistence on the economic, spatial, societal, cultural, and other levels.

Secondly, the spirit of coexistence and how to perpetuate it: the second axis of the conference was devoted to the exploration of ways to materialise the discourse on coexistence through the initiation of actions to safeguard local memory and reaffirm and actualise the spirit of tolerance. Such actions might include the renewal and reinforcement of links between various people interested in coexistence within the city of Sefrou and beyond; increasing awareness of the development of initiatives and of synergies to preserve local memory; identification of the elements of the material and immaterial historic Jewish, Amazigh, and Arab heritage that constitutes the authentic expression of a common past and the guarantee of a better future; and dialogue on the development of projects and the establishment of structures likely to guarantee the preservation of symbols of coexistence in the city of Sefrou in order to assure the durability of its collective memory.

Ladies and gentlemen, the organisation of the present conference in Los Angeles is testimony to the interest this renowned University takes in one of the major figures in the field of anthropology, one whose monumental work has played a determining role in the renewal of and the charting of new directions for this discipline.

The choice of a theme on Islam is an edifying choice, for more than one reason. In the first place, because the comparative study of the formation and the evolution of Islam was one of Professor Geertz's primary scientific preoccupations in his study of Indonesia and Morocco. At this point, I would like to take the opportunity to say that Islam in Morocco is a moderate and tolerant Islam that has adapted to the demands of modernity, progress, and opening.

Secondly, the question of religion in general and of Islam in particular is a key question at the present time and will remain so in the future, as Professor Geertz wrote only a few months before his death. Thus it has become more imperative than ever that religion be a factor of rapprochement and not one of conflict and separation. But that would require more dialogue and more mutual understanding. Your initiative in organising this conference and selecting this theme is in keeping with this spirit.

Before concluding, I would like to thank you again for inviting me to this conference. I also extend my thanks to all those who will contribute to the enrichment of the discussion and the success of this scientific forum through their presentations and their presence over the next few days.

I also wish to thank Paul Hyman for his brilliant exhibition that immerses us in the authenticity and originality of Sefrou and the kindness of its inhabitants.

By way of conclusion, I would like to inform you that in honour of Clifford Geertz and in memory of his friendship and his scientific and sentimental attachment to Sefrou, I will submit to the City Council in the near future a proposal to name a public square or a street after the eminent researcher and friend of Sefrou. May his soul rest in peace.

Thank you all.

Note

Translation by Diane James

Index

www.ingramcontent.com/pod-product-compliance
Ingram Content Group UK Ltd.
Pitfield, Milton Keynes, MK11 3LW, UK
UKHW020355010325
455677UK00021B/474